Viking Pirates and Christian Princes

Viking Pirates and Christian Princes

Dynasty, Religion, and Empire in the North Atlantic

Benjamin Hudson

OXFORD
UNIVERSITY PRESS

2005

OXFORD
UNIVERSITY PRESS

Oxford University Press, Inc., publishes works that further
Oxford University's objective of excellence
in research, scholarship, and education.

Oxford   New York

Auckland   Cape Town   Dar es Salaam   Hong Kong   Karachi
Kuala Lumpur   Madrid   Melbourne   Mexico City   Nairobi
New Delhi   Shanghai   Taipei   Toronto

With offices in
Argentina   Austria   Brazil   Chile   Czech Republic   France   Greece
Guatemala   Hungary   Italy   Japan   Poland   Portugal   Singapore
South Korea   Switzerland   Thailand   Turkey   Ukraine   Vietnam

Published by Oxford University Press, Inc.
198 Madison Avenue, New York, New York 10016
www.oup.com

Oxford is a registered trademark of Oxford University Press

Library of Congress Cataloging-in-Publication Data
Hudson, Benjamin T.
Viking pirates and Christian princes : dynasty, religion, and empire
in the North Atlantic / Benjamin Hudson
p.   cm.
Includes bibliographical references and index.
ISBN-13 978-0-19-516237-0
ISBN 0-19-516237-4
1. Vikings—Ireland—Dublin. 2. North Atlantic Region—Church history.
3. Vikings—North Atlantic Region. 4. North Atlantic Region—History.
5. Vikings—Scotland—Hebrides. 6. Hebrides (Scotland)—History.
7. Ireland—Kings and rulers. 8. Dublin (Ireland)—History.
9. Vikings—Isle of Man. 10. Isle of Man—History. I. Title.
DA995.D75H84 2005
941'.004395—dc22   2004050136

2 4 6 8 9 7 5 3 1

Printed in the United States of America
on acid-free paper

To Alison and Robert

Preface

THERE ARE many books about Vikings as a group, but few about Vikings as individuals. This book reconstructs the history of two Vikings and their families who were active around the North Atlantic before settling in Ireland and Britain at the beginning of the High Middle Ages. These individual Vikings are studied from two unusual perspectives: those of colonists and of dynasty. The history of two Viking dynasties provides insight into changes in political, cultural, and religious orientation. These families were vitally important in the eyes of contemporaries, but they languish in obscurity today. Their story is more than the usual catalogue of battles in the chronicles, because their promotion of literature, patronage of the Church, and construction of commercial empires made them wealthy and powerful. The Vikings colonists did not live in isolation, and their interactions with the native peoples are both important and instructive. One must be prepared to leave the familiar histories in order to search for traces of them among the stories, lists, and artifacts of their neighbors.

The material in this book has been collected over a number of years, during which I have incurred many scholarly debts, and it is a pleasure to acknowledge them. Two people to whom I should very much have liked to present this book were Denis Bethell and Máirtín Ó Briain. Denis Bethell encouraged me to begin research into the Irish Sea Province during the High Middle Ages. During a memorable spring tour around the Irish Sea, his enthusiasm for the region and its history was infectious. Máirtín Ó Briain was a constant source of inspiration and good advice for this book, for its subject was an area that interested him. He read parts of this book in draft and made many wise observations. The vastness of his knowledge was equaled only by his kindness.

This work has also benefited from the kindness of colleagues who read chapters, commented on ideas, and allowed me to consult their work. In particular I wish to thank Dr. Mary Valante and Dr. R. Andrew McDonald for their assistance and helpful contributions that included reading and commenting on drafts of these chapters. Susan Ferber of Oxford University Press has overseen this enterprise with enthusiasm and expertise. Any errors are, of course, my own.

The many years of research for this book allowed me to enjoy the courtesy and helpfulness of the librarians and staff at several libraries: the Pattee/Paterno Library at the Pennsylvania State University; the Bodleian Library, Oxford; the Queen Mother Library of the University of Aberdeen; the Royal Irish Academy; and the Bibliothèque nationale de France. Financial assistance for the completion of this book was provided by the Research and Graduate Studies Office and the Institute for the Arts and Humanities, both of the Pennsylvania State University.

Finally, the heroes of this project are my family. My wife, Aileen, read through what must have seemed endless versions of chapters, making corrections and offering suggestions. Our children, Alison and Robert, have been enthusiastic supporters of the project from the beginning, and to them is this book dedicated.

Contents

Figures and Maps

Abbreviations and Short Titles

See the Selected Bibliography for full publication information.

Aarbørger	*Aarbøger for nordisk Oldkyndighed og Historie*
Acta Sanctorum	*Acta Sanctorum quotquot toto urbe coluntur: vel a catholicis scriptoribus celebrantur*, ed. Bolandus et al., 66 vols.
Adam of Bremen, *Gesta*	*Magistri Adam Bremensis Gesta Hammaburgensis ecclesiae Pontificum*, ed. Schmeidler
Anglo-Saxon Chronicle	Earle and Plummer, *Two of the Saxon Chronicles Parallel*
Annales Cambriae	*Annales Cambriae*, ed. ab Ithel
Annals of Inisfallen	*Annals of Inisfallen*, ed. Mac Airt
Annals of Tigernach	"Fragmentary Annals of Tigernach," ed. Stokes
Annals of Ulster	*Annala Uladh, Annals of Ulster*, ed. Hennessy and MacCarthy, 4 vols.; and *Annals of Ulster*, ed. Mac Niocaill and Mac Airt.
Annals of the Four Masters	*Annals of the Kingdom of Ireland by the Four Masters*, ed. O'Donovan
ca.	circa
d.	died
Domesday Book	*Domesday Book*, gen. ed. Morris, 42 vols.
Dudo, *History of the Normans*	trans. Christiansen
EHR	*English Historical Review*
f(f).	folio(s)
fl.	flourished
Gerald of Wales, *Topographia Hibernica*	Vol. 5 in *Giraldi Cambrensis Opera*, ed. Brewer, Dimock, and Warner

JRSAI	*Journal of the Royal Society of Antiquaries in Ireland*
l(l).	line(s)
Manx Chronicle	*Chronicle of the Kings of Mann and the Isles*, ed. Broderick and Stowell
MGH (SS)	*Monumenta Germaniae Historica (Scriptores)*
ms(s).	manuscript(s)
OI	Old/Middle Irish
ON	Old Norse
PL	Migne, ed., *Patrologiae cursus completus, Patres . . . ecclesiae latinae*
r.	river
Rolls Series	*Rerum Britannicarum Medii AEvi Scriptores or Chronicles and Memorials of Great Britain and Ireland during the Middle Ages*
s.a.	*sub anno*
Saga Book	*Saga Book of the Viking Society for Northern Research*
SHR	*Scottish Historical Review*
TRHS	*Transactions of the Royal Historical Society*
Ussher, *Whole Works*	*The Whole Works of the Most Rev. James Ussher*, ed. Elrington and Todd
VCH	*Victoria History of the Counties of England*
x	between the years
ZCP	*Zeitschrift für celtische Philologie*

Viking Pirates and Christian Princes

Introduction

BATTLES, VICTORIES, AND GIFTS have occupied the thoughts of many writers, among them a tenth-century poet who declaimed, "Hold my horse, young man, and leave me be; the Irish and the Vikings are raiding, their horses are swift across Achall . . . Olaf who seized the kingship of Dublin in a battle at Howth gave me a horse as the reward for my poem." Olaf is the typical Viking warrior, victorious in battle, exalted in status, and generous to his followers. But no Viking poet recited this verse; the author was an Irishman named Cináed ua hArtacáin[1]—an unexpected choice of poet to recite lines of praise about an unusual patron.

The hero of this poem was one of the most famous Viking princes in the British Isles: Olaf Sitricsson, better known as Olaf "Cuaran." His sobriquet Cuaran is Irish *cúarán* "shoe, boot." This Irish name reveals an aspect not often acknowledged in studies of Vikings, their social and cultural transformation under the influence of the peoples among whom they settled. In the tenth century, Olaf and his family were one of two Viking dynasties that became preeminent in the seas between Ireland and Britain. Their rivals, and occasional allies, were the Haraldssons, the family of Godfrey Haraldsson, who built an empire with his brother, Magnus. Olaf and Godfrey were the descendants of men whom native chroniclers dismissed as itinerant brawlers and pagan pirates. Within a few generations, the clergy, merchants, poets, and princes of their Christian neighbors sought the good will of Olaf, Godfrey, and their descendants.

The dynasties of Olaf Cuaran and Godfrey Haraldsson (hereafter respectively the Olafssons and Haraldssons) straddled the Scandinavian and Celtic worlds. They carved out empires that inspired fear and made them fabulously wealthy. Olaf Cuaran and his family transformed a pirate camp in Ireland into the Kingdom of Dublin, one of the important political and commercial centers along the Atlantic coast. They intermarried with Irish, Norwegian, and Welsh royal families while winning and losing kingdoms from Britain to Scandinavia. Their wealth gave them the means to pay for the praises of poets such as Cináed, to patronize the Church, and to purchase the tools of war. Like the Olafssons, Godfrey Haraldsson and his kindred were active in a wide area, from the Hebrides to Ireland to Wales to Normandy. They assembled the Kingdom of the Isles between Ireland and Britain while allying with, and fighting against, princes from Scotland to Normandy. Their Kingdom of the Isles was the longest surviving Viking principate in Ireland or Britain and an important cultural outpost of the Scandinavian world.

The Olafssons and Haraldssons are proof that the great Viking armies or ships' companies left more in their wake than the carnage so well known from monastic chronicles. The descendants of the raiders who terrified British, Frankish, and Irish societies were the settlers after whom were named the Danelaw in Britain, Normandy in Francia, and Fingal in Ireland. Many Viking colonies failed or were destroyed, but among those that survived were some that thrived. This success was due, in part, to the ability of their ruling dynasties who through the decades achieved power and influence surpassing anything their ferocious ancestors enjoyed.

The story of the Olafssons and Haraldssons has received little attention, despite its importance. One reason for neglect has been the problem of fitting their story into the customary histories of this period. Books devoted to the Vikings usually approach the subject with a view from medieval Scandinavia. The widely separated Viking colonies around the Atlantic, from North America to Normandy, are examined primarily for the insight they provide into Scandinavian culture and expansion. In studies of Britain or Ireland, the treatment of the Vikings is predictable. They suddenly appear at the end of the eighth century, behave badly, steal land, and teach the natives some new words. Then, sportingly, they convert to Christianity and disappear from view. Lost from those historical views are the settled Viking dynasties.

Relations between the Viking settlers and the natives were far more complex than historical clichés about aggressors and victims. In the eleventh century, during the reign of Olaf's son Sitric Silkenbeard, a poem titled "Here is a Happy, Graceful History" was composed about St. Patrick and the Vikings. There, the saint is anachronistically a missionary to the Vikings of Dublin. He blesses them with supremacy in womanhood for their wives and supremacy in beauty for their daughters. Later, a Latin *vita* ("Life") of St. Kevin of Glendalough praises the Vikings of Dublin as powerful and warlike, tough in battle, and skillful at handling ships. In a society that idealized physical beauty, glorified valor in battle, and equated wealth with success, their victims regarded the Vikings with a mixture of horror and admiration. Sometimes admiration was more intimate. In the Haraldssons' empire, at Kirk Braddan on the Isle of Man, Thorstein (Norse name) raised a memorial cross in memory of Ófeig (Norse name), the son of Crínán (Irish name).

This book studies the history of the Olafssons and Haraldssons during the roughly one hundred and fifty years from the middle of the tenth century to the beginning of the twelfth, in what has been called the "Second Viking Age." The years 952 and 1113 conveniently illustrate the range of this study with two events that were minor in themselves, but indicative of major changes. In 952 a rival Viking chieftain forced Olaf Cuaran to flee from his kingdom in Northumbria and return to Ireland. His father, Sitric, had preceded him as king, and Olaf was supported by his kinsmen in Britain and Ireland. Subsequent events showed that Olaf's distress was not caused solely by personal failings. His successor, the aptly named Eirik Bloodaxe, was forced to flee the kingdom scarcely two years later, and he was slain during his flight. Olaf's expulsion showed that the days of a sea-warrior conquering and holding a kingdom by force of arms were almost over. The eventual victor was the English king Eadred, who triumphed through better organization, the perception of good government, and greater resources than his more colorfully named rivals. In common with other minor princes, Olaf had a choice: find new ways to compete with his more powerful neighbors or surrender.

In 1113 another king was forced to flee his kingdom. This time it was an Irish prince named Domnall mac Taidc, who was expelled from the Kingdom of the Isles, where he had reigned since 1111. Domnall was the grandson of a previous Viking lord of the Isles named Echmarcach Ragnallsson. More importantly, Domnall had the support of a powerful patron, the Irish high king (and his uncle) Muirchertach Ua Briain. Nevertheless, his successful rival, named Olaf Godredsson, had an even more powerful patron, his guardian the English king Henry I. Although the nominal over-lord of the Isles was the king of Norway, the monarch of England placed his protégé in the kingship of the Isles and demonstrated that he was the real power in the seas between Ireland and Britain. The era of safety in alliances with local princes had ended, and a new chapter in the region's history had opened: English domination.

The years 952 and 1113 are, of course, symbolic and occasionally this study will transgress those limits. Neither Olaf and Domnall nor their contemporaries would have thought the events of those years to be particularly significant, perhaps nothing more than temporary reversals. They do signal that this was not a static era. Change accompanied the passage of time, sometimes dramatically so. The successful prince was the one who recognized that fact.

This study begins with the history of the Viking fortress on the River Liffey, where Olaf Cuaran's father, Sitric, set up his capital. His family connections illuminate Olaf's career in Ireland and Britain, which appears less random and chaotic when it is realized that he was often fighting for what he believed to be his property. The focus then shifts to the Haraldssons. They illustrate the mobility in the North Atlantic of tenth-century Viking bands, and their battles with rival seafarers explode the myth of Viking solidarity. The affairs of the Olafssons and Haraldssons merged in the early eleventh century, when the commercial success of Dublin made it a magnet for ambitious Irish princes such as the famous high king, Brian Boru. His success led, in 1014, to the important Battle of Clontarf where the Olafssons and Haraldssons allied against Brian. Although the Irish records claim the battle as a triumph for Brian, the true victors were those who avoided it.

In the aftermath of Clontarf both the Olafssons and Haraldssons looked for a powerful ally outside Ireland and found one in Cnut the Great, king of the English and Danes. Their alliance brought security and increased financial rewards within the Christian community. At Dublin a bishopric was founded, and the Olafssons made the transition to patrons of the Christian Church. With the death of Cnut, the rivalry between the Olafssons and Haraldssons became open and intense, as the kingship of Dublin passed from one to the other.

The fortunes of both dynasties were at a low point in the mid-eleventh century. An Irish prince named Diarmait mac Máel na mbó seized control of Dublin and the Kingdom of the Isles. The Olafssons and Haraldssons were on the verge of permanently joining the ranks of once-royal families. Their survival was due to several factors: the willingness of the great Irish families to destroy one other; the collapse of the Anglo-Saxon kingdom after the Battle of Hastings; and the temporary decreasing interest of Scandinavian princes beyond the Baltic.

A new era opened for the Viking dynasties at the end of the eleventh century. The fight for supremacy, and political survival, shifted to the islands between Ireland and Britain. In the midst of the struggle appeared the last great Viking prince, King Magnus III of Norway, better known as Magnus Barefoot. He set up his son as king of the Isles and briefly annexed Dublin. Despite his early death in 1103, the Norwegians remained the masters of the Isles.

The Viking Age lingered long in the seas between Ireland and Britain, due largely to the success of the Olafssons and Haraldssons. The Kingdom of Norway extended as far south as the Isle of Man until the mid-thirteenth century. The Viking settlers around the Irish Sea lived in a colonial society that occupied a peculiar position geographically and intellectually. Long after the Vikings in the English Danelaw had become Northumbrians or the pirates of Bayeux transformed into Normans, the Viking colonists in the Celtic lands remained outsiders to their neighbors. From their first appearance they are described variously as "heathens," "shipmen," "Northmen," "Lochlands," and "Summer Warriors." When the Vikings continued to be described as "foreigners" (*gaill*) by the Irish, they were not indulging in mere bigotry. After the English invaded Ireland in the late twelfth century they, too, observed a distinctive Viking society, which they named Ostman (literally "man from the east"). The name survives today in a neighborhood of Dublin called Oxmantown.

This colonial distinctiveness was marked in different ways. There were physical structures such as the Thingmount at Dublin that stood into the seventeenth century. The Thing (ON Þing) was the Scandinavian assembly place; at Dublin, this had been combined with the Irish use of mounds for gathering places. Another aspect was language. Late in the twelfth century Gerald of Wales noted that the Ostmen spoke a language similar to English rather than Irish.[2] Then there is anecdotal evidence, such as the story told of the twelfth-century Irish reformer St. Malachy. One day he was supervising the construction of a stone oratory at Bangor. A hostile neighbor objected to the work, "We are Irish, not Vikings, and do not build in stone." Malachy's tormentor departed with the taunt that the construction was far too expensive for an Irish church, a revealing comment on the wealth of the Viking settlers.[3]

Earthen mounds, languages, and anecdotes supplement the record of royal succession and battles of the Olafssons and Haraldssons. The progression from victory in battle to survival and political domination is a fascinating study. Other aspects of the dynastic fortunes of the Olafssons and Haraldssons must be investigated, however, in order to understand their prominence when the classical Viking Age was ending. One aspect is commerce, which was increasingly visible both in literary claims that the Viking families were wealthy together with archaeological evidence of the material wealth that was being exploited by princes during this period. In agrarian societies, such as those around the North Atlantic, climatic and environmental changes had an impact on trade. Increased grain yields during the European Climatic Optimum (roughly 1000–1315) fed larger populations, which, in turn, competed for scarce commodities such as oak timber. Religious orientation was also a factor in success. Hostility between pagans and Christians was genuine and a barrier to diplomatic and commercial contacts. Religious change did not take place quickly. Even as the Viking colonists accepted Christianity, pagan cults were still potent among them.

There remain many questions, and a sampling indicates their variety. What do literary or artistic productions reveal about the power or social structure of the elites and their subjects? How important was intermarriage between the Viking dynasties and their neighbors? How did the children from these "mixed marriages" identify themselves, and did they attempt to exploit their ancestry? Finally, did diplomatic adroitness (on both the regional and international level) make a contribution to the fortunes of these Viking dynasties?

The search for answers leads to the historical records. The cliché that the history of the Vikings survives mainly in the accounts of their victims becomes less true by the second half of the tenth century. The Vikings "speak" by means of the inscribed and decorated stones they carved during the tenth to twelfth centuries.[4] These stones are particularly abundant on the Isle of Man and in the Hebrides, the kingdom of the Haraldssons. The inscriptions reveal social structure and family organization with messages written primarily in runic script, following formulaic eulogies on the order of "X raised/made this in remembrance of Y."[5] Christians among the Vikings used religious emblems such as crosses. Typical are two crosses, the first at Kilbar (Isle of Barra) commemorating a Thorgerth the daughter of Steinar, the second at Thurso (Scotland), which an unknown man raised in honor of his father, Ingolf. In addition to biological relationships were ties of dependency formed through artificial kinships such as fosterage and sworn friendship. Memorials to fostering can contain unexpected statements of tenderness. In the churchyard of Kirk Michael (Isle of

Man) the inscription on a cross in honor of a foster-mother notes that it is better to leave a good foster-son than a bad biological son. Almost as important as kinship was friendship, and breeches of it could be both violent and treacherous. Inscribed on a fragment of a cross shaft at Kirk Braddan (Isle of Man) is the accusation that Hrossketil ("Horse Ketil") broke faith and deceived his sworn friend.

The memorial stones also indicate how cultures and religions mingled in the domains of the Olafssons or Haraldssons. Change was a slow process, and Viking colonists did not quickly discard their culture. This is seen in the four Christian high crosses on the Isle of Man decorated with scenes from the pagan legend of Sigurd and the Dragon. Sigurd understood the language of birds and animals after he placed in his mouth the finger that had touched a dragon's blood. The legend of Sigurd was popular throughout the northern world among both pagans and Christians. A version of the saga of Olaf Tryggvason, one of Norway's Christian missionary kings and Olaf Cuaran's son-in-law, has an episode in which a poet recites the Sigurd story to his court.[6]

Compositions by and for the Viking settlers in Ireland and Britain include histories, stories, and verses that circulated among islands and headlands.[7] An example is the poem *Darraðarljóð* ("The Banner Song"), an account of the Irish battle against the Vikings at Clontarf from the latter's point-of-view. *Darraðarljóð* differs from Irish accounts by claiming victory for the Vikings led by Olaf Cuaran's son Sitric Silkenbeard.[8] The poem was composed soon after the battle and, while the principals at Clontarf were all Christians, the poem's tone is pagan; its narrators are witches working at a loom. Like the cultural ambiguity of the scenes from the legend of Sigurd that were carved on Christian crosses, *Darraðarljóð* reflects the religious ambiguity of the Viking settlers in Ireland and Britain that is noted in the legislation and literature of their neighbors. Paganism continued to flourish among the Viking settlers well into the eleventh century. Prohibitions against heathen practices are found in the eleventh-century English "Northumbrian Priests' Laws" and laws of Cnut. The Irish eschatological tract called "The Second Vision of Adomnán" (circa 1096) implies that the Viking settlers still practiced idolatry.[9]

There was literary patronage at the highest ranks of Viking society. Olaf Cuaran and his son, Sitric Silkenbeard, made Viking Dublin a thriving literary and historical center.[10] To their courts came both Norse and Gaelic poets such as Thorgils Grouse-Poet and Gunnlaug Serpent's Tongue, as well as the Irishman Cináed ua hArtacáin. In common with other princes, Olaf and Sitric wanted to be remembered for their prowess in battle and for great wealth. Their subjects also had a literary culture. The author of the Irish tract called *Cocad Gáedel re Gallaib* ("War of the Irish against the Vikings") claims that he consulted the Vikings for their version of the history of the Battle of Clontarf.[11] Sometimes information owes its survival to personal reminiscence and piety. An eleventh-century battle between a Viking named Guthorm who occasionally lived at Dublin and the Irish prince Murchad of Leinster is remembered in the miracles of St. Olaf of Norway, because the silver causing that fight was made into a cross and placed in a church dedicated to Olaf. More specific information can be found at the end of the eleventh century in several works by Bishop Patrick of Dublin (1074–84), including accounts of marvels and theological literature.

Viking colonies provided the avenues for literature to travel between the British Isles and Scandinavia. Icelandic verse has important metrical similarities with Irish poetry, while Icelandic *brynjuboen* (short verse prayers for protection, from circa 900) are based on Irish prayers for protection (*loricae*). Aspects of Irish heroes, such as Finn, may be found in Icelandic tales. A possible borrowing from the Irish legend of Suibhne Gelt into the Icelandic *Hávamál* ("Sayings of the High One") may have traveled from Ireland through the Hebrides to the Orkneys and Shetlands before reaching Iceland.[12]

One chronicle that was the result of patronage by descendants of Olaf Cuaran has the modern title *Chronicle of the Kings of Man and the Isles*, briefly known as the *Manx Chronicle*. Now extant in a Latin copy of the fourteenth century, the *Manx Chronicle* was probably compiled on the Isle of Man at Rushen Abbey; its chronology becomes less confused after the entries for the abbey's foundation.[13] Rushen was founded circa 1135 by a descendant of Olaf Cuaran, the aforementioned Olaf Godredsson (King Olaf I of the Isles). There was a French aspect as Rushen initially was part of the Order of Savigny before being received into the Cistercian Order when the two merged in the mid-twelfth century. The chronicle is a compilation of several sources: a saga about the kings of Man and the Isles; brief annals probably composed at Rushen; and a text cognate with the *Chronicle of Melrose*. The orientation toward Scandinavia is apparent from the first entry, which announces the conquest of England by Svein Forkbeard. Unique material first appears for the year 1066 in connection with the Norwegian defeat at the Battle of Stamford Bridge.

The *Manx Chronicle* shows the difficulties faced by authors attempting to combine different traditions of record keeping, especially in chronology. Until the middle of the twelfth century, the chronicle's chronology is often inaccurate in one of three ways. First, there is misdating as in, for example, the Battle of Stamford Bridge placed *sub anno* 1047, nineteen years before the true date of 1066. Second, events from several years are compressed into a single year, such as the successive reigns of Godred Crovan and his son Lagmann, both given *sub anno* 1056, thirty-nine years before Godred's death in 1095. Finally, events are out of order. Immediately following the notice of Lagmann's death is an entry *sub anno* 1073 recording the death of the Scottish king Máel Coluim Canmore, who died two years before Godred Crovan. The chronological confusion eases by the second quarter of the twelfth century, when the chronicle's dating is basically accurate with only slight errors. As the *Manx Chronicle* shows, determining the sequence of events for Viking history could be as confusing for medieval writers as for later historians.

A useful complement to written sources for Viking history comes from material objects. Memorial inscriptions and art are useful for the elites, but the excavations of houses, farms, ships, and towns reveal the minutiae of daily life that are rarely mentioned in records more concerned with powerful individuals. There have been important excavations at Dublin—at Christ Church Place, Wood Quay, and Fishamble Street—and at Whithorn, in southeast Scotland, as well as sites from northern Wales to the Outer Hebrides.[14]

An important type of artifact that has received much attention is coinage. While the minting of coins in Scandinavia began only late in the tenth century, the Vikings in Britain and Francia had taken control of existing mints in regions where they settled. In northern England from the ninth century the mint at York produced coins for Viking lords. Most of these coins have been recovered in buried hoards, and they were not always the loot from pirate raids. In Sweden many coin hoards represent merchants' stocks.[15] The Icelandic *Landnámabók* ("Book of Settlements") tells of a man named Thord who buried his money before sailing, but he died at sea and his wife refused to leave the farm before she found the buried treasure. Analysis of coin weight and refinement gives an indication of local economic conditions. Reducing the weight of coins encouraged exports because it made business costs cheaper for buyers. Compared with the mass of money that must have been in circulation, relatively few coins have survived. In addition to the usual wear, replacement, and re-coinage, coins have been hunted for centuries as the proverbial "buried treasure." *Cocad Gáedel re Gallaib* claims that pagans found buried coins through sorcery, while the *vita* of the Irish St. Ruadan of Lorrha claims that he used divine guidance to help peasants find treasure in a field. On February 1, 1215, William de Tuit was compelled to explain to the King's Exchequer at Dublin the circumstances of his discovery of money, rings, and gold at the castle of Killamlun, an early example of treasure trove.[16]

More frequently used by historians are the notices about the Viking settlers found in the annals, chronicles, and narratives of their neighbors. For a study of the Olafssons and Haraldssons, the most important sources are the Irish chronicles.[17] The dynastic aspects of these records give clues about the alliances of the Viking families. For instance, a southern Irish chronicle known as the *Annals of Inisfallen* is particularly informative about the Haraldssons because they allied with the princely Irish family of Uí Briain that patronized the church where the annals were maintained. In the north, the *Annals of Ulster* have a bias toward the princes of the powerful Uí Néill confederation, and their interest in the Vikings is mainly in contacts with those princes. A chronicle with a midlands view is the so-called *Annals of Tigernach*, for which a cognate text is the seventeenth-century transcription known as the *Chronicon Scotorum*. The *Annals of Tigernach* contain important and unique information on the Kingdom of Dublin and the family of Olaf Cuaran from the late tenth century, but its value is diminished because of several lacunae, one of which extends from the eighth century to the last quarter of the tenth and another from the years 1003 to 1018.

Less reliable, but occasionally more informative, are chronicles surviving in seventeenth-century transcriptions, such as the *Chronicon Scotorum* and the *Fragmentary Annals* (both preserved in transcriptions made by Duald Mac Firbis). A difficult record to use is the *Annals of the Kingdom of Ireland by the Four Masters*, usually known by the abbreviated title the *Annals of the Four Masters*. This is a seventeenth-century compilation created during a period when Gaelic-speaking society in Ireland was under severe stress. The Four Masters, all clerics, labored valiantly to record information from rapidly vanishing manuscripts. At the same time they incorporated information of dubious reliability, such as the career of the fictional ninth-century king of the Isles named Godred mac Fergus.

The English annals and chronicles are better known than the Irish, although for the purposes of this study they are not as informative. The chronicles known collectively as the *Anglo-Saxon Chronicle* are a royal gazette, and the Vikings are the enemy.[18] A western view in a similar historical tradition is the chronicle often attributed to a Florence of Worcester, which was actually written by a man named John. Entries in this chronicle become contemporary in the late eleventh/early twelfth centuries, when a chronicle written by the Irishman Marianus Scotus was used, and it contains useful information about the Irish mercenary fleets that ravaged the English coast in the eleventh century as well as reports from the Welsh borders.

From northern England, the area of most intense Viking settlement, are the records maintained by the community of St. Cuthbert: the *History of St. Cuthbert*, the *History of the Church of Durham*, the *History of the Kings*, and the *Siege of Durham*. They vary widely in date of composition and information, but their main theme is the rights of St. Cuthbert's see. Originally based on the Isle of Lindisfarne, the community fled from Viking raiders in the ninth century and wandered for several years before residing temporarily at Chester-le-Street and then permanently at Durham. Records of land grants, collections of miracles performed by Cuthbert, and annals were all maintained by the community. While several of the tracts are not strictly annals, they attempt to maintain a chronological progress. The Cuthbertines were not uniformly hostile to the Vikings; a bishop of Lindisfarne was instrumental in the elevation to the kingship of Northumbria of a Viking named Godfrey.[19]

Compared with the Irish and English chronicles, the Welsh records are less informative and more difficult to decipher. The chronicles *Annales Cambriae* and *Brut y Tywysogyon* give only brief notices of events, generally concerned with Wales. Nevertheless they are important for the early history of the activities of the Haraldssons during the tenth century and the Olafssons in the eleventh century. Their usefulness is lessened by uncertainties about their chronology and the brevity of their information.[20] They survive in late manuscripts of which the earliest, a manuscript of the *Annales Cambriae*, is twelfth century. Their Irish Sea outlook reflects that both chronicles derive, ultimately, from a southern Welsh compilation, probably kept at St. David's; in the eleventh century it was sending its clergy to Ireland for instruction.

Their reliance on the annals and chronicles has led many historians to dismiss or ignore another important source of information: narrative histories and historical lists. These works do not make a secret of their views, but they are not fictions, and confusions or simple mistakes are all too often read as deliberate attempts to deceive. Like the chronicles and annals, they must be read with care and discernment. An example is the Welsh *History of Gruffudd ap Cynan* (*Hanes Gruffydd ap Cynan*). Gruffudd ap Cynan (1055–1137) was the lord of Gwynedd in the late eleventh and early twelfth century, and from him descended important Welsh princes such as his son Owain Gwynedd. Gruffudd was a descendant of Olaf Cuaran—his mother was Olaf's great-granddaughter—and he was born in Dublin. This history was composed after Gruffudd's death by someone who did not know him, but used informants who did, and the chronology is confused. Nevertheless, there is a great deal of useful information about Gruffudd's Viking ancestors, as well as illuminating asides, such as how mercenaries operating in the Irish Sea were paid. This is not unqualified hero-worship. Gruffudd's desertions of his troops and shifting alliances are recounted, although often with what was clearly Gruffudd's side of the story.

Writers of those histories had access to significant material no longer extant and the details they preserve make them important. For the history of the Olafssons and Haraldssons this is particularly true for the tract known as *Cocad Gáedel re Gallaib* ("War of the Irish against the Vikings"). This late eleventh/early twelfth-century work is a compilation from the reign of the titular Irish high king Muirchertach Ua Briain (died 1119), and it was written in the interests of his dynasty. The first section is based on a late tenth-century chronicle of the Irish wars against the Vikings from the first raids in the ninth century to the Battle of Tara in 980. Added to that material was a second piece, a saga of the Munster king, and later overlord of all Ireland, Brian Boru (Brian mac Cennétig), who is presented as the unwavering foe of the Vikings. Omitted are Brian's alliances with the Haraldssons and his family's later intermarriage with them. The final section is an account of the events leading up to, and culminating with, the Battle of Clontarf, which was fought on Good Friday, April 23, 1014. *Cocad Gáedel re Gallaib* is an important record of cultural and social history. How the Vikings fought, what types of goods were in their markets, what they took for taxes, and the topography of Viking Dublin are described.

The reception of this tract has gone from one extreme to another. One opinion, especially among historians of the nineteenth and early twentieth centuries, believed that it was written soon after the battle by eyewitnesses.[21] More modern scholars have been divided in their assessment of this tract, usually taking extreme views that either reject completely any information that cannot also be found in the annals or accept the tract wholeheartedly as a genuine memoir.[22] Less considered has been the combination of tracts of different ages and purposes in *Cocad Gáedel re Gallaib*. A tract cognate with the tenth-century text is in the twelfth-century encyclopedia called *The Book of Leinster*, while the report of an exceptionally high tide seems to be based on eyewitness accounts.

Sometimes narratives are valuable for comparison and explanation, such as Dudo of St. Quentin's *History of the Normans*. Historians have noted the inaccuracies and exaggerations in this family history of a Viking named Rollo (Old Norse Hrólfr), his son William Longsword, and grandson Richard I. Dudo's work is panegyric and he rarely allowed fact to interfere with a good story. Despite this work's flaws as political history, it is important for the cultural history of Viking settlements of the tenth and eleventh centuries. Dudo's description of a town with a pronounced Viking aspect helps to illuminate other Viking settlements such as Dublin. Battle formations, antiquarian remains, and agrarian information are found in this history. Equally important are the references to rivalries within Viking towns, the importance of country estates, instructions on how to build a church from the initial plans to completion, and information about other families, such as possibly the Haraldssons.

A view of the Viking families in Ireland and Britain from outside the islands is in the *History of the Archbishops of Hamburg/Bremen*, composed by Adam of Bremen. Adam came to Bremen circa 1066 and almost immediately began to collect materials for his history; soon after it was completed circa 1076 he began to make additions to the text. The archbishops of Hamburg/Bremen had pastoral responsibilities among the Scandinavian churches before the twelfth century. That responsibility extended as far west as the British Isles, which is why Adam's view included the Viking colonies in the Irish Sea. Among his written sources were several that are now lost, including a book he describes as the "Deeds of the English" (*Gesta Anglorum*) that supplied him with information about the ancestors of Olaf Cuaran. Another source of information was his personal friend, the Danish king Svein Ulfsson, who was an amateur historian. King Svein collected information about his ancestors and their subjects, including genealogies, reign lengths, and significant events.

Finally, important genealogical information is found in the list of famous ladies known as the *Banshenchas* ("History of Ladies"). Intermarriage between Viking families (such as the Olafssons and Haraldssons) and their neighbors produced offspring who ensured that information about their ancestors found its way into genealogies and biographies. The *Banshenchas* is a list of the names of notable Irish women and their illustrious children.[23] The earliest version was composed using materials from the late eleventh century, and later copies included supplementary material added in the twelfth century. Viking princesses, like their contemporaries throughout Europe, married for the diplomatic purposes of their families. The marriages are rarely revealed in chronicles and annals, but they are important in understanding the seemingly random attacks of individuals who were actually fighting for their inheritance.

Records that look at the Viking families in Britain and Ireland with sympathy rather than as *gennti* ("heathens") or *gaill* ("foreigners") were composed in the twelfth century and later. Descendants of the Viking colonists in Ireland and Britain were interested in the deeds of their forbears, and they were recorded in the Icelandic sagas and histories. Icelandic scholars of the eleventh century such as Ari the Wise and Saemund Sigfússon made collections of memoirs of the early settlers and their families that were used in twelfth-century products such as *Íslendingabók* ("Book of the Icelanders"), and *Landnámabók* ("Book of Settlements"). In addition to famous individuals such as the Hebridean Viking lady named Aud the deep-minded and her husband, Olaf the White, there were obscure individuals such as the brothers, Ketil and Thormod the Old, who emigrated from Ireland to Iceland.[24] Sagas that were being composed in the twelfth century used the history preserved in the verses of earlier court poets, who immortalized their aristocratic patrons by reciting their deeds. *Orkneyinga Saga* ("Saga of the Orkney Islanders"), partly composed before 1190 in Iceland, is a history of the jarls of the Orkneys using skaldic verse as its foundation. The historical view could be broad, as in Snorri Sturluson's *Heimskringla* ("World Encircler"). Even though he is telling the story of the kings of the Norwegians, it extends as far as the Viking colonies in the Shetlands, Orkneys, Hebrides, and Irish Sea.[25]

Genuine historical information is the basis for entertaining narrative literary works such as *Njal's Saga*, *Eyrbyggja Saga* ("Saga of the People of Eyr"), and *Gunnlaugs Saga Ormstungu* ("Saga of Gunnlaug Serpent's Tongue"), written down in the thirteenth and fourteenth centuries. While they were intended primarily as amusement, they preserve ancient verses and present an outline of events in the Hebrides and Irish Sea reflecting the Vikings' remembrance of events. *Njal's Saga*, for example, has the important poem *Darraðarljóð* and the author used a history cognate with the Irish tract *Cocad Gáedel re Gallaib*.[26]

The first history of the Vikings settlers in Ireland as more than foils for native princes was written in the twelfth century by Gerald of Wales in the third book of his *Topographia Hibernica*. He began with the shadowy ninth-century Viking leader Turgeis (whom he confuses with the African king Gormund found in Geoffrey of Monmouth's *History of the Kings of Britain*) and describes the triumph of the Vikings followed by their expulsion. Gerald makes the interesting claim that the Vikings returned to Ireland at the request of the Irish, who wanted towns and commerce.

The final chapter in the preservation of the history of the Irish Vikings came four hundred years later. The seventeenth-century Irish antiquarian known to English-speakers as Duald Mac Firbis (properly Dubhaltach Mac Firbhisigh), the last of a family of historians from Sligo trained in the old Irish schools, raced against time to transcribe the vanishing records of ancient Ireland. One of these was a book of genealogies, completed in 1650, with lineages of the important Irish families. Included in it is a short history of the Vikings in Ireland, which has been given the modern title *Concerning the Formorians and Norsemen*. This is a miscellany of lineage and family saga; a confused and confusing mixture of probable fiction and possible history. Even the more humble were not forgotten; Mac Firbis notes that many of the merchants of Dublin claimed to be descended from Olaf Cuaran.

The Dublin merchants made claims of illustrious ancestry using records that were preserved because a Viking ancestor had financial and legal benefits in Ireland after the Anglo-Norman invasions. Two documents illustrate the point. In 1215 King John ordered an inquiry into the question of the right of the clergy of Christ Church, Dublin, to keep a boat on the River Liffey.[27] The matter, with important financial repercussions for the Church, was decided by a jury drawn from the English and Ostmen of Dublin, but not the Irish. Unlike their "wild Irish" neighbors, the Ostmen had legal rights in the eyes of the new masters of the land, and "English" law was extended to them. This brought safety. In 1295 a man named William the *Teynturer* of *Artfinan* had a suit of disseisin (i.e., to remove him from his land) brought against him by three accusers.[28] They claimed that he was a pureblooded Irishman of servile condition, whose father was named Thomas Omoleyns. In his defense, William asserted that he was a free man by virtue of being an Ostman (*houstmannus*), that his family name was Macmackus (literally "son of Magnus"), and that he had inherited his property legally from his mother, Olyna. William's testimony convinced the court, and he kept his land. Being an Ostman meant being free in thirteenth-century Ireland.

Records are one part of understanding the history of Olaf Cuaran, Godfrey Haraldsson, and their families. Another part is geography. The final settlement of the Olafssons and Haraldssons was in a region of the North Atlantic that is today known as the Irish Sea Province. During the Middle Ages, this region was considered to be the haunt of the adventurer who gained his fortune by courage, calculation, and good fortune. In the Old Icelandic tale known as *Egil's Saga*, a Viking father advises his son to sail to Dublin because that was where a fortune was to be made. Whether this was heroic or barbaric depended on one's point of view. The Irish Sea also had connections with the supernatural in the popular mind. In *Njal's Saga*, a Viking fleet anchored off the Isle of Man is attacked by a phantom army. During three consecutive nights the seamen are attacked by showers of blood, phantom birds of prey, and ghostly weapons; every morning one man is found dead.[29] In the same vein are stories told by Gerald of Wales and Matthew Paris about Irish Sea chieftains who concluded treaties by drinking each other's blood.[30]

The geography of the Irish Sea lent itself to colorful individuals and empire building. This relatively shallow extension of the North Atlantic begins at the North Channel (between northeast Ireland and southwest Scotland) and then extends south to a line just north of Wicklow Head in Ireland across to the Llyn Peninsula in Wales, between latitudes 55 and 53 degrees north.[31] The Irish Sea's width ranges from about 20 miles between county Antrim in Ireland and the Rhinns of Galloway in Scotland to over 100 miles between the Lancashire coast of England and the river Boyne in Ireland. To the south is St. George's Channel, often considered part of the

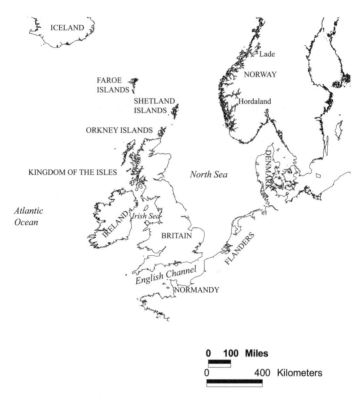

MAP 1. *Northeast Atlantic*

greater Irish Sea Province. To the north are the islands of the Hebrides, also techni-
cally outside the Irish Sea, but in the view of this study part of the Kingdom of the
Isles.

Within the Irish Sea region are few hindrances to travel, none insurmountable.
The Irish coast has natural harbors such as Strangford Lough and Carlingford
Lough, where Viking raids were particularly severe in the ninth century. They are
complemented by rivers such as the Liffey, which rises in the Wicklow Hills before
flowing past Dublin into the Irish Sea. Sailing was not without difficulties and dangers. Whirlpools were a menace, such as Coire Brecáin ("Brecan's Cauldron") in the
North Channel and one off the Isle of Anglesey in the Menai Straits. There are sand-
banks and submerged rock outcroppings throughout the area, which continue to
make coastal navigation dangerous. Vessels entering Dublin Bay, for example, must
plot a course between the Burford Bank to the north and the Kish Bank to the
south.[32]

The Irish Sea anciently was an area for communication among Ireland, Britain,
continental Europe, and the Arctic Circle.[33] In the sixth century a ship that sailed this
route from Italy to the Hebrides was remembered in Abbot Adomnán of Iona's *Life*

of Columba. In the eighth century a storm drove another ship along this route. One of its passengers was the traveler Arculf who provided Adomnán with information about the Holy Land that is preserved in his "armchair traveler" *Concerning Holy Places* (*De Locis Sanctis*). Bede notes that many English students sailed to Ireland. In the late seventh century one of them named Egbert wanted to sail from Ireland south around Britain to *Germania*, but his ship capsized in the harbor, although another man named Wicbert did sail from Ireland to Frisia. More precise sailing directions are given in a Norman charter, issued by the future king Henry II of England circa 1150. This charter of liberties for the citizens of Rouen states that all ships from Normandy to Ireland must sail from Rouen, except one a year from Cherbourg; any Irish ship sailing past Guernsey Head that wanted to trade in Normandy must do so in the town of Rouen.[34]

Sailing times between Britain and Ireland were brief and the actual sailing uncomplicated in comparison with voyages to other areas in medieval Europe. In his *History and Topography of Ireland*, Gerald of Wales notes that the passage from St. David's in southwest Wales to Ireland was one short day's sailing, and that sailing from Ulster to Galloway was half as far. In the Hebrides the distance between some islands is almost negligible. Walter Map tells the story of a Hebridean soldier whose mistress was kidnapped. The soldier swam from his home to a neighboring island, killed the abductor, and them swam home to safety. The eleventh-century Welsh prince Gruffudd ap Cynan made one of his many escapes from Wales to Ireland simply by borrowing the row-boat that belonged to the church at Aberdaron and rowing himself to safety. Within two months he had made three such trips while rallying support for his campaigns in Gwynedd. Sailing times varied, however, with weather conditions and the type of vessel. According to a fifteenth-century Dublin merchant named Bartholomew Rossynell, a heavily laden merchant ship took twenty-four hours to sail from the Isle of Man to Dublin. Sailing from the Irish Sea to the Orkneys took about thirty hours with a good wind; a journey from the north of Ireland to Iceland took five days in good sailing weather.[35]

The ships that sailed these waters made the Olafssons and Haraldssons powerful and wealthy. To be a sailor was an honorable profession, and interest in seafaring began at a young age. Toy ships and boats were made as playthings for children.[36] Excavations in Dublin at Wood Quay have revealed parts of ships or boats, following Scandinavian models, that were reused in the frames of houses, drains, and the town's water-barrier. Literature and art are also informative. For example, by the tenth century ships were built with a hull constructed with overlapping boards held together with iron rivets. This made for sturdier and more seaworthy vessels. The Old English poem on the Battle of *Brunanburh* (fought in 937) describes the defeated Dublin army returning home in ships with nailed sides. The oars and sails of ships are illustrated at the Abbey of Iona on a late medieval monument that shows a descendant of this type of ship under sail.[37] The Vikings were imitated by their neighbors. Ships were included in the ritualized gift exchange practiced by the Irish.

The late eleventh-century Irish treatise on royal dues known as the *Book of Rights* (*Lebor na Cert*) describes brightly colored ships with sleeping bunks.[38]

A helpful comparison of the region where the Olafssons and Haraldssons built their empires is with the northwestern Mediterranean; in a geographical context the Irish Sea has been described as a "British Mediterranean."[39] In the later tenth century, like the principalities of the northern Mediterranean lands, the Irish and Welsh were politically fragmented and various principalities contested among themselves despite owing allegiance to a nominal high king. The turmoil was caused by a sophisticated and violent aristocracy, despite the best efforts of an intellectually vibrant clergy to reduce the bloodshed. Similar to the north Mediterranean ports, the commercial centers around the Irish Sea were cosmopolitan and thriving. Coins circulated throughout the region. To the east, kings from a single dynasty of the West Saxons were completing their monopoly of kingship over a unified Anglo-Saxon kingdom that was a wealthy and administratively progressive domain. At the same time it was a major supplier to, and important market for, the goods traded and produced outside its borders. As in Byzantium, wealth and stability did not guarantee the English protection from military disaster. And finally, just as the Islamic merchants/adventurers/settlers were both a stimulus and disruption in the Mediterranean, so, too, were Vikings such as the Olafssons and Haraldssons. At the same time that they were a military threat to their neighbors, they were also contributing to their commercial and cultural development.

Of course, those interesting similarities must not be pushed too far. England was not Byzantium, nor did it have the ancient and smoothly functioning administration that was available to the Greeks. The thriving settlements on the shores of the Irish Sea, such as Chester and Dublin, were not comparable in amount of goods traded, number of merchants, or area of influence to wealthy cities such as Venice or Genoa. Nevertheless, like societies around the northern Mediterranean, the peoples around the Irish Sea during the tenth century were experiencing tremendous political, economic, and cultural changes. The answer to the question of who was a pirate and who was a prince varied according to the observer, and both labels were applied to the families of Olaf Cuaran and Godfrey Haraldsson.

1

Two Rivers and the Origins of Olaf Cuaran

T HE FIRST FACT about Olaf Cuaran is that his father, Sitric, was active in Ireland and Britain in the first quarter of the tenth century. This simple statement helps to explain Olaf's career and the preoccupations of his descendants. Like his parent, Olaf ruled kingdoms in two islands, married princesses from among his enemies, and entered legend.

The ancestry of Sitric and two other Vikings named Ragnall and Godfrey has been a matter of dispute. Irish writers describe Sitric, Ragnall, and Godfrey as the "descendants of Ivar" (*Uí Imair*) or the "kindred of Ivar" (*clann Imair*).[1] Are these descriptions of family lineage, or are they a generic designation of Vikings whose ancestry is otherwise unknown? In the contemporary record in the *Annals of Ulster* the designation "descendant of Ivar" is used only during a period of forty-two years, from 896 to 937. This actually overstates matters a bit. Prior to 914 the phrase is used twice, in 896 for an *Amlaim h[ua] Imair* and in 904 for *Imar h[ua] Imair*. From 914, and for the next twenty-four years, this identification is used for only four men: Sitric, Ragnall, Godfrey, and Godfrey's son Olaf. Godfrey's other sons are described as "sons of Godfrey."

Who was Ivar? He is generally thought to have been one of the powerful chieftains of the first Viking colony in the Liffey Valley in the mid-ninth century. Ivar is first mentioned in the Irish annals in 853 and he made expeditions throughout Ireland in 871 and 872 before dying a Christian in 873.[2] Ivar ruled with two other princes (which the *Fragmentary Annals of Ireland* describe as his brothers) named Ausil and Olaf. Olaf was the most famous of the trio, the "son of the king of Lothlind," who took lordship over the Vikings in Ireland according to the *Annals of Ulster* and became the model for Olaf the White of the Icelandic sagas; a ninth-century Irish verse calls him "Olaf the good king of Dublin."[3] The reigns of Ivar and Olaf marked the high point for Viking fortunes in the ninth century. After their deaths (Olaf in Scotland in 875), the Vikings of the Liffey fell on evil times, leading to the destruction of their camp in 902.

Another version of Sitric's ancestry comes from genealogies in later medieval Welsh texts, such as the *History of Gruffudd ap Cynan*. They claim that he was a son of Harald Fairhair, the late ninth/early tenth-century prince who, by the twelfth century, was credited with the formation of the Norwegian kingdom. This lineage seems unlikely to be correct because neither contemporary histories nor later medieval Norse sagas are aware of a connection between Sitric and Harald Fairhair.[4] The pedigrees in the Welsh materials bear the marks of historical revisionism intended to give the Welsh descendants of Olaf Cuaran a connection with the Norwegian kings.

A third and more precise lineage is given by the eleventh-century historian Adam of Bremen in his *Gesta Hammaburgensis Ecclesiae Pontificum* ("History of the Archbishops of Hamburg/Bremen").[5] He notes that early in the tenth century there were three brothers ruling in England named Ragnall, Sitric, and Olaf; they were the sons of Godfrey Hardacnutsson. All four men are known from other records. Godfrey ruled Northumbria for about thirteen years, from circa 883 to 896; Sitric and Ragnall have been introduced. Olaf was actually a grandson, not son, of Godfrey, and a son of Sitric's brother, Godfrey; the same name for father and son led to the confusion. Olaf the son of Godfrey the son of Godfrey Hardacnutsson, nephew of Sitric and Ragnall, was far more famous than his father, ruling briefly in Northumbria before his death in 941.

Adam's source was an "English book" that he quotes elsewhere for information about northern England. His claims of kinship among Godfrey, Ragnall, and Sitric are supported by the twelfth-century English historian William of Malmesbury and the fourteenth-century Scots historian John of Fordun. Fordun claims that Ragnall was the son of Godfrey Hardacnutsson, and that Sitric was his kinsman. William of Malmesbury claims that Sitric was a kinsman of Alfred the Great's Viking opponent named Guthrum. William of Malmesbury and John of Fordun both confuse Godfrey of Northumbria with Guthrum of East Anglia who died circa 890. Geffrei Gaimar (using a now-lost northern English chronicle) gives a complementary piece of genealogical information that Ragnall had an English mother.[6] Godfrey Hardacnutsson's parentage of Sitric does not necessarily contradict the Irish chronicles, since Irish *ua* can mean "grandson" or have the wider meaning of "descendant."

As noted, Godfrey Hardacnutsson (ON Guðröðr Hörðaknútsson) was king of Northumbria circa 883 to 896. The little that is known of him comes mainly from the records of the community of St. Cuthbert. Despite being forced to abandon the church at Lindisfarne because of Viking attacks, and wandering in northern Britain for years, the head of the Church, the bishop of Lindisfarne, was instrumental in the elevation of Godfrey to the kingship. The *History of St. Cuthbert* claims that St. Cuthbert appeared in a dream to Bishop Eadred of Lindisfarne and announced that a youth in the Danish army was to be the king of Northumbria.[7] Eadred went to the army, at that time camped above the River Tyne, brought forth Godfrey, and had him recognized as king by placing a golden ring on his right arm in a ceremony witnessed by the troops.

After the death of Godfrey Hardacnutsson in 896, control of Northumbria was contested between the Vikings and the English. The political situation appears to have been complicated, although the details remain obscure despite the use of historical records, coin inscriptions, and archaeological materials in efforts to illuminate the two decades after the death of Godfrey. In 913 the Irish annals record the death of Eadulf "king of the North Saxons." He might have ruled just the northern part of Northumbria, the old Kingdom of Bernicia, although it is not impossible that he ruled all Northumbria.

Studies of Ragnall, Sitric, and Godfrey have assumed that the three men were originally resident in Ireland before invading Northumbria.[8] Using the information given by Adam of Bremen and historians in Britain, Ragnall and his brothers were immediately connected with Northumbria. After Eadulf's death, Godfrey Hardacnutsson's son Ragnall appears in the *History of St. Cuthbert* circa 914. His base of power seems to have been in the southern part of Northumbria, the region of Deira where his father granted lands. He sailed his fleet up the Tyne as far as Corbridge (just south of Hadrian's Wall, near Hexham) to seize the lands of Eadulf's son Ealdred. Ealdred fled north to the Scots where he enlisted the aid of King Constantine to recover his lands. Kinship may explain the alliance. The name of Constantine's son Idulf is a Gaelic form of Eadulf, the name of Ealdred's father. Ealdred and Constantine led an army to Corbridge but were defeated by Ragnall, "I do not know because of what sin," lamented the chronicler.

The goodwill from the community of St. Cuthbert to Godfrey did not extend to his family. Their records are careful never to connect Godfrey with Ragnall, Sitric, or Godfrey the younger. Ragnall is described simply as a "king of pagans" who led his pirates on raids. This coyness is not surprising, since the community staunchly supported the conquest of Northumbria by the southern English family of Alfred the Great, even going so far as to state that Alfred was the first of his dynasty to hold lordship over Northumbria. Any hint that a Viking dynasty ruled in Northumbria from the ninth to tenth centuries is carefully avoided, despite the fact being clearly evident in the records prepared with the patronage of Alfred's family.

The hostility of the Cuthbertine records reflects land disputes with Godfrey's family. The community had lost much land during the ninth-century Viking wars, and the succeeding centuries were devoted to replenishing the loss. Godfrey Hardacnutsson granted estates to the bishop of Lindisfarne in the vicinity of Durham and Hartlepool: Hesleton, Horden, Castle Eden and Little Eden, Holam, Hottun Henry, and Willington.[9] The bishop redistributed those lands to a noble named Alfred son of Birihtulfinc, who had fled to the eastern coast in order to escape Viking pirates. Some of his father's lands later were retaken by Ragnall Godfreysson, who, in turn, gave Castle Eden and Little Eden to his commanders Scula and Onalafball ("Olaf the Bold"). Onalafball acquired a special place in the local demonology as "the son of the devil" who appeared at a church and taunted the congregation by asking why they prayed to a dead Cuthbert when his gods—Thor and Odin—were so much stronger. Ragnall's land confiscations/retrievals together with the paganism of his followers ensured that the Christian clergy who wrote the records wasted little sympathy on him or his kinsmen.

Land hunger was also helped by turmoil in the Irish Sea, which was infested with pirates in the opening years of the tenth century. A fleet led by a Viking named Ingimund raided from Wales to Chester and beyond. The attacks were so severe that a pact of mutual aid, remembered in the *Fragmentary Annals*, was made among the English, Scots, and Britons of Strathclyde. Not all the pirates were Vikings; some were Irish. In 913 the Viking settlers of Cumberland and Lancashire defeated a fleet from northeastern Ireland. The *Annals of Ulster* note: "A battle gained by the heathen over a new Ulaid fleet on the shores of the land of Saxons, where many were slain." Among the slain was an Irish prince named Cummascach, son of Máel-mochéirgi of Leth Cathail, a kingdom located on the coast of county Down.

Adding to the confusion in the Irish Sea Province were the movements of Viking fleets between Britain and Francia. In 914 a fleet sailed from Brittany to southwestern Britain under the command of two chieftains named Ottar and Hraold. According to the report in the *Anglo-Saxon Chronicle*, after the fleet sailed from Brittany, it raided around the Severn and throughout southern Wales. The pirates captured Bishop Cyfeiliog of Archenfield (located between Hereford and Gloucester), who was ransomed by the West Saxon king Edward the Elder for forty pounds of silver. After Hraold was slain, the invaders were forced out of Britain. They sailed first to Dyfed (southwest Wales) and then on to Waterford in Ireland. Parts of that fleet may have sailed farther. In 914 Ragnall led a fleet into the Irish Sea where, off the Isle of Man, he fought a sea battle against Barid, son of Ottar (probably the same man who led the fleet from Brittany), who was slain together with many of his men.

The pirates in the Irish Sea led to a flight of the Anglo-Saxon aristocracy from the region. Abbot Tilred of Heversham (in Westmorland) abandoned his church and purchased either Castle Eden or Little Eden, which were presented to the community of St. Cuthbert for his admittance. Tilred succeeded Cutheard as bishop in 915. There was also Alfred son of Birihtulfinc who, "fleeing pirates," came from beyond the western mountains. Bishop Cutheard gave him all the lands that Godfrey had assigned to the community as well as Easington, Shotton, Billingham, and Sheraton. A third refugee was Eadred son of Rixinc who murdered *Eardulfus principus*, apparently the Eadulf mentioned in the *Annals of Ulster*. Afterwards, Eadred abducted Eadulf's widow (although without popular approval, as the *History of St. Cuthbert* primly notes) before retiring south of the River Tyne to the sanctuary provided by lands belonging to the Cuthbertine community. Eadred faithfully paid rent to St. Cuthbert's community for three years until he attacked Ragnall at Corbridge, where he was slain circa 916. With a generosity of spirit that did him credit, Ragnall first seized the lands for himself but then gave them to Eadred's sons Esbrid and Æthelstan to honor their ferocious fighting in the battle. Eadred himself appears to have had noble status, for his son Æthelstan is described as a count.

In 917 Ragnall and Sitric led fleets to southeast Ireland. Their arrival was heralded by comets and terrifying thunderstorms. Precisely why they were in Ireland is uncertain. Possibly they had some connection there or Sitric might have desired his own kingdom, and Ragnall assisted him. They landed in the southeast and made an alliance with the fleet anchored at Waterford. Sitric led his ships up the River Barrow to a place called *Cennfuait* (probably near St. Mullins) while Ragnall remained on the Suir at Waterford. The Irish were aware of the danger the Vikings presented, and the High King Niall *Glúndub* ("Black Knee") mac Áeda moved against them with an army composed of the Uí Néill and the men of Munster. An inconclusive battle was fought on August 22 near Clonmel. The Leinstermen attacked Sitric's camp at *Cennfuait*, but they were repelled with heavy losses. In the wake of his victory, Sitric led his troops to the River Liffey, where he established a base that became Dublin.

The Irish were carefully watching Ragnall and Sitric. A tract from the first half of the tenth century with the modern title "The March Roll of the Men of Leinster" gives instructions for the deposition of the province's warriors in case of attack by, among others, the Vikings.[10] The men of Osraige were to contain the Viking invaders in the south, apparently a reference to Waterford, while the other men of the province were to hurry to the east to face the "gentiles" coming across on the currents of the great sea.

Sitric and Ragnall divided their forces in 918. Ragnall sailed from Waterford back to Britain, never to return to Ireland. The reason for his departure was renewed hostility from the Scots. Ragnall led his forces northwards, but the Scots were waiting for him. In a battle fought on the banks of the Tyne (probably the Haddington Tyne in Lothian rather than the southern Tyne), the Vikings and Scots fought to a draw. The *Annals of Ulster* seem to have used a brief saga of the battle that reveals Ragnall's tactics, which were probably the same used by his brother in Ireland. He divided his forces into battle groups of four, of which the fourth was held in reserve. When the battle began to go badly, the reserve forces were used to force a stalemate.

Sitric remained in Ireland. Realizing that success depended on diplomacy as well as military preparation, he made an alliance with his northern neighbor Máel Mithig mac Flannacáin, who ruled Brega (extending from northern county Dublin to southern county Louth) from his fortress of Knowth, perched above the River Boyne. Máel Mithig had made this alliance for defense against his Irish enemies although, as the *Annals of Ulster* point out, "it helped him not at all."

Dublin became the main Irish base of operations for Sitric and his family. Situated in the middle of the eastern Irish coast, the town was located near the crossing of the River Liffey known as "the ford of the hurdles" or *Ath Clíath* in Irish. The ford was an important crossing place and is mentioned in seventh-century records connected with the saints Columba and Patrick. Place-name legend (OI *dindshenchas*) explains its name.[11] One legend claims that the ford had been built by the men of

Leinster, who had controlled lands north of the Liffey, in order to herd their sheep to the rich grasslands of what is now northern county Dublin. Another story states the ford was formed from the breastbone of a monster named Matae that had been thrown into the River Boyne (north of the Liffey), drifted out to sea, and then floated into the Liffey, where it lodged.

Sitric was not the first pirate to have sailed up the Liffey. Somewhere around the river was Casse, where the legendary Irish Sea pirate named Lóegaire was slain. He gave up piracy after hearing a prophecy that he would die between Ireland and Britain. The elements of nature were sureties for his good behavior. Lóegaire eventually broke his vow and returned to his former life. So his sureties the sun and the wind took their revenge, and they killed him near the Liffey between the hills Ériu (Ireland) and Alba (Britain) in Casse (possibly modern Mullacash). South of the Liffey along the coast was the site of the famous hostel of Dá Derga, the scene of action in the Old Irish tale *Destruction of Dá Derga's Hostel* (*Togail Bruidne Dá Derga*). In this saga a prince named Conaire rules peacefully and prosperously until he unwittingly violates his taboos (the restrictions on the actions of a king), which leads precipitously to doom when pirates attack him from the Irish Sea.

The first Viking settlement along the Liffey had been built in the ninth century. Originally an anchorage for the raiding parties that attacked the rich Irish midlands, a ship fort (*longport*) was constructed circa 841.[12] The exact location of the early fort is obscure, but the later Viking fortress was built at a secure anchorage on the south side of the Liffey, at the confluence with the River Poddle. These early riverine settlements provided refuge for raiders, a convenient harbor for the ships, and a secure holding place for loot. Such a position could be quickly and easily fortified, needing little more than an earthen work defensive barrier.

One attraction for Vikings was the many churches in the vicinity of Áth Clíath.[13] They suffered severely. A few miles north of the Liffey was the church of Glasmor where the entire community had been killed in one night during a Viking raid. The ruins were still standing in the twelfth century. Terror of the Vikings is found in the remains of a service book from the church of Clondalkin (south of the Liffey) where a ninth-century Viking fortress was build. Among the surviving scraps is a prayer for deliverance from the flood of foreign peoples and pagans.[14]

Other religious houses were more fortunate, such as the famous church of Tallaght, home of the important Céli Dé ("Clients of God") reform movement developed by Máelruain in the late eighth century, just prior to the arrival of the Vikings. South of the Liffey, near the ford, was the church of Kilmainham. A Viking cemetery was discovered near here in the nineteenth century, and the Vikings might have used the church at some time as a camp. Some churches were immediately connected with the Olafsson dynasty. North of the Liffey was the church of Finian (*Cell Finnend*) located in Fingal. This was probably the "house of Finian" where Olaf Cuaran's granddaughter was a nun. East of Finian's church was the church of Swords. For a long time it was on Dublin's border and, depending on where the border shifted, the Olafssons were occasional plunderers and sometimes protectors. After becoming permanently within Dublin's territory, together with a church farther north along the coast at Lusk, Swords was the school attended by Olaf Cuaran's Welsh descendant Gruffudd ap Cynan.

By the later half of the ninth century the Vikings, under the leadership of Ivar and Olaf, had built several forts close to the Liffey. In 865 two Irish princes named Cennidigh mac Gaithin and Máel Ciaráin mac Ronáin captured one such fort, known as Olaf's fort, at Clondalkin. There was another fort close by, where a hundred Viking chieftains were slain on the same day. Those small, isolated settlements were vulnerable to a determined attack and could easily be swept away by one powerful prince. In 866 the High King Áed Findliath ("Aed the handsome warrior") destroyed the Viking colonies along the northern coast from Cenél nEógain to Dál nAraide (in modern terms, from the Inishowen Peninsula to Larne Harbor).

After the deaths of Ivar and Olaf there was infighting among the Vikings of the Liffey. The disruption was made worse by the tendency of close (and distant) relations to kill each other with alarming casualness. In 888 a son of Ivar named Sicfrith was killed by his brother in what seems to have been a fight for supremacy. By the last decade of the century the hostility had become so intense that bands of Vikings were leaving Ireland. The *Annals of Ulster* claims that in 893 there was a division among the Viking colonists. One group remained in Ireland with a chieftain named Sicfrith the jarl, while a second group left under the leadership of a man called only "the son of Ivar," who was probably the Sitric later slain in 896 by his own people.

Racked by disputes and apparently without a substantial proportion of its former population, the fortress at the "ford of the hurdles" was an easy prey when it was captured in 902 by Máel Findia mac Flannacáin of the southern Uí Néill dynasty of Síl nÁedo Sláine of Brega (located just to the north of Dublin) and Cerball mac Muricáin of Leinster. The subsequent flight of the Vikings was hailed in the Irish annals, which note that they fled so hurriedly that they left behind their dead. Probably only the nobility departed, with the commoners remaining under Irish domination. There might not have been many exiles, for the annals remark that many ships remained. The old Viking kingdom along the Liffey was ended.

The geographical and political conditions that had attracted the first wave of Viking settlers remained. The Irish considered the plain of the Liffey (OI *Mag Life*) to be one of the three most fertile plains in Ireland. The rich farmland of the Liffey plain was well guarded on two sides. Curving on the west are the Dublin Hills, also mentioned in the Irish triads, while to the south are the Wicklow Hills. The early Viking settlements depended on farming, and leaders rewarded their followers with land. The Viking chief Halfdan made a famous land-sharing in 876 in Britain, according to the *Anglo-Saxon Chronicle*, so that his followers could plow and make a livelihood for themselves. Sometimes the indigenous population remained to support the new overlords. *Cocad Gáedel re Gallaib* claims that Vikings settled in Munster took foodstuffs, especially milk and eggs, from the local farms as taxes. The Vikings also kept herds and flocks. As part of his destruction of the Viking settlements along the northern Irish coast, the High King Áed Findliath drove away their cattle and sheep. The herds of the Dublin Vikings were so important in the late tenth century that they were moved into hiding at the threat of invasion.

Political geography provided another reason for a Viking camp along the Liffey. By the ninth century the river was the border between two rival groups. To the north were the Uí Néill kingdoms, and to the south was the province of Leinster. The Liffey had been the border between them only a little more than a century before the Viking settlement. As late as the mid-eighth century the Uí Néill and Leinster princes were fighting for control of the lands around the Liffey. The fortress of Dublin was on the southern bank of the Liffey, and within the province of Leinster. The Vikings were a buffer between the rival Irish princes and, on occasion, were useful allies.[15]

A third equally, if not more, important reason is that the Liffey basin was an ancient trading place, both international and coastal.[16] The Liffey is mentioned in the "Geographical Guide" of the second-century A.D. geographer Claudius Ptolemeus of Alexandria, where it is called *Oboka*. There had been a trading station on Dalkey Island, just south of the Liffey, where artifacts from throughout the northern Atlantic and Mediterranean have been uncovered. After escaping from his Irish master, St. Patrick might have fled to the mouth of the Liffey where he met sailors preparing to sail across the Irish Sea.

The River Liffey was connected with the interior of Ireland by major roads. Four of the great Irish highways known as *slige* (a road large enough to accommodate two chariots traveling side by side) either crossed over, or ended at, the Liffey. These roadways were "the Great Highway" (*an tslighe mhóir*) from Dublin to Clonmacnoise (on the banks of the River Shannon), "the Highway of the Assembly of the sons of Umhar" (*slige dhála meic Umháir*) from Dublin to Limerick (also on the Shannon), "the Highway of Midluachra" (*slige Midluachra*) from Dublin through Anagassan to Dunseverick, and "the Highway of Cúala" (*slige Chúalann*), which ran from Dublin past Da Derga's hostel to Waterford. Three of those four roads connected the Liffey with places—Limerick, Anagassan, and Waterford—where other Viking settlements would be made. Roads were important and information about them was collected in a medieval guide or "book of roads" (*lebar sliged*) found and copied by St. Lasrianus.[17]

With his capture of the old Viking settlement on the River Liffey, Sitric set his men to construct a stronghold on the south bank of the Liffey at the confluence with the River Poddle. The original fort was likely neither elaborate nor complex, possibly little more than an earthen rampart. The Vikings at Rouen, for example, had made a simple earthen fortress with a large gap serving as a gateway, according to Dudo of St. Quentin, who had seen its remains. The fortress was built on a ridge above a small bay called *dub lind* ("the dark/black pool"), giving its name to the modern city of

Dublin. An Irish legend claims that the pool was named for an elf, Dub. She had a competitor for the affections of her husband, Énna. So Dub chanted a sea spell that caused her rival to drown. In her moment of triumph, however, Dub was killed by a shot from the sling of her victim's servant. She fell into a pool, which was afterwards called Dub's pool.

From the start, the settlement seems to have been a planned community, with carefully laid out streets and residences. While boundaries within other Viking towns such as Waterford could change as much as five times during the centuries, the divisions at Dublin appear to have remained constant into the nineteenth century. The defensive design of the fortress was based on contemporary English models. The town was completely enclosed by a wall, which differed from the Scandinavian method of fortifying only the landward sides while leaving open the side along the water.[18]

As a fortress was being built, the territory around it was being subdued. The theater of operations is described by the Irish poem "There Were Yielded out of Fair Inis Fail" (*Roddet a hinis find Fail*), a political geography of the important principalities in Ireland that was composed in the early tenth century.[19] A stanza on the Vikings of Dublin, called the army of Thor, recounts that they looted *Cuille*, foraged as far as the River Suir, and fought a battle at *Indiuin*. A tentative identification of these places is suggestive. *Indiuin* is correctly *Indeóin*, located somewhere west of the Howth peninsula. *Cuille* seems to be what is now Rathcoole in southwest county Dublin. The Suir is far to the south, flowing past Waterford. The raids of these new Vikings were in a corridor extending from Waterford through the midlands to Dublin. Comparing this list with the annals shows that Ragnall and Sitric were not leading random raids, but coordinating a well-directed operation.

A more local guide to Viking settlement in the plain of the Liffey is given by the *Tripartite Life of Patrick*. The purpose of this information is to claim that Patrick founded churches whose revenues would be paid to his successors (*comarbai* "heirs") at Armagh. The narrative explains the contemporary situation through prophecies attributed to the saint. As Patrick is made to travel around the Liffey Valley, he stops at Leixlip (remembered by Gerald of Wales in his *Topographia Hibernica* for its salmon leap), where he foretells that those people will be under the rule of a foreign prince. When the people living near Ballymore Eustace refuse to obey the saint, he warns them that foreign families will take their lands.[20] These pseudo-prophecies reveal a mixed aspect to the reestablishment of a Viking force on the Liffey. In some places the change was nothing more than the substitution of one lord for another. In another place the local population was being displaced so that newcomers could take the land.

The Irish High King Niall Glúndub decided to attack Sitric late in 919. Although they fought beyond the fortress, probably in the vicinity of what is now Island-bridge, the conflict is known as the Battle of Dublin. Niall was supported by princes from the north and Sitric received aid from new allies, the men of Leinster. The

Leinster princes and the Uí Néill were resuming an older contest, the fight for control of the lands around the Liffey. An added dimension was political domination, as Leinster was almost an Uí Néill satellite from the ninth century. Now the southern princes saw their opportunity to throw off that lordship.

The outcome of the Battle of Dublin was a complete victory for Sitric and his allies. Niall was slain, together with the king of Ulaid and numerous other princes, including the fickle Máel Mithig of Brega. A list of the slain reads like a roll call of the powerful northern Irish lords. News of the battle reached Britain, where it was garbled in the lost "Northern Chronicle" (parts of which survive in the *Anglo-Saxon Chronicle* versions D and E) that Sitric and Niall were brothers.

Despite triumphs in Ireland, it is clear that their territories in Britain were the more valued parts of the brothers' empire. When Ragnall died at York in 920, Sitric promptly left Dublin to take his place, while his brother, Godfrey, succeeded to the kingship of Dublin. Now their royal neighbors were prepared to treat them as equals. According to the earliest surviving version of the *Anglo-Saxon Chronicle*, known as the Parker Chronicle, Edward the Elder of Wessex (to which he had added the lordships of Mercia and East Anglia) made peace with them. This information is found in a eulogy on Edward on the announcement of his death in 924. The entry must be retrospective because it claims that Edward made his treaty with Ragnall, who had died several years earlier. Although the chronicle presents this information in a form flattering to Edward, who is called "lord and father," the clear implication of the entry is that the English needed some respite from the competition with Godfrey Hardacnutsson's successors.

The most obvious indication that the English princes accepted Ragnall and Sitric as their social equals is given during the reign of Edward's son and successor Æthelstan. In January 926 he gave his sister in marriage to Sitric. William of Malmesbury states that he had searched for the name of the lady, but was unable to find it. He does give one piece of information about her: she was Æthelstan's full sister, the child of "Ecgwynn." A century later, Sitric's wife is called Orgiue in the thirteenth-century chronicle copied by John of Wallingford, which incorporated a now-lost earlier northern record. The chronicle claims that Orgiue and Sitric had a son named Olaf who later ruled Northumbria: this is Olaf Cuaran. For what it is worth, in the legend of Olaf Cuaran's alter ego Havelok the Dane, Geffrei Gaimar claims that Havelok's mother was named Alvive.[21]

The matter of Olaf's mother seems to have been controversial by the thirteenth century. The chronicle copied by John of Wallingford is not the only record that gives Sitric's queen a name. John's contemporary Roger of Wendover, followed by Matthew Paris, who also used northern English materials, appears to have been aware of the claim that Olaf Cuaran's mother was an English princess. He insists, however, that the marriage of Edward's daughter, whom he calls Eadgytha, to Sitric was childless, and the widow retired to Polesworth (Warwickshire) where she died a virgin. This tale seems to begin with Roger, because earlier the Yorkshireman Roger of Howden, who used similar northern records, is unaware of Sitric's saintly bride.[22] There was a church at Polesworth whose foundation was credited to an Eaditha, but she lived in the ninth century and was the daughter of Ecgbert of Wessex (died 839). Roger might have confused Sitric's wife with her sister-in-law Æthelgifu, the wife of her younger brother, Edmund, who was revered as a saint.[23]

Clearly there was unique material about Olaf Cuaran's ancestors circulating in northern England. The name of Sitric's wife, possibly Eadgytha, was known to the compiler of John of Wallingford's chronicle and to Roger of Wendover; apparently both were aware of claims that she was the mother of Olaf Cuaran. There is no obvious reason why the chronicle copied by John of Wallingford would fabricate this information, and it was more critical toward its sources than Roger. Olaf was no more than a name to the chronicler. If we accept the account of John of Wallingford, Olaf was not only a member of a Viking dynasty but also the nephew of the West Saxon kings Æthelstan, Edmund, and Eadred.

Sitric died suddenly in 927, his death heralded by a brilliant display of the northern lights. His brother-in-law Æthelstan seized the opportunity to annex Northumbria. There he had to face Sitric's brother, Godfrey, who immediately returned from Ireland according to the *Annals of Ulster*. A number of legends arose from this episode. Some claim that Godfrey fled his kingdom and sought shelter with the Scots, while other stories claim that he was defeated in battle by Æthelstan. All agree on the result: Godfrey was forced to retreat to Ireland. At a meeting with the men of Northumbria on July 12, 927, at a place identified only as the confluence of the rivers (*æt ea motum*) Æthelstan was proclaimed king, and the Northumbrians agreed to outlaw paganism. Now confined to Ireland, Godfrey consoled himself by leading raids throughout the island. On his death in 934 he was described as a "most cruel king of the Northmen."

The successes of Ragnall, Sitric, and Godfrey in Britain and Ireland led to colonists from England going to Ireland. Emigration from Britain explains curious statements in two Irish works. The first statement is attributed to St. Patrick in the *Tripartite Life*. In the famous episode where the saint "bargains" for the salvation of the Irish, Patrick asks for several divine favors in connection with the Last Days. These include the sea flooding Ireland seven years before the final day (in order to spare the Irish the horrors of the approaching end), and Patrick to be allowed to judge the Irish at the Last Judgment. In addition, Patrick asks that the Saxons, that is, the English, not be permitted to live in Ireland forever.[24] The second statement comes from "The Colloquy of the Two Sages," another tenth-century work. Two learned men compete to determine the wiser, and they give a list of the horrors of their age including "screeching Saxon women." The presence from England in Ireland was becoming noticeable.[25]

The restoration of a Viking camp at Dublin led to fresh attacks on prominent Irish churches. Sitric attacked the church at Kildare in 917 and again in 918, while Godfrey made an infamous attack on Armagh on November 10, 921. Their successes sent the Irish clergy looking to King Æthelstan for an English alliance. This opened a period of friendly contacts between the Irish and the English. The famous volume known as MacDurnan's Gospels, once belonging to Abbot Máel Brigte mac Tornáin of Armagh (died 927), was given to King Æthelstan. Another important churchman, Bishop Dubinsi of Bangor (died 953), was a visitor to the English court, where he learned a game called "Gospel Dice."[26] The Irish needed an ally when Godfrey was succeeded in 934 by his son Olaf. For three years Olaf Godfreysson went from strength to strength in Ireland, forcing kingdoms as far west as the River Shannon to pay taxes to him and camping at the church of Clonmacnoise for two nights in 936.[27]

In Britain Æthelstan's policy of taxation was leading to general unhappiness among his non-English subjects. The Welsh in particular chafed under his exactions. The mounting tensions sparked a wave of diplomacy that is reflected in a poem called *Armes Prydein* ("Prophecy of Britain") composed circa 934. The poet calls upon the Scots, the Vikings, and the Irish to join the Welsh and rise up against the "Great King."[28] The Scots had their own reasons when, in 934, Æthelstan attacked them by land and sea. If the goal had been to instill fear, it had the opposite effect: King Constantine plotted revenge. Across the Irish Sea another prince was watching events in Britain, while nursing his own grievances against Æthelstan. Godfrey's son Olaf, now the undisputed leader of the Viking settlers in Ireland, saw the opportunity to take what he considered to be his patrimony in Northumbria. Old foes became new allies as the Scots, who had been the leaders of opposition to Olaf's family, made common cause with their former enemies. John of Worcester, writing in the twelfth century, even claims that Constantine gave his daughter in marriage to Olaf.[29]

In 937 Olaf and Constantine moved against Æthelstan in a battle at a place known as *Brunanburh*. The battlefield's location has been placed from southern Scotland to the River Humber and even the place name is uncertain, called *Dun Brune* in the *Scottish Chronicle* and *Vinheath* in the thirteenth-century Icelandic *Egil's Saga*. The battle was, in the words of the *Annals of Ulster*, "a most cruel and bloody conflict." Almost all the details about the battle are found in an Old English poem that is preserved in the *Anglo-Saxon Chronicle*. The contest was fiercely fought, and victory for Æthelstan and his teenage brother, Edmund, was closely run. In the end they prevailed over Olaf and Constantine. Æthelstan had won more than a battle, however. He had established his supremacy throughout Britain. Olaf fled back to Dublin "in ships with nailed sides." The Irish annals gleefully announce Æthelstan's victory over the Vikings of Dublin. When Æthelstan died in 939, the *Annals of Ulster* describe him as the pillar of dignity of the western world.

By the twelfth century a legend circulated that Olaf Cuaran was present at *Brunanburh*. William of Malmesbury tells the story that before the battle, Olaf had spied on the English by disguising himself as a skald and offering his services in the royal tent.[30] There he listened to the English plans for the campaign while he performed. Discovery of his mission came only after Olaf had departed and his "reward," a bag of coins, was discovered under his seat. His audience knew that no gen-

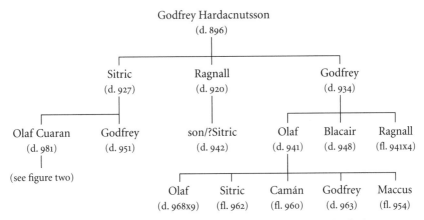

FIGURE 1. *Descendants of Godfrey Hardacnutsson.* Key: —, *descent;* d., *died;* fl., *flourished;* x, *between the years.*

uine skald would have discarded his pay. If there is any historical basis to this story, Olaf Cuaran clearly is confused with his cousin Olaf Godfreysson.

After Æthelstan's death on October 27, 939, the kingship was taken by his half-brother, Edmund. Not everyone had been pleased to be part of the West Saxon empire, and in Northumbria discontented factions took advantage of the changed circumstances to separate from the southern lord. Almost immediately Olaf Godfreysson returned to Britain, possibly at the request of the Northumbrians themselves. His power in Ireland had been undiminished by his misadventures in Britain. When the High King Domnall son of Flann laid siege to the fortress of Dublin in 939, he had to retire without taking the town. The Irish army had to be content with devastating the lands westwards to Ath Truisten, a ford on the River Greece near Mullaghmast (county Kildare), which the *Annals of the Four Masters* claim was within the domain of the men of Dublin. Olaf's return to Northumbria was brief. He died two years later, in 941, just after he raided a church dedicated to St. Baldred in Lothian.

A brief study of the origins of Olaf Cuaran and the early history of Dublin together places his career and that of his dynasty in a context. The establishment of Viking camps along the Liffey merely followed ancient sailing patterns that had made the region a trading center of antiquity. The combination of religious houses, fertile land, and a disputed political boundary contributed to the success of a settlement. They did not, however, guarantee survival, as the first Viking colonists had learned.

The second Viking colony at Dublin was entirely a family triumph. Olaf Cuaran's father, Sitric, had settled his followers there, defeated an attempt by the Irish to expel him, and had passed Dublin intact to his brother, Godfrey. The English aspect to this family is pronounced. Sitric's father, Godfrey, had ruled Northumbria, and his son's expeditions had been from Britain to Ireland, not the reverse. Dublin fortress was constructed in a fashion similar to that found in England, and contemporary Irish texts show that Sitric's followers had been recruited from Britain. Sitric had quickly left Dublin to succeed Ragnall in Northumbria, and his marriage to a West Saxon princess demonstrated his intention to remain in Britain. After his death, Godfrey's inability to take what he must have considered his rightful patrimony explains why two Olafs from the family—his son and his nephew Olaf Cuaran—devoted so much effort to retaking their ancestral lands in Britain.

The career of Olaf Cuaran followed many of the paths made by his kinsmen. Like his father, Sitric, he too would rule in Ireland and Britain. Like his cousin Olaf Godfreysson, he would impose his authority into the Irish midlands. Olaf Cuaran took full advantage of his inheritance.

2

Battle, Marriage, and Empire

ONE OF THE MAJOR CHARACTERS of Middle English literature is Havelok the Dane. The earliest version of his legend is found in a mid-twelfth-century French verse history composed by Geffrei Gaimar, who seems to have lived in the southern English Danelaw in Lincolnshire. The story begins with an orphan princess named Argentille who is forced by her wicked uncle to marry a kitchen servant named Cuaran, supposedly the son of a fisherman. Cuaran pays no attention to his bride, and at night insists on sleeping face down. Eventually Argentille discovers the reason for her husband's shyness: he has a flame issuing from his mouth. They visit Cuaran's family and learn that his real name is Havelok and that he is the son of the king of Denmark. Havelok returns to Denmark and after various adventures is restored to his patrimony.[1]

What is the connection of a Middle English story with tenth-century Vikings? The answer is in the name. Havelok is a francophone rendering of Olaf, and Cuaran is the Irish word *cúarán*.[2] Only one other man had those names: the tenth-century prince Olaf Cuaran. Olaf Cuaran was sometime king of Northumbria and Dublin, twice married to Irish princesses, a patron of Irish and Icelandic poets, and he died in religious retirement after a lifetime of attacks on churches. From the mid-tenth to twelfth centuries, his dynasty dominated the Viking settlements around the Irish Sea. If importance is measured by longevity, then Olaf's descendants in Wales, the Hebrides, and the Isle of Man are testaments to dynastic success. By the twelfth century both the lords of Gwynedd and the kings of the Isles proudly traced their ancestry to him. Having only minor resources compared with his rivals, Olaf Cuaran exerted an influence in the affairs of Ireland and Britain that far surpassed the size of his realm. More important than a mere tally of battles was the economic growth of Dublin during his reign. Olaf's fleets controlled the Irish Sea while enriching his domain through commerce and trade.

Olaf Cuaran's career began after the death of his cousin Olaf Godfreysson in 941. Olaf Cuaran and Olaf Godfreysson's brother, Ragnall, shared the kingship of the

Northumbrians. Divided rules were considered recipes for disaster during the Middle Ages, often leading to war between the princes. Age might be an explanation for Olaf and Ragnall. If Olaf had been born late in the year 926, he would have been about 15 years old in 941, just barely an adult by Viking standards. Ragnall might have been his foster-father. The English records treat Olaf as the more important partner, another indication that he was the nephew of the West Saxon king. While he might have appealed to those Northumbrians supporting an English connection, his immediate right to rule came from his father, Sitric, a previous king.

Olaf's first known action as king was to lead the Northumbrians south in 943 in an attack on Tamworth. The raid turned disastrous when Olaf and the archbishop of York were trapped by King Edmund inside Leicester. They had to wait for dark to escape from the town. The failure of his southern expedition appears to have led to a change of tactics. After his return to Northumbria, Olaf journeyed south again, this time to be baptized with King Edmund acting as sponsor. This was clearly a politically motivated act, and it does not necessarily mean that Olaf was not already a Christian. Sponsorship was a recognized method of sealing an alliance with a dominant individual. Alfred the Great, for example, sponsored the Christian Welsh prince Anarawd ap Rhodri after he had been received at the hands of a bishop.[3] Edmund's reception of Olaf from the baptismal font meant that the young Viking was now a part of the English king's spiritual family. Later that same year Ragnall was also received from the font by Edmund.

While the political and theological aspects of religious conformity are well known, less so are the economic implications. The Irish priests who departed after meeting the Viking settlers in Iceland were not alone in wishing to avoid contact with pagans. Christians throughout Europe often refused to conduct trade with pagans unless elaborate securities were arranged. A ninth-century law of Alfred the Great states bluntly that there was to be no trade between his subjects and the Danes unless hostages were exchanged at prearranged times. Part of the problem seems to have been human sacrifice. Dudo claims that the devotees of Thor sacrificed captives to the god and used the blood to entice fair winds. A similar belief is found in the Irish "Law of Sunday" (*Cáin Domnaig*), which tells of heathens who carry people into bondage and sacrifice them to their gods.[4]

Animosity by Christians was reciprocated by the heathens. The story of the pagan Onalafbald taunting Christians was preserved for centuries as an example of religious persecution. The gods he names—Thor and Odin—had devotees throughout the Viking settlements of Britain and Ireland.[5] Thor was one of the most widely popular deities in the pagan north. As the peoples of Scandinavia began to convert to Christianity in ever greater numbers, he became the symbol of resistance to the innovations of the southern religion. A literary echo is found in *Njal's Saga*, where a missionary named Thangbrand is confronted by a lady named Steinunn. She tells him that Thor and Christ fought a duel, but Christ ran away. The cult of Odin is less visible, although it seems to have been particularly prominent in the Orkneys. There

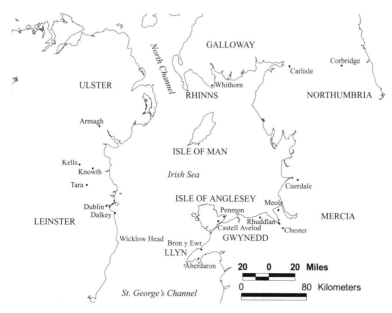

MAP 2. *Irish Sea Region*

was a rock called the Stone of Odin at Stenness, while a literary echo comes from *Orkneyinga Saga*, which claims that Jarl Sigurd, who died in Ireland at the Battle of Clontarf in 1014, had a magical raven banner; ravens were the messengers of Odin.[6]

An expedient compromise for many Viking merchants was "prime-signing." *Egil's Saga* remembers that Vikings who wanted to conduct trade with Christians would be "prime-signed," that is, they would take the first steps toward conversion to Christianity. This allowed them entrance to the Christian communities and merchants. The commercial prosperity of Dublin increased dramatically after it had a king who was at least nominally Christian.

Despite their baptism, the following year (944) Olaf Cuaran and Ragnall Godfreysson were driven from Northumbria to Dublin.[7] The circumstances are not entirely clear. In the contemporary (Parker Chronicle) version of the *Anglo-Saxon Chronicle*, Olaf and Ragnall were expelled by Edmund during his invasion of Northumbria. A different view is given by the chronicler Æthelweard, a nobleman of the late tenth century who was a distant kinsman of the royal family. He claims that Olaf fled as the result of a coup d'état led by Archbishop Wulfstan of York and an unnamed ealdorman of Mercia. Regardless of the exact reason, Olaf is next found at Dublin. There he displaced Ragnall Godfreysson's brother, Blacair, from the kingship, a move that has been seen as a triumph for Christianity.[8]

Olaf's return to Ireland came at a low point in Dublin's fortunes. In 944 Dublin was destroyed by Congalach son of Máel Mithigh of Brega and the Leinster prince

Bróen son of Máel Mórda. Congalach of Knowth (his sobriquet was his family's fortress above the Boyne) was a dynast of Síl nÁedo Sláine, and his father, Máel Mithig, had been briefly the ally of Olaf's father, Sitric, before making the disastrous change of allegiance prior to the Battle of Dublin in 919. The destruction of Dublin in 944 was primarily plundering; the *Annals of Ulster* note that Congalach and Bróen took away many valuables. According to the *Annals of the Four Masters*, the survivors sailed eight miles south to Dalkey.

For the next five years Olaf remained in Ireland. His northern rival, the powerful Uí Néill confederation, was in turmoil. Two dynasties, Cenél nEógain in the north and Clann Cholmáin to the south, had monopolized the overlordship since the eighth century. Their domination temporarily ended in the mid-tenth century when the High King Donnchad son of Flann, a dynast of Clann Cholmáin, died in 944 without a clear choice of successor. His heir-apparent, the Cenél nEógain dynast Muirchertach of the Leather Cloaks (the son of Niall *Glúndub*), had been killed the previous year in a fight with the men of Dublin. Muirchertach's extensive campaigns had culminated in his famous "Circuit of Ireland" in 942, when he took hostages throughout the island. According to a verse history of the expedition, when Muirchertach received the submission of the fortress of Dublin he was assisted by its unnamed (and probably imaginary) queen who had fallen in love with him.[9]

In this political vacuum began a competition between two men from Uí Néill dynasties that had been in obscurity for several centuries. The first prince was Ruaidrí Ua Canannáin of Cenél Conaill, located in the extreme north of what is now county Donegal. His rival was Congalach. Like their fathers, Olaf and Congalach became allies. In 945 they attacked Ruaidrí's army as he campaigned on the eastern coast in the territory of the Conaille Muirtheimne (county Louth). The allies were victorious, and Ruaidrí was forced to retreat. During the lull in hostilities, Olaf spent his leisure time attacking churches throughout the midlands, from modern county Meath to the eastern shores of the river Shannon. Meanwhile Ruaidrí plotted a return to the east. In 947 he fought Olaf and Congalach at Slane, in the midst of Congalach's lands. Ruaidrí won the battle after a slaughter of Olaf's troops. This setback might have cost Olaf temporary control of Dublin. When the Dublin army was next led out, their captain was Olaf's cousin Blacair.

In the report of the Battle at Slane, the *Annals of Ulster* give the earliest attestation of Olaf's distinctive nickname *cúarán*. Although the word often is translated as "shoe" or "sandal," the footwear was more distinctive. The name *cúarán* is an adaptation of *cúar* "crooked or bent" suggesting a boot rather than a shoe. A description of a *cúarán* is given in the twelfth-century satire *Aislinge Meic Con Glinne* ("The Vision of Mac Conglinne"), where it is made of brown leather that has been folded seven times, and the toes are pointed. The folding might refer to the method of waterproofing the footwear. When Mac Conglinne arrives at his destination he cleans the dust off his shoes by dipping them in his bath water. Waterproof also meant retaining liquid inside the shoe, and *Scél Baili Binnbérlaig* ("Story of Baile

Binnberlag") describes the *cúarána* being used as drinking vessels in place of a goblet.[10]

The *cúarán* does not seem to have been antique. There is no mention of it in the earliest Irish laws, although it is found in the later medieval commentaries and texts. In a twelfth-century version of the poem called "Here Is a Happy, Graceful History" (*Atá sund seanchas suairc seang* in the *Book of Uí Maine*, f. 69 ra. 23), a description of the craftsmen at Dublin includes the *sutaire* "cobbler" who owes a *cúarán* in payment of his taxes. Olaf's nickname refers to a new type of footwear being manufactured at Dublin that was markedly different from the shoes being worn by the Irish.

After the miseries of 947–948 events conspired in Olaf's favor, although the precise chronology is unclear.[11] A member of the Norwegian royal dynasty with the picturesque name of Eirik Bloodaxe seems to have been set up as king in Northumbria possibly as early as 945. Eirik was one of the sons of the famous Norse king, Harald Fairhair, whose family had maintained good relations with the West Saxon dynasty. Eirik's brother, Hakon, had lived for a time at the court of Æthelstan, and was known as Æthelstan's Fosterling. In the interval between the departure of Olaf and the appearance of Eirik, King Edmund, circa 945, had led an army through Northumbria to Strathclyde. He devastated the kingdom and blinded two sons of its king, Dynfwal. Then he assigned lordship of the kingdom to the Scots king, Malcolm I, on the condition of an alliance.[12] After Edmund's death in 946, Malcolm renewed the alliance with his brother, Eadred. If Eirik had been ruling in Northumbria just prior to mid-century, he was forced to abdicate by 949, when Olaf returned to Northumbria.

Olaf was able to return to Britain because his cousin Blacair was dead. When Olaf was defeated at Slane in 947, Blacair retook the kingship. His tenure lasted about a year, for he was attacked at Dublin by Olaf's ally Congalach and slain together with sixteen hundred men. Blacair's successor was Olaf's brother, Godfrey. When Olaf was absent in Britain, Godfrey faced the return of Ruaidrí Ua Canannáin in 950. Ruaidrí raided between the rivers Boyne and Liffey for half a year. Finally, on November 30, Godfrey marched against Ruaidrí and fought him at a place called Móin Brocaín. Godfrey was defeated, leaving six thousand of his men dead on the battlefield, but Ruaidrí was slain. The next year Godfrey replenished his wealth with raids on churches in Meath, including Kells, Ardbraccan, and Donoughpatrick. Three thousand people were taken captive (those not ransomed probably sold into slavery) together with gold, silver, cattle, and horses. Godfrey had little time to enjoy his triumph, for he died soon afterwards, possibly during the outbreak of disease at Dublin, described as leprosy and dysentery by the *Annals of Ulster*. Olaf Cuaran's flight from Britain the following year might not be entirely coincidental.

From 949 to 952 Olaf held onto an increasingly precarious kingship in Northumbria. He was faced by enemies north and south. Malcolm of the Scots honored his alliance with Edmund and in 949 attacked Northumbria as far as the river Tees, which was remembered in the Scottish Chronicle as the "raid of the White Ridges."

A second invasion, circa 951, was less successful. An invading force composed of Scots, men of Strathclyde and Anglo-Saxons was defeated. In 952, however, Olaf fled the kingdom and he returned permanently to Ireland. His rival Eirik returned to Northumbria and reigned for two years until 954. Then he, too, was forced to abdicate. In his flight he was slain in Westmorland, on Stainmore Heath, by a son of Olaf Godfreysson named Maccus.[13] Although it was not obvious at the time, the independent Viking kingdom in Northumbria died with him.

When Olaf Cuaran returned to Dublin for his second, and final, sojourn, much had changed in Ireland. While he was absent in Britain, following the death of his old foe Ruaidrí ua Canannáin, Olaf's former ally Congalach was the undisputed high king. Now, however, relations between the two men had changed for the worse, and they continued to deteriorate during the few years before Congalach was assassinated in 956. His death reveals the dangers awaiting any overlord who affronted the sensibilities of his subordinates, in this instance Leinster and Dublin. Ritual and display were important in medieval Ireland, and Congalach ignored them at his peril when he went into Leinster and presided over the Fair of Carman, held the first week of August. This fair was an archaic survival of pre-Christian funeral games, where athletic competition was held in a cemetery so that the dead ancestors could partake in the festivities. By the tenth century there was also a commercial aspect, with several markets held in conjunction with the games. The presidency of the gathering was one of the rights of the provincial king of Leinster. Congalach's intrusion into the festivities was a sign that he intended to rule the province directly, rather than be merely a distant overlord. He might have had grander dreams that extended beyond Ireland.[14] Within Ireland Congalach was becoming too powerful and too intrusive for either the Leinstermen or Dubliners.

In the face of this threat, the princes Leinster and Dublin formed an alliance. Neither wished to chance another pitched battle with Congalach, so they decided to ambush the high king. Details of the trap are revealed in a poem on the deaths of heroes by Cináed ua hArtacáin, whose patrons included Olaf Cuaran.[15] After presiding over the games at Carman, Congalach began the return to his fortress of Knowth. The high king's entourage stopped at the ancient fortress of Ailenn, stronghold of the kings of Leinster and now known as Cnoc Ailinne ("the hill of Allen"). This was an unfortunate choice, for it had last been used by an Uí Néill prince in 770 as a base for ravaging Leinster. Congalach rested at a house called *Tech Giugrand*, literally "the house of the barnacle goose" or "house of Giugra."[16] There he was attacked and slain by the men of Dublin and Leinster.

Olaf's role in the ambush might have had less to do with Leinster and more to do with marriage. Sometime after his final return from Britain, Olaf married a princess from the northern Uí Néill kingdom of Cenél nEógain named Dúnflaith; both her father, Muirchertach of the Leather Cloaks, and grandfather, Niall Glúndub, had been slain by the Vikings of Dublin.[17] Like many princesses throughout medieval Europe whose marriages were diplomatic, not romantic, Dúnflaith was a "peace weaver." Olaf was her second husband. Previously she had been the wife of Domnall of Clann Cholmáin (d. 952), the son of the High King Donnchad. That union had been dictated by their family's efforts at peaceful coexistence because the rivalry between their fathers was famous. Dúnflaith's marriage to Domnall produced Máel Sechnaill II, the future Irish high king circa 948.

Olaf and Dúnflaith wed probably soon after 952, the year Domnall died and Olaf returned to Ireland. They had two children whose names are known: a girl who was given the Norse name Ragnhild, and a boy with the Irish name Glúniairn ("Iron Knee"). Glúniairn ruled Dublin after the abdication of his father in 980, a task for a mature warrior. If he was about twenty-five years old in 980, then his birth was sometime around the year 955.

The marriage of a Viking prince from Dublin to an Irish princess from Cenél nEógain brought benefits for both parties. Since their territories were distant from each other—Cenél nEógain in the extreme north and Dublin on the eastern coast—immediate conflicts were more likely over extension of influence rather than the annexation of land. There could have been a territorial aspect to the marriage that looked beyond Ireland. Cenél nEógain was situated within easy striking distance of the Hebrides whose Viking settlers raided Ireland, and where Dúnflaith's family had hereditary claims. Her grandfather Niall's mother was Máel Muire the daughter of Kenneth mac Alpin, the founder of the Scottish kingdom. The coast and islands south of Ardnamurchan had been part of the kingdom of Dál Riata, Kenneth's ancestral home. In 941 Muirchertach led a fleet to the Hebrides and collected a tax or tribute, in other words he asserted his lordship over the area. This voyage became famous and the eleventh-century historian Flann of Monasterboice noted Muirchertach's raid was a famous deed.[18]

The alliance with Dublin also brought Cenél nEógain an ally on the borders of the southern Uí Néill principalities, especially its main rival Clann Cholmáin. By the tenth century any cooperation between them was based on pure self-interest rather than distant memories of kinship.[19] As the less powerful Uí Néill dynasties—Cenél Conaill and Síl nÁedo Sláine—controlled the high kingship from 944 to 956, it must have been impressed on Cenél nEógain how easily they, too, could be relegated to the ranks of "outsiders."

There could also have been an economic aspect to the union of Olaf and Dúnflaith. Her dynasty of Cenél nEógain had a particular need for a commercial alliance. Muirchertach's grandfather, Áed Findliath, had destroyed the Viking bases in the north of Ireland, from the Inishowen Peninsula to county Antrim. His hostility was continued by his successors, and the reward for military prowess was economic stagnation. In contrast, the distribution of coin hoards throughout the lands of the southern Uí Néill dynasties of Clann Cholmáin and Síl nÁedo Sláine suggests that the southern families were sharing, to some extent, in the prosperity that was emanating from their Viking neighbors. The northern kingdom might have wanted access to a southern market.

Economic considerations extended beyond the commercial to contests for the kingship. Fights for political supremacy were so fierce because the benefits to the monarch, and his family, were substantial. An indication is given in a tract called "The Rights of Every King" (*Cert Cech Ríg*) attributed to Fothad na Canoine (d. 818).[20] After the successful prince has taken hostages to ensure the good behavior of his subjects, he collects taxes in cattle and swine, and demands that his subjects provide food and shelter for his livestock and troops while they are on the march. Subject peoples were less able to compete with the king because their own resources were being used to support him. In tenth-century Ireland there was only one way to circumvent this brutal reality of an agrarian society. That was to have access, or have an ally who had access, to wealth being generated in another way, such as trade.

Advantage in a wise marriage was not limited to one party. His marriage to Dúnflaith gave Olaf a northern alliance and the goodwill of a powerful Uí Néill dynasty. In 956 Dúnflaith's brother, Domnall Ua Néill (reigned 956–80), succeeded Congalach as high king. Cooperation between Domnall and Olaf had begun circa 954 when the *Annals of the Four Masters* note that Domnall's raid on the lands of Brega, immediately north of Olaf's territory, was planned in cooperation with the Vikings.

There may have been benefits outside Ireland. Although Olaf's expulsion from Northumbria in 952 (and the subsequent collapse of the independent kingdom two years later) appear in hindsight as decisive events, contemporaries did not know that. Olaf possibly cherished hopes of recovering his former domain in Britain. Cenél nEógain would be useful allies for such an enterprise. Their ability to carry out a sea-raid had been demonstrated by Muirchertach when he invaded the Hebrides, and his tactics were continued by his son Domnall, who was famous for his naval expeditions. More importantly, the Scots ancestry of Dúnflaith's family might have given them some influence with princes in northern Britain. From 954 to 962 the southern Scots were ruled by Idulf whose father, Constantine, had been the ally of the Dublin army at the Battle of *Brunanburh*.

An astute marriage did not end all Olaf's troubles. Factionalism reappeared among the Viking settlers of the Liffey plain, the type of disorder that had contributed to their expulsion in 902. Olaf's reinstatement as king of Dublin after his return from Northumbria in 952 had been to the loss of his cousins, the family of Olaf Godfreysson. They were forced to flee from Dublin and initially seem to have gone to the Hebrides. In 960 Olaf Godfreysson's son Camán was slain on the river Duff in Donegal, within easy striking distance of the Hebrides. In 962 a "fleet of Lawmen of the Isles" (*longes Laghmuind*) raided Munster led by a "son of Olaf." Olaf Cuaran is unlikely to have had any children old enough to command a fleet at this time, and this individual seems to have been another son of Olaf Godfreysson.[21] The family of Olaf Godfreysson did not stay in the Hebrides, but moved south to Wales, to the Isle of Anglesey, following raids on Holyhead and Llyn by "sons of Olaf," circa 960, that are remembered in the Welsh chronicle *Brut Y Tywysogyon*. Their new home put them in position for raids on Dublin. The *Annals of the Four Masters* note that in 962 a son of Olaf raided the island of Ireland's Eye (off Howth), and the captives were taken to *Mon Conain* in Britain, that is, to the Isle of Anglesey. This was probably the same attack as a following notice of a raid around Lusk (county Dublin) by Sitric *Cam[m]* ("the Crooked"), who was intercepted by Olaf Cuaran. Olaf was wounded through the thigh by an arrow and Sitric was able to escape. The element of revenge is obvious.

The attacks on Olaf Cuaran by his cousins are another reason why he needed allies. The expulsion of Olaf Godfreysson's family from Dublin led to their being denied royal status. Among the Vikings, as among the Irish, kingly status was easy to lose, but difficult to regain. The idea of "kingship" among the Vikings in Ireland and Britain is reflected in the Old Norse poem "The Lay of Rígr" (*Rígsþula*). Three classes of society are listed in the verses: the slaves (*þrælar*), the freemen (*karlar*), and the aristocracy (*jarlar*). There is no separate royal or "kingly" class, but at the end of the poem there is the description of an extension of nobility known as the king (*konungr*), who is descended from the jarl. How to interpret this poem depends on when it was composed. Dates have been proposed from the ninth to thirteenth century. A tenth/eleventh-century date seems best to fit the archaic material. What makes this poem particularly pertinent in a discussion of Vikings in Ireland is the Irish word for king, *rí*, in the title, and its description of hospitality to guests that is similar to custom in Ireland.[22]

The rapid succession of kings among the Vikings of Ireland and Britain suggests that their idea of monarchy was in the process of development. The war leader was developing into a prince with sacral and stabilizing aspects. This might not have occurred quickly, but the nuances of change would not have been noticed in the Irish records. For the Dublin Vikings, their leader might have been viewed as a hybrid territorial chieftain and war leader, but the Irish clergy maintaining the records described the process of rule in the form familiar to them, as kingship. The development of the office of king, in turn, brought with it a particular problem for would-be Viking lords in Ireland. High status in the north Atlantic world needed a considerable outlay of stock and goods. Among the Vikings in Ireland, who lacked both large areas of territory and vast numbers of people, there were two obvious remedies, for which allies were very useful. One was to acquire plunder in battle or raids. Much of the seemingly endemic warfare among the Irish was simply self-enrichment at the neighbors' expense. A problem with this solution is that the outcome of conflict is always unpredictable, and even if successful, the vanquished might regroup and attack in their turn. The other choice was more dependable and profitable: commerce.

By the tenth century trade and manufacturing around northern Europe were increasing. Literary expression is found late in the century when the Anglo-Saxon writer Ælfric, in his *Colloquy*, included the merchant among the occupations useful for society. The merchant imported wine, cooking oil, cloth, clothes, copper, tin, and glass. Manufacturers are the shoemaker and the blacksmith; the former turned hides and skins into shoes, harness and bags, while the latter produced plowshares, fishing hooks, and needles. The Irish Sea shared in the revival. There was a flourishing mint at Chester and harbors were built on the Isle of Anglesey. During Olaf's reign Dublin's commerce becomes vaguely visible. The Dublin Vikings may have turned to trade if raiding was becoming less remunerative, while their relatively limited territory did not allow for extensive farming.[23]

Commerce brought wealth that was more reliable and safer than the plunder from raiding. For the Viking colonists, trade became as important as the battles. Their skill as sailors was matched by their "eye for business." They were responsible for making the Irish Sea a wealthy trading zone, and an important economic area in the North Atlantic by the late tenth century. Northern and southern Europe met in the Irish Sea. At towns such as Dublin raw materials and worked goods from Scandinavia were exchanged for the foodstuffs and luxury goods of Ireland, Britain, and western continental Europe. International trade bestowed prestige. A twelfth-century monk named Lucian noted that ships from Aquitaine, Poitou, Normandy, and Flanders called at Chester, which he cited as proof of the town's international importance and sophistication.[24]

Little more than an outline of commercial activity is visible for this period at Dublin. Material remains give some indication, but certain types of materials are more likely to survive than others, and random discoveries can provide a distorted picture. These remains are difficult to place into precise chronology, although there are often efforts to do just that. Sometimes the evidence comes beyond this period, but it appears to represent a long tradition. Nevertheless, excavations in Dublin at Wood Quay and at Winetavern Street provided evidence of some of the goods manufactured or traded in the town.[25] A few examples give an indication of commercial activity at Dublin during Olaf Cuaran's reign.

The Vikings' ships followed the trading lanes that had been used for centuries with the types of cargoes that had an ancient history. Clothing provides one example. At least by the eighth century there was a trade in Irish clothes and shoes to the Loire Valley, mentioned in the eighth-century *vita* of Philibert of Jumièges. The Viking colonists are probably the clothes merchants from Ireland who were at Cambridgeshire in the late tenth century. Olaf Cuaran's son, Sitric Silkenbeard, rewarded the poet Gunnlaug Serpent's Tongue with clothes. Shoes, and leather goods in general, became well known Viking productions. The Old Norse word for skin or hide (*skinn*) was borrowed into Middle Irish as *scing*, and subsequently it acquired the extended meaning of clothes or cloaks. Borrowing moved in either direction. Olaf Cuaran's sobriquet is Irish *cúarán* "boot" and pieces and workings from hundreds of shoes have been found at Dublin, especially in the excavations of the shoemakers' workshops at the Wood Quay. In the twelfth century Gerald of Wales remarks that dressed hides from Ireland were being shipped to Poitou.[26]

More valuable than clothes or shoes were furs, prized throughout Europe. Furs from Ireland were exported to England and the continent. Gerald of Wales mentions the abundance of martins. Their pelts were shipped to northern England (where there are no martins), and the Chester Domesday survey mentions the ancient custom that ships calling at the port with cargoes of martin skins must not unload before the king's representative made his selection. In the twelfth century, the charter issued by the future Henry II of England reveals that Irish furs were being traded in Normandy as a monopoly of the town of Rouen. The charter states that once a ship from Ireland had passed Guernsey Head, it must take its cargo to Rouen.[27]

The Vikings were also importing foodstuffs and, like their Irish neighbors, Olaf and his subjects enjoyed their food. They imported walnuts from southern Europe. Again, this was an ancient trade. The Old Irish legal text called "Sea Judgments" (*Muirbretha*), composed long before the arrival of the Vikings, mentions exotic nuts as part of a cargo carried across the sea, while another ancient law tract called "Judgments about pledge interests" (*Bretha im fuillema Gell*) describes the nuts as coming from the east. Cultivated plums from southern England were also imported. Among his many complaints about the Irish, Gerald of Wales remarks that they are too lazy to plant foreign fruit trees; a somewhat similar comment is made by Warner of Rouen in his attack on the Irish scholar Moriuht, when he notes that Ireland is fertile, but the Irish will not cultivate it.[28]

Domestic wares, cloth, and ivory were also imported. Soapstone (steatite) bowls were imported from the Shetlands and possibly Norway. Pottery was brought from western Britain, particularly from Chester. Luxury textiles came into Dublin from the Mediterranean, probably via English ports, such as gold braids, silk tabbies, patterned compound silks, and worsted wares. From Scandinavia came walrus ivory. The archaeological record is echoed in literature, and Ælfric's merchant specifically mentions silk, unusual clothes, and items of purple as trade goods.[29]

Wine was a valuable import, and it was crucial for Christian worship. In the sixth century Abbot Columba of Iona could expect ships from southern France to call at Iona, probably with cargoes of wine for the church. Ships probably followed the same schedule in the early Middle Ages as later, when wine from Bordeaux was brought into the Irish Sea from October to December. Wine was the drink of choice of the aristocracy, and the Irish were particularly fond of it. Gerald of Wales, in an aside on the wealth of the Irish, remarked that there was so much wine available in Ireland that one scarcely noticed that no vines were cultivated.[30] A ship from England carrying wine and wheat was caught in the midst of a battle at Wexford in 1169.

Together with finished items, raw materials were imported. The craftsmen of Dublin needed materials not available in Ireland, especially for making jewelry. Jet probably was brought from England, where it is found around Whitby in Yorkshire. Glass and glass beads were brought into Ireland. Amber was imported into Dublin from either eastern England or Denmark. The craftsmen of Dublin were the main producers of amber goods for Ireland and Britain; despite its proximity to the deposits in eastern England, there seems to have been relatively little amber worked at Viking York. Precious metals were also imported. Gerald of Wales claimed that almost all the gold in Ireland was imported, and that it was greatly desired by the Irish. Some of the precious metals mentioned in the records probably were intended for manufacturing purposes, such as the six ounces of white silver that were part of the ransom for Olaf Cuaran's grandson in 1029. When the Dublin settlements at the river Tolka, north of the fortress, were raided by the men of Leinster in 1024, among the spoils were gems and silver, all necessary for the production of jewelry.[31]

Craftsmen then, as now, had to follow changes in fashion. Jewelry shows how abruptly styles could be replaced. During the tenth century the Vikings in Ireland produced four main designs: arm rings, penannular brooches, kite-shaped brooches, and thistle brooches. Arm-rings seem to have gone out of fashion after the mid-tenth century, while the penannular and thistle brooches continued to be produced rather longer. By the mid-tenth century a ringed pin usually described as "Hiberno-Norse" was being produced throughout the Irish Sea region, but especially at Dublin and the Isle of Man.[32] This pin was popular throughout the north Atlantic, and it has been found in the Viking settlement in North America. Even though there could have been a thriving market for jewelry within Dublin, the majority of items manufactured in the town were probably made for export.

Excavations in Dublin at Wood Quay and Fishamble Street suggest that manufacturing relied on native materials as well as imported raw materials. When the High King Máel Sechnaill II freed the southern Uí Néill from paying tribute (*cáin*) to the Vikings of Dublin after his victory at Tara in 980, the goods rendered could have included raw materials for manufacturing in addition to the customary food stuffs. The lord of Dublin took some of his dues in goods such as malt, which was used for brewing. Many of the non-precious metals used in the workshops of Dublin are found locally; copper and lead deposits, for example, are found in county Wicklow, south of Dublin. Iron might have come from local Irish suppliers, although some might have come from as far away as Norway, and there is evidence for iron smelting in Galloway, at Whithorn.[33] Iron was used to manufacture goods as varied as farming implements, riding tack, swords, fish hooks, and nails. The metal was so important that the early tenth-century tract called "Cormac's Glossary" has a translation of the Viking's pronunciation of iron, *hiarn*, which the glossator notes "i.e. [the word] iron in the Northmanish language" (*.i. iarn in nortmannica lingua*). Iron production at Dublin might have employed the latest technology. Iron production changed dramatically in the late ninth century, when a new type of furnace was developed, which became widely popular in the mid-tenth century, because it produced a cheaper and better quality of iron.[34]

Not all items manufactured in Dublin were glamorous or complicated. For domestic consumption and sale to their Irish neighbors there were agricultural implements such as plowshares and spades.[35] Roughly contemporary with Olaf Cuaran's father, Sitric, was the introduction of a new type of plow in Ireland. The earlier "scratch plow" that used only a plowshare was replaced by a larger implement that had a coulter (for slicing the sod) mounted above it. The plow irons were valuable items that were removed from the frame after work was finished, and reattached when needed. The Vikings may have introduced this new type of plow to Ireland, for a similar development was occurring at the same time in England. Craftsmen at Dublin also produced items considered vile by the Irish, such as hair combs and dressed hides. The Old Irish law tracts place leather workers and comb-makers lowest among all artisans. Deer antler and bone used for making combs were gathered locally. An antler recovered from excavations at Dublin has a runic inscription that appears to state where it was found.[36]

Dublin became an important producer of wooden goods during the reign of Olaf Cuaran. Unlike elsewhere in Europe, Ireland remained densely forested throughout the Middle Ages. There was forest so dense southwest of Dublin that an army moving north to attack the town in 1170 traveled along the coast in order to avoid it, in part because of the possibility of ambush. Timber was used to pay tribute; Olaf Cuaran's brother-in-law, Máel Mórda, escorted such a payment prior to the Battle of Clontarf (1014) according to *Cocad Gáedel re Gallaib*. Excavations at Dublin have revealed evidence of a thriving lumber-based industry that produced utilitarian goods such as furniture, gaming boards and pieces, spoons, and bowls. There were also shipyards in which were built and repaired vessels of all sizes, everything from small rowboats to oceangoing ships.[37] Lumber was not cheap, even in Ireland. Damaged boat parts were reused in the construction of interior and exterior drains as well as loftier uses such as roof rafters.

Finally, slaves were an ancient and valuable commodity. Irish, Welsh, Norse, and Anglo-Saxon societies all practiced slavery, and the Irish Sea was their central meeting point. In the fifth century, the apostle of Ireland, St. Patrick, was brought to the island from Britain as a slave. The slave trade circulated throughout the North Atlantic. The Norse sagas mention revolts of Irish slaves in Iceland, and the Irish *Book of Rights* mentions slaves in Ireland who did not know Gaelic. By the eleventh century, slaves were part of the ritual gift exchange practiced by the Irish, such as the eight foreign slaves who the Irish high king gave to the king of Ardgal (county Meath).[38]

Coins suggest the direction of Dublin's trade. Until coins were minted in the town at the end of the tenth century, most of them found around Dublin are English, and it is difficult to believe that all of them are loot from raids.[39] Coins probably were used to purchase raw materials such as amber from the Danes. The coins in Ireland are only a fraction of the total that circulated because coins were also used as a source of precious metals. Some of the silver used for manufacturing in Dublin could have come from mines within Ireland, but most of it probably came from outside the island. Much of the silver circulating around the Irish Sea and Scandinavia came from Kufic coins, which were used as bullion throughout the northern world until the supply began to diminish in the later tenth century.

As the lord of a commercial center, Olaf profited from a commodity that only he could supply: security. The Icelandic *Lœxdala Saga* has an episode, supposedly contemporary with Olaf, in which there is panic on a Norwegian ship when the crew realizes that they were off the coast of Ireland, but not near the harbors or marketplaces where foreigners could land safely and peacefully.[40] Merchants demanded security to conduct their business and safety for their wares.

A prince guaranteed peace and, in return, his officials collected a toll, which could be a percentage of the goods or their selling price. How Olaf Cuaran profited is suggested from the twelfth-century revision of the poem "Here Is a Happy, Graceful History"; comparison with commercial tracts elsewhere shows its value for the tenth century. Taxes were paid in various ways. Dublin craftsmen usually paid in the commodity they produced: mead from a brewer, combs from the comb maker and, as noted above, *cúarán* from a cobbler. Merchants also paid for the right to trade at Dublin, once again probably with some proportion of their goods for sale. Royal success, and lack of it, in exploiting commerce is illustrated across the Irish Sea in the legislation of the English kings. An early tenth-century law attributed to Edward the Elder ordered that all commercial transactions had to be carried out in the confines of a port, with a port-reeve as witness. Enforcement was difficult, as illustrated by two laws issued by Edward's son Æthelstan. The code known as II Æthelstan exempts transactions of less than 20 pence from being carried out in a port, while a later code, IV Æthelstan, eliminates the restriction altogether.[41]

Royal exploitation was hampered by the casual manner in which trade was conducted. The Anglo-Saxon law tract II Æthelraed (composed circa 994) mentions merchants who set up temporary booths from which they sold their wares.[42] The Arab traveler Ibn Fadlan gives a more complete description of a similar practice among the Swedish Vikings, known as Rus, who traded with the Bulgars.[43] The Rus anchored their ships along the Volga and then built wooden houses on the shore, where they displayed their wares (in this instance slave girls).

Their fortified towns with craftsmen and imported wares were part of the reason why, by the later tenth century, Viking colonists were at the same time economically important and militarily threatening to their neighbors. Considerable commercial activity was omitted from the written sources, and now is known only from excavations. An example is the important trading center in western Britain at Meols. Hiberno-Norse coins have been found there, showing its importance for the Irish Sea trade and the Olafssons.[44]

As Dublin became an important commercial center, Olaf Cuaran was becoming more involved in Irish affairs. After the exclusion of his cousins from the rule of Dublin, Olaf actively campaigned throughout the eastern midlands. His success is visible in incidents such as the execution of Carlus son of Conn, a dynast of Clann

Cholmáin, in Dublin in 960. He also raided south into Leinster, attacking the famous church of St. Brigit at Kildare in 964 and again in 967.

By 967 the marriage of Olaf and Dúnflaith seems to have ended, and with it the familial alliance. When Olaf and the Leinster prince Cerball son of Lorcan raided Brega in that year, there was a retaliatory attack in 968 by Dúnflaith's brother, the High King Domnall, who laid siege to Dublin for several months, but eventually was forced to withdraw. Olaf then took the offensive. In an abrupt reversal of previous policy, he allied with Domnall, the son of his former foe Congalach. They attacked the high king at Kilmona (Kilmoon, county Meath) in 970 and won a celebrated victory. Domnall Ua Néill managed to escape with his life, but some of his prominent supporters were not as fortunate, such as the kings of Ulaid and Airgialla. He was, however, harshly criticized for fleeing from the battle; an eleventh-century pseudo-prophecy known as *Baile in Scáil* ("The Phantom's Frenzy") described it as the "womanly flight."[45]

The defeat at the Battle of Kilmona was only one in a series of disasters for Domnall. The most famous was a devastating famine that swept through Ireland in 965, when the *Annals of Ulster* claim that a man would sell his children for food; *Baile in Scáil* claims that it lasted several years. Although Domnall could not be held personally responsible for a famine, it was widely believed that a king's "luck" was the cause of success or failure, and affected his subjects. The eleventh-century historical poem known as the *Prophecy of Berchán* directly associates him with the famine and describes Domnall's reign as being without grain, without milk, without gentleness.[46] If the high king fared badly in his encounters with Olaf, so, too, did other members of his family. In 977 his son Muirchertach was captured by the men of Dublin, together with Congalach the son of Olaf's former ally Domnall son of Congalach. They were both executed on Olaf's orders.

Olaf needed allies to replace the Uí Néill. He might have looked to the English king Edgar, with whom he had family connections. Edgar's father, Edmund, had been Olaf's godfather, and if Olaf's mother was the daughter of Edward the Elder, then he was Edgar's cousin. These ties had not prevented Edmund's involvement in Olaf's flight from Northumbria in 944. In a medieval context, however, the connections were significant. An artificial kinship such as religious sponsorship would have been comprehensible to Vikings as a parallel to sworn friendship. Edgar enjoyed good relations with the Viking settlers in Britain and northern Francia. His laws gave the inhabitants of the Danelaw an impressive amount of self-determination, while he was one of the patrons of the church of St. Ouen's, Rouen. Edgar is also one of the two tenth-century English kings whose death is noted in the medieval Irish annals.

Interesting in this context is a charter known from its initial word as *Altitonantis* that claims to be a grant of lands and confirmation of rights by Edgar to the monastery of Worcester. The preamble states that Edgar was the overlord of Dublin through hereditary right because of the conquests of his predecessors.[47] The document is now extant only in a twelfth-century copy, and there is controversy about its authenticity. The preamble has been used in the debate about the date of the charter's composition, but its information that Edgar claimed to be overlord of all Britain, the surrounding islands, and Dublin with a great part of Ireland has been ignored; other tenth-century documents make similar claims. Setting aside the English aspect, the political geography described in the charter fits only the later tenth century. A "great part of Ireland" was tributary to Dublin's king Olaf Cuaran, from the river Shannon to sea, and his capitol was a flourishing commercial center. As will be discussed in the next chapter, Edgar seems to have had an interest in the Hebrides and Isle of Man. At the end of the eleventh century the islands on the west of Britain were formally Norwegian territory while Dublin was a port city in decline whose rulers controlled little beyond the bounds of the modern county.

Coins support the claims of *Altitonantis* for Edgar's interest in Dublin. English coins have been found throughout Ireland, and during Olaf's reign many of them came from the Chester mint. More significant is the name of the prince in whose name they were produced; Edgar's coins in Ireland "outnumber those of all other English kings put together."[48] They could be loot from raids, the pay of mercenaries, or the profits from trade. The reign of Edgar was noteworthy for its peacefulness and for the beginnings of the periodic recall of all coins so that new issues could be made. Trade is one obvious way the coins came into Ireland, and it is worth remembering the cloth merchants from Ireland who were selling at Cambridge. There might be another explanation for the coins. If Edgar had made an alliance with Olaf Cuaran, he could have supplied him with funds in order to pay for mercenaries so that he could maintain himself in Ireland, and stay out of Britain. Olaf would have used the coins for his own purposes, hastening their distribution.

More certain is Olaf's alliance with the Uí Dúnlainge confederation of northern Leinster. There were three divisions: Uí Dúnchada, Uí Fáeláin, and Uí Muiredaich. These families circulated the provincial kingship among themselves from the eighth to eleventh century.[49] This arrangement was not dissimilar from the alternation of the Uí Néill lordship between Cenél nEógain and Clann Cholmáin, and it was based on military parity rather than a sense of kinship. Olaf allied with Uí Fáeláin, whose king was Murchad son of Finn. In 970 Olaf and Murchad raided Brega, where they plundered the monastery of Kells before winning a Battle at Ardmulchan (county Meath). In 976 the Dublin army captured Augaire son of Tuathal, the king of Leinster and a dynast of Uí Muiredaich. Augaire was in captivity less than two years, for he was free in 978 when he was defeated and slain by Olaf at the Battle of Belan (county Kildare).

Olaf continued his campaign of terror against two of the three clans of Uí Dúnlainge in 979, when he captured the new king of Leinster, Domnall Clóen ("the crooked") of Uí Dúnchada. There may have been an element of revenge involved, for Domnall had slain Olaf's ally Murchad son of Finn in treacherous circumstances in 972. Or there might have been a more self-serving motive. Previously, Uí Dúnchada had controlled the lands south of the Liffey, including the land now occupied by Olaf's subjects. The Vikings pushed the Irish away from the Liffey, and now it seems that Olaf wanted their lands to the south, which provided good grazing. While the king of Leinster languished in his prison, Olaf could assert his lordship. Domnall remained in captivity less than a year before he was released by Máel Sechnaill II after the defeat of Dublin at the Battle of Tara in 980.

The alliance with Murchad of Leinster in 970 marks another milestone in Olaf's career: his second known marriage. This time the bride was Murchad's daughter Gormflaith (died 1030), called his "clever child" in the *Banshenchas*. Gormflaith was remembered for marrying well, and her romantic adventures were summarized in the verse: "Three leaps leaped Gormflaith, which a woman will never leap again: a leap into Dublin, a leap into Tara and a leap into Cashel, the mound of the plain over everyone." Each place name represents a different husband. The choice of the word "leap" looks to heroic verse, in which warriors leap into a conflict as a demonstration of their fearlessness. The poet apparently thought that there were similarities between combat and matrimony.[50]

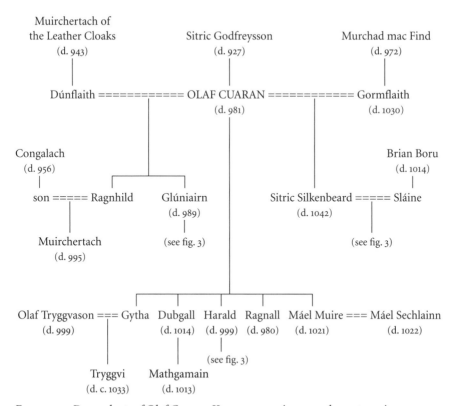

FIGURE 2. *Descendants of Olaf Cuaran.* Key: ==, *marriage*; —, *descent*; c., *circa*; d., *died.*

The order of place names in the verses indicates that Olaf was Gormflaith's first husband. Their son was Sitric Silkenbeard, who succeeded his half-brother, Glúniairn, as king of Dublin in 989. Gormflaith's second husband was Máel Sechnaill II, the son of Olaf's previous wife Dúnflaith. Their son was Conchobar, who succeeded his father as lord of Clann Cholmáin. Gormflaith's last husband was the king of Munster and Irish High King Brian mac Cennétig, better known as Brian Boru or *Bóruma* ("of the cattle-tribute"). According to *Cocad Gáedel re Gallaib*, she was still married to him in 1013, the year when Dublin and Leinster revolted against his lordship, although *Njal's Saga* claims that Gormflaith was divorced from Brian before the battle and was in Dublin during the conflict.[51] Their son Donnchad eventually succeeded to his father's kingship in Munster, but he never realized his ambition to reign over all Ireland.

The marriage of Gormflaith to Olaf began military and economic accommodation between the kingdoms of northern Leinster and the Vikings of Dublin that endured into the eleventh century. The relatively few attacks from Leinster on Dublin in the late tenth century, together with the Viking settlements along the coast of what is now county Wicklow give testimony to a more peaceful co-existence between the Vikings and their Irish neighbors than the Irish annals suggest. The Dublin–Leinster alliance is also a sign that Dublin was increasingly unable to defend itself from the northern Leinster kingdoms and did not want to live in a constant state of war. Geography was part of the problem. The fortress of Dublin was on the south side of the Liffey, within easy reach of the powerful Leinster princes.

Economic aspects of Gormflaith's marriage to Olaf are arguably as important as the military alliance. The Uí Fáeláin and the Vikings of Dublin had been rivals for control of the lands around the Liffey, a rivalry that was, at least in part, for the resources of the neighborhood. Dublin was dependent on the surrounding countryside for hides, timber, fuel, wool, as well as some materials for manufacture. The population of Dublin also needed vast supplies of foodstuffs.[52] There was not enough land under the control of the Dublin lords to produce the quantities necessary for the needs of the town, especially in an age of low grain yields and slow maturation of livestock. Even though northern county Dublin is well suited for grain cultivation, a larger area would need to be cultivated in order to compensate for relatively low yields, and Gerald of Wales remarked on the small kernels of Irish grains in comparison with varieties found in Britain.

There was also the need for grazing land, and the union of the king of the Dublin Vikings with a Leinster princess seems to have led to a settlement between the two peoples on the question of grazing rights. In his *View of the Present State of Ireland*, Edmund Spenser remarked on the good grazing in the hilly areas south from Dublin.[53] Before the Battle of Glen Mama in 999 cattle from Leinster herds were sent into Dublin territory for safety. The bones excavated in Dublin at Fishamble Street show that over 60 percent of the cattle were slaughtered after the age of thirty-six months and the majority of those slaughtered were females.[54] Sheep were also being raised for the trade in woolens that was flourishing throughout the northern Atlantic region. The poem on the circuit of Ireland by Muirchertach of the Leather Cloaks notes that a colored mantle (*brat datha*) was given to each of the princes in his army by the men of Dublin.

By the mid-tenth century, Dublin was also an important food-processing center.[55] The poem on Muirchertach's journey through Ireland notes that the tribute taken from Dublin included items such as bacon, wheat, meat, and cheese. These were basic provisions for the troops on the march or crews of ships. Dudo of St. Quentin mentions that provisions for crews sailing around Normandy included grain and bacon, and the Billingsgate Tolls note that ships calling at London could purchase three pigs.[56] Trade in foodstuffs between the Vikings and the Irish is reflected by Old Norse loan words in Irish. The Old Norse word for a sheaf of grain *bundin* had passed into Middle Irish as *punnan* by the tenth century, when it is found in the versified biblical tract *Saltair na Rann* ("Metrical Psalter"), while the Old Norse word for beans *baunir* became *pónair* in Middle Irish.[57] Wheat, beans, and cows may have been in his thoughts as Olaf pondered the desirability of marriage to a Leinster princess.

By the fourth quarter of the century, there appeared a far more worrisome foe than Olaf's previous opponents. This was his stepson, the king of Clann Cholmáin named Máel Sechnaill II, the child from Dúnflaith's first marriage to Domnall of Clann Cholmáin. His energy and ability were timely for the Uí Néill. Even before retiring to the church of Armagh, where he died in 980, the High King Domnall Ua Néill had become ineffective. Máel Sechnaill served notice of his determination to seize the high kingship when, in 975, he attacked Dublin. Although he could not breach the fortress, he destroyed the grove known as *Caill Tomair* ("Thor's Wood").

In 980 Olaf carried the fight to Máel Sechnaill, a battle that was the Irish prince's greatest triumph and the last defeat of Olaf Cuaran. An army drawn from Dublin and from the Hebrides challenged Máel Sechnaill in what became known as the Battle of Tara. The Vikings were led by a son of Olaf named Ragnall, whom the Irish annals style the *rígdamna* "royal stock" or "crown-prince."[58] Jointly commanding troops with Ragnall was Conamhal mac Gilla Mairi of the Isles. To medieval writers this was one of the major battles between the Irish and the Vikings, and it took its place in popular legend alongside the Battle of Dublin in 919 and the Battle of Clontarf in 1014. The choice of Tara as the battlefield had an unmistakable significance, for now it was associated with sovereignty over the entire island.

The fighting at Tara was furious, and Máel Sechnaill triumphed. Among the slain, according to the *Annals of Tigernach*, was a man called "the orator" (Middle Irish *Irlabraigh*) of Dublin. This orator is clearly the Old Norse "lawspeaker," who recited the customary law at every gathering of the assembly or Thing (*Þing*). Máel Sechnaill took advantage of his triumph to attack Dublin. The countryside was ravaged and, after a siege of three days, Dublin surrendered. Máel Sechnaill forced the Vikings to pay tribute, in the form of 2,000 head of cattle and movables such as jewels.

Greater fame was gained from his liberation of the Irish hostages held by Olaf. These included Domnall Clóen, the king of Leinster, and hostages from the Uí Néill. There was literary recognition in the statement attributed to Máel Sechnaill: "Let everyone of the Irish in the Viking's lands go in peace to his own land." With pardonable overstatement, the *Annals of Tigernach* refer to it as the Babylonian captivity of Ireland. More significant than the release of prisoners was the loss of a source of revenue for Dublin from the payment of tribute by the southern Uí Néill, "from the river Shannon to the Irish Sea," that is the southern boundary of Uí Néill confederation. Now the lord of Dublin had even fewer resources for competing with his rivals, and the resurgence of the southern Uí Néill established a dangerous rival in Dublin's neighborhood.

That the Battle of Tara was, in part, a fight over control of territory provides a historical background to the poem that introduced this study, Cináed Ua hArtacáin's verse *dindshenchas* of Achall (the Hill of Skreen near Tara) now known by its first line "Achall beyond Tara" (*Achall ar aicce Temair*). The verses explain the mythological history of the hill, which was named after a princess named Achall who died of grief when her beloved was slain, before turning to the battles of the Irish and the Vikings around Achall.

Tribute or taxes, called *cáin* in Irish and *skattr* in Norse, were paid in a variety of goods, and they could be collected by Vikings for a long time. In the ninth century, the contemporary Scottish Chronicle notes that the ninth-century Olaf collected taxes for a number of years from the Scots and that he was slain there in 875 while gathering that tribute.[59] *Cocad Gáedel re Gallaib* claims that the Vikings took their payments in a combination of foodstuffs and precious metals; the quantity of silver was called a nose tax, because the penalty for not paying was to have the nose cut off.[60] Occasionally Viking prince and native lord clashed over the right to collect these dues. *Orkneyinga Saga* records vicious fights between the Vikings and the Scots in Caithness over the collection of taxes.[61] The Vikings used a specific official to collect these taxes similar to the Irish *maer* ("steward") who collected dues and oversaw his master's interests. When Brian's elder brother, Mathgamain, conquered the Vikings of Limerick, one of his first acts was to expel their officials from Munster.

The Battle of Tara ended the long career of Olaf Cuaran. After almost four decades of winning and losing kingdoms on either side of the Irish Sea, this defeat proved to be too much for Olaf, and the old warrior abdicated in favor of his son Glúniairn. Even though much of his career had been plundering churches, for his retirement Olaf chose the famous monastery of St. Columba at Iona. Olaf died there, in repentance and pilgrimage, in 981. Olaf's choice of a church famous for its association with St. Columba is not surprising. Scattered around Dublin were several churches dedicated to the saint. A famous church was Skreen, close by Tara, on the hill praised by Cináed Ua hArtacáin. North of Dublin was the church of Swords and, off the coast, was the church on Ireland's Eye.

Olaf's influence can be measured by more than a recitation of his military triumphs or defeats. The future fortunes of Olaf's family depended on their ties to princely families. His descendants are found scattered throughout Ireland, Wales, and the Isles. Their success explains why so much information survives in so many genealogical collections, such as the descent of the Lords of the Isles from Olaf outlined in Welsh genealogies.

Olaf had three daughters whose names and marriages are known: Gytha, Ragnhild, and Máel Muire. Gytha married the Norwegian prince Olaf Tryggvason. Her sister, Ragnhild, has been introduced. She married a son of the High King Congalach of Knowth. His name is unknown, but he might have been the Domnall son of Congalach (died 976) who fought on the side of Olaf in 970 during his victory at the Battle of Kilmona over Domnall Ua Néill.[62] Ragnhild's marriage was apparently part of the alliance between Olaf and the family of Congalach that was made fifteen years after the ambush and death of the high king in 956. Ragnhild had a son named Muirchertach who maintained amiable ties with his mother's family. He joined the men of Dublin on a raid against the church called *Domnach Mór Pátraic* (Donaghpatrick, county Meath) in 995. The Irish chronicles gleefully attribute his death a month later to divine punishment for the desecration of the church. A preoccupation on the part of Olaf's dynasty with affairs in Brega, the territory controlled by Congalach's dynasty, is a reflection of their ties with a branch of the royal dynasty.

The third daughter, Máel Muire (the name means "Servant of Mary"), was the wife of the High King Máel Sechnaill II and died in 1021. The ties of Máel Sechnaill to Dublin were quite intricate. He was the brother-in-law of Olaf's sons and successors Glúniairn and Sitric Silkenbeard, the half-brother of Glúniairn, and one of the husbands of Olaf's wife Gormflaith. The multiple marital connections of Máel Sechnaill with the family of Olaf illustrate why the ecclesiastical reformers in the late eleventh and twelfth centuries devoted so much of their criticism to the problem of marriage irregularities, especially within the prohibited degrees of kinship.

Olaf's sons were a force in Irish political life for almost a century and their careers are discussed in detail throughout the following chapters. He was succeeded immediately by Glúniairn, who reigned from 980 to 989. Glúniairn's successor, and the most famous of Olaf's children, was Sitric Silkenbeard, Gormflaith's child. Two other sons were Ragnall, who died at the Battle of Tara in 980, and Dubgall, who was slain in 1014 at the Battle of Clontarf. A particularly important son was named Harald, and he was slain at the Battle of Glen Mama in 999. Described as *maith Gall* ("a noble of the Vikings") in the *Annals of Ulster* and *Annals of Tigernach*, but *rígdamna* ("royal stock") in *Cocad Gáedel re Gallaib*, both titles stress his kingly ancestry. Harald's son Ivar was king of Dublin from 1038 to 1046. Ivar's son was the king of the Isles named Godred Crovan, whose descendants ruled there in the twelfth and thirteenth centuries.

Olaf Cuaran and his career provide a useful insight into the upper level of Viking society in Ireland and Britain. He demonstrates how the popular image of a Viking prince as merely a savage pirate needs modification. Olaf lived in violent times, and he was as ruthless or bloodthirsty as any contemporary. Allies were made or discarded as dictated by self-interest. Ambush, assassination, and imprisonment were all tactics used by Olaf and his rivals. Kinship was important, but it counted for little when it interfered with his plans. Olaf did not hesitate to exile his cousins, the sons of Olaf Godfreysson, upon his final return from Britain, and he was quite prepared to kill them when they reappeared in Ireland. Even his marriages were politically, not romantically, motivated, and contracted for whatever gain they brought. Exactly the same idea motivated the families of his wives Dúnflaith and Gormflaith.

Clichés about illiterate Vikings are even less apt in light of Olaf's patronage of Irish and Scandinavian poets. The Irish verses of Cináed Ua hArtacáin reveal that Olaf was bilingual; there was little to be gained by composing a poem in a language the audience did not understand. Olaf maintained connections with the Scandinavian literary world as the patron of the Icelandic poet Thorgils "Grouse-Poet." Thorgils might have received his sobriquet while in Ireland, for "grouse" is used in Irish verse for a powerful warrior. There is general scholarly consensus that Irish metrical forms influenced Old Norse verse, and Olaf's court was one of the places where those contacts could be made.[63]

Olaf Cuaran's immediate ancestors are found among the Vikings settled in Britain. He was the grandson of the obscure ninth-century king of Northumbria named Godfrey Hardacnutsson. An Irish connection with Godfrey is possible, although nothing can be certainly stated. For almost a generation after his death in 896 Godfrey's family was in obscurity. When they emerge in the written records circa 914, their leader is his son Ragnall. For three years Ragnall consolidated his hold over Northumbria and on the eastern shores of the Irish Sea, and is recognized as king. When, in 917 Ragnall and his brother, Sitric (Olaf Cuaran's father), began their campaigns in Ireland, they did so from a base in Britain. Sitric's capture of the old Viking base along the Liffey began thirty-five years in which he and his extended family tried to hold kingdoms in two islands. By 952 only the Irish kingdom remained after Olaf Cuaran was forced to flee from Britain.

Battles, trade, religion, and marriages are all important for understanding the career of Olaf Cuaran. During his reign Dublin was transforming into an important commercial center. Imported goods were sold at Dublin as well as items made there with local and foreign materials. Olaf's military and material concerns are visible in his marriages. The Irish in general, and the Uí Néill in particular, were far less isolationist than they are popularly thought. Despite their reputation as foes of the North-men, they welcomed marriages with powerful Viking dynasties. Olaf was married to Dúnflaith of Cenél nEógain, his daughter Máel Muire was married to the southern Uí Néill High King Máel Sechnaill II, and her sister, Ragnhild, was the wife of the son of Congalach of Síl nÁedo Sláine. Olaf Cuaran's decision to retire to Iona in 980 may have been influenced by his Uí Néill contacts. Even the Leinster princes, who had suffered as much as anyone at the hands of the Vikings, were enthusiastic about peaceful ties to the Vikings and became the main allies of Olaf's family.

The union with a princess of the Cenél nEógain during the reign of her brother, the High King Domnall Ua Néill, shows Olaf looking beyond Dublin's immediate neighborhood in the Liffey Valley in order to establish influence with the powerful overlords of the north. His second marriage to Gormflaith was the outwardly secured alliance with the Uí Fáeláin of Leinster, revealing the changing nature of his goals. To the military dimension—safeguarding the southern boundaries of Dublin—was added an economic purpose. Access to supplies of foodstuffs and raw materials, both of which were needed in vast quantities by a manufacturing and trading town like Dublin with a growing population, was just as important as security. There was also a personal concern for Olaf in his marriages: support against his own cousins, the family of Olaf Godfreysson. The rivalry continued for decades and moved from Ireland to Wales, where the establishment of the family of Olaf Godfreysson on the Isle of Anglesey placed them in a perfect position for attacks on Dublin.

Equally interesting is the question of economic benefits. While the population of Dublin was dependent on the surrounding regions for supplies of foodstuffs, fuel, and raw materials, such a trade made the surrounding countryside, in turn, eco-nomically dependent on Dublin. Not all the goods collected by the Vikings of Dublin were necessarily for their own use. The commercial value of a commodity such as the woolen mantles is obvious, but there was also something to be gained by sup-plying stores to the ships sailing in the Irish Sea. Trade followed politics. His ties to northern England helped Olaf's subjects make an important trading connection there, illustrated by the English coins of Edgar's reign from the Chester mint found in Ireland.

Olaf Cuaran was a complex man. Ruthlessness in the pursuit of his own interests is only part of the picture. He was a Christian, who enriched himself by pillaging churches, yet he chose to die in religious retirement. Olaf was a man of literary tastes who could understand and appreciate poetry composed in Old Norse and Irish. His antiquarian interests are revealed in the mythology contained in the poem on the Hill of Skreen. Olaf could recognize merit in verses that were more than just flattery. He was also a diplomat, who knew the limitations of his own military and economic resources, which he attempted to remedy through alliances. Much of the credit must go to Olaf for the changes at Dublin. From its refoundation in 917 as a base for raiders, it had developed into a major commercial and manufacturing center. Havelok the Dane might have done worse than to take Olaf Cuaran for a model.

3

Pirate Kings of the Islands

As Olaf Cuaran and his dynasty were becoming entrenched in Ireland, another empire was being assembled in the islands and headlands of the Irish Sea. In the third quarter of the tenth century two brothers named Magnus and Godfrey Haraldsson raided in Ireland, Scotland, and Wales. Within two decades Godfrey was described as the "king of the Isles" between Britain and Ireland. Little, however, is known of these men. Their ancestry and origin are matters for speculation, as is the location of their base of operations, and even what precisely is meant by "the Kingdom of the Isles" at a particular time. None of these obscurities is unique, but the search for answers reveals how widely and casually Viking families roamed.

In the popular medieval imagination there was a perception of mystery surrounding the islands between Ireland and Britain, and this is found even in the records from antiquity. The grammarian Demetrius of Tarsus claimed to have visited unspecified sacred isles off the northwestern coast of Britain, while several islands are included in the "Geographical Guide" of Claudius Ptolomaeus, and in the seventh-century Ravenna Cosmography (using earlier imperial documents).[1] An interpolation (possibly Irish) to the third-century miscellany of C. Julius Solinus claims that the Hebrides, called *Ebudes*, formed a single kingdom. The king had no personal property, but enjoyed all the possessions of his subjects, including their wives. Without any hope of enrichment or heirs, the prince reigned for the benefit of his people rather than personal gain.[2]

The pagan Irish believed that some of their deities resided in the Irish Sea region. The sea-god Manannán mac Lir was believed to dwell on the Isle of Man, where the eleventh-century Irish historian Flann of Monasterboice placed the slaughter of three gods of the Tuatha Dé Danann. The mythical earthy paradise known as the "Land of Promise" was thought to be either in or just beyond the Hebrides. One legend has the hero Conn of the Hundred Battles relieving Ireland from famine by sailing beyond Howth from one island to another for more than a month guided only by the stars until he came to the Land of Promise. These associations lingered, and

56

late in the Middle Ages women on the Isle of Man were rumored to practice witch-craft by selling knotted ropes that supposedly released breezes when untied.[3]

Christian writers explained away and replaced pagan gods with reference to missionaries/saints such as Brendan and Patrick, or possible reflections of Viking activity.[4] In his glossary composed circa 900, the Irish scholar cum prince Cormac mac Cuilennáin described Manannán as a merchant living on the Isle of Man, a comment that seems to reflect nascent Viking trade and commerce in the Irish Sea. The voyage of St. Brendan the Navigator along the western coast of Britain followed the same route used by Viking ships. The conversion of the Manx to Christianity is attributed by the seventh-century hagiographer Muirchú to another sailor named Mac Cuil, who had persecuted St. Patrick and, after becoming a Christian, sailed from Ireland to the Isle of Man in a boat with no oars and no sail. By the twelfth century, St. Patrick was credited directly with the conversion of the Manx in his *vita* written by Jocelin of Furness whose patron, the adventurer John de Courcy, was married to the Isles princess Affrica, a descendant of Olaf Cuaran.

The most famous saint in the Hebrides, Columba, founded the church of Iona where Olaf Cuaran died. Iona was in the Kingdom of Dál Riata, a maritime state with similarities to the later Viking empire. Dál Riata was originally a kingdom in Ireland (county Antrim) from where settlers had moved across the North Channel to Britain circa A.D. 500. The British lands eventually extended from Ardnamurchan Point to the Isle of Arran, with a ceremonial center at Dunadd, in the Moss of Crinan. The sea was a highway connecting a distance of only thirteen miles between county Antrim in Ireland and the Mull of Kintyre. Late in the eleventh century Dál Riata was incorporated into the Kingdom of the Isles when it was ceded by the Scots king Edgar to the Norwegian king Magnus in 1098.

Geography emphasized differences in the Kingdom of the Isles. Bede had claimed that the Isles of Man and Anglesey were a single entity called the Menevian Isles. Man was important because of its central position in the Irish Sea, and both the Anglo-Saxons and the Irish had fought to control it. The sixth-century Irish prince Báetán mac Carill, the king of Ulaid (in northeast Ireland), raided the Isle of Man while early the next century it was invaded by the Northumbrian king Edwin. An equally important geographical reality was the Highland/Lowland division, which bisects the Isle of Bute. From Kintyre north to the Outer Hebrides is the mountainous region, while the southern (Lowland) zone has the more prosperous Rhinns of Galloway and the Isle of Man. During the Middle Ages this Highland/Lowland divide was the line between poverty and prosperity. The difference is clear in the thirteenth century, when rule of the kingdom was divided between the princes Ragnall Godredsson and his half-brother, Olaf. Olaf's court was on the Isle of Lewis, where there was little cultivated land and the inhabitants lived through hunting and fishing. He complained that the island's poverty prevented him from an establishment appropriate to his status, unlike the more comfortable existence of Ragnall's court on the Isle of Man.[5]

Viking settlers arrived in the Outer Hebrides in the eighth century according to the geographical treatise *The Measure of the World*, composed by the Irish scholar Dicuíl circa 825. In the first half of the ninth century the Vikings fought with the Scots for control of the southern Hebrides and the lands south of Ardnamurchan. In 839 the Dál Riata prince Eóganán mac Óengusa, leading the men of the Pictish Kingdom of Fortriu, was slain while fighting a Viking fleet that sailed from a raid on the Liffey Valley. According to the Scottish Chronicle, in the last decade of the ninth century the Scots defeated Vikings in a battle around the River Sheil. As the Scots emigrated eastwards into the richer lands of the Picts, Dál Riata received settlements of farmers and fishers from Scandinavia and from the neighboring isles.[6]

Details about Viking settlement in the Hebrides are found in Icelandic works as varied as *Landnámabók* and *Eyrbyggja Saga* that preserve tales of uneven historical reliability about pirates/warriors who lived in the Hebrides.[7] Usually they begin in the mid-ninth century with a Viking named Ketil Flat Nose (*Flatnefr*), who was allegedly sent to the Hebrides by the Norse king Harald Fairhair. Ketil became a pirate, and Harald led a naval expedition against him. The chronology of this story is difficult to reconcile with the historical records, but Ketil was the ancestor of several important Icelandic families.

Occasionally connected with Harald's expedition is a medieval legend found in Irish, Norman, and Icelandic sources claiming that the Isle of Man was completely depopulated at one time and then resettled.[8] The Irish legend "Siege of the Men of Falga" (Falga is another name for the Isle of Man) claims that the hero Cú Chulainn attacked the island and killed all the men in a single battle. The Icelandic *Orkneyinga Saga* claims that Harald Fairhair destroyed settlements in the Hebrides in order to end assaults on Norway from the west. Snorri Sturluson expanded on this, remarking that the Isle of Man was inhabited until Harald's expedition, when his appearance in the Irish Sea so terrified the inhabitants that they abandoned the island. Slightly different is the story recounted by the Anglo-Norman historian Orderic Vitalis in his twelfth-century *Ecclesiastical History*. He claims that the Norwegian king Magnus Barefoot found the Isle of Man uninhabited upon his arrival in the Irish Sea in 1098 and established settlers there.

The Haraldssons built their kingdom in this region associated with pagan gods and nautical missionaries. The first record of Magnus and Godfrey Haraldsson is in the Welsh chronicles' account of their raid in North Wales on the Isle of Anglesey. Anglesey was an inviting target for any sea raider, a prosperous island jutting into the Irish Sea. Magnus raided Penmon (in northeast Anglesey) circa 971 according to the *Annales Cambriae*, and the following year Godfrey extorted what is politely called "a tax" from the inhabitants.[9] Their description as raiders while gathering "taxes" suggests that the Haraldssons were not based on Anglesey. In their exploitation of the people of the region, Magnus and Godfrey appear to have kept some distance from their victims.

Their Welsh interests brought the Haraldssons into conflict with another Viking family: the descendants of Olaf Godfreysson, who had settled in Wales after leaving Dublin. Conflict between them apparently began several years before Magnus and Godfrey appear in the records. A passage in *Cocad Gáedel re Gallaib* gives a fragmentary account of a joint venture, circa 968, between a son of Olaf Godfreysson named Olaf and a Viking from Ireland named Ivar of Limerick.[10] Ivar had led a fleet to western Ireland circa 960, when he seized the islands in the River Shannon. Like the Irish aristocracy, the Vikings either made allies with their neighbors or enriched themselves with loot from raids on them. One of Ivar's allies was Mathgamain mac Cennétig of Dál Cais (county Clare, north of Limerick). Mathgamain became the provincial king of Munster in 963, possibly with Ivar's help. Mathgamain felt strong enough to dispense with his colleague by 967. Ivar fled Ireland and the Irish prince destroyed the Viking fortress at Limerick after looting it of gems, precious metals, and saddles, and enslaving the Viking women. They were taken to the hill of Saingel (now Singland, county Limerick) and placed in a circle where they stooped with their hands on the ground. Then the youths who looked after the horses drove them along, for the benefit of the souls of the dead Vikings. This arcane ritual might have a connection with the horse cults of Scandinavia.[11]

Ivar fled to Wales, called Britain in Irish texts. There he allied with Olaf the son of Olaf Godfreysson. For a year, from 968 to 969, they raided around the Irish Sea. During that year Olaf was killed by someone called simply a British king. Olaf is the last known member of his line, and the family of Olaf Godfreysson disappears from view. Ivar returned to Limerick after raiding in eastern Ireland.

The "British king" probably was either Magnus or Godfrey Haraldsson. If he had been Welsh, it probably would have been mentioned in the insular records. The disappearance of Olaf's family at the same time as the sudden appearance of the Haraldssons in Anglesey suggests that there had been a battle over the exploitation of the Welsh that was won by the Haraldssons. An Irish record can be excused for not realizing that the victor in a battle fought in Wales could be a Viking rather than a Welsh captain. Conflict between Olaf son of Olaf Godfreysson and his ally Ivar of Limerick with Magnus and Godfrey Haraldsson explains why Magnus led his fleet on a great circumnavigation around Ireland to the Shannon in 974. There he stormed Inis Cathaig (Scattery Island) and captured Ivar.[12] A fight between Viking chieftains that might have begun in Wales was finished in Ireland.

On his Irish expedition Magnus had the assistance of the "Lawmen" (*Lagmenn*) of the Isles. That was not their first visit to Ireland. A "fleet of Lawmen" (*longes Laghmuind*) had been part of an extensive raid on the Irish in 962 when their leader was a "son of Olaf," possibly Olaf son of Olaf Godfreysson.[13] They attacked the eastern coast, raiding Howth and Ireland's Eye before moving northwards to county

Down. The "Lawmen" then went south to Munster where, among other targets, they sailed up the Blackwater to raid Lismore before sailing along the River Lee for an attack on Cork. The raids were, in part, revenge for the death of one of their number named *Oin*. The expedition was not entirely successful. While the Vikings were raiding between Cork and Lismore, the Irish attacked the Vikings, who lost three hundred and fifty of their number with only the crew of three ships escaping.

The "Lawmen" pose an interesting question: was this a family that allied with the son of Olaf or was it a fleet supported by a number of chieftains? The personal name Lagmann is preserved in Baly Lamyn ("farm of Lagmann") on the Isle of Man. Among chieftains the lawman (ON *lögmaðr*) was an individual well versed in the traditional laws, about which he was consulted as an authority. From the ranks of the lawmen was selected the "law speaker" (ON *lögsögumaðr*) who recited the laws at the assembly called the Thing.[14]

With their rivals eliminated, Magnus and Godfrey became involved in Welsh dynastic politics. Godfrey probably led the Vikings who raided Powys in 979 and killed the prince named Iago. He was certainly in Gwynedd the next year when he allied with the Welsh prince Custennin ap Iago. Together they ravaged the Llyn Peninsula and the Isle of Anglesey, but Custennin was slain by a rival named Hywel ap Ieuaf. Several years later, circa 982, Godfrey moved farther south to attack Dyfed, with raids on St. David's and Llanweithefawr.[15]

The attacks on the Welsh may have been only a part of the Haraldssons' activities. From 980 to 982 there are several raids that were probably carried out by Magnus or Godfrey Haraldsson. Chester was ravaged in 980 by a "northern ship fleet." The devastation was severe, with some areas temporarily abandoned. There was also a decline in the number of moneyers and a reduction in the output of the Chester mint. Also in 980, Southampton was raided by pirates (called Danish by John of Worcester), who then sailed on to attack Thanet followed by, the next year, raids on Cornwall and Devon, with the church of St. Petroc's singled out for destruction. In 982 nine pirate ships of Danes attacked Dorset and then ravaged Portland.[16] That was the same year Godfrey Haraldsson led his raids on southwest Wales. Reasons for suggesting the Haraldssons as involved in these actions include their intolerance of rivals in this area, the extent of devastation at Chester (which was fortified and prepared for attack because of its mint), and, finally, the labeling of some of the raiders as Danes, as were the troops of the Haraldssons.

The Viking raids after 979 are one reflection of the deteriorating political situation in England, after the murder of the young English king, Edgar's son Edward the Martyr, killed in 979 by the supporters of his half-brother, Æthelraed. A more impressive glimpse of the Haraldssons' power is visible in 984. Their success in the Irish Sea had a parallel in Ireland in Brian Boru, the brother of Mathgamain. Brian took the provincial kingship of Munster in 978 after slaying Máel Muad, one of the conspirators in his brother's murder. He steadily extended his power by taking the submission of Osraige and Leinster in 983. Then he prepared to launch raids in the eastern Irish midlands. Toward that goal he sought the assistance of the Haraldssons. Brian and the Haraldssons made an alliance in 984 at the town of Waterford. The only record of the conference is preserved in the *Annals of Inisfallen*. The phrasing of the entry suggests that the Haraldssons were not based in Ireland, for they made a naval expedition to the town, "a great sea-expedition by the sons of Harald to Waterford."[17] After the customary exchange of hostages, the allies agreed to attack several Leinster kingdoms, with the ultimate aim of capturing Dublin. The Haraldssons ravaged the coast of Leinster with attacks on the Kingdom of Uí Chennselaig, while Brian's troops marched overland; if Dublin was attacked, there is no record of it. This is the first notice of the alliance between the family of Brian and the Haraldssons that would endure into the twelfth century.

Waterford as a meeting place might have been the choice of Magnus and Godfrey. Evidence of a marriage alliance between the Haraldssons and the royal family of Osraige comes from the version of the *Banshenchas* preserved in the *Book of Lecan*, a late medieval codex. A lady named Máel Muru, called the daughter of Harald son of Godfrey (*Aralt mac Gofraid*), married King Gilla Patraic mac Donnchada of Osraige (reigned 976–996). They had a son named Donnchad who reigned from 1003 to 1039 and added the lordship of Leinster to that of Osraige. Gilla Patraic's search among Vikings for a wife was a family tradition by this time and they had been intermarrying with the Vikings in Ireland for generations; according to *Landnámabók*, he had relatives among several powerful Icelandic families.[18] There are various possibilities for the identity of Máel Muru's father, but the most likely one is that his name is a reversal of the name Godfrey son of Harald. Miswriting names is found in later manuscripts, even for prominent individuals such as the Isles prince Godred Crovan. Kingly Irish families were ever mindful of their status, and they did not make unions with nonentities or mere pirates. There were levels of marriage among the Irish, and the inclusion of Máel Muru in the *Banshenchas* shows her at the highest level, a primary wife or *cétmuinter*.

Máel Muru's name ("servant of Mary") indicates that at this date some Viking princesses were Christians. From the Isle of Man to the Hebrides, conversion of the Viking settlers to Christianity is documented in illustrations and inscriptions on grave markers and crosses.[19] The monastery of Iona became a mausoleum for the seafaring chieftains, where representations of the great war-galleys are engraved on memorial stones set up in the churchyard. A grave slab on Iona with a runic inscription from the second half of the tenth century announces that Kali Olvisson laid the stone over his brother, Fogl. On the Isle of Man a runic inscription shows the newcomers taking the names of their Celtic neighbors. A father with the Norse name of Thorleif erected a cross in memory of his son who had the Irish name Fiach.

Conversion was a slow process. This is reflected in two late tenth- to eleventh-century carved stones on the Isle of Man that employ scenes from Nordic mythology.[20] A blending of Christian and non-Christian is found on a dressed stone found at Kirk Andreas. On one side of the Manx stone, which has elements of the Borre style (angular animal designs with ribbon motifs and knotwork, flourishing in the tenth century), there is a scene from Ragnarök (the end of the world) in which Odin is devoured by Fenrir the wolf. On the other side there are the Christian symbols of the cross and fish. The longevity of paganism is seen in an ornamented stone from Maughold exhibiting elements of Ringerike style (using intertwined animal and plant motifs, from the eleventh century) with three figures that have been identified as the pagan gods Loki, Odin, and Hœnir.

After 984 only one Haraldsson, Godfrey, is mentioned in the chronicles. The date when Magnus died is unknown, although the *Annals of Inisfallen* insist that more than one son of Harald was at Waterford in 984.[21] He might have been one of the first victims of the plague that swept through Britain in 986 and reached Ireland the next year, with a second plague in 993. Irish and English documents, such as *Saltair na Rann* and the *Anglo-Saxon Chronicles*, remarked on the mortality. Weakened victims were too irresistible for Godfrey, and he began a new series of raids. Godfrey probably led the unsuccessful attack in 986 by Danes on the men of Dál Riata, in which 140 of the brigands were captured and hanged. The location was Dál Riata in Scotland, because later that year, on Christmas night, the Danes returned for an easier target. They attacked the monastery on Iona where they killed the bishop, the abbot, and thirteen other senior members of the monastery.[22] The next year (987) a Haraldsson (probably Godfrey) turned south and led his army of Danes in the conquest of the Isle of Man. But Wales, particularly Anglesey, remained an inviting and rewarding target. That same year, Godfrey again raided Anglesey with his army of "Dark Foreigners" (i.e. Danes), where he captured two thousand men and defeated the prince Maredubb ab Owain, who fled south with the other survivors. In 989 Maredubb was back in Anglesey, when he was forced to pay a tax to the "Dark Foreigners." A raid on Watchet, on the North Devon coast, in 988 by Danes was probably the work of Godfrey. Watchet had a mint, from which coin dies would be taken to Ireland and used as the model for the earliest coins struck at Dublin. In the battle at Watchet two of the leading Devon nobles—Goda and Strenwald—were slain, but the Danes were defeated.

By 989 Godfrey was at the height of his power as he raided throughout the Irish Sea Province and beyond. He controlled the Isles of Anglesey and Man as well as an indeterminable section of the Hebrides. In addition, Godfrey was the ally of the rising power in southern Ireland, Brian Boru, and probably the father-in-law of the king of Osraige. His ships roamed at will through the waters between Ireland and Britain. Nevertheless, he was not immune to the fortunes of war. There was still a score to be settled, and that was his downfall. Godfrey led his troops into Dál Riata where he was slain. The *Annals of Ulster* acknowledged his power by styling Godfrey "king of the islands of the Foreigners." He was even more important, for Godfrey founded a dynasty that controlled the region for another century.

A recitation of Magnus and Godfrey Haraldsson's careers is quickly given. But this is only part of the story. Now comes a more difficult task: trying to understand the fragmentary records. For the tenth century they are notoriously sparse. Many of the individuals mentioned in the chronicles are names; they make a brief appearance before retiring into obscurity. Nevertheless, this can be known for certain: Magnus and Godfrey were important and powerful individuals. They raided over a vast area, from the Isle of Man to the western coast of Ireland, and from the Hebrides to the south of Wales (and probably farther). Monarchs treated them as equals, and Godfrey is called "king" in a contemporary Irish record that wastes no love on Vikings. Only two pieces of personal information about them are known: their father was named Harald, and their followers were called Danes.

Magnus and Godfrey Haraldsson were active in a North Atlantic zone that extended from Ireland to Britain to Francia. Vikings moved through this region with extraordinary ease during the tenth century. They raided, settled, and resettled wherever the opportunity presented itself. The chronicler Æthelweard noted that at the beginning of the tenth century a Viking force based in northern Francia was raiding around Britain. Raids ran in both directions. Two Vikings named Bard and Eirik who sacked Tours in 903 had been in Ireland; they were possibly among the refugees from Dublin. In 942 a Viking band arrived in Normandy led by a Sitric (*Setric*) who might be the same man as the Sitric who is named on two coins minted in York. There is the possibility that the obscure Viking lord from Northumbria named Cnut had been at the mouth of the Canche early in the tenth century because coins with his name found in the hoard at Cuerdale were minted at Quentavic. People captured by the Vikings were carried great distances from their homes, and the Breton cleric Johannes of Landévennec "served the cause of repatriation among the barbarians, Saxons and Northmen on both sides of the sea" (that is, between England and Francia).[23]

In addition to raiders, there were also Viking settlers moving throughout this region, occasionally with the support of local princes. According to the oldest version of the *Anglo-Saxon Chronicle*, in 914 a Viking named Thurketil and his army submitted to the West Saxon lord Edward the Elder. Two years later Thurketil decided not to renew his agreement, so he and his men moved to Francia with Edward's aid and protection.[24] At roughly the same time a Viking fleet from Brittany that had raided around southern Britain and Ireland settled at Waterford, where it was briefly joined by Olaf Cuaran's uncle Ragnall. There were also mercenary bands. Writing a century and a half after the event, Hugh of Fleury claims that men from Deira, the southern part of Northumbria, served in the army of Duke Richard I of Normandy circa 962.[25]

Population movement from Ireland to Britain to northern Francia is visible in place and personal names.[26] A distinct Anglo-Saxon element is present in the Pays de Caux, perhaps reflecting settlement of Deiran mercenaries. In the Cotentin is evidence of Vikings who had been in Ireland or in Gaelic-speaking Britain. A famous Viking chieftain of the Cotentin had the name "Niel" that, like the Icelandic name Njál, is ultimately Irish "Niall." Then there are three curious statements made by

Dudo of St. Quentin. First, he insists that the tenth-century Viking settlements around Rouen were supplied from England, and, second, that the English and Irish obeyed both William Longsword and Richard I, so much so that Duke Richard made peace between them. These are usually dismissed as overwrought sops to Norman vanity, yet they do make sense if read as referring to Viking bands in Britain and Ireland. Interestingly, Dudo makes no such claims of influence for the Normans in their own neighborhood, and he was composing his work at a time when that influence was considerable. The third statement is in an episode from the period 962–65, when Richard I was fighting Count Theobald of Blois-Chartres and his ally the Frankish king Lothar. Dudo has Richard include the Norse, Danes, and Irish in a list of the members of his army. The inclusion of the Irish makes sense only if this, once again, means the Vikings in Ireland or the Gaelic-speaking regions.[27]

Communication between the Irish Sea region and northern Francia is claimed in connection with the Viking chieftain Hrólfr or Rollo, the famous founder of Normandy. Dudo states that Rollo had lived in England before leading his followers to the continent. Medieval Scandinavian historians claim that Rollo was active in northern Britain or in the Hebrides before settling in Normandy.[28] The late twelfth-century composition "History of Norway" (*Historia Norvegiae*) says that Rollo raided Northumbria from a base in what is now Scotland. Snorri Sturluson has Rollo emigrating from the Hebrides to northern Francia. As is also found in *Orkneyinga Saga*, he states that Rollo was the son of Ragnall of More, and that Ragnall had been given the Orkneys and Shetlands by the Norse king Harald Fairhair. A Hebridean connection might be suggested by Richer of Rheims, who calls Rollo the son of Catullus, the Latin equivalent of the Old Norse name Ketil, the same name as Ketil Flat Nose the Hebridean chieftain.[29]

Ties to Britain, Ireland, and the Irish Sea region are suggested by Rollo's children. He had two whose names are known: a son, William Longsword, and a daughter, Cadlinar. William was slain on December 17, 942. A contemporary Frankish eulogy, called "Lament for William," says that William was born overseas, and that while his father was a pagan, his mother was a Christian who insisted that her child be baptized and raised in her faith.[30] A generation later, Flodoard describes William's mother as a *concubina Brittanna*. This appears to mean "a Breton concubine," but the statement in "Lament for William" that he was born overseas indicates that William's mother came from Britain. Rollo's daughter Cadlinar had a direct link with the Irish Sea. *Landnámabók* states that her husband was a king named Beollan, and their daughter Nithbeorg married the Icelander Helgi Ottarsson (the reason why this information is preserved).[31] Beollan was the Irish prince Beollan son of Ciarmac, the king of Lagore (county Meath), who, with his son, was captured by Magnus Haraldsson's rival Ivar of Limerick and slain in 969. Beollan's Viking connection is seen in the nickname *lítil* given to him in the *Annals of Inisfallen*. *Lítil* is Old Norse for "little." Nithbeorg had a sister named Deichter who is remembered in the *Banshenchas*, where their father is called the "king of south Brega, of the treacherous Vikings."

✠

The search for Magnus and Godfrey's father, Harald, must extend over a wide area of the North Atlantic. No record preserves more information about this Harald than his name. The traditional answer to the question of Harald's identity was advanced in the nineteenth century by James Todd. He claimed that the father of Magnus and Godfrey was a Viking named Harald Ua Imhar who was slain in Connacht in 940. The *Annals of the Four Masters* claim that he was the son of Sitric Ua Imhar of Limerick. No medieval work knows this Sitric, which suggests that he is the product of learned speculation. This has not prevented expansion on Todd's theory, including the theory that Harald's ancestor was the Viking named Ivar who died in 873.[32] The argument continues by making Magnus and Godfrey distant members of Dublin's ruling dynasty, cousins of Olaf Cuaran, and clients of the Dublin dynasty who were set up in the Isles as part of Olaf Cuaran's efforts to maintain links with Northumbria. The connection of Magnus and Godfrey with this Harald is based on nothing more than a matching of names. There is no evidence that the Haraldssons were members of a cadet branch of Olaf Cuaran's kindred. The maneuvers of the Haraldssons against Dublin in 984 argue against it. While a contingent from the Kingdom of the Isles did ally with the men of Dublin at the Battle of Tara in 980, there is no indication that either Godfrey or Magnus was involved. The leader of the Isles contingent had the completely Gaelic name Conamal mac Gilla Maire with the nickname "the Viking."[33]

A second suggested familial link is that Magnus and Godfrey were the sons of King Harald Bluetooth (died 987) of the Danes, the son of Gorm the Old.[34] That would make them at least the half-brothers of Harald's son Svein Forkbeard, the future king of the Danes and English. Once again the link is based solely on the similarity of names. Tenth-century records are sparse, and arguing from the silence of the sources is dangerous for any era, but the establishment of a royal Danish dynasty in the Isles would be expected to provoke some comment. Furthermore, Svein Forkbeard attacked the Isle of Man in the last decade of the century, not an action necessarily to be expected if he were a close kinsman of the Haraldssons.

These theories have ignored an important Viking chieftain in a region with ties to the Irish Sea. His name was Harald and he ruled in northern Francia. This man was not the Danish prince Harald Bluetooth, despite Dudo of St. Quentin's description of Harald as "king of *Dacia*" in noting his alliance with William Longsword's son Richard I. He was the Viking chieftain called Harald (Hagroldus) of Bayeux in the chronicles of the tenth-century Frankish historians Flodoard and Richer of Rheims.[35] Harald ruled the area from Bayeux to Coutances, part of the region that had been ceded to the Vikings by King Raoul circa 933. He first appears in the Frankish records circa 942 and disappears after 954.

Harald was a formidable warrior, and initially an ally of Rollo's family. Soon after his arrival in Normandy he became embroiled in the complex political competition of the region. Duke Hugh the Great, the most powerful of the northern Frankish nobles and whose descendants ruled France for centuries, invaded Bayeux in 944. The next year Harald captured Hugh's ally the Frankish king Louis IV as he campaigned in the region. The prisoner was particularly well connected with Britain. Louis was the son of the Frankish king Charles the Simple and Eadgifu, the sister of the English kings Æthelstan, Edmund, and Eadred. After Charles's death in 929, Louis lived in England with his mother. In the palace at York, the capital of the independent Viking Kingdom of Northumbria, Æthelstan received envoys from the Franks asking for the return of his nephew Louis. The capture of Louis by Harald led to English involvement in Frankish affairs. Almost the last meeting of Æthelstan's brother, Edmund, in 946, several weeks before his murder at Pucklechurch, was with ambassadors from his former brother-in-law Emperor Otto I about the ransom of Louis.[36]

Harald's ability to withstand an attack by Hugh the Great or hold King Louis for ransom shows that his position was more than that of commander of a few boatloads of pirates. Only a powerful lord could play "the great game" with these rivals. For Hugh, too, had a connection with the kings of England. He married their sister, Eadhild, in 926. Hugh conducted his courtship with sumptuous gifts: the lance of Charlemagne (thought to be the weapon that had pierced the side of the crucified Christ), a sword believed to have belonged to the Roman emperor Constantine with a nail in its hilt that was claimed to have come from the Cross, as well as gems, horses, perfumes, and a diadem set with jewels. By 954 Hugh was also the father-in-law of Richard of Normandy, who was then married to his daughter Emma. That same year Hugh the Great again attacked Harald, this time with an assault on his fortress at Bayeux, where he found the defenses poorly prepared.[37] The attack on Bayeux suggests that Hugh and Richard were eliminating a common rival. After that campaign Harald of Bayeux disappears from the records. Dudo of St. Quentin insists that Harald left Francia, which he mistakenly thought had occurred soon after the restoration of Louis.

Dudo describes Harald of Bayeux as a Dane who was a recent arrival in northern Francia, and who was not a Christian. Conditions within tenth-century Denmark were propitious for the emigration of a well-connected family. There had been an exodus leading to what has been called the second "Viking Age."[38] Political chaos among the Danes in the ninth century had been halted in the early tenth century by Gorm the Old. Despite the success of Gorm, military organization on the northern frontier of the Empire by the Emperor Otto I meant that the southern Danish aristocrats were increasingly under pressure from their German neighbors. By 934 they were paying tribute to the emperor.

There was also internal conflict among the Danes. Gorm's son and successor Harald Bluetooth attempted to build a powerful Christian monarchy in Denmark. He announced his success in the famous memorial at Jelling that proclaimed "he united Denmark and Norway under himself and made the Danes Christian." Another reason for dissatisfaction was financial. As was occurring in Britain (and beginning in

Ireland), Harald was building fortresses to guard his lands. These were expensive, and the taxes needed to pay for his forts enraged some of Harald's subjects. The price for such a policy was opposition, some of which came from within his family. Toward the end of the tenth century, Harald's son Svein Forkbeard became the leader of the "pagan" party. Later commentators have suggested that Svein was less anti-Christian than anti-German, and that his campaigns were designed to prevent the archbishops of Hamburg-Bremen from interfering in Danish affairs.[39] Svein was able to rally considerable support among the disaffected Danish aristocracy and defeat his father's forces in battle. Soon afterwards Harald died, circa 987. Svein's triumph was brief, and he was forced into an exile that lasted for several years.

The Danes and the early rulers of Normandy were well disposed one toward the other.[40] Harald of Bayeux could have been one of the disaffected Danish nobles who decided to seek his fortune in northern Francia. Emigration from Scandinavia often took the form of a powerful chieftain departing with his family and followers, which gave him a ready army. There has been no quarrel with Dudo's description of Harald as the leader of a Danish force. Vikings continued to organize themselves into what their neighbors described as "armies" even during the process of settlement, and not all Danes were in Denmark. Late in the ninth century, when Bishop Eadred of Lindisfarne sought the future Northumbrian king Godfrey Hardacnutsson, he went to what the *History of St. Cuthbert* describes as the "Danish Army." The name "Danes" was also attached to the army of Magnus and Godfrey Haraldsson.

Alliances between Viking bands, such as Harald of Bayeux and the Vikings of Rouen, were helped by mutual enterprises. This need not have been limited to cooperation in battle. Rouen was famous as a place where loot from Viking raids could be dispersed. This business was so profitable that even papal intervention could not bring it to a halt. Pope John XV was called upon to reconcile Æthelraed of England and Richard I of Normandy in 991 with an agreement that they not give aid to each other's enemies (a polite way of saying that Richard would not help the Vikings raid England). Æthelraed's marriage with Richard's daughter Emma furthered efforts to ensure peace. This agreement was soon set aside by Richard's successor, Richard II, whom William of Jumièges claims made a treaty with the Danish king Svein Forkbeard so that the booty Svein took from raids could be sold at Rouen.[41]

Ties between the Vikings of Bayeux and the early dukes of Normandy extended beyond military alliances. The young Richard I was fostered at Bayeux, where he had been sent, in part, to learn to speak a purer variety of Old Norse than was spoken at Rouen. Eloquence was a virtue especially for a Viking commander who had to persuade, rather than order, his troops. The residence of Richard at Bayeux for elocution lessons indicates that Harald of Bayeux and his Danes were more recent arrivals from Scandinavia. Another connection was Richard's second wife, the formidable Gunnor who might have been related to Harald. Gunnor's home in the Cotentin is known from a donation of lands her brother, Herfast, gave to the church of St. Père of Chartres in the early eleventh century. The church took care to ensure that it did not receive stolen property, so Herfast carefully noted that the estates were his private property that he had received as an inheritance.[42]

By 954 it must have been clear to Harald of Bayeux that the descendants of Rollo at Rouen would be the dominant Viking dynasty in northern Francia. The future seemed to offer two choices: stay as a subordinate or lead his followers to a new settlement. Dudo is adamant that Harald departed, and there is no reason to doubt him. Harald might have been looking for a new home before 954, which would explain why Hugh the Great found the defenses so poor at Bayeux. What happened to Harald and his followers is unclear, but fifteen years later there abruptly appear in the Irish Sea two powerful Vikings named Magnus and Godfrey who are the sons of a man named Harald.

That Harald of Bayeux was the father of Magnus and Godfrey is argued by the ties between the Kingdom of the Isles and Normandy that are visible into the eleventh century. According to William of Jumièges, a king of the Isles named Lagmann (described in the *Cocad Gáedel re Gallaib* as the son of Godfrey Haraldsson) fought for Duke Richard II of Normandy in the first quarter of the eleventh century. Adémar of Chabannes records that circa 1018 a fleet from the Irish Sea region joined a Danish fleet for a raid on St. Michel l'Herme, in Aquitaine. Among the captives was the Countess of Limoges, who was released only through the intervention of Duke Richard II of Normandy. In 1014 warriors from Francia fought in Ireland at the Battle of Clontarf, where Lagmann's son Olaf died fighting for Olaf Cuaran's son Sitric Silkenbeard. Political or military ties were one avenue for artistic contacts, such as the similarities between reliefs at Evrecy in Normandy and designs found in the Hebrides and Orkneys.[43]

Coins also show a link between the northern Irish Sea region and northern Francia.[44] Coins from continental mints are found throughout Britain and Ireland until circa 922. Then there are none for almost forty years until circa 965. When continental coins reappear, most are in the Irish Sea region and the lands in contact with it: Ballaqueeny (Isle of Man); Chester; Lough Lerne (county Westmeath); Derrykeighan (county Antrim); and Islay (Scotland). From circa 986 to 1000, deniers (pennies) from Norman mints appear in areas where the Haraldssons were active: Iona, Inchkenneth (Argyllshire), and Knochmaon (county Waterford). Beyond the Haraldssons' immediate area of influence are continental coins at Tarbat (Ross, Scotland) and Burray (Orkneys). After the millennium there is another gap until circa 1025 when coins from Norman and other continental mints are found in a widely distributed pattern throughout the British Isles. There are not many deniers in any insular hoard before 1025, but there are few in any of the contemporary hoards discovered outside Normandy. That the coins minted in Normandy were not the residual from raids is suggested by their overwhelming representation among the Frankish coins because mere loot would be expected to provide a wider sampling of mints. This suggests that a trade route ran from Normandy through the Irish Sea into the Hebrides that is exactly contemporary with Magnus and Godfrey Haraldsson.[45]

Appearing in the Irish Sea region contemporary with the Norman coins and the Haraldssons are settlers described as Danes in the contemporary records. One of the Haraldssons is described as the leader of a Danish army in the *Annals of Ulster* that, throughout the entire medieval period, use the term "Dane" only in the period 986–90: in 986 when Danes landed in Dál Riata; their attack on Iona at Christmas 986; a battle fought on the Isle of Man by a (unspecified) son of Harald and the Danes in 987; the attack on the Danes that same year in revenge for Iona's raid; and in 990 an attack on Derry, Ireland. The ravages of the Danes are specifically mentioned in the contemporary verses in the *Saltair na Rann* ("Metrical Psalter"), a poem on biblical history composed late in the tenth century, a date revealed by verses describing contemporary princes and a great cattle plague. The princes reigned in the last quarter of the century, when there were two plagues, in 987 and 993.[46] The first prince is the Scottish king Kenneth II (reigned 971–994) followed by the kings of Leinster, Munster, Connacht, Uí Néill, the English, the West Franks, the emperor, the *comarba* of Armagh, and, in conclusion, the king of Strathclyde. Then follows an interesting comment on the Vikings in the Irish Sea: "At that time took place the expedition of the cropped heads, multitude of crimes, intent on every savage deed, Danes from the land of Denmark."[47]

The phrase "Danes from the land of Denmark" in an insular document of the last quarter of the tenth century is significant. From the end of the ninth century "Denmark" was being used as a geopolitical term. These include the description of the northern world by sailors Othere and Wulfstan in the Old English version of Orosius' *Seven Books against the Pagans*; the *Denimarca* used in the chronicle of Regino of Prüm for the year 884; and, later, the Jelling memorial erected on the orders of King Harald Bluetooth that describes his mother Thyra as "the jewel of Denmark."[48] The author of the *Saltair na Rann* is making clear that he is referring to a specific group of pirates and is not using Dane as a general term for any Viking.

The implication in the *Annals of Ulster* and *Saltair na Rann* that there were newcomers to the ranks of the Irish Sea Vikings is supported by runic inscriptions. At the millennium there are pronounced changes to the runic inscriptions on the Isle of Man.[49] One of these changes is the appearance of runes that seem to be strongly influenced by Danish orthography, even though scholars are hesitant to call them "Danish" runes. An interesting aspect to runic inscriptions from this period is the argument that they were more than just memorials, that they were statements of kinship that were important for claiming inheritance.[50] Such statements would be especially necessary in times of settlement and political transition, as new arrivals were anxious to make known their claims to territory and status. So the act of setting up Manx rune stones could have had an economic as well as commemorative purpose among new arrivals.

Political events, verse, chronicles, coins, and runic inscriptions all give evidence of a new force in the Irish Sea in general and the Isle of Man in particular. Art produced in the Isles bore similarities to that from the Viking colonies in northern Francia, and coins from Normandy are found in the Haraldsson's domain. Like Viking settlers in northern Francia, the Haraldssons led an army of Danes. Runic inscriptions begin to show affinities to Danish. The simplest explanation is that Harald of Bayeux led his Danes to the Irish Sea region after 954, and that he was succeeded by his sons Magnus and Harald.

The second half of the tenth century was a propitious time for a Viking band from northern Francia to move into the Irish Sea region. This was a period of turmoil as the family of Alfred the Great consolidated their control of the English. The grandsons of Alfred the Great had made the permanent reduction of Northumbria in 954, the same year that Duke Hugh led the assault on Harald of Bayeux's fortress. At roughly the same time there began a movement from the English Danelaw into southwest Scotland that can be traced from place names. The settlers followed an old route that had been opened during Northumbrian annexation of the region in the seventh century. That earlier movement began at Carlisle (where St. Cuthbert had his vision of Ecgfrith's defeat by the Picts in 685) and it reached the North Channel by 750, when the Northumbrians conquered the lands as far as the Plain of Kyle in Ayrshire. An Anglian bishopric was established at Whithorn early in the eighth century, and it continued to flourish into the ninth. As late as the last quarter of the ninth century, according to materials maintained by the Cuthbertine community, refugees from the Viking attack on Lindisfarne resided briefly at Whithorn while attempting to flee to Ireland.

The westward movement of English settlers has implications for the question of where Magnus and Godfrey Haraldsson resided. The, admittedly spare, records simply do not place them in any particular location. They spent two decades raiding the Welsh, but they did not live in Wales, because they arrived there for their raids. Even though they are usually listed by modern scholars among the rulers of the Isle of Man, their first recorded appearance on the island was in 987, when Godfrey raided it. The only real evidence for locating them in the Hebrides is the accompaniment of the Lawmen of the Isles with Magnus on his circuit of Ireland in 974, but the Haraldssons apparently were not participants in the Isles contingent that fought on the side of the men of Dublin at the Battle of Tara in 980.

There are reasons for placing the Haraldssons among the settlers in what is now southwestern Scotland. The obituary in 1065 for Godfrey's grandson Echmarcach by the contemporary chronicler Marianus Scotus describes him as "king of the Rhinns (of Galloway)." In 1096 Echmarcach's grandson, Olaf, died fighting in the Rhinns. This region was in the heart of the very area the Haraldssons were raiding. Place-name forms found in Galloway indicate a "Danish" element in the settlement. Name elements such as -*bagh* from ON *vágr* "creek, inlet," -*bhig* from ON *vík* "bay," and *nis* from ON *nes* "headland" are found across Galloway, especially from Whithorn to the

Rhinns. The date, designation, and location of some of those names suggest that at least some settlers were coming from northern England.[51] One model for Viking settlement in Britain, based on similarities in artistic styles from Cumbria to Dumfriesshire to Man, has proposed a zone encompassing northwest England, Dumfriesshire, and the Isle of Man.[52] After the mid-tenth century, decorative styles employed on the Isle of Man reflect contemporary developments in York or Scandinavia, and not until almost the second quarter of the eleventh century did they look towards Ireland. Finally, southwestern Scotland is the one area where the Haraldssons did not raid, and it was convenient to the Irish Sea, the Hebrides, and for sailing to the west coast of Ireland.

Westward emigration from the Danelaw to the northern shores of the Irish Sea coincided with new "Danish" influence in northern England. York might have been enriched from Denmark.[53] Adam of Bremen, whose informant was the Danish king, claims that there was direct Danish involvement in northern England at this time, that Harald Bluetooth had a son named *Hring*, who was killed in a battle fought in Northumbria.

The English monarch at this time, Edgar, is particularly associated with Viking settlement as well as being a contemporary of Harald of Bayeux, and Magnus and Godfrey Haraldsson. By the twelfth century, Edgar was regarded as the English Solomon, and his reign was the standard by which all others were measured. These generous estimations begin to appear soon after his death. In part this was due to his patronage of the Church that went outside the kingdom to Rouen. There is only one matter that is raised in criticism of Edgar. Early eleventh-century verses composed by Archbishop Wulfstan of York and embedded in the *Anglo-Saxon Chronicle*'s D and E manuscripts *sub anno* 959 (following a northern English source), complain that Edgar invited harmful foreign peoples into his realm. By the twelfth century, William of Malmesbury claimed that the numerous foreign visitors to Edgar's court corrupted the English.[54]

Edgar's family had been well disposed to the Scandinavians. His uncle Æthelstan, the conqueror of Olaf Godfreysson at the Battle of *Brunanburh*, was the foster-father of the Norse prince Hakon, the son of Harald Fairhair. Æthelstan had no objection to dealing with the Vikings in Britain. He gave an estate at Amounderness to the Archbishop of York that he had purchased from two Vikings. In 957, two years before the death of his brother and predecessor Edwy, Edgar was chosen as king by the people of Northumbria and Mercia, regions heavily settled by Vikings. Edgar remembered his debt by enacting legislation that ensured the virtual legal self-determination of the Danelaw. This is visible in the law code IV Edgar, issued circa 963 and addressed to the English, Danes, and Britons in his domain. He gave the Danes the right to choose their laws and punish any royal official who violated them; this autonomy, it has been suggested, helped to ensure peace in his domains.[55] His good will extended to the Vikings of northern Francia, and he made donations to the church of St. Ouen at Rouen.

These contacts help to explain why there is not a catalogue of battles for Edgar's reign. Why was peace enjoyed by the English during Edgar's reign, while the Irish and Welsh were attacked by the Haraldssons? Edgar's answer to the problem of defending the northwest coast of England may have been to establish his clients in the region. This is precisely claimed in a sixteenth-century Welsh history following a twelfth-century exemplar, noting that Edgar allowed Magnus Haraldsson and his followers to settle in England. English territory in the ninth century had extended as far west as the Rhinns of Galloway. This could explain why there was "a period in which, for the first time since the reign of Egbert, England was free from the imminent threat of foreign invasion."[56]

A guide to Edgar's interest in the Irish Sea Vikings comes from the charter *Altitonantis*, which has been discussed earlier for its claims of lordship over Dublin. The charter claims that Edgar's rule extended to all the island kingdoms around Britain, as far as Norway. Norway, at this period, ended at the Orkneys. The legends that Edgar's fleets circumnavigated the seas around Britain appear in the twelfth-century chronicle of John of Worcester and are clearly revisionism. Neither *Orkneyinga Saga* nor any contemporary English documents are aware of those voyages, and the Orkney Vikings were unlikely to have allowed an English fleet to invade their lands without a response.

The passage in *Altitonantis* becomes more sensible if "island kingdoms" is read as "the Kingdom of the Isles," the Haraldsson domain according to contemporary Irish accounts. Magnus Haraldsson is particularly associated with Edgar. Magnus appears in the legends of Edgar's rowing on the River Dee after his coronation at Bath in 973, which appear in the twelfth-century histories of John of Worcester and William of Malmesbury. There are also two charters, dated to the reign of Edgar but extant only in later copies, which have Magnus among the witnesses.[57] The first charter is a grant from Edgar to Glastonbury, dated 971. The second is a grant from Edgar to Canterbury, dated 966 but probably intended for 973. Both charters have been rejected as forgeries. This is obviously true for the Canterbury charter, but the Glastonbury charter is more complex.

The Glastonbury charter, acknowledged to contain contemporary material, has a witness list that is not likely to have been forged at a later date.[58] A *Marcusius archipirata* ("Magnus the great pirate") is found among the witnesses together with *Cinadius rex Alban* ("Kenneth king of Scotland," the same man found in the *Saltair na Rann*). The names of both men are given after the royal family, but before the clergy. Each man is designated king (*rex*), and there is no claim of subordinate status, such as the "underking" (*subregulus*) that is used for Welsh princes in the English charters. The designation of Magnus as *pirata* evokes the classical meaning "pirate," but by the tenth century there are less villainous translations such as "seafarer or sailor."[59]

Magnus' presence at Edgar's court circa 971 is sensible in light of the English prince's generally benevolent attitudes toward the Vikings. To the material of uncertain authenticity in *Altitonantis* and the Glastonbury charter can be added a more definite witness to English interest in the Irish Sea: coins. On the Isle of Man, fifteen hoards have been recovered that were buried during Edgar's reign. In three of those coin-hoards, 123 out of 172 coins were from his reign.[60] Nine of the fifteen hoards were concealed by circa 970. The date of concealment for English coins can be dated closely after this time because coins were being recalled on a six-year cycle when a new issue was placed in circulation. The Manx coin-hoards might represent the loot from raids, yet other than the ravaging of Westmorland by the Yorkshire nobleman Thored Gunnarson in 966, a region lacking mints and large trading centers, England during Edgar's reign is conspicuous by its peacefulness. So it is possible that the coins were used in trade with English ports or were the pay of those in the employ of Edgar.

The reigns of Edgar and the Haraldssons were propitious for peaceful contacts. The climatic warming in northern Europe that was to become pronounced by the eleventh century was already becoming noticeable. From Scandinavia to the Irish Sea, land that had previously been too marginal for cultivation was being brought into production. In eastern Sweden it has been estimated that there were between 1,000 and 2,000 farms in the eighth century that increased to 4,000–5,000 farms circa 1100. Most of this expansion took place on marginal land.[61] An example of cultivation on new land comes from the Isle of Man. A Viking farm at Doarlish Cashen, occupied about the year 1000, was located on ground that is now, and had been earlier, too marginal for use.[62] Together with this warmth there was moisture. Examination of the moss at Bolton Fell (northeast of Carlisle) has revealed that the period from circa 900–1100 was very wet.[63] This was a great benefit for agrarian societies because more land could be cultivated with less danger of drought. The benefits were not limited to farming, for the increased food production freed more people to pursue other occupations at the same time that a steadily increasing level of wealth provided the means to afford the goods.

The inhabitants of the Kingdom of the Isles were prospering during this period. One indication is the circulation of English coins minted during Edgar's reign. Another sign is silver, and on the Isle of Man almost as much silver "ring money" has been found as in all of Ireland. Of the eighteen major silver hoards found on the Isle of Man, for example, five of them were concealed during the time Godfrey and Magnus were active in the region.[64]

Some of this wealth was generated by manufacturing. Metalworking appears to have been a profitable occupation in the tenth and eleventh centuries. A Viking grave on the Isle of Man at Knock-y-Donee contained the tools of a blacksmith—hammer, tongs, and cauldron—as well as fishing weights (possibly a product of his shop) in addition to the expected sword, axe, knife, spear, and shield-boss. Tenth-century trade between the Isle of Man and Ireland is revealed by ring pins found on Man with Irish designs. Trade in metalware provides one commercial explanation for the Anglo-Saxon coins found in the Isles. Fragments of an armband and brooch found at the Castle Esplanade hoard at Chester, buried circa 988, show similarities to items found in a hoard at Ballyquayle on the Isle of Man, and they might have been manufactured on Man. Craftsmen were rich and important. The famous cross at Kirk Michael was made by sculptor named Gaut for a Melbridgi (OI Máel Brigte), the son of Athakan the Smith.[65] This glorification of artisans was a phenomenon found throughout the region, and in Ireland the death in 1004 of Náemhan mac Máel Ciaráin, "the chief artificer of Ireland," was remembered in the *Chronicon Scotorum*.

Momentous changes occurred in Britain and Ireland after Edgar's death in 975. He was succeeded by his son, Edward, who became known as Edward the Martyr after he was murdered in 979 by the retainers of his younger half-brother, Æthelraed. Æthelraed began his reign as a minor who was dependent on a deeply divided English aristocracy. In Ireland the ineffectual high king, Domnall Ua Néill, died at Armagh in 980 and was succeeded by the hero of the Battle of Tara, Máel Sechnaill II. But a far more important change was waiting in southern Ireland, in Munster. From the southwestern Irish dynasty of Dál Cais the famous Brian Boru wrested the high kingship from the Uí Neill and would be remembered as the conqueror of the Vikings.

There was also change in Scandinavia, which had its own influence to the west. Among the Danes, the tensions between the Christian king Harald and his subjects reached a breaking point. Conflict between Harald and his son, Svein Forkbeard, led to the former's death in 987. In Iceland, the great period of the "land-taking" was coming to its end, closing one area for Scandinavian expansion. Latecomers to the island were forced to take lands that were marginal even in the comparatively balmy conditions of the day. Efforts to establish colonies in Greenland, and later Vinland, signaled the ending of the great age of Scandinavian emigration. In Britain and Ireland the Viking colonists were fighting among themselves. The preeminence of Olaf Cuaran's family among the Irish Viking settlers was challenged by rivals into the eleventh century.

Among the chieftains at large was the future conqueror of England and Danish king Svein Forkbeard, then in exile somewhere in Britain or Ireland. Adam of Bremen (whose informant was Svein's grandson) remarks that the Swedish king Eirik forced Svein to flee Denmark in 992, during the episcopate of Bishop Lievizo of Hamburg (988–1013), and that he did not return until after Eirik's death in 995.[66] Svein fled first to the Norse aristocrat Tryggvi, father of Olaf Tryggvason. Then he went to the court of Edgar's son Æthelraed "the Unready." Æthelraed refused to receive him, so Svein then fled to the court of the Scots king, whose identity is unknown. The king of the southern Scots, the dynast of Cenél nGabráin, was Kenneth II. There is no other indication that Kenneth had such a well-placed visitor. Adam might have meant a king in Ireland, but again there is no record of such a visitor. There is the possibility that the king of Scots in Adam's narrative was Godfrey Haraldsson's son, Ragnall, who succeeded him as king of the Isles; his location in the Irish Sea might have led Adam to believe he was Irish.

Svein was active in the Irish Sea circa 996 when he raided the Isle of Man. He was not alone. Another Scandinavian prince had preceded him: Olaf Tryggvason. According to his saga in *Heimskringla*, Olaf fought several battles in the Hebrides, Man, and Cumberland before setting up a base in the Scilly Isles; the saga information is corroborated in part by contemporary English records.[67] If remembrances found in the later Icelandic sagas are accurate, there was a third force active in the Irish Sea during this time: Jarl Sigurd Hlodvisson of the Orkneys, also known as "Sigurd the Stout." *Orkneyinga Saga* claims that Sigurd raided the Hebrides, and *Eyrbyggja Saga* states that his raids went as far south as the Isle of Man where he laid a tax upon the natives and left men there to collect that tax. *Njal's Saga* supplies the additional information that Sigurd's opponent was King Godfrey, a mistake for Godfrey's son, Ragnall, and that Sigurd's agent was his brother-in-law, Gilli.[68] There has even been the suggestion that Manx coin-hoards containing pennies of King Edgar were concealed during Sigurd's attack(s) on Man. Something traumatic was occurring. Coins disappear from the Isles circa 1000, to be replaced by armbands, while a chair back pommel made at Dublin shows similarity of design with the Skaill brooches found in the Orkneys that were probably made on the Isle of Man.[69]

Sigurd's actions in the Kingdom of the Isles were part of his much wider empire building. His attempts to annex Caithness, Sutherland, and Ross brought him into conflict with the Scots, more precisely with the kings of Cenél Loairn who ruled north of the Grampians. What Sigurd could not conquer by the sword he gained at the altar when he married the daughter of Malcolm mac Máel Brigtí, who would later be king of the Cenél Loairn.[70] Their son was named Thorfinn and he continued the Orkney interest in the Irish Sea after the second quarter of the eleventh century.

There might have been a Scottish aspect to turmoil in the Isles.[71] In 1005 Malcolm II (the son of Edgar's ally Kenneth II) came to the throne after he defeated and killed his cousin Kenneth III. Malcolm was the real architect of the later medieval Scottish nation as he added Strathclyde (and possibly some kind of lordship over Galloway) to his domains as well as having his overlordship acknowledged by his northern rivals of Cenél Loairn. Prior to his accession to the throne Malcolm had been expelled from the kingdom and retreated to the Hebrides, to Islay and Arran in the lands of Scottish Dál Riata, from where, according to the *Prophecy of Berchán*, he led naval raids. Malcolm had a continuing interest in the region, as seen in two events. The first was the Battle of Clontarf, when one of his nobles named Domnall mac Eimhin, the mormaer of Mar, died fighting for Brian Boru. The second incident was in 1031, when Ragnall's son, Echmarcach, was a member of Malcolm's retinue during his negotiations with Cnut, a sign of Malcolm's overlordship.[72]

The turmoil in the Irish Sea explains why Godfrey Haraldsson's son, Ragnall, was in Ireland when he died in 1005. The Irish chronicles style him "king of the Isles" and give genealogical information: the *Annals of Inisfallen* call him the "grandson of Harald," while the *Annals of Ulster* have "son of Godfrey, king of the Isles." There is no indication of any raid, so Ragnall apparently was an exile in Ireland when he died, possibly residing at the old Viking fortress of Limerick, which had been in the hands of Brian Boru for almost twenty-five years. His residence in Ireland might explain the statement in the *Cocad Gáedel re Gallaib* that Brian took tribute from the Welsh, English, Argyll, and Lennox.[73] At first glance that list of places appears to be little more than bombast on the part of an over-enthusiastic supporter of Brian. Yet the Haraldssons had been active around those regions. Both Magnus and Godfrey Haraldsson had taken tribute in northern Wales, out of the Isle of Anglesey. Godfrey's raids on Dál Riata could account for Argyll and possibly Lennox. The seventeenth-century antiquarian Roderic O'Flaherty, a student of Duald Mac Firbis, in his *Ogygia* claimed that Brian recruited heavily among the Gaelic-speaking aristocracy of northern Britain, especially from Lennox, before the Battle of Clontarf.[74] The raid by the English king Æthelraed on the Isle of Man in 1000 could have been retaliation for earlier raids by the Haraldssons on England. So this section praising Brian could reflect his patronage of Ragnall.

By the millennium, at least part of the Kingdom of the Isles was actively supporting the Danish monarch Svein Forkbeard. In 1000 the *Anglo-Saxon Chronicle* notes that the English king Æthelraed II attempted to ravage "Cumber land" by land and sea, but the fleet was unable to sail there because of contrary winds, so it ravaged the Isle of Man. "Cumber land" might have been what is now modern Cumberland, but in the tenth and eleventh centuries it could also could also refer to the Kingdom of Strathclyde, which here is suggested by the abandonment of the naval assault; the fleet attempted to sail through the North Channel to the firth of Clyde, but was unable, and returned via the Isle of Man. If winds were so strong that ships could not reach the coast of Cumberland, it is unlikely that they could have reached the Isle of Man opposite. The change of plan may have been less casual, perhaps also retaliation for past English raids by the Haraldssons.[75]

This raid makes more sense when put in the context of Svein's network of allies. Prominent was Duke Richard II of Normandy. The Anglo-Saxon chronicler notes that Svein's "hostile fleet sailed to Richard's domain" in the summer of the year 1000. The use of his ports for the disposal of loot from Svein's raids brought Richard to the brink of war with Æthelraed. William of Jumièges claims that about this time Æthelred sent an expedition against Normandy because Richard was allowing the English plunder gathered by the Danes to be sold in Norman markets.[76] William also claims that Svein and his son Cnut sent mercenaries to the dukes of Normandy in the early eleventh century. Two soldiers of fortune hired by the Normans are known by name: the future Norwegian king and saint Olaf the Stout and Ragnall Godfreysson's brother, Lagmann. The chronology is not entirely clear, but they seem to have fought for Duke Richard II in two campaigns. The first was an invasion of Brittany in 1009, while the second was an attack on Odo of Blois-Chartres in a campaign that began in the fall of 1013 and lasted until the following spring. Odo, the son of a famous foe of the Normans named Theobald, had been married to Matilda, the daughter of Duke Richard I and Gunnor. Matilda's dowry had been half of Dreux, but when she died childless, Odo refused to give up his claims to the region, which precipitated the conflict.[77]

The two mercenaries are a study in contrasts. Olaf was certainly in Normandy in 1014, but at that time he was an ally of Æthelred, although previously he had fought for Svein. His earlier career was rehabilitated when, after his death, he was recognized as a saint throughout the Scandinavian world. Lagmann, on the other hand, was obscure even in his day, and William refers to him as *rex Suerorum*. This might mean "king of the Swedes," but there is general scholarly agreement that it is a garbled attempt to reproduce *rex Suðriorum*, "king of the Sudreys" from *Suðreyjar*, the Norse name for the Kingdom of the Isles.[78] Lagmann's son Olaf was killed in 1014 at the Battle of Clontarf, and in *Cocad Gáedel re Gallaib* his lineage is spelled out—Olaf son of Lagmann son of Godfrey—and he is described as one of the chief lords of the Vikings. So Lagmann, son of Godfrey Haraldsson, succeeded his brother, Ragnall, as King of the Isles in 1005.

The Haraldssons built their empire in a manner that was similar to their neighbor Olaf Cuaran. They demonstrated their abilities as captains with successful raids over a long period of time, during which they enriched themselves and removed rivals. Their attacks on regions as far-flung as Anglesey, Limerick, the Isle of Man, and Dál Riata reveal focused military minds beyond that of mere brigands. The family of Magnus and Godfrey appears to have been based in Normandy prior to their appearance in the Irish Sea, and the father of the two men was probably Harald of Bayeux. This helps to explain the contacts between Normandy and the Kingdom of the Isles.

Magnus and Godfrey were more than casual pirates as alliances with Brian of Munster and Edgar of the English show. Edgar might have introduced the Haraldssons to the Irish Sea region, apparently in southwestern Scotland, during a general movement that included emigration from the Danelaw. The collection of tribute on Anglesey demonstrates how the Haraldssons secured a source of income. Empire building on the part of the Haraldssons explains their participation in a proposed attack on Dublin in 984, if their share of the spoils was to have been control of a major port town. If so, it would have to wait two generations for Godfrey's grandson, Echmarcach. The alliance of the Haraldssons with Brian began a long period of good relations between their families that endured for generations.

In building alliances, one of the important aspects was selecting an ally. The cooperation between the Haraldssons and Brian Boru in 984 might be a sign of the former's need for a new powerful friend after the death of the English king Edgar in 975. This situation was not improved by the division into warring camps of the

Anglo-Saxon aristocracy. The factionalism led to the murder of Edgar's son Edward and the subsequent accession of his brother, Æthelraed. Unlike his father, Æthelraed felt threatened by the Danelaw; legal revisions clearly show that he did not share his father's respect for the self-determination of the region.[79] As his raid on the Isle of Man in 1000 indicates, Æthelraed included the Haraldssons among his foes. In that context their alliance with Brian might be a sign that the Haraldssons were willing to forge ties in Ireland to replace the ties with England. Brian's alliance with Vikings such as the brothers Haraldsson was one aspect of his career that his descendants and their historians tried to ignore. *Cocad Gáedel re Gallaib*, assembled during the reign of his grandson Muirchertach Ua Briain, presents Brian as the constant enemy of the Vikings, not as their sometime comrade-in-arms.

After the death of Godfrey, his son, Ragnall, was faced with powerful opponents. The traditions preserved in *Orkneyinga Saga*, *Eyrbyggja Saga*, and *Njal's Saga* remember the turmoil in the Irish Sea in the last decades of the tenth century. A new power, Sigurd of the Orkneys, succeeded in extending his influence southwards in the Isles. The Haraldsson dynasty, in the person of Godfrey's son, Ragnall, may have sought aid from Brian Boru against Sigurd, a renewal of the earlier alliance made by his father. The advantage might not have been all Ragnall's. At the end of the tenth century, Brian was campaigning throughout Ireland for recognition as high king. While the main obstacle was removed when Máel Sechnaill II recognized Brian as his overlord in 1002, this came only after campaigns throughout the island. Brian needed an ally in the Irish Sea to watch those eastern and northern Irish kingdoms that made no secret of their dislike for him.

The Haraldssons were not the only dynasty fighting for supremacy in the seas around Britain. In the east, from Denmark, Svein Forkbeard invaded England with a national army and set the foundations for a Scandinavian empire that came to fruition under the leadership of his son Cnut. From the Orkneys, Sigurd the Stout launched his campaign to take command of the Irish Sea. Finally, the Scots were fighting for control of the region. Malcolm II would move south into Strathclyde, Galloway, and southern Lothian. In the north, the Cenél Loairn king Findláech, the father of Macbeth, fought with Sigurd of the Orkneys for control of Caithness, Sutherland, and Ross. The Haraldssons built their empire in a busy part of Europe.

4

Sitric Silkenbeard

THE UNSKILLED SAILOR will frequently find himself shipwrecked," Dudo of St. Quentin sagely warns, "just as the merchant who is not skillful at purchasing or bargaining will be ruined."[1] This little observation in the midst of a panegyric on the Norman dukes illustrates the increasing importance of commercial aptitude in the equation of political success. What was true along the banks of the Seine was equally applicable farther north, on the shores of the Irish Sea. The years around the first millennium witnessed an increasing prosperity throughout northern Europe. Villages and ship forts were developing into towns, and these towns were becoming economically important. The expansion of commercial activity around the North Atlantic benefited from changes in the climate since the ninth century. The improvement was pronounced by the beginning of the eleventh century. Winters were milder and the growing season was extended. Ships had more time to sail to lands around the Arctic Circle with less danger from drift ice, a particular worry for Icelanders. Agricultural productivity grew as farms were established up to the utmost limits of arable cultivation, and cereal cultivation increased to feed an expanding population with more wealth to spend on goods.

The Olafsson and Haraldsson dynasties shared in this prosperity. The Viking settlements around Britain and Ireland became commercial emporia that produced a range of goods, from household wares to luxury items; this wealth paid for impressive works of art such as the sculpted stones on the Isle of Man. Among all the western Viking settlements this was a golden age of culture and commerce. Literature, art, and political alliances—remembered in Icelandic verses, physical remains, and insular chronicles—testify to the pre-eminence of the entrepreneurs. Just as important was the continued conversion of the Viking families to Christianity. They became a respectable and acceptable element of society in the eyes of their contemporaries. The bold merchant on the sea joined the brave warrior in replacing the image of the Viking as demon. Dudo uses the seafaring merchant traveling with his wares from one port to another as an allegory for the voyage of the soul after death, while

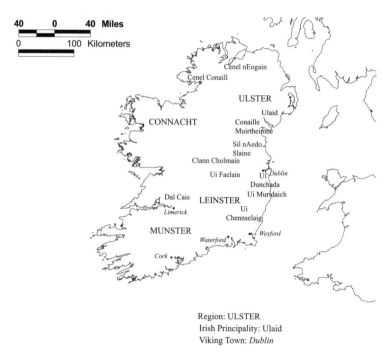

Region: ULSTER
Irish Principality: Ulaid
Viking Town: *Dublin*

MAP 3. *Viking Towns and Irish Principalities*

his contemporary Ælfric describes a merchant as someone who sails with his goods across perilous seas, constantly in danger of shipwreck.[2]

Under the rule of the Olafsson dynasty, Dublin was well on its way to becoming an economic powerhouse. This prosperity owed something to changes in warfare. Towns in Ireland and Britain were not only trading with each other, but they were also supplying local fortresses, which provided ready markets for goods.[3] Early in the tenth century, the West Saxon king Edward the Elder and his sister, Æthelflaed of Mercia, oversaw the construction of a series of fortresses to meet the threat from the Vikings in Northumbria and the Irish Sea. Towns such as Chester became commercial and financial centers for these garrisons that ensured a ready market for essential commodities to feed and clothe the troops. Later in the tenth century a similar system of forts/garrisons was constructed in Ireland, as the princes of the relatively minor Munster dynasty of Dál Cais used fortifications to maintain their control in southern Ireland. Part of the attraction of the Viking towns for the most successful member of the Munster family, the high king Brian Boru, must have been their ability to provide the goods that maintained the garrisons of those fortresses.[4] The incorporation of Irish Viking towns in Brian's empire provides an indication of their importance: Limerick in 967, Waterford by 984, and Dublin in 1000.

By the late tenth century, the seas between Ireland and Britain were an international trading zone. Like politics, commercial self-interest made strange bedfellows, and old enemies became new friends. Dublin's prosperity was partly due to its commercial contacts with towns controlled by the Olafssons' former foes. English ports such as Chester, now under the control of the West Saxon dynasty that had expelled Olaf Cuaran from Northumbria, were crucial to the Olafssons' good fortunes.[5] This wealth brought its own dangers. Mercantile success attracted unwelcome attentions from ambitious princes motivated less by military threat and more by the opportunity to exploit a town's wealth. Throughout Europe, the successful commander no longer relied on baubles from loot as his source of funds. He needed a dependable and continuous source of revenue to pay for the maintenance of forts, the building of fleets, and the troops to man them.

This prosperity was not enjoyed equally. Whether or not England was sharing in this commercial "boom" is not certain. Their importance as trading partners for the Olafssons' domain ensured that commercial woes of the English ports had repercussions in eastern Ireland. For over a generation, from circa 980 to 1020, the English economy had to endure raids on the kingdom and the payment of Danegeld.[6] Its resilience, and the importance of the Irish Sea trade, is illustrated by the revival of urban life on the western coast of England, especially at Gloucester, along the River Severn. Gloucester was part of the Irish Sea trading network, and in 1081 Archbishop Lanfranc of Canterbury was met there by a messenger from Ireland. This had been an important town in Roman Britain, but it was little more than a ruin for centuries.[7] By the beginning of the eleventh century, however, Gloucester was a flourishing commercial center and a royal residence. What makes Gloucester so interesting is that its wealth was based on iron production, part of which was being used in shipbuilding; according to *Domesday Book* (f. 162a) Gloucester paid 100 iron rods annually to the king for his ships.

Other western British towns appeared and prospered. Farther north, the physical bounds of Chester had been expanding during the tenth century. The area within the town walls had been filled, and latecomers among the merchants set up their shops outside. The Viking raid on Chester in 980 was particularly devastating on those houses/shops beyond the town walls.[8] Turning south, not far from Gloucester, in the mid-eleventh century Bristol suddenly appears in the chronicles as a thriving port, arising from nowhere, so it seems, to become Chester's economic rival.

The economic and political fortunes of his family changed after the abdication of Olaf Cuaran in 980. Rule over Dublin was taken by his son Glúniairn ("Iron-knee"), whose mother was the Uí Néill princess, Dúnflaith, the daughter of Muirchertach of the Leather Cloaks.[9] Glúniairn's relations with his half-brother, Máel Sechnaill, reveal the very real benefits of kinship. Máel Sechnaill might have been crucial in

Glúniairn's elevation to the kingship of Dublin, for the new king had several half-brothers who must have had their own ambitions. During the following years, Máel Sechnaill assisted Glúniairn against his Leinster rivals of Uí Dúnchada. By this time the fight clearly was about land. In 983 they defeated Domnall Clóen of Leinster and his ally Ivar of Waterford in a "battle-rout" (*cathroiniudh*) that left Ivar's son Gilla-Patraic among the slain. Then Glúniairn's troops attacked the church of Glendalough, which might have been supplying Domnall Clóen. Finally Máel Sechnaill swept right across Uí Dúnchada territory, harrying Leinster as far as the sea according to the *Annals of Tigernach*.

In 989 Glúniairn was murdered by his servant Colbain. He was survived by at least two sons: Gilla Ciaráin, who was slain in the Battle of Clontarf; and Sitric, who might have been the "son of Glúniairn" who killed his cousin Godfrey, the son of Sitric Silkenbeard, in Wales in 1036. Glúniairn might have been slain on behalf of a rival faction. Factionalism was a vice indulged in by many Viking settlers, with potential rivals waiting in the shadows.[10] Suspicion that the circumstances of Glúniairn's death were more complex than the drunken brawl remembered in the Irish annals is raised by the actions of an enraged Máel Sechnaill, who promptly attacked Dublin. He defeated the Vikings in a battle, but then had to besiege the town for twenty days before the defenders surrendered, mainly because the drinking water was exhausted. The *Annals of Tigernach* claim that Máel Sechnaill took a payment of his choice, apparently for Glúniairn's murder, in addition to an ounce of gold from each *garrda* or house plot to be paid every Christmas Eve, acknowledging his overlordship. The payment appears to have been a fine known as an *éraic*, in this instance paid to the kindred of the slain individual. Máel Sechnaill was Glúniairn's kinsman and possibly also took the *trian tobaig*, "enforcer's third," a fee taken by the individual powerful enough to ensure that the fine was paid.[11]

The terms between Máel Sechnaill and the Dubliners give an insight into the price of property within the fortress of Dublin. The term used to describe a unit of land within Dublin, *garrda*, is from Old Norse *garðr*, which means an enclosure, yard, or house. The payment from every *garrda* to the high king has similarities to what is known of property transactions elsewhere in Ireland. Land in Ireland was valued in units of ounces of precious metals. Some idea of eleventh- and twelfth-century land prices comes from Kells, the ecclesiastical community north of Dublin, in three charter notes found in the *Book of Kells*.[12] Gillachrist mac Mancháin purchased a tract of land north of the church from Cú Uladh mac Beolláin and his brother, Máel Ciaráin, for 480 ounces of silver, which, in the valuation of that day, was equivalent to 20 ounces of gold. A priest of Kells named Ua Breslen purchased land northeast of modern Navan from a man named Ua Riamán for 20 ounces (probably of gold). The church officials of Kells sold for an ounce (again, probably gold) a semi-detached house that had formerly been owned by a craftsman named Mac Áeda.

Using the guide provided by the *Book of Kells*, the ounce of gold taken from each household within Dublin by Máel Sechnaill seems to be the value of a house and its

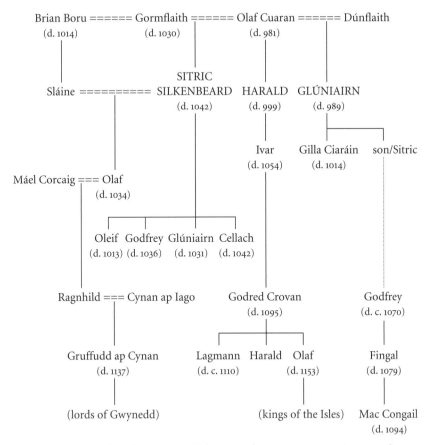

FIGURE 3. *The Sons of Olaf Cuaran and Their Families.* Key: ==, *marriage;* —, *descent;* …, *suggested lineage;* c., *circa;* d., *died.*

plot within Dublin. In other words, to buy a house inside the town of Dublin in the late tenth century cost an ounce of gold or 12 ounces of silver or 12 cows. The claim that the inhabitants of Dublin paid every Christmas Eve reflects the use of religious festivals as the date when payments were due. In early eleventh-century London, at the Billingsgate quay, merchants from the Holy Roman Empire paid for their special privileges at Christmas and Easter.[13]

Glúniairn was succeeded by his paternal half-brother, Sitric. He has the descriptive sobriquet "Silkenbeard" in the Icelandic sagas.[14] Sitric's mother, Gormflaith, was the princess from Uí Fáeláin of northern Leinster whose matrimonial conquests provoked the admiration of her contemporaries. Sitric's long reign spanned forty-six years, until his abdication in 1036.

There is curiously little information in the Irish chronicles about Sitric, his family, or Dublin during the first five years of his reign. The reason for this silence is connected with a man who passed into legend in Scandinavian literature: the future Norwegian king Olaf Tryggvason. His career in Britain is popularly known through the Old English poem on the battle at Maldon (in Essex on the Blackwater estuary), where Olaf fought an Anglo-Saxon noble named Brythnoth. Less known is Olaf's connection with the family of Olaf Cuaran and his residence in Ireland, which explains why Sitric Silkenbeard was left in peace.

Olaf's career in the British Isles is described in literature. His skald named Hallfred Ottarsson *vandræðaskald* ("troublesome poet") listed the areas where Olaf was active.[15] These were England, particularly Northumbria, Scotland, Ireland, the Isle of Man, and Wales; the accompanying prose narrative expands upon this with the addition of Francia. While raiding around the Irish Sea Province, Olaf married Olaf Cuaran's daughter Gytha, Sitric Silkenbeard's sister. The marriage is announced in *Orkneyinga Saga* and Olaf's saga in Snorri Sturluson's *Heimskringla*; the former claims that Gytha was Olaf Cuaran's sister, the latter calls her daughter of a king in Ireland. Gytha could not be Olaf Cuaran's sister because his father, Sitric, had died sixty-three years earlier. There might be an Irish origin for this error, because a similar confusion of Olaf with his son Sitric is found in *Cocad Gáedel re Gallaib*.[16] Olaf and Gytha lived at Dublin, where Olaf was found by messengers asking him to return to Norway. They had a son named Tryggvi who, circa 1033, attempted to claim the kingship of the Norse.

The courtship of Olaf and Gytha is an amusing romantic episode in his saga that gives an insight into the social structure of the Olafssons' world. Olaf's first wife Geira had died, and his voyage to Britain was undertaken, in part, as a distraction. One day he landed near a village in England where an assembly had just been called. A widow named Gytha intended to remarry and, as was her right, wanted to select her husband. Olaf, dressed only in his working clothes, and his men sat at a little distance from the gathering in order to watch the fun. After surveying all others, Gytha approached the party of seamen and, pointing to Olaf, announced that she chose him, to which Olaf consented. With all the reservations that literature is not history, an episode such as this had to have been believable to its audience, demonstrating the freedom enjoyed by a wealthy widow.

Olaf Tryggvason's residence at Dublin during the early part of the reign of Sitric Silkenbeard explains numismatic material. A comparison of the earliest known coins from the Dublin mint, found in hoards from Ireland to Scandinavia, with contemporary English pieces, shows that a die of the *Crux* issue of Æthelraed (circulating 991–997) was copied at Dublin.[17] The mint in question was Watchet, and Olaf Tryggvason was active in the area during the last decade of the tenth century, a time that would correspond with the date of the coin issue. The minting of coins indicates that the volume of business being conducted at Dublin had increased to the point where a local currency was needed to service it.

But was this coin-die taken as loot from a raid, or was it received as part of a trade agreement? Before his return to Scandinavia, Olaf negotiated a treaty with King Æthelraed of the English in 994, the previously mentioned treaty II Æthelraed.[18] This pact touches on matters found in other compacts between Vikings and territorial princes. There are two concerns: trade and violent crime. The treaty specifically refers to merchants associated with Olaf. Their ships are free to conduct trade with the English, the crews are not to be molested, and their goods must not be seized, unless the ship was wrecked. Plundering of ships that were not wrecks was one of the abuses that persisted throughout medieval Europe. *Laxdœla Saga* reflects this in an episode where a ship sailing from Norway to Ireland is grounded off the Irish coast and attacked by Irish claiming it as a shipwreck.[19] The treaty continues by guaranteeing the safety of merchandise if it is in the hands of the merchants or stored among men who are party to the treaty. There is also a description of a merchant preparing to open for business. He draws his ship upon the bank and builds a shed or pitches a tent. This type of shipside market, mentioned in Icelandic sagas such as *Eyrbyggja Saga*, must have been commonplace. The treaty implies that theft was open, because there is a provision that if a merchant is robbed and he knows which ship's crew is responsible, he can bring suit against the steersman, who represents his shipmates.

What merchants did Olaf represent? He did not control territory in England, and until his return north, the Norwegians were under the lordship of the jarls of Lade, acting as the agents of the Danes. The date and terms of this treaty suggest a look towards the Irish Sea Province. The making of a commercial treaty between Olaf and Æthelraed coincided with increased trade between Ireland and England that made an Irish mint possible at Dublin, but producing coins that would be recognizable by a main trading partner.

The residence of Olaf Tryggvason at Dublin explains the silence of the Irish records about the Olafssons or Dublin. A powerful Viking leader was an effective deterrent to Irish raids. Even the mighty Máel Sechnaill would hesitate before provoking a captain whose troops had raided throughout Britain. Olaf might have been weakening Sitric Silkenbeard's foes by plundering them, which could be the scene for a story in *Heimskringla*. One of Olaf's plundering parties gathered a herd of cattle. They were followed by a farmer, who begged Olaf to let him keep his cows from the herd. Olaf agreed, and the Irishman called to his dog that separated his beasts, the same number of cows claimed by the farmer, all with the same mark. Olaf was so impressed that he purchased the dog for a gold ring, and called him Vígi. The factual basis of this story is revealed in two matters. First, the Irish did mark, or brand, their cattle on the ears or horns. Such marking was necessary in a land where livestock grazed outdoors all year around, often in groupings of several farmers' herds that were run together under the care of the cowherds. Second, the Irish used dogs for herding and the law tracts mention specialized tasks for different types of dogs. Irish dogs were famous for being both intelligent and brave.[20]

The return of Olaf to Norway circa 994 coincided with the temporary exile from Dublin of his brother-in-law Sitric Silkenbeard, forced out by the king of Waterford named Ivar who earlier had been defeated by his brother, Glúniairn. Ivar's attack shows the limited scale of warfare, he had three ships with probably about one hundred and twenty men; when three pirate ships attacked Dál Riata in 986 their combined crews of one hundred and forty men were killed, while a century later in 1098 three ships from the Isles had combined crews of one hundred and twenty men when they were captured in Ulster. Sitric was back in the town within the year. As has been suggested for the murder of Glúniairn, his expulsion may have been helped by a rival faction in the town.

Sitric Silkenbeard learned that the wealth of Dublin enriching him also attracted other princes who wanted it for their own empire building. The connection of wealth with violence was not limited to Ireland. The revival of urban life at Gloucester, for example, was accompanied by the rebuilding of its walls. Sitric needed more than walls: he needed powerful friends. Events of the past two decades had shown that Dublin and its countryside were unable to provide the resources for competition with powerful Irish princes. Vigilance was necessary because from the southwest Brian Boru was leading campaigns for recognition as *imperator Scottorum* ("emperor of the Irish").

The need for an ally is clear from events between 995 and 998. Sitric and his nephew, Muirchertach Ua Congalaich, attacked the church at Domnach Patraic (Donaghpatrick, county Meath) in 995. In retaliation, Máel Sechnaill entered Dublin and took the ring of Thor and the sword of Carlus (who was killed at Dublin in 960). Sitric attacked Kells and Clonard in 997, and in 998 Brian and the high king Máel Sechnaill forced Sitric to recognize their lordship by giving hostages.

Sitric's search for an ally took him to his mother's family, to his uncle, Máel Mórda mac Murchada, king of Uí Fáeláin of north Leinster. In the year 999 Sitric and Máel Mórda joined forces twice. The first time they defeated the provincial overlord of Leinster named Donnchad, son of the Domnall Clóen rescued from Dublin by Máel Sechnaill in 980. Like his father, Donnchad was made a prisoner at Dublin. The attack had the intended effect of Máel Mórda's succession to the provincial lordship.

The second alliance of Sitric and Máel Mórda was in December, when they faced the invasion of Leinster by Brian at *Glen Mama*, near Newcastle Lyons. The Dublin–Leinster army was defeated, and two days later Brian's troops captured Dublin and destroyed the pagan sanctuary of Thor's Wood. The chronology of this brief period is not clear, but contemporaries thought it significant. *Cocad Gáedel re Gallaib* has two versions of events. First, that Brian was in Dublin from Christmas Day to Epiphany (*nodlaic mór co nodlaic becc*, December 25, 999, to January 6, 1000). Later in the narrative Brian remains in Dublin from Christmas to the Feast of Brigit (February 1), after which three months pass before Sitric makes his submission and is reinstated in Dublin. The report in the *Annals of Inisfallen* dates Brian's capture of Dublin to January 1, 1000.

Sitric Silkenbeard fled the city; according to *Cocad Gáedel re Gallaib* (where Sitric is confused with his father, Olaf, as in *Orkneyinga Saga*) he traveled north to the Ulaid and then to Áed of Cenél nEógain. Both times his request for aid was refused. With no help to be found in Ireland, Sitric acknowledged Brian's overlordship and was reinstated in Dublin. The slight suffered at the hands of the Ulaid was not forgotten. Two years later Sitric had his revenge when his troops ravaged their lands. Before returning to Dublin, Sitric might have turned pirate and been responsible for a Viking raid in Wales at St. David's.[21]

Brian's destruction of Thor's Wood indicates that paganism remained in the Christian Sitric's realm. Thor's Wood (Ir *caill Tomair*) was on the north bank of the Liffey across from Dublin. Shrines dedicated to Thor and other pagan gods were found throughout the regions of Scandinavian settlement. Thor was especially venerated at Dublin because he was considered a mighty warrior, who traveled great distances and was able to kill giants. He was particularly associated with rivers. The Viking settlers at Dublin are described as "Thor's Army" early in the tenth century, and they were still described as "the nobles of Thor" a century and a half later in the *Book of Rights*.[22] Active worship, rather than antiquarianism is behind the *Annals of Tigernach* notice that Máel Sechnaill took "Thor's Ring" from Dublin in 995; this is probably the same type of item as the sacred oath ring that the Vikings used in England when they swore to Alfred the Great that they would leave his lands in 876. Repeated attacks on Thor's Wood (earlier it had been destroyed by Máel Sechnaill in 975) show that it contained an active pagan sanctuary, not just a memory of former worship. A sanctuary had wooden idols before which votive offerings were placed. These offerings could be grisly. Dudo of St. Quentin and Adam of Bremen both mention animal sacrifices in connection with pagan cults; Adam claims that animals' were not the only flesh hanging from trees.

The breaking of Thor's Wood was not idle vandalism. Christian princes in Britain as well as Ireland had been deliberately attacking paganism in all its manifestations. The actions of Brian and Máel Sechnaill can be compared with those of the descendants of Alfred the Great, who had been trying to eradicate paganism in the English lands during the tenth century. Their lack of success is revealed in eleventh-century works, such as the great Anglo-Saxon archbishop and jurist Wulfstan of York and Worcester's "Sermon of the Wolf to the English" (composed circa 1014), with its condemnation of the Vikings' faithfulness to their false gods. The Irish were particularly sensitive to the importance of forest shrines and sacred trees because they, too, used them. Brian's dynasty of Dál Cais had their inaugural site at Mag Adhair (now Moyare Park, county Clare), a large level mound on which stood a sacred tree; groves were dedicated to saints such as Kevin (Cóemgan) of Glendalough.[23]

By the early eleventh century, however, attitudes toward paganism and Christianity were more ambivalent throughout the northern Atlantic than suggested by legal codes or raids on shrines. As the image of the evil Viking gave way to the brave seaman, also visible is the virtuous pagan in contrast with the sinful Christian. In his "Sermon of the Wolf to the English," for example, Wulfstan compares the heathen Vikings who faithfully pay their dues to false gods, respect their temples, and protect their priests with the English Christians who avoid paying tithes, defraud churches, and hold the clergy in contempt. Religious ambiguity was not limited to the Viking colonies of Britain and Ireland. The same year that Thor's Wood in Ireland was burned by the high king Brian, the Icelanders agreed to convert to Christianity through legislation, with the provision that anyone who wished to remain a pagan could do so and practice rites in secret. The previous year the Norse prince Olaf Tryggvason died in the Battle of Svold (leaping from his longship into the sea, according to later stories) after a brief reign in which his efforts to oversee the conversion to Christianity of his subjects had met with mixed success. While Olaf's Christianity is emphasized in later histories, Adam of Bremen, writing before hagiographers made him a missionary, remembered him as a pagan believer in omens named "Crack-a-bone" after his favored method of divination.[24]

A brief glimpse into mercantile Dublin at the beginning of the millennium is provided by *Cocad Gáedel re Gallaib*, an important and neglected source for cultural history. The first mention of a market (*margad*) at Dublin is in connection with Brian's residence in the town in 1000. The market seems to have been recently set up because it is not mentioned when Máel Sechnaill attacked Dublin in 980. The beginnings of the Dublin coinage probably coincided with the regularizing of commerce with the opening or expansion of a market. Viking markets in Ireland seem to have been located outside the town walls; this saved the market at Limerick in 1108 when a fire engulfed the town. The attack on the market in 1000 is the last known time that the site was raided. Even battles, such as Clontarf, were fought away from it.

Cocad Gáedel re Gallaib gives two lists of goods found by Brian's troops when they entered the town. The second list is briefer and has the expected luxury items such as gold, gems, goblets, fine cloth, and horns. The first and longer list is in a poem celebrating Brian's victory. The goods in that catalogue are a combination of the luxurious and utilitarian: fine, silken-like cloth (*siric*); feathers (*clúmh*); bedding (*colcaid*, possibly a reference to quilts); livestock (horses and cows); and slaves. Feathers were used for insulated bedding, their trade is mentioned in the Irish law tracts and it seems to have been common throughout the northern Atlantic. In the late ninth century feathers were among the items collected for the "Lapp Tax" around the Arctic Circle.[25] The Irish anciently imported horses, and the "horse from overseas" (*ech allmuir*) was assigned a special value in the law tracts, probably because it was used to improve the native stock. Horses from Scotland are mentioned in the eleventh-century *Book of Rights* (*Lebor na Cert*), along with luxury goods such as foreign shields, foreign slaves, gold, and undefined "wealth."[26] The inclusion of slaves among the livestock gives us a glimpse of the mentality behind the idea of servitude.

A third statement of the plunder is found in the seventeenth-century transcription of earlier annals now known as the *Chronicon Scotorum*, where it is stated that gold and cloaks (*braitt*) were taken. The standard outer garment found among the Irish, cloaks were produced by all the Viking settlements of the west, from Ireland and the Hebrides as far north as Iceland. The cloaks produced in the Viking settlements were slightly different from the Irish variety, and they were greatly prized throughout the northern world at this period. A description of the Viking cloaks is preserved in the *vita* of the Welsh St. Cadog, composed circa 1100. They had prominent tufts or hair-like coils that from a distance gave the appearance of fur.[27] Among Norse-speakers this type of weave was known as *röggr* and the cloak was known throughout the Scandinavian world as *röggvarfeldr*.

Careful attention was paid to the loot by the victors because there were immediate uses for it. First, it paid the troops. Brian used mercenaries far more extensively than was usual in Ireland, and they were customarily paid with a percentage of the captured goods. According to *Cocad Gáedel re Gallaib*, Brian's men received cloth as part of their wages. Another use for this plunder was in the ritualized Irish gift exchanges known as *tuarastal* "stipend," which sealed political ties between lord and follower. When Brian took the submission of the Ulaid, he received taxes from them in the expected form of livestock: cattle, hogs, and sheep; a necessary source of protein

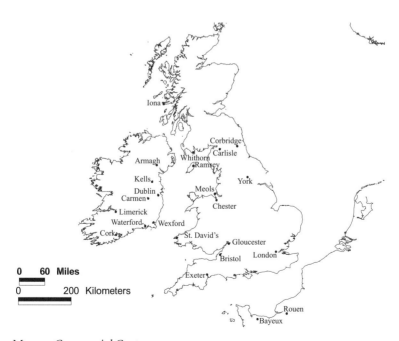

MAP 4. *Commercial Centers*

for troops on the march. In return, he gave them horses, precious metals (gold and silver), and cloth.[28] All of these goods—especially the horses and metals—could have been supplied by Brian's Irish subjects. The quantity of cloth needed to make it a suitable gift may have come from the Viking towns. The similarities between the goods taken by Brian at Dublin and the items he gave to the Ulaid are interesting.

The high quality of goods from the Irish Sea region is suggested by their distribution throughout the North Atlantic. As Scandinavian settlement expanded westwards, toward Greenland and North America, trade items from the Irish Sea are found. A Hiberno-Scandinavian type of plain ringed, polyhedral-headed pin has been found at the Viking settlement uncovered at L'Anse aux Meadows in Newfoundland. A direct Dublin connection is suggested by *Eirik's Saga*, in the manuscript of the Icelandic lawman Hauk Erlendsson (died 1334). Ireland is mentioned as the western point of reference for those seeking the North American settlements of Vinland and Markland, and that the news of their discovery first reached Europe via Dublin.[29]

The success of a market at Dublin depended on several conditions.[30] First, there had to be security for the merchants at the market as well as travel to and from it. Next, there had to be an agreed medium/rate of exchange. Finally, the market had to be held on or very near to easily accessible routes, ideally where two commercial regions intersected. Sitric Silkenbeard ruled a town where these criteria were met. The Dublin fleet provided security by controlling the waters around the town. Not until the end of the eleventh century, when Dublin was under Irish control, is there evidence of piracy in the Irish Sea. The medium of exchange was provided by the production of coins at Dublin. Finally, Dublin was at the intersection of the northern and southern trading zones. The raw materials of Scandinavia were traded for the luxury foodstuffs and manufactured items of Ireland, Britain, and continental Europe. The conjunction of several major Irish roads at the River Liffey gave access to the interior of the country, while the east–west sailing avenues communicated directly with the English markets.

Prior to the beginning of a mint at Dublin, the coins circulating around the town were mainly English. The commencement of a market might have been only part of the reason why a separate coinage was needed. By the tenth century there was a shortage of silver throughout northern Europe, possibly in part reflecting a deficiency of production in the ninth century and in part because the Islamic sources began to fail. New sources were coming into production such as the mines at Rommelsburg in the Empire, which supplied the Anglo-Saxons.[31] So economic growth at Dublin combined with silver shortages probably made the English coins more costly than the traffic could bear. Adding to the difficulties of anyone who made English coins the basis of their currency was the English practice, begun during the reign of Edgar, of issuing new coins every six years and forbidding the circulation of older coins. Dishonest merchants attempted their own currency manipulation by resorting to the counterfeiters (*falsarii*) and procuring underweight coins.[32] To ensure royal control, the dies were collected from a central administration. Manipulation of coin weight could quickly and easily increase the crown's own reserves of money. Not only was this an effective measure against counterfeiting, but it was also a simple way to allow for inflation or deflation of the currency. Such considerations must have been known in Ireland, and the stylistic changes in the Dublin coinage probably were made for similar reasons.

The coin produced at Dublin was a silver penny that imitated contemporary English coins. The earliest Dublin penny was a copy of the *Crux* issue of Æthelraed II on which the name of Sitric was impressed.[33] The weight and quality of the Dublin coins were not identical to their English models, but they were closely comparable during the early part of Sitric's reign. Licensing the right to mint coins was profitable. The poem "Here Is a Happy, Graceful History" claims that the twelfth-century Dublin moneyers paid a scruple (traditionally equivalent to a twenty-fourth of an ounce) for their dues, but this seems inaccurate and too modest when compared with other lands. In eleventh-century England the moneyers at Hereford paid 18 shillings when they collected their dies and 20 shillings a month after returning home, while the Worcester moneyers paid 20 shillings upon receiving their dies; south of the Alps the moneyers of Pavia paid 16 pounds of pennies annually, while retaining 2 pennies from every 12 they produced.[34]

The production of coinage testifies to the administrative sophistication of Sitric Silkenbeard's government. At the very time when one might expect to see an economic crisis at Dublin complementing its political decline, there was the very antithesis of a crumbling empire—the issue of a strong and stable currency. A mint at Dublin argues for powerful royal control. Strong government was necessary to enforce the tax collection that made coins desirable, and also to ensure that its coins were accepted. As has been noted for England, and it was just as true for Ireland, such a financial system "was not run from a box under the bed."[35] When Brian's troops took gold and silver at Dublin, this may have included stockpiles of bullion used by the town's moneyers. The use of precious objects as bullion is seen in the reign of Henry III. In 1245 the king ordered the keeper of the Mint at Dublin to give from his stocks a silver chalice worth between 15 and 16 pence to Bishop Geoffrey of Osraige, to replace one that the bishop earlier had given to the king.[36]

Coins were used to pay harbor tolls as well as the tax that was levied on merchants who sold at the market. How this operated in practice in Dublin at this time is unknown, but examples from other regions offer some suggestions. In southern Wales in the mid-eleventh century, according to the *Life of St. Gwynllyw* (composed circa 1130), English merchants who traded at the mouth of the River Usk paid their toll when the market closed. Failure to pay meant that they were not permitted to take their goods farther up river. The toll was collected by the nephew of the region's then overlord Gruffydd ap Llywelyn. There was a similar practice at the fair at Champagne in the twelfth century. Merchants kept careful note of their sales and purchases, then procured the necessary amount of local currency in order to pay their bills and tolls. There may be evidence of commercial bills from Scandinavia. A rune-stick found in excavations at Hedby in the ninth-century *stratum* appears to be the record of a sales contract.[37]

Coins were not the exclusive method of payment, and dues could be collected in-kind before the merchant was allowed to trade. A comparison with English ports is instructive. At London, the Billingsgate tolls note that a small ship paid a half penny toll, a large ship paid a penny, and a ship carrying planks paid one plank. There was also a variation for individual merchants. Sellers of hens, eggs, and blubber fish gave a percentage of their goods, but those selling butter and cheese paid in cash.[38] The Cheshire Domesday account notes that the king's tax on furs was collected by the royal official before the merchant was allowed to trade.

Tolls were paid at different places. Ships and their cargoes paid at dockside. Merchants traveling overland paid at specific locations. One place where tolls were collected was called the *via regis* "royal way," or "king's highway." This highway was maintained at the king's expense (often with a better surface than other roads), and royal officials were stationed there to collect taxes. At Dublin the "king's highway" is mentioned in a thirteenth-century complaint made by the citizens of Dublin to King Henry III of England, while several charters use the king's highway as a boundary marker.[39] The complaint of the Dubliners was that the justiciary had erected a pillory on the highway, taking what belonged to the king.

Commerce contributed to a growing population at Dublin. In the tenth century the population had been between one and two thousand inhabitants; by the middle of the eleventh century the population was approximately four to five thousand people.[40] By eleventh-century standards it was large. While population figures for this time are always estimates and must be read as merely informed guesses, a comparison might be useful. Dublin had roughly the same population as the English towns of Oxford, Lincoln, and Norwich. Each of the English towns had an average population of 4,000–5,000 and about 1,000 properties. Dublin was much larger than its main trading partner Chester, which had only about 1,500 people with about 283 properties, but it was smaller than York with its 1,500 properties and a population of possibly 9,000 in 1066.[41] Dublin was a populous town not just in terms of Ireland, but also in comparison with settlements throughout the northern Atlantic.

As the population increased, so too did the number of houses in Dublin. Space for building was at a premium. Excavations have revealed that within the fortress there was an undeveloped bit of ground in the mid-tenth century that had been covered by houses and their gardens by the beginning of the eleventh century. A particular problem for the houses of Dublin was surface water, which was caused by the poor drainage of the town's soil. Inside and outside many houses were elaborate systems of drains. Efforts to remove standing water belie the popular image of medieval towns as carelessly filthy. There was a genuine effort towards cleanliness at Dublin, and the floors of the houses were swept regularly.[42]

By the reign of Sitric Silkenbeard the organization of manufacturing becomes visible.[43] The makers of specific goods gathered together on particular streets. Fishamble Street, for example, was lined with butchers' and cloth makers' shops. Cloth working was one of the main industries, and there is evidence that flax was grown locally. Brian's capture of Dublin yielded fine linens smooth as silk and multi-colored cloth, almost identical to the report of the types of cloth taken at the capture of Limerick a generation earlier.[44] By the end of the tenth century there appears to have been an explosion in the demand for woolens from Ireland and the Hebrides, especially for *röggvarfeldr.*

An interesting view of the Vikings in Ireland about the middle of the eleventh century comes from an Iberian source.[45] The geographer al-ʿUdhri describes Ireland (Irlandah) as the capital of all the Vikings. The people wear rich mantles, some of which are decorated with pearls. They hunt whales off the coast during the months of October to January, a revealing comment because the Irish did not hunt whales, although a whale stranded on the shore was considered valuable community property.[46] The Viking whalers enticed a whale calf to their boat by clapping their hands. Then, as they rubbed its head, a harpoon was hammered into the animal's head. If the mother attempted to rescue it, the sailors sprinkled garlic to confuse her. An interesting parallel is in the eleventh-century Norwegian legal code known as the Gulathing Laws that mention whales being shot with arrows from the shore. Anyone could hunt whales on the water. If the animal is killed there, then the hunter retained full ownership, but if it was driven to the shore, the owner of the land received half.[47]

Another aspect of Dublin's wealth was a thriving agricultural community around the town. The plain of the River Liffey (Mag Life) was one of the three great (i.e. productive) plains of Ireland.[48] The farms of the Viking colonists surrounded Dublin, and individuals are remembered in their names. Ballyfermot was the *baile* (MI "farmstead") of a man named Thormund, while Turkilby is Thorkel's *býr* ("farm").[49]

Together with farmland were tracts of valuable woodlands. Thor's Wood was a remnant of the oak forest that once had covered the Liffey River Valley. Irish oak was prized for shipbuilding, such as the eleventh-century ship found in Denmark in Roskilde Fjord known as Skuldelev II. South of Dublin there was a thick forest. As late as the twelfth century, armies attacking Dublin would make a detour to avoid traveling through that forest where ambushes were a danger. There is evidence that woodlands were being managed. Groves of ash and yew trees were planted around the cemetery of a church in Fingal.[50] An aside in *Cocad Gáedel re Gallaib* compares the combat at Clontarf with the clearing of underbrush from Thor's Wood. This suggests that coppicing was being practiced, in which rods were being harvested after ten years growth, while mature trees would be taken as needed.[51] These woods were not spared the ever present danger of fire, and the same aside compares the flashing of weapons with that of the wood on fire, possibly a reference to Brian's troops setting alight Thor's Wood.

Even though it is customary to speak of "Viking" Dublin, the half-Irish Sitric and his subjects were not living in isolation from their neighbors. The houses in Dublin were constructed more similarly to structures built by Irish carpenters rather than the Vikings.[52] Even the style of Dublin's houses is similar to those found among the Irish themselves, rather than the typical Viking long houses, such as those found in the Outer Hebrides. The wealth of Sitric was dependent on, at least partly, the raw materials supplied by their Irish neighbors. Some of the timber used in Dublin probably came from Leinster. *Cocad Gáedel re Gallaib* mentions that Sitric's uncle Máel Mórda mac Murchada paid part of his tribute to the high king Brian in timber. Trade between the Irish and the Vikings might explain political change in Leinster, which had been a battlefield between the Uí Néill and Munster during much of the ninth and early tenth centuries. By Sitric's reign, Leinster become increasingly powerful and assertive, probably reflecting a new wealth produced, in part, by supplying their Viking neighbors who paid cash. About two-thirds of all Viking Age coin hoards in Ireland have been found in Leinster.[53]

Wealth paid for artistic and literary patronage, something the creative community was not slow to realize. A remembrance of Sitric's reign comes from verses preserved in a late medieval Icelandic romance known as the saga of Gunnlaug Serpent's Tongue (*ormstunga*) Illugason. Gunnlaug was a professional court poet, or skald, whose vicious satires gave him his sobriquet. He traveled throughout the northern world and served as a court-poet to Jarl Eirik of Lade and King Olaf of Sweden in the first quarter of the eleventh century. In verses composed circa 1002, Gunnlaug tells of his journey around Britain and Ireland, a type of poem that has been described as a versified travelogue. He visited King Æthelraed of England, Sitric Silkenbeard of Dublin, and Jarl Sigurd of the Orkneys. Only fragments survive of the verses Gunnlaug composed about Sitric, known as *Sigtryggsdrápa* ("the *drapa* of Sitric").[54] *Drápa* is a composition with at least twenty stanzas and a refrain recurring at regular intervals. *Sigtryggsdrápa* is even more interesting because it was composed in a rare meter called *runhenda* that has end-rhymes, also found in Middle Irish verse composition.[55]

In Gunnlaug's verses Sitric is praised for his descent from kingly ancestors and his father, Olaf Cuaran. The poet concludes by requesting a gold ring as the reward for his poem. The prose narrative of the saga elaborates on Gunnlaug's visit to Sitric's court. Sitric considered rewarding Gunnlaug with a ship and much gold, until cooler heads prevailed and the poet was given a new suit of clothes. The impression given of Dublin in Gunnlaug's saga is of a bustling and thriving port that could accommodate a somewhat naive young king who wanted to be praised as a great warrior. All this can be discarded as a mere literary edifice built upon ideas suggested in the verses, but gold, ships, and clothing all have been uncovered in excavations at Dublin and are mentioned in connection with the town in the historical records.

There was also entertainment of a less literary variety. Games were being manufactured at Dublin, and pieces for these games from circa 1005 have been discovered. The Dubliners also kept pets, one of which was used as the model for a weaving toggle that is carved in the form of a dog playing with a ball. Children's toys were produced, including toy swords and toy horses. From a tenth-century level in the excavations a toy boat has been found.[56]

A brief tour through the domain of Sitric Silkenbeard shows that he ruled more than a few pirate boats guarding a shanty town on the shore. Dublin enjoyed a dozen years of peace while Sitric's troops were in the armies of the high king Brian. They served on Brian's northern campaigns against the Ulaid in 1002 and 1005 and against the Northern Uí Néill in 1006 and 1007. In order to secure Sitric's genuine cooperation, rather than his begrudged help, Brian used a traditional method of sealing alliances; he wed his daughter to Sitric. Their marriage is noted in *Cocad Gáedel re Gallaib*, but her name, Sláine, is known only from the pedigree of their great-grandson Gruffydd ap Cynan.[57] There were additional family ties. Brian's marriage to Gormflaith made him Sitric's stepfather, and Sitric was the half-brother of Brian's son Donnchad, who succeeded his father as king of Munster. Thus the bitter pill of submission was sweetened, somewhat, by the fact that it was administered by "one of the family." Yet natural and artificial ties could not prevent conflict.

Brian's efforts to be recognized as high king throughout Ireland were completed by 1011 when the last of the Northern Uí Néill kingdoms, Cenél Conaill, submitted to him. His empire was short-lived, however, and it began to disintegrate almost as soon as Brian returned to Munster. In 1012 the Northern Uí Néill kingdoms revolted and they were joined the following year by Dublin and Leinster. Not all of the high king's supporters deserted him. The Southern Uí Néill remained loyal to Brian, and Máel Sechnaill ravaged Dublin's territory in 1013. The expedition was not a complete success as Sitric's troops defeated his troops at Drinan (county Dublin) where they killed Máel Sechnaill's son Flann. A few lines of verse in the margin of a copy of the *Annals of Ulster* note that the battle was fought on a Monday when the Vikings "welcomed the army of Meath on their journey to Drinan."

Then the offensive was taken by Sitric, who sent a fleet led by his son Oleif south to Munster where it burned the Viking settlement at what is now Cork and attacked Cape Clear. The raid shows that Sitric believed a fleet from Cork aided the high king materially, so he destroyed part of Brian's naval power. He appears to have been both perceptive and successful, for Brian's next moves were by land. Brian sent his troops through Leinster in order to besiege Dublin. They encamped outside the town for several months from September 9 until Christmas, but the siege ultimately failed and Brian's troops returned home.[58] In the quiet of the winter months, son-in-law and father-in-law recruited allies for another confrontation, a battle that would be fought at Clontarf.

The Battle of Clontarf was one of several important conflicts in the northern Atlantic during the eleventh century. The battle was fought on Good Friday, April 23,

1014, in a field on the north bank of the River Liffey called *cluain tarbh* ("the bulls' meadow"); it is now a neighborhood in the eastern part of the modern city. Unlike obscure contemporary conflicts, there were historical remembrances and legends about the Battle of Clontarf circulating for centuries throughout northern Europe, from Francia to Iceland.[59] Those writing history in Ireland took the date of the Battle of Clontarf as a standard chronological marker. In the *Annals of Ulster* the dates attached to the entries are one year behind the true date until the entry for the year of the Battle of Clontarf, when a correction is made by skipping over an entire year. Entire chronicles, such as the *Annals of Loch Cé*, take the Battle of Clontarf for their starting point.

Among the medieval Irish, the Battle of Clontarf came to be seen as the decisive moment in the destruction of the Vikings as a military threat. For the descendants of Brian, who took the collective name *Uí Briain* ("descendants of Brian"), the Battle of Clontarf was enshrined in their mythology, and they labored to give their ancestor pride of place in the political hagiography of Ireland. Their patronage produced the tract *Cocad Gáedel re Gallaib*, in which a selective history of the Vikings in Ireland (hence the title "War of the Irish against the Vikings") was combined with a saga of Brian. The battle is the climax of the narrative, and Brian is presented as the liberator of the Irish from the Viking menace.

Medieval literary explanations for the battle point to one person. In both the Irish *Cocad Gáedel re Gallaib* and the later Icelandic *Njal's Saga*, the blame for the revolt of Sitric and Máel Mórda is placed on Sitric's mother, Gormflaith, Brian's wife.[60] In *Cocad Gáedel re Gallaib* Gormflaith incites her brother, Máel Mórda, to revolt against Brian's overlordship because his submission would cause a permanent clientship of Leinster to Munster. Máel Mórda enlists his nephew Sitric as an ally, who then recruits other Vikings to their cause. *Njal's Saga* omits Máel Mórda; Gormflaith is roused to fury when she is divorced by Brian, and she takes revenge by provoking her son Sitric into a battle against her former husband. Gormflaith's appearance in *Cocad Gáedel re Gallaib* and *Njal's Saga* is familiar to students of folklore as the malevolent woman/wife, who has been described as the "female inciter."[61] These stories also ignore the fact that Gormflaith's supposed involvement in a plot against Brian took place after the rebellion had begun, as Leinster and Dublin were late arrivals to it. They do illustrate one point: the loyalty of aristocratic women to their kindred. Even if this is only a literary embellishment, it must have been believable to an aristocratic audience. Some historians have followed, and see Máel Mórda attempting to free Leinster from submission to Brian.[62]

The question remains, why did Sitric join the rebellion? There is no indication that Dublin had suffered during Brian's overlordship; quite the opposite seems true. Other than a few skirmishes with its neighbors, Dublin was relatively undisturbed from 1000 to 1013, and it was prosperous, as demonstrated by its coinage that was of very good quality. A look towards Britain, however, suggests another reason for the battle.

In the second half of the year 1013 the English king Æthelraed was battling un-successfully against the Danish king Svein Forkbeard. For almost two decades Svein had raided around Britain, and the incompetence of Æthelraed, together with the revival of separatism among the formerly independent regions such as North-umbria, resulted in political instability among the English.[63] When the final Danish assault on England began in the summer of 1013, it must have been apparent to any objective observer that Svein would prevail. Merchants from England undoubtedly brought news of the conflict to the ports that they visited, and Svein might have sent agents to Dublin in an effort to recruit troops. In November of 1013 Æthelraed, who was married to Emma of Normandy, fled to the refuge offered by his wife's family in Rouen. Svein was recognized as king of the English. His empire would not long sur-vive, however, for he died in February of 1014. Although his son Cnut was in England at that time, he was unable to hold together the coalition of Danes and English who had supported his father and was forced to flee back to Denmark. Æthelraed returned from Normandy, after giving the strictest assurances that he would rule justly. Among his first actions was to ravage mercilessly the areas, such as Lindsey, where Svein had received support.

In light of the Danish successes in England, Sitric and his uncle, Máel Mórda, may have thought the time ripe for their own attempt at empire building. They would have been encouraged in their plans by the fragility of Brian's alliances. His rise to power had upset the established Irish political order. The submissions given to him by the Irish princes usually had been offered as a temporary escape from a difficult situation. Even the alliance of Máel Sechnaill and Brian was only a neces-sary evil for the former, as was illustrated by his apparent desertion of Brian before the Battle of Clontarf. The situation was slightly better for the high king in southern Ireland, but even there Brian maintained control with fortresses overseen by his offi-cials.[64] The precarious nature of Brian's supremacy is clearly visible on the day of the battle. Other than his troops from Munster, only a few Connacht princes (Brian's mother came from southern Connacht) and some mercenaries fought for Brian. Among those mercenaries were men from the Viking settlements according to *Njal's Saga* and *Cocad Gáedel re Gallaib*.

For the Viking settlers of Ireland and Britain this presented an opportunity for a common cause. Sitric obtained the aid of one of the most powerful Viking lords in the west, Jarl Sigurd the Stout of the Orkneys. Sigurd might have fought to maintain the independence of the Hiberno-Scandinavian towns, but such selflessness is ab-sent from his career. There is little evidence that the scattered Viking settlements thought of themselves as belonging to a single community. More realistic is the possi-bility that Sigurd and Brian were fighting for control of the Irish Sea trade. Sitric might even have acknowledged the jarl's lordship in return for his help. *Njal's Saga* states that Sigurd was promised marriage to Sitric's mother and the kingship of Ire-land in return for his service. The former part of the statement can be dismissed as romantic fiction, but the latter part of the bargain sounds believable. The bait to lure him as far south as Dublin could have been the promise of an Irish addition to his empire. This would explain the contemporary verses in *Orkneyinga Saga* claiming that Sigurd's son Thorfinn (died circa 1064) was lord of a region that extended as far as Dublin.[65] Thorfinn never seems to have visited the town, but the statement makes sense if based on an earlier submission made by Sitric to Sigurd.

The Olafssons and Haraldssons fought as allies at Clontarf. Among the slain were Olaf son of Lagmann son of Godfrey, Dubgall son of Olaf Cuaran, and Gilla Ciaráin son of Glúniairn son of Olaf Cuaran. Olaf's father, Lagmann, was the son of Godfrey Haraldsson and he was the king of the Isles who fought in Normandy in 1009 and 1014. Whether the Haraldssons were fighting independently or as part of Sigurd's Orkney contingent is unknown. Sigurd by this time controlled at least part of the Kingdom of the Isles. Dubgall and Gilla Ciaráin were members of the Olafsson dynasty, respectively the son and grandson of Olaf Cuaran.[66]

In addition to Sigurd of the Orkneys, Sitric looked for allies elsewhere among the Scandinavian colonies around Britain. Irish records and later Norse remembrances give some idea of the extent of the insular Viking world of Ireland and Britain. The list given in *Cocad Gáedel re Gallaib* includes mercenaries from France, Cornwall, Wales, and Northumbria. This catalogue is more realistic than it is generally considered. A particularly interesting ally of Sitric was named Brodor. *Njal's Saga* claims that Sitric traveled to the Isle of Man to recruit Brodor, whose paganism is presented in stark contrast to the Christianity of Brian.[67] There was a Brodor who fought and died at the Battle of Clontarf, but *Cocad Gáedel re Gallaib* calls him Brodor of York. Ties between Dublin and York continued long after political separation. The devastating fire at York in 1032 is known only from the *Annals of Tigernach* and *Chronicon Scotorum*; the *Anglo-Saxon Chronicle* merely states that there was a wild fire that did damage in many places.

The historical Brodor becomes, in the thrilling story told in *Njal's Saga*, an apostate who compounds his sin with sorcery. A thoroughly bad character, the literary Brodor insists that he, not Sigurd, be wed to Sitric's mother and also that the deception be concealed from the Orkney lord. For three nights, as his ships lie at anchor off the Isle of Man, Brodor and his men are attacked by a phantom army. They are scalded with boiling blood on the first night, attacked by their own weapons on the second, and ravens set upon them the third night. Every morning one man is found dead. The literary embellishments are interesting because the phantom army is well known in Irish literature. *The Song of Dermot and the Earl*, written in the late twelfth century, includes an episode when Dermot's Anglo-Irish army is attacked by phantoms while on an expedition near Wexford.[68]

The main outline of the preliminaries and combat at Clontarf given in *Cocad Gáedel re Gallaib* is generally accepted. Brian's own troops approached from the northwest of the town and camped on a ridge on the north side of the Liffey, opposite the fortress. His allies arrived in individual groups, so he paused on the *faithce átha clíath* ("*faithce* of Dublin") to assemble the different divisions. *Faithce* has various meanings, but in this instance it seems to refer to something similar to a "green belt," an open space outside the town.[69] The Leinster–Viking army had its rendezvous at Howth and set up camp in *Mag nElta*, a plain extending to the west of Howth, where Clontarf was situated. At this time it was open country, and the name of Clontarf, "the bulls' meadow," indicates that it was grazing for the cattle of Dublin. Prior to the battle Brian's son Donnchad took troops to ravage the lands just south of Dublin as a diversionary tactic, and the Leinster–Viking army could see the flames as they prepared for battle.

On the day of the battle Brian's army was at less than full strength because, according to *Cocad Gáedel re Gallaib*, his ally Máel Sechnaill did not fight. No plausible reason is ever given in the contemporary or near-contemporary records, leaving ample room for speculation. Perhaps Máel Sechnaill's personal relationships dictated his actions. He was married to Sitric's sister, Máel Muire, and had been the second husband of Sitric's mother, Gormflaith. A curious episode in *Njal's Saga* describes an unidentified man on a gray horse talking intently to Gormflaith the night before the battle. This might have a connection with the accusation made in *Cocad Gáedel re Gallaib* that Máel Sechnaill plotted with the Vikings the night before the battle and agreed not to attack them if they did not attack him. These stories seem to reflect a widespread and persistent belief that Máel Sechnaill saw the looming battle as his opportunity to be rid of Brian and regain the high kingship. Such ambitions are not too far-fetched. Little encouragement might have been needed from someone such as Gormflaith, acting in Sitric's interests, to persuade her former husband to stand aloof from the fighting. Noble ladies did play such a diplomatic role, as did Gormflaith's contemporary in England. Thietmar of Merseburg claims that after the death of the English king Æthelraed in 1016, his Norman-born queen Emma opened negotiations with the Danish army on the behalf of the English people.[70] Did Gormflaith, like Emma, take advantage of her personal connections to engage in diplomacy?

Brian did not personally take part in the fight. He was an old man for the time; according to the *Annals of Ulster* he was born in 941, so he was about seventy-three years old. On the day of the battle Brian's son and heir-designate Murchad was his field commander. Both sides divided their troops into battle groups, fighting in ethnic or dynastic groups. Like the Vikings, there was an international aspect to Brian's army and the mercenaries fighting for Brian were under the command of ten mormaers ("great-stewards"). Murchad, a mature and experienced commander, personally led one group, and another was led by Domnall mac Eimhin the mormaer of Mar in Scotland. Mac Firbis claims that Domnall was a descendant of a Viking named Ivar the Old. The Leinster–Viking coalition was commanded jointly by Máel Mórda and Sigurd, although the Icelandic sagas claim that Sitric also led troops.

As the combatants prepared for battle, they donned their armor and readied their weapons. These varied according to the manufacturing practiced by each group. This information comes from *Cocad Gáedel re Gallaib*, and it is the type of material least likely to be deliberately fabricated for an audience of warrior-aristocrats. The Irish fought with little or no body armor, although high status warriors such as commanders wore a helmet. For defense they used shields, probably similar to the *targed* later used by the Highland clans. The high-status warriors carried swords, which apparently functioned more as clubs than as blades, as well as Viking axes for cutting. The rank and file fought with spears, and probably used some type of knife for close fighting. Some of the spears could have been the Irish "jabbing" spears used throughout the Middle Ages. All their weapons were carried on the body; later in the eleventh century, Guibert of Nogent commented on the Gaelic-speaking warriors whose weapons dangled about them.[71]

The Vikings wore heavy body armor made of both iron and brass that, together with their weapons, seems similar to that used in northern Francia and described by Dudo (an exact contemporary of the Battle of Clontarf).[72] This armor is described as *lúirech* in the *Annals of Ulster*, which can mean specifically "breastplate" or more generally "armor." *Cocad Gáedel re Gallaib* describes it as *tredúalach*, which can mean either that the metal was worked into three strand cables or was formed into many loops such as chain mail. Dudo notes that Norman warriors wore a mail of triple thickness, probably similar to that illustrated on the Bayeux Tapestry. The armor covered the upper torso and extended to the head, but it is unclear if this meant that it included the equivalent of a metal hood or if the Vikings wore separate helmets; Dudo claims that contemporary Normans were wearing helmets. This body protection allowed them to dispense with shields. They used spears and swords in addition to bows and arrows, but not the axes that contemporaries considered to be particularly "Viking" weapons. According to Dudo, spears were thrown in the first onslaught of battle, and then swords were wielded.

The Battle of Clontarf began early. In the closely fought contest the advantage passed initially from the Leinster–Viking forces to the Munster troops by the afternoon. After the initial clash the combat degenerated into a series of personal combats. Much of the fighting took place near, or on, the wharves and piers along the northern bank of the Liffey. The report in *Chronicon Scotorum* mentions that the fighting ranged from the River Tolka east as far as Howth. There were individual tragedies in addition to acts of daring, and occasionally the circumstances illuminate a commercial aspect of Viking Dublin. To take one example, during the battle a grandson of Brian named Tairdelbach drowned after he was knocked unconscious under a weir. Weirs were a relatively recent development in the northern Atlantic. As the size of cargo vessels increased from about eight to thirty tons during the tenth century, deeper water was needed to accommodate them. This weir obviously had been built to accommodate the larger ships bringing the wealth that made Dublin a prize worth winning.

Two minor episodes found in *Cocad Gáedel re Gallaib* give an insight into the international aspect to the combat. One is the recruitment by Sitric of two warriors named Carlus (who fell in battle) and Ebric, who are called the sons of the king of the Franks. They may have been Normans, possibly merchants or mercenaries from Rouen; the *Annals of Tigernach*'s obituary for Duke Richard of Normandy in 1027 describes him as "king of the Franks." The second episode is a duel, illustrating bilingualism, between Brian's ally Domnall the mormaer of Mar (Scotland) and a warrior from Scandinavia named Plat (an Irish rendering of ON *flatr*, "flat").[73] Plat calls out in Old Norse, "*faras Domnaill*" ("where is Domnall?"), which Domnall hears and understands, but he replies in Gaelic, "*sund snithing*" ("here, serpent"). Each dies with the other's sword piercing him. Behind the literary aspect of these episodes is an international aspect to the battle.

One feature of the battle that easily lent itself to legend was the employment of banners. Both sides used them so that the commanders could follow the movement of troops, while any soldiers who became separated from their comrades could return. *Cocad Gáedel re Gallaib* claims that Sitric observed the progress of the battle by standing on the ramparts of his fortress, where he could watch the movement of the standards. Among Brian's troops were 70 banners, including a "lucky" banner that was variegated in color and had led men to victory in seven previous battles. The Irish were not the only ones with a banner that brought good luck. *Orkneyinga Saga* describes a magical raven banner made for Jarl Sigurd by his Irish mother, Eithne. This banner brought victory to the troops that followed it, but death to the person who carried it. Sigurd's men refused to touch the banner, so he was forced to carry it and lost his life. Ravens were the symbols of the Norse god Odin, who had two named *Huginn* and *Muninn* to bring him news from all the world. Raven banners are found elsewhere, such as the Viking army in Devonshire in 878 that had a standard called Hræfn ("Raven"). Sigurd's banner is similar to the banner of Cnut. In times of war the figure of a raven appeared on the plain white silk background. There would be victory if the bird's beak was open and wings flapping, but defeat if it was drooping.[74]

This leads to the question, did Sitric Silkenbeard actually fight at Clontarf, or was he merely a spectator? *Cocad Gáedel re Gallaib* insists that he remained within the fortress, where he watched the battle with his wife. *Orkneyinga Saga*, followed by *Njal's Saga*, states that Sitric fought in the battle, and that his flight from the combat was the reason for the scattering of the Viking forces. Finally, there is the poem *Darraðarljóð*, composed soon after the battle, which claims that a "Young King" (i.e. Sitric) fought valiantly. The Scandinavian materials are probably correct that Sitric did fight. The author of *Cocad Gáedel re Gallaib* appears to be indulging in historical revisionism because elsewhere the text claims that all the Vikings who fought at Clontarf perished in the battle. Since Sitric did not die for another twenty-eight years, he had to be placed away from the battle.

The combat at Clontarf lasted for hours, and the outcome was not decided until late afternoon. The decisive contest occurred at a place known as *drochat Dubgaill*

("Dubgall's Bridge"), probably located at the same place as the "Old Dublin Bridge" (connecting Bridgefoot Street with Oxmantown) that was the sole bridge crossing of the Liffey until the seventeenth century.[75] The bridge might have been post-humously named as the place where Sitric's uncle Dubgall was slain. Among the Vikings, the building or naming of a bridge in honor of a family member was considered a pious deed. As the defenders of the bridge scattered, the Leinster–Viking force broke. They were virtually leaderless after Sigurd of the Orkneys and Máel Mórda of Leinster were slain. The Vikings tried to retreat to their ships, but the escape turned into a slaughter. Their vessels had been beached above the usual high water mark, but an exceptionally high tide, which has been confirmed mathematically, reached the ships and caused them to float into the middle of the river. The stranded seamen could either try to swim to the ships in mid-channel, not an easy task when encumbered with armor, or they could remain on the shore and fight it out with Brian's forces.

Disaster struck the Irish as well. Brian's son Murchad was slain, while Brian was cut down by Vikings who had become separated from the main battle, led by Brodor of York. The story in *Cocad Gáedel re Gallaib* that they came upon Brian as he was praying is also remembered by the chronicler Marianus Scottus.[76] The Vikings were about to pass by (believing Brian to be a priest) when one of them, who had previously served as a mercenary in his forces, recognized the high king. Brian was surrounded and slain. When evening came the Munstermen held the field, but they were only slightly better off than their opponents. Even though the Leinster–Viking coalition had been broken, Brian's troops were unable to exploit their survival. Too decimated by the slaughter to attempt to storm the fortress of Dublin, the survivors were led home by Donnchad, Brian's younger son. According to *Cocad Gáedel re Gallaib*, he had to content himself with butchering some of the Dublin oxen on the green in front of the fortress, before his army literally fought its way to Munster.

The remnants of the Viking fleet sailed away. In the aftermath developed tales of unexpected mercy and courage. They are not history, but examples of the type of stories that became attached to the Battle of Clontarf. Two of the legends preserved in *Njal's Saga* are worth repeating. The first concerns a Viking named Hræfn ("Raven," like the banner), who was among the survivors fleeing from the fray. He was a Christian who had made several pilgrimages to Rome. As Hræfn tried to swim out to the ships, he saw devils pulling him under the water. So in despair he prayed to St. Peter, "Twice your dog has run to Rome, and he will do so again if you allow it." Immediately the devils loosened their grip and Hræfn escaped to fulfill his vow. The second story is about a Viking named Thorstein, who paused in the midst of his flight to the ships in order to tie his shoelace. When his Irish pursuer asked why he stopped, Thorstein replied that he had no reason to be in a hurry, because his home was in Iceland and he could not reach it by nightfall. His pursuer generously gave him quarter.

✠

Who won the Battle of Clontarf? The medieval Irish records are in no doubt that Brian was the victor. In this they are followed by modern scholars and even some medieval Icelandic sagas. *Orkneyinga Saga* says bluntly that Brian died, but won the victory. Ignored is the fact that Brian's troops did not capture the town of Dublin, and that Sitric was free from the lordship of Brian's family in the aftermath of this battle. A more ambiguous appraisal comes from *Njal's Saga*. There are two accounts of the battle: a very long prose narrative that claims the battle was an Irish victory and a poem.

The poem is called *Darraðarljóð*. Composed, probably in Ireland, in the years immediately after the Battle of Clontarf, it is quite accurate in its limited account.[77] *Darraðarljóð* has eleven stanzas. The first three stanzas describe a weaving by Valkyries who are making a "web of battle" on a loom in which the threads and devices are replaced by weapons and human entrails and limbs. The fourth stanza moves on to the battle of a "young king" whom the Valkyries will follow into battle. This king survives behind bloodstained shields, but others are less fortunate. Among the slain are a great king and a jarl who is killed by spears. A great grief is inflicted on the Irish by a people who once clung to the coast, but now rule great stretches of territory. The poem concludes by claiming that news of the battle will be broadcast widely, and the young king hailed by songs of victory. Identification of the poem's allusions is easily made. The verses describe a people who once clung to the coast now holding vast territories: they are the Viking settlers of Dublin. The young king of the poem is Sitric Silkenbeard, the jarl is Sigurd of the Orkneys, and the great king is Brian.

The pagan tone of *Darraðarljóð* is more evidence of paganism persisting among the Vikings, while the character Brodor in *Njal's Saga* is a reminder that lapsed Christians also were not unknown. This is not a literary affectation. In one of the few personal letters from the Anglo-Saxon period, preserved in an eleventh-century manuscript, an unnamed writer urges his brother, Edward, to abandon the heathen practices he has acquired.[78] He points out that this is a disgrace and insult to his countrymen, and particularly mentions the pagan practices of countrywomen that he encounters.

Like *Darraðarljóð*, another story claims a victory for the Vikings at the Battle of Clontarf. This is the adventure of a man from Dublin called the "White Merchant" that survives in an English synopsis in the Book of Howth.[79] According to this tale, the conflict was caused when the "White Merchant" went on a trading expedition, leaving his wife in the care of the Irish high king Brian. During his absence, Brian's son Morcke (Murchad) committed adultery with her. They were found asleep together by the merchant when he arrived home early. The injured husband quietly exchanged his sword for that of Morcke. He then complained to Brian, who allowed him to choose a form of compensation. The merchant's choice was a battle with the

Irish prince at Clontarf on the same day the following year. The merchant then sailed to Denmark to recruit troops because it was "whence his generation came." On the appointed day the two sides clash. The initial advantage is with the Irish who drive the Danes to "collis," which is Irish for woods. The Danes return, however, and defeat the Irish, killing Brian and leaving Morcke for dead north of the "stynging" stream, which seems to mean the River Liffey. The story continues with an episode in which a priest came to look for his son on the battlefield and learned that he had fled from the fight, which led to the Irish defeat. The severely injured Morcke was put to death because he might reveal the treason, but before this he wrote a message to his brother, Donogh (Donnchad), on a token. The treason was revealed and the priest's son was executed. Then follows another, separate, story explaining why the Battle of Clontarf was lost.

Literary remembrances aside, one of the undoubted victors of the Battle of Clontarf was Máel Sechnaill. Brian's death led to his recognition again as high king. Less clear is the benefit of Clontarf to Brian's family. Brian was slain, his army had to fight its way home, and several years passed before a Munster king influenced events again outside the province. The difficulties of his son Donnchad on the return home were largely with his erstwhile allies who saw an opportunity to break the supremacy of the upstart Dál Cais. In the north, Sigurd of the Orkneys was dead, temporarily ending the prominence of the Orkney jarls in Britain, and his sons fought among themselves for supremacy.

For the Olafssons and Haraldssons, the answer to the question of gain or loss is mixed. Sitric saw his troops slaughtered, his allies scattered, and members of his family slain. For more than a dozen years, the Olafsson dynasty continued its decline in Irish political affairs. On the other hand, the town of Dublin was not destroyed or plundered, and Sitric was still alive. Regardless of any treaty he had made with Sigurd, the latter's sons were in no position to enforce it. The Haraldssons saw one of their princes slain, and it may be assumed that the contingent from the Isles suffered many casualties. There was one bright spot for them. Domination from the Orkneys was broken and no threat came from Dublin.

In the years immediately following his discomfiture at Clontarf, Sitric endured a series of reverses in Ireland. Sometimes it must have seemed that even nature was collaborating with his enemies. In 1015 a plague ravaged Dublin and Leinster. Seizing his chance, Máel Sechnaill marched south and burned the town's suburbs. Family alliances became frayed. While the Vikings of Dublin allied with Leinster for an unsuccessful attack on Odba (county Meath, near Navan) in 1017, the alliance between Dublin and the Uí Fáeláin of Leinster collapsed the next year when Sitric blinded his cousin Bróen (the son and heir of Máel Mórda) in Dublin.

Military reverses had economic consequences too. One sign of this comes from the coinage issued at Dublin. After the Battle of Clontarf, the Dublin moneyers began to produce a silver penny that was a reduced-weight imitation of the English

Long-cross pennies of Æthelraed (issued between 997 and 1003). The reduction in weight suggests that business was not going well at Dublin and that there was a deliberate attempt to stimulate it with the equivalent of a currency devaluation. In addition to the reduction in weight, there was a stylistic change in the Dublin coinage, which suggests that the amount of coin in circulation had declined sharply and there was a rush to produce more money. A virtue could have been made of necessity, as the lighter Dublin coins would have lured English traders, whose heavier coins gave them an advantage in currency exchange. Lighter coins encouraged exports (which were cheaper) while discouraging imports (which were more expensive). Apparently the problem was not limited to the western shore of the Irish Sea, for a similar currency adjustment was occurring in England. In both England and Dublin light coins suggest economic depression. These changes do suggest that the Dublin market was being managed in an adroit manner, necessary for any successful emporium. Adam of Bremen recorded how easily a market could be ruined, when heavy taxes imposed at the port of Bremen drove away the merchants.[80]

Economic problems at Dublin were not all due to the Battle of Clontarf. There was turmoil throughout its trading zone at this time. The unexpected death of Svein Forkbeard in February of 1014, only a few months after winning the Kingdom of England, was responsible for a great deal of the upheaval. Despite the support of the Danish army, Svein's son, Cnut, was forced to return to Denmark when the English nobles recalled Æthelraed from his exile in Normandy. Despite his pledges of fair government, Æthelraed and his son Edmund "Ironsides" busied themselves with taking revenge on those who had supported the Danish regime. A particularly destructive punishment-raid took place in 1016, when Edmund and Earl Uhtred of Northumbria ravaged Mercia as far as Chester because the Mercians had refused to come out against the Danes. There are few details about the attack, but the damage must have been severe, and Chester began its gradual economic decline. An additional element of disaster for the English was the Scottish annexation of Lothian to the River Tweed either in 1016 or 1018 after the victory at the Battle of Carham by the Scots king Malcolm II.[81] The Tweed became, as it remains, the boundary between the Kingdoms of England and Scotland.

In Scandinavia the Danish overlordship of the Norse had endured, off and on, since the tenth century. The brief reign of Olaf Tryggvason in the last years of the tenth century inspired a younger generation of Norse aristocrats. The main Norwegian allies of Svein Forkbeard were the jarls of Lade, now Eirik Hakonarson assisted by his son Hakon. This family was powerful and respected, but they were to be challenged, circa 1015, by a prince who had spent most of his young life fighting as a mercenary in Britain and Francia. His name was Olaf the Stout, but he is better known today as St. Olaf. Olaf had his claims to rule recognized in Norway, but his success also fueled a reaction against Danish lordship that led to repercussions by the middle of the century.

⚜

The first quarter of the eleventh century had not been a happy time for the Olafssons. Their weakness in comparison with the great Irish princes was revealed at the Battle of Clontarf. The massed might of the Viking colonists in the British Isles together with the armies of Leinster were unable to defeat an Irish army representing, at most, a third of the island. In the immediate aftermath of the battle, the Olafssons were militarily weak and Dublin was economically depressed. The same was true outside Ireland. As far north as the Orkneys, there is a great silence about the Vikings of the southern and northern Isles. Jarl Sigurd of the Orkneys, whose empire building had reached as far as the Irish Sea, passed into legend. One story claims that his ghost was seen riding into the side of a hill in Caithness.

The year 1014 marked a change throughout the northeast Atlantic littoral. In Ireland and England there was a brief return to the political status quo that had prevailed before the storms of the eleventh century. The Danish supremacy in England collapsed after the unexpected death of Svein Forkbeard and the Anglo-Saxon monarch Æthelraed was restored to his throne. His return owed much to his foes, for without confusion among the Danes and their supporters, there is little doubt that Æthelraed would not have died in possession of his throne in April 1016. Challenge to the Danish lordship among the Norse, with the return to Norway of Olaf in 1014 or 1015 led to the restoration of independent native rule. In Ireland, the death of the high king Brian at Clontarf allowed his rival Máel Sechnaill to regain his former supremacy for a few more years.

Soon, however, this political status quo would be completely upset again. The sons of Sigurd of the Orkneys began to raid the Irish Sea region two-dozen years after the Battle of Clontarf. In Ireland, after Máel Sechnaill's death in 1022, the mighty Uí Néill confederation temporarily became insignificant, mainly because of factional rivalries. This ushered in a period of political competition throughout Ireland as various princes, among them Brian's son (and Sitric's half-brother) Donnchad, fought for recognition as high king. The most important change was in England where, by December 1016, Æthelraed and his son Edmund were dead. The new master of the land was Svein Forkbeard's son Cnut. He immediately began to consolidate his control of the country, and to assemble what almost might be called a pan-Atlantic empire. By the second quarter of the eleventh century, Cnut was ready to turn his attention to the Olafssons and Haraldssons.

5

From Dublin to England and Norway

İN BOTH IRISH and Viking literature, Clontarf was more than just a battle, it was a meeting of this world with the supernatural. *Cocad Gáedel re Gallaib* has witches, goblins, and demons howling and gibbering when the armies clashed. Even the champion of Christianity is included, and on the night before the combat a banshee visited the high king Brian to tell him that he would die the next day. In the Viking poem *Darraðarljóð*, the atmosphere is almost entirely pagan. As a man looks into a window, he sees Valkyries/witches chanting verses while they work at a loom. Human heads are the weights, a sword is the beater, and an arrow is the shuttle. The Valkyries chant that they move through the battle with drawn swords, deciding who will live and who will die.

By the end of 1014 the Olafssons and Haraldssons must have felt that the swords of the Valkyries had been hovering very close to them. They had lost kinsmen and supporters at Clontarf. The following years were difficult. Even before Clontarf the Viking supremacy seemed to be waning. The death of the Danish conqueror Svein Forkbeard in February of 1014 had cleared the way for the reinstatement of his foe, the English king Æthelraed. When, two months later, Sitric Silkenbeard and his allies were bloodied at the Battle of Clontarf, contemporary observers could be forgiven for thinking that it was the end of an era. They were almost right.

Within a dozen years, however, circumstances had changed and the fortunes of the Viking settlers again were in the ascendant. Svein Forkbeard's son, Cnut, returned to England where military campaigning led to his acceptance as king by all the English late in 1016. Once again the orientation of the kingdom turned towards the north. Scandinavian literature and crafts circulated throughout the northern Atlantic. Icelandic poets journeyed south to England and made it, briefly, an important center for skaldic verse.[1] Decorative styles from Scandinavia flourished in Ireland and the Isles, where some of them survived longer than in their homelands. The style known as Ringerike appeared in Ireland very soon after its development in Scandinavia, and it came to Dublin directly from England; elements of it were continuing to be used into the twelfth century.[2] The Icelandic historian Snorri Sturluson, writing two centuries later, tells us that many powerful men joined Cnut because they were overwhelmed by the splendor of his court and the wealth he lavished upon his friends. There was peace throughout his domain. Among the Norwegians who had initially welcomed Cnut's rival Olaf as their king, many came to feel that he acted as a tyrant.

The Olafssons enjoyed a period of success in the second quarter of the eleventh century. Their economic and military reverses receded as they achieved a level of influence equal to any known by their ancestors. Commerce prospered at Dublin, and its coins are found throughout the North Atlantic region. Sitric Silkenbeard became embroiled in affairs beyond the Irish Sea, and his fortunes were more heavily influenced by events in Britain and Scandinavia than at any time since the tenth century.

The influence from England and Scandinavia on a Viking family in Ireland leads to one of the many uncertainties about this period: Sitric Silkenbeard's relationship to Cnut. Did the king of the Danes and English add the Olafssons to his clients? The question is prompted partly by Cnut's career, which was international in outlook. Cnut was recognized as king first by the English of Northumbria and, by the end of 1016, was king of all England; to which he added the kingship of the Danes in 1019, after the death of his elder brother. By 1028 he was king of the Norse, and there is the occasional claim that he held lordship over some of the Swedes. During the last years of his reign, there were claims that he was the overlord of the Scots, while his authority among the Welsh is suggested by various records. Through marriages and betrothals, Cnut had ties to noble families of continental Europe. Negotiations for the engagement of his daughter Gunnhild to the future Emperor Henry III may have begun as early as 1029.[3] Cnut's personal ties to Normandy began in July of 1017 when he married Emma, the daughter of Duke Richard I and the widow of Æthelraed. They were briefly expanded when his sister Estrid (known as Margaret in Norman records) was married to Duke Robert, the grandson of Richard, who later repudiated her and fled to Jerusalem on a pilgrimage to escape Cnut's wrath.

In the years immediately after the Battle of Clontarf, Sitric Silkenbeard behaved like a minor Irish princeling. He raided Kells in 1018 and carried off many captives, either to be ransomed or sold into the flourishing slave trade that was a prized source of revenue in eleventh-century Ireland.[4] The collapse of the Leinster alliance provided Sitric with the opportunity to lead a raid south in 1021, but he was defeated at Delgany (county Wicklow). That same year the high king Máel Sechnaill's wife, Máel Muire, Sitric's sister, predeceased her ailing husband. Her death removed whatever restraining influence she might have had on her spouse and his subjects. In 1022 the Dublin fleet sailed north against the Ulaid, but it was decimated during the ensuing sea-battle against the ships commanded by Niall mac Eochaid. The crews were taken into captivity together with their ships.

Matters went from bad to worse for Sitric after Máel Sechnaill died on September 22, 1022, at the age of 73. The great Irish princes began to compete for recognition as high king. The political situation was chaotic because there was no clear choice for supremacy among the Irish, a situation reflected in the historical records. The contemporary verse-history *Prophecy of Berchán* remarks that Ireland was in evil times after Máel Sechnaill's death, while the tract "On the Reigns and Times of Ireland after the Faith" states that there was no single dominating overlord.[5] Dublin became a prize for those who would rule Ireland and wanted the town's wealth to finance their ambitions.

In 1023 Sitric allowed Donnchad Ua Duinn, the prince of his northern neighbors the Síl nÁedo Sláine of Brega, to be abducted from the Dublin assembly and carried eastwards across the sea to an unidentified location. This assembly was the "Thing," and Dublin's Thingmount ("assembly hill") stood about seventy feet high when it was sketched in 1682.[6] At this assembly the "lawspeaker" (*lögsögumaðr*), one of whom was called the "orator" on his death at the Battle of Tara in 980, would have recited a portion of the traditional laws. This glimpse into the organization of Sitric's domain shows it had some of the administrative machinery familiar throughout the northern world.

In 1025 Flaithbertach Ua Néill, king of Cenél nEógain and the new overlord of the Uí Néill, took hostages from Sitric in support of his bid for the high kingship. The next year Sitric's half-brother, Donnchad, the son of Brian, took hostages from Dublin as part of his efforts to seize the high kingship. The giving of these hostages brought no security. In 1026 Dublin was raided by Niall mac Eochada of Ulaid in

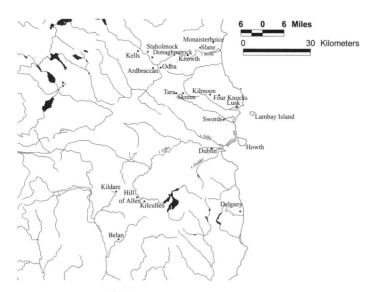

MAP 5. *Eastern Irish Coast*

revenge for the naval attack of 1022. With Niall on that expedition was a certain Roen, a prince of Clann Cholmáin, of the dynasty of Máel Sechnaill. Sitric was forced to make a new alliance with the men of Brega. In 1027 Olaf, the son of Sitric and Sláine, joined King Donnchad of Brega in a raid on *Scrín Moholmoc* (now Staholmock, county Meath); Sitric and Donnchad fought a battle at Lickblaw where Donnchad and Roen of Clann Cholmáin were slain.

In retrospect, Sitric's reign from 1000 to 1028 may be divided into two periods, before and after the Battle of Clontarf. In the first period, Sitric was the client of Brian Boru and Dublin was relatively peaceful. The standard of its coinage was good and closely mirrored English issues. The second period began with the revolt of 1013, leading to the Battle of Clontarf, and lasted until 1028. After throwing off the overlordship of Brian Boru, during the second period Sitric was harassed constantly by his neighbors. Contestants for the high kingship camped outside Dublin's gates demanding hostages. Sitric's military expeditions were generally unsuccessful, and he could barely defend Dublin. The town's wealth continued to make it a tempting target, but those riches depended on security and stability. The reduction in weight of Dublin's coinage after the Battle of Clontarf suggests that the conflict had precipitated economic decline. Attacks on Dublin would not entice merchants to bring their wares to the town, and the general economic malaise in Britain did nothing to improve matters.

Sitric Silkenbeard experienced a significant change in fortunes for the last eight years of his reign. From 1028 until his abdication in 1036 he was as successful as previously he had been unsuccessful. His troops were victorious and the extent of his domain increased, both within and without Ireland. The usual round of petty warfare continued, of course, and not everything went Sitric's way. His son, Olaf, was captured by the men of Brega in 1029 and held for ransom, while another son named Glúniairn was killed during a raid into Brega in 1031.

Alongside those misfortunes were the types of victory that the Olafssons had not seen for almost two decades. In 1032 Sitric, fighting without allies, won a victory at the estuary of the Boyne against a coalition of three principalities: the Conailli Muirtheimne, the Uí Dortháin, and the Uí Méith. At the same time his targets in the endemic local warfare become more impressive. In 1031 Sitric raided the celebrated church of Ardbraccan (county Meath) for captives and cattle. He burned two hundred men in the stone church before carrying off into captivity another two hundred. Four years later he returned, but this second attack led to retaliation from his half-brother Conchobar, the king of Clann Cholmáin, who was the son of Máel Sechnaill and Sitric's mother, Gormflaith. Conchobar raided the church of Swords, in the northeast of Dublin's territory, taking away cattle and captives. Unlike earlier raids, however, Conchobar did not attempt to attack the town itself. So secure was Sitric that he could revive his feud with the Vikings of Waterford in 1035. In what might have been an evening of ancient scores, the king of Waterford named Ragnall son of Ragnall, a grandson of the Ivar who had forced Sitric to flee in 994, was executed in Dublin.

Many of the people captured during raids were held for ransom. In 1029, his occasional alliance with the southern Uí Néill kingdom of Brega again ended when Sitric's son, Olaf, was seized by a man whose son was being held hostage by Sitric. The avenging father handed Olaf to the new king of Brega named Mathgamain Ua Riagáin, who set the terms for the princeling's release. Among the Irish, as elsewhere in Europe, the ransom of well-born captives was important, both to gain revenues and as a means of exhausting the victim's resources. The individual Irish annals give different details about the price of Olaf's freedom, but when read together they give a glimpse of the wealth at Sitric's disposal. The ransom was set at sixty ounces of gold, sixty ounces of white silver, twelve hundred cows, the release of the son of the man who had taken Olaf, the sword of Carlus, one hundred and twenty British horses, and the hostages that Sitric held from kingdoms in the north of Ireland and Leinster. Added to this total were eighty cows that were paid to the man who made supplication for Olaf's release.

The capture and ransom of Sitric's son, Olaf, illustrates how traditional forms of political manipulation were becoming influenced by economic prosperity. Some items in the ransom need no explanation, such as the gold and silver. They might have come from private holdings or, in the case of the silver, from the same stores as the bullion found in Dublin when the town was captured in the year 1000. Other demands are less obvious, but informative. At first glance the inclusion of British horses seems unusual. Irish horses were famous throughout the Middle Ages for their superior conformation, speed, and stamina. Chrétien de Troyes' "Story of the Knight of the Cart," written during the first generation of the Anglo-Norman invasions of Ireland, mentions noble youths who had the best of everything, including good Irish steeds. The importing of horses from Britain into Ireland was, however, an ancient trade, and the foreign animals were avidly sought. Late in the eleventh century horses from Scotland and "foreign horses," including a horse from Francia, were considered high status goods.[7]

The demand for British horses suggests that by the eleventh century Dublin was one of the ports for importing livestock from abroad, and there might have been a horse market in the town at this early date. When Sitric's troops attacked Máel Sechnaill at Tara in 1000 as part of Brian Boru's army, they were mounted. Sitric and his family could have been involved in horse breeding. Horses require large tracts of land for grazing and are expensive to feed if stabled. Those resources were available only to the wealthiest members of society. Olaf Cuaran might have maintained a stud near the Hill of Skreen, from which he gave a horse to the poet Cináed ua hArtacáin. The number of horses paid for his son's ransom suggests that Sitric was personally involved in the horse trade.

Olaf's ransom was a great treasure, especially when compared with other large-scale payments. According to the *Annals of Tigernach*, when Máel Sechnaill seized Dublin after the Battle of Tara in 980 he took two thousand cows in addition to jewels and unidentified goods. The *Chronicon Scotorum* notes that when the Airghialla plundered Armagh in 995 they took two thousand cows as loot; and when Brian of Munster sought the goodwill of Armagh for his claim to be high king, he placed an offering of twenty ounces of gold (equivalent to 240 cows) on the altar. In 985 Máel Sechnaill absconded with the shrine of Patrick at Armagh, and in compensation for his offense he awarded to the church the visitation of Meath, a banquet for every fort, and seven cumhals (equivalent to three cows). Looking ahead, the *Annals of the Four Masters* claim that the ransom for the king of Dealbhna Mór in 1096 was thirty ounces of gold and one hundred cows in addition to eight hostages.

The ransom for Olaf also can be placed in a wider context. Looking to the south, an interesting comparison can be made with the tolls paid by English merchants every three years to the king of the Lombards, listed in a treatise on the imperial customs stations. This included 800 ounces of pure silver, 2 greyhounds with collars, 2 each of shields, swords, and lances with a supplemental fee of 2 fur coats and 32 ounces of silver to the official in charge; the supplementary might have been roughly 10 percent of the total value of goods traded.[8] For the early eleventh century, it is difficult to give more than an estimation of the comparative value of a mix of goods and livestock, although some important studies are available for guidance.[9] Among the Gaels, gold was valued at twelve times that of silver, and a milk cow was equivalent to an ounce (*unga*) of silver. The value of imported ponies is uncertain. When turning back to the ransom of Olaf, the value of the gold and silver combined was roughly equivalent to 780 ounces of silver. Adding to this the equivalent value in silver of the cattle raises the total to 1,980 ounces. So the value of just the precious metals and cattle in the ransom for Olaf was roughly—very roughly—twice the value of the silver paid in tolls every three years by the English merchants in Lombardy, and very close to the value of the two thousand cows taken by Máel Sechnaill in 980. Little wonder that a town capable of giving up wealth on this scale was a magnet for ambitious princes.

The amount of Olaf's ransom might not have been arbitrary. While we know little about the details of Dublin's commerce at this time, the ransom might have included a refund to the men of Brega for the cost of doing business with the men of Dublin. A similar idea might be behind an obscure item in the *Book of Rights*, which notes that the king of the foreigners (i.e. Vikings) paid 300 suits of clothes and 50 horses for admitting (apparently Irish) women and children to their land.[10] Special privileges for specific groups of people were commonplace, and the late tenth-century commercial treaty between Olaf Tryggvason and Æthelred is one example. Sometimes the conditions for trade were purchased. At London, for example, the Billingsgate tolls set different tariffs for merchants from Rouen or Flanders. The subjects of the Emperor paid a fee of cloth, pepper, vinegar, and gloves to enjoy the freedom of the market, which was collected at Christmas and Easter.

Selected Irish principalities might have been allowed to sell their wares at the Dublin market, for a fee. Some of the Irish hoards containing coins struck at Dublin could contain the profits from commerce.[11] Many of the hoards are located in a

semi-circle from north of the river Boyne to south of the Wicklow mountains, including a cache of coins deposited circa 1027, at Fourknocks (county Meath) in the
plain of Brega, which also has a silver ingot.

There were Irish markets around Dublin, and Vikings traded at them. A charter-
note (circa 1106–1153) in the Book of Kells mentions a market at the church of Kells,
and the lord of Meath is described as "the king of Meath of the market" (*rí Midi in
marcaid*) in the *Book of Rights*.[12] South of Dublin was the fair of Carman, which is
described in a poem composed between 1033 and 1079.[13] This gathering was held the
first week of August every third year. In addition to sports and recitations, merchants
were allowed to sell their wares. The poem on Carman lists three markets. There was
one market for food, another for livestock, and a third that was the "great market of
the screeching foreigners" (*margad mór na nGall ngréc[h]ach*). The poem specifically mentions their gold and fine cloth (*ór is arddetach*). By gold the poet means
gold jewelry rather than bullion, although ornaments could be used as sources for
metal. At Dublin, gold bracelets and a gold ring have been found in the tenth- and
eleventh-century strata of excavations, and the verses of Gunnlaug Serpent's Tongue
ask Sitric Silkenbeard for a gold ring as a reward for his poem.[14] The Dublin excavations have also produced several types of imported fabrics that could be considered
"fine cloth." These include diamond twills woven in England, silk tabbies from
Byzantium, patterned silk from Byzantium or Persia, and gold braids that were possibly produced in central Asia.[15]

During this period Sitric was prospering as the population and territory under
his control were increasing. The physical presence of Dublin was an oddity in Irish
society, but this fact did not provoke hostility. Quite the contrary, by the twelfth century Irish poets included the town among the wonders of Ireland.[16] Prior to the
twelfth century, one can only speculate as to the precise bounds of what the Icelandic
sagas describe as "Dublinshire," but topographical information gleaned from the Irish
records allows some estimation for the eleventh century. The traditional southern
boundary was the River Dodder, separating Dublin from the kingdom of the Uí
Cúala Laigen. This had been surpassed by the mid-tenth century, when Dublin's
territory extended as far south as the modern town of Dalkey, where survivors fled
from the attack on the fortress.

Geography dictated Sitric's routes for expansion, and the most promising direction was north along the coast in the region that became known as Fingal (Ir *Fine
Gall*). By the middle of the eleventh century Fingal extended from Dubgall's Bridge
(*Droichat Dubgall*) on the Liffey north as far as Lusk.[17] The rapidity of land annexation is demonstrated by events at the church at Swords. The body of the high king
Brian was waked at Swords in 1014, and the church was burned by Sitric's men in
1020. By 1035 Swords was within Sitric's territory when his half-brother, Conchobar,
burned it in revenge for Sitric's raid on Ardbraccan in 1031.

Sitric's personal residence might not have been within Dublin, but on an estate
several miles away. Living conditions within towns were not always pleasant, and

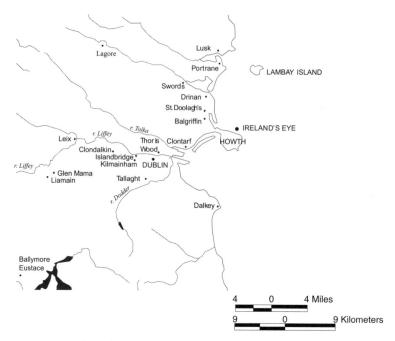

MAP 6. *Kingdom of Dublin*

Dublin was so crowded by the eleventh century that houses were built outside the town walls. Two eleventh-century poems and the *Book of Rights* mention a royal estate south of Dublin.[18] The first poem is "Here is a Happy, Graceful History" (*Atá sund seanchas suairc seang*). This composition is complete historical revisionism, intending to give Armagh the right to take revenues from Dublin's churches with the claim that St. Patrick visited the Vikings of Dublin and converted them to Christianity centuries before they settled along the Liffey. Twice in the poem a place called Liamain is mentioned in connection with the lordship of Dublin. First, the tithes the Dubliners were to render to St. Patrick's church (i.e., Armagh) were to be paid from Liamain. Second, there would be constant warfare between Tara and Liamain, symbolizing the conflict between the Irish and the Vikings. The second poem, "Meath, Homestead of the Clan of Conn" (*Mide maigen clainni Cuind*), is a list of the kings of Meath of the dynasty of Clann Cholmáin, Máel Sechnaill's kindred. Twice (stanzas 36 and 42) verses refer to warfare against Liamain that was undertaken by the Irish princes. Finally, among the stipends listed in the *Book of Rights* are 30 ships and 30 horses to the warriors of Liamain. Here they seem to be separate from Dublin, which receives only 10 each of women, ships with beds and horses.

There are two places called Liamain nearby Dublin. One is Newcastle Lyons, the scene of the famous battle of Glen Mama. The other, more likely, candidate is Lyons Hill, about 5 miles southwest of the center of Dublin, not far from Tallaght. The hill is a prominent feature of the landscape and from its summit there is a panorama of the surrounding countryside. The identification with Lyons Hill fits the description of Liamain in the poem on the kings of Meath where it is described as "peaked Liamain."

What caused the sudden reversal of Sitric's fortunes? At least part of the answer is suggested by a pilgrimage. In 1028 Sitric and his northern neighbor Flannacán mac Cellaich, king of Brega (who was succeeded by Olaf Sitricsson's captor Mathgamain Ua Riagáin), made a pilgrimage to Rome. Sitric's visit to Rome was brief, while Flannacán remained behind. The speed of this trip illustrates how much faster travel had become since the early Middle Ages. In the seventh century the return journey from Ireland to Rome took three years; Sitric traveled to Rome and returned home in the same year.[19]

Sitric and Flannacán were only two of the travelers who journeyed to Rome after Cnut's famous pilgrimage of 1027, in what has been seen as his effort to be admitted to the "civilized fraternity of Christian kings."[20] This was more than a demonstration of personal piety, for Cnut timed his visit in order to be present at the coronation of Emperor Conrad II in March. Cnut was a great admirer of the Empire, and a number of materials connected with him show the influence of imperial insignia. The encomiast of Cnut's queen, Emma, writing in Flanders between 1035 and 1040, recalled seeing the king when he visited St. Omer on his way to Rome. There Cnut, well known for his ostentatious generosity, prayed and placed gifts on the altars.

Cnut also had economic reasons for his journey. This point was noted in the letter of self-congratulation that he sent to his English subjects, which is preserved in the chronicle of John of Worcester.[21] He names two achievements. The first was the greater ease of travel to Rome for his subjects. Towards that end, Cnut had secured freedom from hindrances on the road, such as tolls, and he specifically notes that this was done both for pilgrims and for merchants. This was not a minor issue. The writer of the treatise on the imperial customs stations remembered the ferocious fights between English merchants and imperial officials. Cnut's second accomplishment also had an economic aspect, a reduction in the payments made by English clergy for their offices to the papal treasury. Glaringly obvious in the letter is the importance of commerce for Cnut. Through the payment of tolls and the making of treaties with the Emperor Conrad II and his wife's uncle King Rudolf III of Burgundy (the princes through whose lands those roads ran), Cnut was making a southern trade route more convenient for his subjects and clients.

Sitric's pilgrimage of 1028 might have been undertaken, in part, to obtain the necessary papal approval for the establishment of a bishopric at Dublin. The story of the foundation of the see of Dublin is preserved in the history of Holy Trinity, now Christ Church, in the Black Book of Christ Church.[22] Credit is given to Sitric Silkenbeard as the instigator and main financier of the project. He donated the site for the cathedral, along with gold and silver to pay for its construction, and estates to provide an income. The history claims that the church was constructed over the ruins of an older building, fantastically attributed to St. Patrick, but possibly a confused reference to construction carried out by the Bishop Patrick (1074–1084). While the building was underway, the bishop's chapel might have been in the royal palace. Private chapels were not uncommon among the Christian Vikings in Ireland, and one was maintained by a twelfth-century lord of Cork named *Gillebert*.[23]

The pope in 1028 was John XIX (1024–1032). John's death in 1032 is recorded in the *Annals of Tigernach*, one of the few papal obituaries in the Irish annals. Unusually, the *Annals of Tigernach* announce his death with his name in the world *Romanus papa Romae*; before his election he was known as Romanus "the Senator." This familiarity argues that Pope John gave permission for a bishop at Dublin. He was an obscure pontiff, despite being the brother of his predecessor Benedict VIII. His appearance in an Irish chronicle is noteworthy. He is the only pope mentioned by name in the medieval Irish annals for the eleventh century, although the *Annals of Ulster* repeat a vague story, without names, in the year 1048 when his nephew Benedict IX supposedly poisoned his successor Damasus II. John is not mentioned in the *Anglo-Saxon Chronicle*. Unfortunately no papal notice about the creation of a bishopric at Dublin survives, but this is a reflection of the poor preservation of papal records in the early eleventh century. For John's pontificate of nine years fewer than 50 rescripts survive. Part of the problem was physical. While the use of parchment was begun during the pontificate of Pope Benedict VIII, much continued to be written on papyrus, a fragile medium, and there was no contemporary papal register between the ninth century and the pontificate of Gregory VII.[24]

The establishment of a diocese at Dublin depended on the goodwill of the Holy Roman Emperor Conrad II. The Tusculan popes—as John, his brother Benedict VIII, and their nephew Benedict IX have been styled—were supporters of the emperor; and John was very much Conrad's creature. His involvement suggests why Conrad appears in the Irish annals. Both the annals of Tigernach and Ulster note the death of Emperor Henry II followed by the succession of Conrad. This is placed among the events of 1023, a year earlier than it actually occurred, which indicates that it was added some time later, unlike Conrad's battle with Odo of Blois in 1037 that the *Annals of Ulster* place under the year 1038. The Irish annals are interested in secular affairs on the continent for particular reasons. The information about Conrad suggests an interest in him personally rather than in the Empire generally.[25]

There were reasons why Conrad might be interested in Ireland. His center of power was at Worms, but his family originally came from the Moselle region of Upper Lotharingia. They had founded the monastery of Hornback, in the Bliesgau, which had been placed under the direction of St. Pirmin, who in the eleventh century was believed to be an Irishman. Another Irish connection was at Metz, whose counts were relatives of Conrad's mother, Adelheid. There was the monastery of St. Clement, a destination for Gaelic-speaking clergy since the tenth century Scottish reformer Catroe (d. 978) moved there at the direction of Bishop Adalbero, a patron of the

Gaelic-speaking clergy. In 992 Adalbero successfully petitioned Emperor Otto III to confirm his right to the restoration of an abbey outside the town walls that was dedicated to St. Symphorian.[26] The first abbot, Finenius, was an Irishman, and admission was restricted to Gaelic-speakers; only if their numbers failed were other nationalities to be introduced.

Dublin was originally designated a metropolitan, and its incumbent was an archbishop. Later in the eleventh century this was changed to a bishopric. The archbishop of Dublin was named Dúnan, and he took Donatus as his name in religion. No one is known to have preceded him and he died in 1074. If he became bishop circa 1028, then he served for 46 years before his death in 1074. His age is unknown, but if he received the pallium when he was 30 years old, he would have been 76 years old at the time of his death. Long lives and careers were not unknown. Abbot Dub-dá-leithe of Armagh died in 998 at the age of 73, Bishop Domnall Ua Énna of Dál Cais was 76 years old when he died in 1098, and in 1185 Bishop Amlaim Ua Muirethaigh of Armagh died at the age of 86. Tenure could also be long. *Orkneyinga Saga* claims that the twelfth-century William "the Old" of the Orkneys was bishop for 66 years, while, more contemporary with Donatus, Archbishop Guifred of Narbonne had a reign of 63 years (1016–1079), after being elevated to the archiepiscopal dignity when he was 10 years old. Archbishop Hugh of Rouen served for 47 years (942–89), and his successor Robert for 48 years (989–1037).

Archbishop Donatus oversaw extensive construction. He had built a church dedicated to St. Michael, but his main work was building the nave of the cathedral with two attached structures as well as the chapel of St. Nicholas in the northern part of the church. He also had the base constructed for a cross with an image of the crucifixion. Two legends became associated with the cross in the twelfth century, both told by Gerald of Wales. The first legend claims that the cross spoke when a merchant did not fulfill a contract that had been sworn on it. The other legend claimed that when the Dublin aristocracy was preparing to flee to the Isles as the Normans were capturing the city, they tried to take the cross with them, but it would not be budged.[27]

Donatus also collected relics. A list is preserved in the book of obits and martyrologies from Christ Church. There, in an ecclesiastical calendar at July 31, is the record of the relics collected by Donatus and deposited in a special container by the twelfth-century Bishop Gregory. The items included relics of St. Humber of Cologne, St. Olaf of Norway, and St. Audoen of Rouen, in addition to relics of Our Lord, the Apostles Peter and Andrew, and other saintly individuals. The relics indicate the international political and economic interests of Sitric's realm, with two interesting omissions: Ireland and Britain.[28]

Sitric gave to the cathedral community three estates north of the River Liffey: St. Doulough, Portrane, and Lambay Island. St. Doulough (or Cell Duilig) is within the parish of Balgriffen, also known as Grangegorman; the parish contains about 1,000 acres. Portrane is farther north and east, on the coast between Rush and Malahide, a little over four miles northeast of the famous monastery of Swords. The modern parish has more than 2,500 acres, but the land is poor quality. Directly opposite Portrane is Lambay Island, which is almost 600 acres in size. Despite its small area, this little island was valuable in the Middle Ages, with good soil and good fishing. Seals used to breed on the island and there is a well dedicated to the Holy Trinity (the original dedication of Christ Church). So the donations were a mixed lot, with varying values.

Piety need not have been Sitric's sole motivation for establishing a bishopric. Throughout Europe the usefulness of the bishop as a royal ally had long been known. Among the Scandinavian aristocracy, the Christian clergy built upon local hierarchies in order to make, or bolster, a central monarchy.[29] An example of this is Cnut's treasurer in England named Henry who became successively bishop of the Orkneys circa 1035 and bishop of Lund circa 1060, during the reign of Cnut's nephew Svein Ulfsson; he might be the same man as a Bishop Henry who was in Iceland at some unspecified time.[30]

While Sitric's journey was not the first from Ireland to Rome by any means (in 1024 a priest of Clonmacnoise named Fachtna died at Rome on his pilgrimage), he opened the way for other princes. In 1030 the Uí Néill prince Flaithbertach Ua Néill made a pilgrimage to Rome and returned in 1031, while in 1034 Sitric's son Olaf was killed in England while on his way to Rome, probably with a detour to the court of Cnut. Two routes from Ireland to the continent went across Britain, one across Northumbria and the other in the south.[31] In 1051 the king of Gailenga (one of the Irish client-kingdoms of the Vikings in Fingal) named Laighnen took his queen with him on a pilgrimage to Rome.

The setting up of a bishopric in Ireland with a precise geographical mandate suggests that Sitric's model came from Scandinavia or, more probably, England. The prominence given to the bishop of Dublin in an Irish setting and the grant of lands for his household are significant. Among the Irish at this time, the primary importance of the bishop was spiritual, and the control of estates left largely in the hands of laymen. There was an increasing dissatisfaction among some elements of the Irish clergy about this situation, especially as they came into contact with clergy from elsewhere in Europe. Dublin was one of the ports used by clergy traveling to and from continental Europe. The Life (*vita*) of Colmán mac Lúacháin, for example, mentions three clerics who made a pilgrimage to Rome via Dublin.[32]

One question about Archbishop Donatus has provoked debate: was he consecrated by the archbishop of Canterbury? His successors were. Their professions of obedience survive, as do details of their consecrations. The records of St. Mary's, Dublin, note that Donatus' immediate successor Patrick gave his profession "according to ancestral custom." In announcing Patrick's consecration, Archbishop Lanfranc of Canterbury declared that he did so as was the custom of his predecessors. In other contexts this phrase signifies earlier ecclesiastical dependence. For example, a letter from Archbishop Thomas of York to Archbishop Lanfranc of Canterbury notes the former's consecration of a bishop of the Orkneys on the basis of a letter from the jarl which notes the precedent (*Ac ille antcessorum tuorum ordine custodito*), probably a reference to the earlier Bishop Henry.[33]

The archbishop of Canterbury during much of Cnut's reign was Æthelnoth "the Good" (1022–1038). Æthelnoth's services were sought by clergy from outside England, and his labors on behalf of the churches among the Scandinavians were famous or infamous, depending on the view of the writer.[34] Adam of Bremen complained bitterly that Æthelnoth consecrated bishops for areas where the jurisdiction properly belonged to the archbishops of Hamburg-Bremen. This technicality did not seem to bother the princes of the land, as both Cnut and his rival Olaf of Norway recruited clergy from England.

The establishment of a bishopric at Dublin need not be a sign of hostility toward the Irish churches by Sitric. His family had connections with those churches, and it could be argued that the Olafssons were oriented towards the churches connected with St. Columba. Sitric's father had retired to Columba's church at Iona, while his great-grandson Gruffudd ap Cynan was educated at the major Columban church of Swords, only a few miles to the north of the town. There was some variation, and Sitric's daughter Ceallach (who died in 1042, the same year as her father) was a nun in a house dedicated to St. Finian. This was probably *Cell Finnend* ("church of Finian") in Fingal. A miracle at this church was attributed to St. Brigit of Kildare. A side of bacon was offered to the saint's community during a visit to the church, but they left without it and the bacon remained in Cell Finnend for a month. A dog guarded the bacon, without touching it and would not allow any other animal near it.[35]

Sitric is the first member of his family who is known to have made a pilgrimage to Rome. Sitric left Dublin peacefully and his subjects were unmolested during his absence. In light of his troubles in the previous years, why was Dublin not attacked the moment Sitric departed? The answer is suggested by a poem.

Among the contemporary verses in praise of Cnut are several composed by a skald named Ottar the Black (*svarti*). In his description of Cnut's empire, Ottar gives a list of his subjects: "Let us greet the king of the Danes, the Irish, the English and the Islanders; his praise travels through all the lands under heaven."[36] The precise date of this verse is uncertain, but the omission of the Norwegians suggests that it was composed before King Olaf's expulsion from Norway in 1028, after which Cnut could claim lordship.

There is little doubt about the poem's accuracy. Ottar was not an uncritical partisan of Cnut. Since the poem was intended for public recitation, any fictional inflation of his empire would have been considered satirical. What happens when those restraints are removed can be seen in the next century when an assessment of Cnut's domain by the nationalistic Danish chronicler Svein Aggeson expands it to include Francia and Italia.[37]

The Irish (*Irsk*) of Ottar's verses refers to the inhabitants of Ireland, not the Gaels of Scotland; by the eleventh century Old Norse verse is careful to distinguish between them.[38] *Irsk* is not necessarily limited to the "native" Irish, but it could also refer to the Viking colonists. A broad application of "Irish" is found in a coin imitating the *Quatrefoil* issue of Cnut that has the legend *Sihtric rex Irum*, "Sitric, king of the Irish." The die for this coin appears to have been made in England, and Chester has been suggested as its place of manufacture. So by the eleventh century Sitric and his subjects were considered "Irish" by their contemporaries outside Ireland. The manufacture in England of a coin-die for a king of Dublin is significant because the production and distribution of those dies were royal monopolies. Interestingly, this copy of the *Quatrefoil* issue ended the imitation at Dublin of Cnut's coins. The Dublin coinage reverted to a copy of the *Long Cross* type of Cnut's predecessor Æthelraed.[39]

Coin-dies made in England for Sitric indicate an international dimension to the trade that made the Olafssons wealthy and powerful. Another sign of the extent of Dublin's commercial sphere of influence comes from London, where there might be evidence of a colony of Dublin merchants.[40] During the rapid expansion of London in the tenth and eleventh centuries, settlements of foreign merchants were made outside the western walls. Just west of the River Fleet (remembered today in Fleet Street), on the site of a former Roman cemetery, was the church dedicated to St. Bride, better known as St. Brigit of Kildare. St. Brigit was one of the Irish saints venerated by the Dubliners, and they had built a church in her honor no later than the twelfth century. Excavations at Viking Dublin have uncovered a number of coins in the eleventh-century stratum with London mint signatures. Contemporary with the coins are disc-brooches uncovered at Viking Dublin identical to disc-brooches discovered in the excavation of a workshop at Cheapside.[41] Material from London where there was a church dedicated to a saint venerated at Dublin suggests that Sitric Silkenbeard's subjects had a merchant colony at London. If so, such a settlement could have been made only with royal permission.

Military cooperation between Sitric and Cnut is revealed by the *Annals of Tigernach* that record a raid on Wales by ships from England and Dublin in 1030. While Dublin's fleet often served as a mercenary force after the late eleventh century, this is the first unambiguous record of its involvement in a raid outside of Ireland since the battle of *Brunanburh* in 937. The attack appears to have been carried out in order to give Sitric a base on the Isle of Anglesey, which he certainly possessed sometime before 1034. His fortress was called *Castell Avloed* ("Olaf's castle"), which is now Moel-y-Don Ferry, located in the southeast of the Isle of Anglesey along the Menai Straits.[42] The fortress was named after Olaf, the son of Sitric Silkenbeard and Brian's daughter, Sláine.[43] That the "Viking prince" Olaf was three-quarters Irish is a useful illustration of how the integration of the two societies had progressed. Olaf continued this trend when he married a princess from northern Leinster named Máel Corcraig of Uí Muiredaig.[44] Their child, a daughter named Ragnhild, married a Welsh prince named Cynan, the son of Iago the king of Gwynedd. Their son was Gruffudd ap Cynan.

Olaf Sitricsson's tenure at *Castell Avloed* benefited from earlier political turmoil that shows Cnut's authority, and intervention from Ireland, in the area. A pretender from Powys named Llywelyn ap Seisyll took the kingship of Gwynedd circa 1018, and then faced attacks from rivals, one of whom was an Irishman named Reyn (Rhain), who claimed to be the son of Maredudd ap Owain, the opponent of Godfrey Haraldsson.[45] In 1022 Reyn led a fleet from Ireland to Wales, ships possibly supplied by Sitric. After some early successes, he was defeated by Llywelyn in a battle at the River Guili and returned to Ireland. After Llywelyn's death in 1023, there appeared Rhydderch ap Iestyn. The *Book of Llandaff* preserves a document setting out the bounds of his lordship: all Wales except for Anglesey, which was held by Iago ab Idwal.[46] Iago was the father of Ragnhild's husband, Cynan. The grants were secured by guaranties from Archbishop Æthelnoth of Canterbury and with letters from Cnut. Cnut's consent for a Welsh land transfer is not a detail that a Welsh writer would invent in the twelfth century, and his authority is claimed in the contemporary *Encomium* of his queen Emma.[47]

The defeats Dublin endured in the early eleventh century must have forced Sitric to consider how to contend with the great Irish lords.[48] A colony in Wales provided a safe haven should an escape be needed, and such a colony could also protect the merchant ships sailing between Dublin and Chester. How long Dublin controlled the colony at *Castell Avloed* is not known, but Sitric's son, Godred, was slain in Wales in 1036 by his cousin, identified only as the son of Glúniairn, almost certainly in a fight for control of *Castell Avloed*. Olafsson interests in Wales are suggested by Viking/Irish activity recorded in the Welsh chronicles *Brut y Tywysogyon* and *Annales Cambriae* between 1032 and 1049. Rhydderch was slain in 1033 by the Irish, who might have been Sitric's Vikings. Vikings captured Meurig ap Hywell circa 1038 and Gruffudd ap Llywelyn circa 1042. A Viking force was defeated by Hywell ab Edwin circa 1042, who then allied with them two years later for an attack on Gruffudd ap Llywelyn at the River Tywi. Finally, in late July 1049 a fleet from Ireland allied with Gruffudd ap Rhydderch for attacks in South Wales.

Coins, verses, and raids need to be set within the context of Sitric's presence at Cnut's court. This is found in three charters connected with the see of Crediton (later transferred to Exeter).[49] The first charter is a grant of lands at Abbots Worthy, Hants., to Bishop Lyfing of Crediton and is dated 1026. The second charter is the grant of half a hide of land at Meavey, Devon, to Æthelric *minister*, circa 1031; it was in the archives at Canterbury by the twelfth century. The final charter is a grant of land at Stoke Canon, Devon, to a Hunuwine *minister*. All three charters appear to be genuine, although there are chronological difficulties with the first two.[50] The charters were composed at Crediton and were witnessed by *Sihtric dux*.

Is this *Sihtric* to be identified with Sitric Silkenbeard of Dublin? The dates of the charters correspond with Sitric's dramatic change of fortune in Ireland. Crediton was located in an area with trading connections to Ireland, as revealed by artifacts uncovered at Dublin that point to trade with southwestern England. This contact becomes more visible later in connection with the English aristocracy, especially with Harold Godwinsson, earl of Wessex and the last Anglo-Saxon king, and his family.[51] An argument against the identification of the Sihtric of the charters with Sitric Silkenbeard of Dublin is that the former is styled *dux* rather than *rex*. There was flexibility in the use of titles for lesser princes, as seen for Sitric's contemporary, the famous Scottish prince Macbeth. He is called a "king" when he submitted to Cnut in 1031, but is styled *dux* in Marianus Scotus's record of his murder of Duncan I in 1040. An apparent loss of status from *rex* to *dux* reflects political reality. Sitric may have had an English moneyer minting coins that described him as king, but such would have counted for little in the estimation of powerful lords at Cnut's court. A tradition that Dublin was ruled by counts becomes visible in the early thirteenth century. The documents giving the history of the foundation of Christ Church, Dublin, describe Sitric as the son of Count Olaf of Dublin.[52]

Two English documents—a writ and a will—mention an Earl Sitric. An argument based on this material suggests that he flourished in the eleventh century, held lands in Hertfordshire, and is the same man as the Sitric of Cnut's charters.[53] The first text is a writ circa 1045–1049 claiming to be from the reign of Edward the Confessor (1042–1066), confirming his grant to Westminster Abbey of an estate at Aldenham (Hertfordshire). The form of the text and some of the words are unusual, which is attributed to a legal dispute with the abbot of St. Albans concerning the right to the land, also explaining why a brief history of the estate is given in the writ. The history begins with an Earl Sitric who gave the land to Abbot Ælfric of Westminster (d. 956). Previous commentators on this writ were unaware of any noble named Sitric in the mid-tenth century, and so they read Ælfric as a mistake for Ælfwig, the name of the abbot for twenty years after circa 997. That change did not completely solve the problem, since it placed Ælfwig's death circa 1017, a decade before the appearance of Sitric as a charter-witness. In order to make the connection with the Sitric of Cnut's charters, Ælfwig's tenure was shifted by another 10 years. All this was done in order to make the Sitric who granted lands to Westminster, Ælfwig, and the Sitric of Cnut's charters contemporaries.

The changes are sensible, but unnecessary. Numismatic evidence together with Frankish and Irish chronicles produces several men named Sitric who were contemporaries of Ælfric. Minted at York in the mid-tenth century were coins for a man named Sitric. He was not king of York, but was an important noble of the type who donated land to a religious house. This Sitric was an exact contemporary of Abbot Ælfric of Westminster and was very possibly the donor mentioned in the historical passage in the charter. Several other men with that name also were active in the mid-tenth century. A "Setric" led a raid into northern Francia circa 943 and was defeated. In Ireland, according to the *Annals of the Four Masters*, a Sitric was ruling Dublin when Muirchertach of the Leather Cloaks received hostages from the town during his famous "Circuit of Ireland." Twenty years later a Sitric Cam led an attack on Dublin from a base in Britain.[54] The writ concerning Aldenham needs no arbitrary revision of a tenth-century donation by a man named Sitric.

More interesting is the second document: a will made by a man named Wulf. The original is lost. All that survives are a thirteenth-century Latin abstract made by Matthew Paris, and an eighteenth-century transcription supposedly of an English text from a now-lost cartulary of St. Albans abbey. The date of this will is unknown. Matthew Paris claims it was written in the time of Edward the Confessor, but there is no date in the English text, so the chronology seems to have been Paris's addition. In it, Wulf distributed ecclesiastical materials (mass vestments, mass book, chalice), monies, horses, and land among institutions and individuals. The religious houses receiving gifts are St. Albans, Ramsey, the principal churches in England, and St. Peter's, Rome. Several of the bequests might be settlements of debts. A man named Dagfinn is left a mark of gold or more if he should deserve it. The wording of this passage suggests the Scandinavian legal practice of self-judgment (*sjálfdæmi*), when an aggrieved party defined what would satisfy him in order to reach a settlement, rather than an invitation for a beneficiary to take a larger share of the estate than is his due. In the English, but not Latin, text one of the individuals who receives a half mark of gold is Earl Sitric.

A clue to the interpretation of this charter is provided by the names of the beneficiaries. Several of them—Æthelric and Edward—are commonplace. The others are more informative: Dagfinn, Æfinn (probably a misspelling of Ælfwine rather than the Norse names Auðfinnr or Eyvindr), Sihtric, Thorod (for Thored), Osgod, Othin (also spelled Odda, probably the Norse name Auðun), and Saxa. The names are similar to those found among nobles connected with the court of Cnut.[55] Three of the names—Odda, Osgod, and Ælfwine—are the same as men who were witnesses with Sitric to Cnut's charter of 1026; a possible addition to that group is Thorod, if the Ðorð of the charter is a variant spelling of his name. Osgod was Cnut's retainer Osgod Clapa who held estates in Suffolk and possibly in Norfolk, Oxfordshire, and the Isle of Wight. Odda held lands in the region of Dorset. Thored was connected with the southeast and gave an estate in Surrey to Christ Church, Canterbury. The Ælfwine who witnesses Cnut's charters is obscure, while Saxa and Dagfinn are not mentioned in any document connected with Cnut. The Wulf/Ulf who made this will might be the brother of Earl Eglaf who is listed in the *Liber Vita* of Thorney and is called a Danish count by John of Worcester.

This Sitric and the witness to Cnut's charters are almost certainly the same individual; again, probably Sitric Silkenbeard. Wulf seems to have been part of Cnut's court, and his legatees were other men who waited upon the king. There is no need to limit the search for Sitric to Hertfordshire, just as there is no reason to do so for the other men. The will is international in its distribution of gifts, from Rome to the farthest ends of England. Friendships were made at the king's court, and Wulf's will gives an insight into them.

✠

Why would Cnut trouble himself with a prince such as Sitric? An obvious reason is commercial. Dublin was a major port and manufacturing center not just for the Irish Sea, but for the northern Atlantic. The town also offered a valuable entrance into the Irish market. Cnut's reign in England was less benign than it generally has been assumed, and his financial extractions were burdensome.[56] His concern for commercial benefits is made clear in his letter from Rome. The good relations he cultivated with Emperor Conrad had an important goal of assisting trade from his domains to pass from northern to southern Europe.

Cnut also needed an ally among the Viking settlers around Ireland and Britain to stop raids.[57] Cnut was away from Britain for long periods of time. He continued his family's interests in Norway that extended back to the tenth century when his grandfather Harald Bluetooth intervened in the struggle for supremacy among the descendants of Harald Fairhair by supporting the family of Harald's son Eirik Bloodaxe against their cousins. The fifteen-year ascendancy of jarl Eirik of Lade owed much to the support of Cnut's father Svein Forkbeard. Cnut's own struggle with the Norwegian king Olaf the Stout, the future St. Olaf, ended in success, helped both by Cnut's bribery of the Norse and Olaf's enemies among the aristocracy. Olaf's expulsion in 1028 was followed two years later by his attempt to regain his throne through force of arms, but he was defeated and slain in the battle of Stiklestad on July 29, 1030.

The aftermath of the slaying of St. Olaf illustrates why Cnut needed allies. In life Olaf's fortunes had been mixed, but in death he was invincible. Soon after the battle of Stiklestad, miracles began to be attributed to Olaf and, although never officially canonized, he was revered as a saint throughout the Scandinavian world. Friend and foe alike were called upon to recognize his power. A poem addressed to Cnut's son Svein, who was his regent in Norway, advises him to pray to Olaf for protection.[58] A church dedicated to Olaf was at Dublin, on the west side of Fishamble Street near the first of the double bends that are visible in John Speed's 1610 map of Dublin. By the twelfth century, Dublin had a parish dedicated to St. Olaf; and there was another St. Olaf's parish at Waterford. Archbishop Donatus of Dublin collected some of the clothing belonging to Olaf, which was venerated as a relic, and the saint's feast day (July 29) was included in the cathedral's calendar.[59] In 1055 Earl Siward of Northumbria, a Dane and a trusted servant of Cnut, died at the church of Galmanho that he had built and dedicated to Olaf.[60] The cult of Olaf transcended ties of loyalty.

Cnut also needed an alliance with Sitric because men from the Viking colonies around Ireland and Britain were leaving to fight in the wars between the Norse and Danes according to *Orkneyinga Saga*. One of them was Sitric's nephew Tryggvi. Tryggvi, the son of Sitric's sister Gytha and Olaf Tryggvason, invaded Norway circa 1033. There he was confronted by Cnut's son Svein, his child by an English concubine named Ælgifu of Northampton, with whom he also had his son Harold, the fu-

ture king of England. The few details about Tryggvi's campaign come from a contemporary poem called *Tryggvaflokkr* composed by Sigvat *skáld* ("the poet").[61] The
verse calls Tryggvi a king, although the accompanying prose passage notes that there
were some who said that Tryggvi was really the son of a priest. Rumors that a chal-
lenger to Svein was preparing a fleet in the west were circulating in western Norway
before Tryggvi arrived. Most people thought that the initial landing would be in the
Vík. Tryggvi actually landed first in the west at Hordaland, but soon sailed south to
Rogaland to find Svein. Svein had been searching for him and they fought a battle in
the Sóknar Sound, where Tryggvi and many of his men died. Some verses composed
for Svein refer to their battle, which was fought on a Sunday morning. While there
is no indication that Sitric supported his nephew, and Tryggvi would have found
plenty of aid outside Ireland, this episode shows why Cnut needed to tie the Olafssons
to him.

Returning to the Irish shore, the benefits gained by Sitric in a good relationship
with Cnut are obvious. He was free to carry on Dublin's trade with its main markets
in England. The Irish Sea region's economic health depended to a great extent on
England, and by the second quarter of the eleventh century this extended even to the
silver that was circulating in the area.[62] Access to continental trade with bases in England, such as a merchant colony in London, might also have been made available
to Sitric. Sitric and Cnut were aware of the economic advantages of trade with the
Empire or northern Francia, especially Normandy. They needed customers to buy
finished goods or raw materials for manufacturing or trade, and they monitored the
financial fortunes of the market. The *Annals of Tigernach* note the dearth and devastation at Cologne and Rouen in 1045; paupers were poor customers. The emperor
and the Norman duke entertained similar thoughts about the benefits of an expanding economy. During Conrad's reign there was a rapid expansion in urban life
and trade, and the commercial interests of the Norman ports were expanding, in
part towards the north.[63] The Danish and English connections with Normandy are
well known, but less so is the Irish aspect. Dudo of St. Quentin's references to the
Irish in his history of the Norman dukes reflect the importance of those contacts.[64]
That Dudo's Irish were the Vikings of Ireland is suggested by a coin where Sitric is
described as a "king of the Irish."

On November 12, 1035, Cnut the Great died. The empire that he so carefully assembled was collapsing even before his death. He had not been able to prevent the return to Norway of a native royal dynast, St. Olaf's son, Magnus the Good, about the
year 1034. Danish rule in England ended within seven years. The years remaining to
Cnut's direct descendants were marred by hostilities between his sons, the half-
brothers Hardacnut and Harald, neither of whom lived to middle age. Cnut had intended that Hardacnut, his son with Emma of Normandy, would succeed him both in
Denmark and England. Hardacnut was hard pressed to hold Denmark from Magnus

the Good, however, and postponed his return to England. There were attempted invasions from Normandy by the Anglo-Saxon exiles Alfred and Edward, Emma's sons with Æthelred. Alfred was captured and killed while Edward won a battle in Southampton, but was unable to exploit his victory.[65]

By 1037 the English nobility tried to end the turmoil by declaring Cnut's son Harald as king. That only exchanged one problem for another, as Hardacnut plotted a return, assisted by his mother's diplomatic efforts in Flanders. Not until Harald's death in 1040, with an invasion fleet being assembled in Denmark, did Hardacnut fulfill his father's plans. The appearance of Harald's obituary in the *Annals of Ulster* suggests that he was supported by the Olafssons. Hardacnut seems to have had no interest in either Dublin or the Isles during his short reign. He did make a treaty that would be the justification for Norwegian attacks on England (involving Ireland and the Isles) during the following twenty-five years. In order to end the war with the Norwegian king Magnus the Good, the two monarchs agreed that whoever survived the other would inherit both kingdoms.[66] Within two years Hardacnut was dead and the English throne was occupied by his "Normanized" and middle-aged half-brother Edward, remembered as "the Confessor." The Norwegians, however, did not forget the treaty made with Hardacnut. During the next twenty-five years there would be two invasions of England by them in pursuit of their claim to the English kingship.

The political chaos among the Danes and their allies after Cnut's death had consequences for the Olafssons and Haraldssons. While Cnut ruled in England the jarls of the Orkneys (the sons of Sigurd the Stout) were absent from the Irish Sea region, an area that had held a fatal fascination for their father. After Cnut's death, one son, Thorfinn took advantage of Hardacnut's absence in Denmark to attack the Hebrides, Galloway, and the northwestern English coast.[67] There were far greater repercussions for the Olafssons. In 1036, within a year of Cnut's death and after a reign of almost half a century, Sitric was driven from Dublin by Echmarcach Ragnallsson. Sitric abandoned the island, and the *Annals of Tigernach* note that he "went across the sea," the usual phrase for exit from Ireland. When he fled from Dublin, Sitric was at least 55 years old, and probably closer to 65. An old man by the standards of the day, Sitric lived for six more years before dying in 1042, within a month of the death of his daughter Ceallach, his last known child.

The location of Sitric's home in exile is unknown, but it was somewhere in communication with Ireland, since news of his death is found in the *Annals of Tigernach*. His refuge might have been the Dublin colony on Anglesey, which would explain why Sitric is remembered in Welsh literature in a garbled passage about Sitric and his maternal half-brothers Donnchad mac Briain (correctly named) and Conchobar (incorrectly called by his father's name Máel Sechnaill). They are said to be the sons of Murchad, who was actually their grandfather Murchad mac Find, and described as the greatest and swiftest men in Ireland.[68]

Sitric Silkenbeard had become a client of Cnut the Great in the second quarter of the eleventh century, probably by the year 1026. A coin-die from England, a verse by an Icelandic skald, an Anglo-Dublin raid on Wales, and several English charters all argue that Cnut played a part in the sudden reversal of Sitric's fortunes. The English chronicles never directly connect Cnut with Sitric, but they are not so complete to allow for a conclusive argument from silence. To take one example, without the evidence from continental records, the date of Cnut's pilgrimage to Rome in 1027 would still be a matter of controversy. English chroniclers little cared which nest of Irish pirates, as Dublin would have been considered, was allied with Cnut. The Irish were interested in Cnut and his son Harald, whose obituaries are found in the *Annals of Ulster* (Cnut and Harold) and the *Annals of Tigernach* (Cnut). They are the only two eleventh-century kings of the English whose deaths are recorded in the medieval Irish annals. The inward gaze of the Irish historical records argues that Cnut and Harald had a recognized position in some portion of society in Ireland. The death of Sitric's son, Olaf, in 1034 in England while traveling to Rome indicates that his heir-apparent was visiting the court of his overlord. Through their connection with Cnut and his family, the Olafssons became part of a political sphere that extended as far as the Baltic. As will be discussed in the next chapter, they were joined by the Haraldssons. This had repercussions for the Irish Sea Viking families for generations.

The career of Sitric Silkenbeard illustrates some of the ways the Viking families became powerful and maintained themselves. Allies were an important part of the Olafssons' strategy, and as Cnut shows, they did not need to be in Ireland. Whether this support was military or financial is unknown, but possibly a combination. After the tenth century these alliances become a significant factor in the safety of the Olafssons. Commercial alliances contributed to the wealth available to Sitric. As the economy of northern Europe expanded, manufacturing and trading towns such as Dublin benefited from the new opportunities. Sitric used that wealth to buy friends for himself and his dynasty. This could take the form of largess to visiting Icelandic poets or lands and funds to establish a bishopric. That wealth could also attract unwelcome attentions, but even then, as the ransom of Olaf shows, the sheer scale of it must have inspired awe.

Sitric Silkenbeard did not die full of honors in the city that he ruled for almost half a century. He died in exile from Dublin, and in that he followed his father, Olaf Cuaran, who died on the Isle of Iona and his grandfather, Sitric, who died in Britain. After a lifetime of ironies, there was a final one waiting after Sitric's death. Despite his fame as the monarch of the Vikings of Dublin, Sitric would not be the ancestor of a line of sea kings. Instead, he became the progenitor of the later medieval lords of the Welsh, the princes of a people who had been the victims of the Viking raids.

6

The Brief Ascendancy of the Haraldssons

By the time of his death in 1042, Sitric Silkenbeard could have offered some interesting comments on a favorite medieval theme: the wheel of fortune. From an unsteady beginning to mature survival, Sitric had a career of extremes. Then, in a final turn, after a decade of economic prosperity, ecclesiastical progress, and military success, he was forced into exile. With Sitric's abdication, for the first time since the mid-tenth century, the family of Olaf Cuaran did not rule Viking Dublin. The new lord of the town was Echmarcach Ragnallsson from the rival dynasty of Haraldsson. Henceforth there was direct competition between the Olafssons and Haraldssons, first for Dublin and then for the kingdom of the Isles.

The rivalry between the Olafssons and Haraldssons was only one of several duels in the North Atlantic during the years after Cnut's death. By 1042 all of Cnut's sons were dead. In Denmark the dynasty of Svein Forkbeard continued with his grandson Svein, son of his daughter Estrid. In England, the family of Edgar made a brief return to power with his grandson Edward "the Confessor," the son of Æthelraed the Unready. In the north, among the Scots, a more famous figure came to power: Macbeth. After Macbeth killed Duncan in a battle in August 1040, his dynasty of Cenél Loairn eclipsed their southern rivals Cenél nGabráin. Finally, in Ireland, there was a power vacuum. The contest between the northern Irish Uí Néill and the family of Brian Boru in the south had exhausted both groups. The way was open for the rise of a Leinster prince named Diarmait mac Máel na mbó. Within 25 years he ruled both Dublin and the Isles.

Since 917, with only brief absences, Dublin had been ruled by members of the same dynasty. In 1036 that changed, and the new ruler was Echmarcach Ragnallsson. His name reflects the mingling of Gaelic and Norse societies. Echmarcach is a compound of two Irish words *ech-* + *marcach*, meaning "horse rider," while Ragnallsson is Old Norse *Rögnvaldsson*, "Rögnvald's son." There have been two theories about

Echmarcach's background.[1] The traditional view, dating from the nineteenth century, is that Echmarcach was a member of the Olafsson dynasty, the son of Olaf Cuaran's son Ragnall who died at the Battle of Tara in 980. This is almost chronologically impossible. Echmarcach would have been at least 81 years old when fighting his last battle, on the Isle of Man in 1061; and 85 years old when he died at Rome. Brian Boru was 73 years old at the Battle of Clontarf in 1014, and his great age was a reason why he did not actually fight.

The second theory is that Echmarcach belonged to the dynasty of Ivar of Waterford (d. 1000), the man who forced Sitric to flee Dublin in 994. Ivar had a son named Ragnall who ruled Waterford after him and died in the year 1018. Ragnall had a son also named Ragnall who ruled Waterford from 1022 to 1035, when he was slain in Dublin on the orders of Sitric. If Echmarcach were the brother of Ragnall II, then his expulsion of Sitric could have been revenge for the death of his sibling. Echmarcach, however, is not known to have had any contact with the town or people of Waterford. In 1037, the year after Sitric's abdication, the king of Waterford was Cú-in-main Uá Raband. When Waterford was burned that year the culprits, according to the *Annals of Inisfallen*, were other Vikings.[2] Echmarcach made no effort toward taking control of Waterford militarily nor, it would seem, economically. Preliminary archaeological excavations in the town indicate that significant trade did not occur until the late eleventh century.[3] By 1040 Waterford was controlled by a prince who would be the most powerful Leinster king of the eleventh century, Diarmait mac Máel na mbó, then beginning his rise to the domination of the eastern coasts of Ireland.

The surviving evidence points outside Ireland to the Haraldsson dynasty of the Isles for the origins of Echmarcach.[4] He was ruling the Isle of Man in 1061 when defeated by Diarmait mac Máel na mbó's son Murchad. The contemporary Irish chronicler Marianus Scotus, writing on the continent, calls Echmarcach the "king of the Rhinns" of Galloway on his death in 1065. This is sensible for a son of the Ragnall the son of Godred Haraldsson and king of the Isles who died in Munster in 1005. If Echmarcach had been born in the year 1000, several years before Ragnall's death, he would have been about 65 years old when he died in 1065; in comparison Brian Boru and Máel Sechnaill II were in their mid-seventies when they died.

Echmarcach emerged as the leader of the Haraldssons after they had endured two decades of obscurity. Like the Olafssons, the Haraldssons' fortunes had been mixed since the Battle of Clontarf. There was even a period when their ascendancy was in danger of ending. Evidence that a Norwegian noble ruled the Isles circa 1016 to circa 1030 comes from the tract *Ágrip af Nóregs Konunga Sögum* ("Summary of the Norwegian Kings' History"). *Ágrip* claims that St. Olaf expelled from Norway to the Hebrides a rival named Hakon of Lade, the son of Eirik Hakonarson. The chronology within *Ágrip* is vague, but this episode is placed soon after Olaf returned to Norway. When Hakon is sent to the *Suðreys* ("the south islands," i.e., the Hebrides) to take

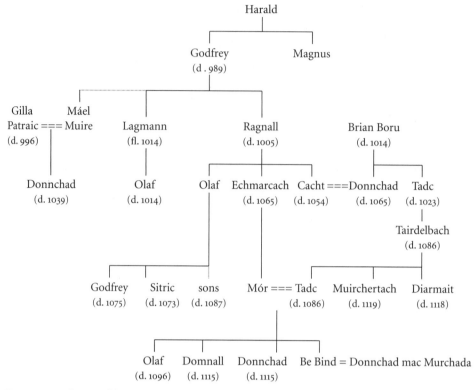

FIGURE 4. *The Haraldsson Dynasty.* Key: ==, *marriage;* —, *descent;* …, *suggested lineage;*
c., *circa;* d., *died;* fl., *flourished.*

the kingship, he is assured that Olaf would support him: "Holy Olaf gave to him,
Hakon, the south islands [i.e., the Hebrides], as some say, and strengthened him thus
that they were his to hold; and there was he king while he lived."[5]

Many scholars have dismissed this passage from *Ágrip* as "unhistorical," and "un-
supported and obviously impossible."[6] While not without a patriotic bias, the author of *Ágrip* was well informed and trying to write an accurate history. *Ágrip* used
earlier poetry for its information, seven stanzas or parts of stanzas are quoted directly, including a poem about Hakon's grandfather; the alliteration in the passage
on Hakon and the Hebrides suggests that it is based on verse.[7] This occasionally en-
tailed reconciliation or conflation of materials, as seen in this extract by the phrase
"as some say." The reigning monarch at the time of the tract's composition was probably Sverrir (reigned 1177–1202), who traced his official descent to the Kingdom of
the Isles or Ireland through a (possibly fictitious) connection with Harald Gille, the
illegitimate son of Magnus Barefoot.

The statement that St. Olaf gave to Hakon rule of the Isles is unique to *Ágrip*, but
the author is clear that he did not invent or welcome this information. A story in

which St. Olaf acts as the patron of Hakon is unexpected. Hakon was not quite a national villain by the late twelfth century, but rather a man of dubious loyalty who collaborated with the oppressor Danes. The future St. Olaf of Norway was involved with the Irish Sea Vikings. Olaf was a comrade-in-arms of King Lagmann of the Isles, so the Vikings of the Irish Sea knew him. This could explain a passage in *Cocad Gáedel re Gallaib* that lists the Vikings who were approached to fight for Sitric Silkenbeard and his allies at the Battle of Clontarf. Brodor of York is mentioned, as well as an Olaf the son of the king of Lochland (i.e., Norway). Both men are described as the earls of *Cair* and all northern England.[8] Olaf's father was not a king, but a similar mistake is made by Adam of Bremen who claimed that St. Olaf's father was Olaf Tryggvason. Olaf was in Britain at the time when *Cocad Gáedel re Gallaib* claims messengers from Dublin arrived to recruit troops, after St. Patrick's feast (March 17). As part of Æthelred's retinue, Olaf returned to England from Normandy during Lent of 1014, so he was in Britain sometime after March 10.

Olaf returned to Norway after Hakon's father Eirik had joined the army of his brother-in-law Cnut, probably early in 1015, leaving Hakon in Norway.[9] After his expulsion, it is usually assumed that Hakon joined his father in Cnut's service. He appears as a witness to English charters in 1019 with the status of earl over some unidentified region, usually thought to be Worcester, although there is no clear indication. When Cnut took lordship over the Norwegians in 1028, Hakon became his regent. He drowned off the Orkneys, in the Pentland firth, circa 1030.

Hakon had the ancestry to be accepted as a king in the Isles. The Islanders had been supporters of Svein Forkbeard, and the Isle of Man was attacked by the English when Svein sailed to Normandy in 1000. Hakon was the grandson of Svein; Hakon's mother Gytha was Svein's daughter and Cnut's sister. His family, the jarls of Lade, ruled as kings in all but name from the late tenth to early eleventh centuries.[10] The dynasty of Lade enhanced their prestige with claims of descent from the pagan gods of Scandinavia, which were broadcast by poets such as Gunnlaug Serpent's Tongue and Hallfred the Troublesome Poet. Another poet named Eyvind the Plagiarist composed a piece known as *Háleygjatal* ("Catalogue of the Halgoland Chieftains") in which he traced the family's origins to the union of a son of Odin with Skadi, a giant's daughter.[11] Eyvind's *Háleygjatal* was one of the sources used in *Ágrip*.

Two other works claim a Danish presence in the Isles. The first is the verse of Ottar the Black on the bounds of Cnut's empire, which includes Islanders among Cnut's subjects. The reference is unlikely to be to the Shetland or Orkney Islanders, who were part of the Norwegian domain. In this context "Islanders" appear to mean the inhabitants of the Kingdom of the Isles. Ties between the Danes and Islesmen at this time are noted by a second work, the contemporary chronicle of Adémar of Chabannes. Adémar claims that circa 1018 a Viking fleet from Denmark and *Iresca regione* raided St. Michel en l'Herm. The "Irish region" was not simply Ireland; it was the Irish Sea Province.[12] The spelling of place names shows that one of his informants was an Old Norse speaker. Adémar was an exact contemporary of the raid; he was about 30 years old at the time of the raid. An interesting aside is the capture in this raid of the countess of Limoges, who was released only through the intervention of the Norman duke.

A Norwegian history, a contemporary Icelandic poet, and a contemporary French chronicler provide information about the Kingdom of the Isles in the years after the Battle of Clontarf. The deaths within a year of Lagmann Godfreysson in Normandy and his son Olaf at the Battle of Clontarf had left the Isles without a suitable leader. This eased the way for an outsider such as Hakon Eiriksson to be intruded into the kingship of the Isles circa 1016, and rule there until his death circa 1030. Hakon's descent from Svein Forkbeard together with the support of his uncle Cnut would have muted much opposition. Cnut gave him the title of earl; the exact bounds of his authority are today unknown. Hakon's father, Eirik, was earl of Northumbria, so Hakon had parental support in the north of England. Hakon added to his lordship in the Isles when he was made regent in Norway by Cnut in 1028 after St. Olaf's flight. Hakon's support from Olaf would have been a reasonable price for the former's quiet departure from Norway.

Hakon died in either 1029 or 1030, drowning in the Pentland Firth. The Haraldssons regained control of the Isles in the person of Echmarcach Ragnallsson. Echmarcach first appears in the historical records in connection with Cnut's journey to northern Britain. In 1031 Cnut led an expedition to Scotland. The *Anglo-Saxon Chronicle* states: "In this year Cnut went on a pilgrimage to Rome, and when he returned he went north to Scotland where he was met by the Scots king Malcolm and two other kings, Maelbaethe and Iehmarc."[13]

This meeting is also known from another record, the verse commemoration by the skald Sighvat "the Black" (*svarti*) Thórdarson in his *Knútsdrápa* ("*drapa* about Cnut"), composed circa 1038: "The heads of famous foreign lords journey to Cnut— out of Fife in the midst of the north—a peace buying was that. Olaf never sold himself in this world to anyone in that way; often was victory to the Stout." The reference to heads is a poetic indication of political submission rather than decapitation.[14] Thanks to Sighvat's desire to show off his geographical knowledge—he liked to remind his audience that he had lived in Britain (during the years 1025–1026) by including place names in his works—the location of the meeting is known to have been Fife. Sighvat might have composed the poem with the Viking colonists in mind. The vocabulary and syntax are simple, suggesting that it was intended for recitation to people whose Old Norse was basic and old fashioned. In a largely illiterate society, the comprehension of listeners was reflected in a piece's complexity.[15]

The kings are easily identified.[16] The leader of the trio was the Scots monarch Malcolm II (Máel Coluim mac Cináeda, reigned 1005–1034), one of the most famous and successful of the early Scottish kings. His mother was Irish, from northern Leinster, and the *Annals of Tigernach* call him the "glory of the whole west of Europe." Malcolm's contemporary, the historian Rudolfus Glaber, writing at the great monastery of Cluny, described him as a most Christian king against whom Cnut battled unsuccessfully. Cnut and Malcolm never fought each other, but Glaber is referring to the Battle of Carham (circa 1016) when Malcolm defeated the Northumbrians and annexed Lothian as far south as the River Tweed. Malcolm's power is revealed when, soon after Carham, he annexed the Kingdom of Strathclyde, later giving its lordship to his grandson Duncan I (Donnchad mac Crínáin).

The other kings with Malcolm were Macbeth and Echmarcach. Maelbaethe is a variant spelling of Mac bethad, more familiar in its modern contracted form Macbeth. Although his Shakespearean namesake is better known, the historical Macbeth had been king of Cenél Loairn (the Scots located north of the Grampians and around the Moray Firth) since the death in 1029 of his cousin Malcolm (Máel Coluim mac Máel Brigtí), the grandfather of Jarl Thorfinn of the Orkneys. Macbeth was probably Malcolm's grandson; the fourteenth-century *Chronicle of Huntingdon* claims that Macbeth was Malcolm's *nepos* "grandson." Echmarcach's identity is obscured by the chronicler's "Iehmarc," a phonetic spelling of Echmarcach.

His companions are proof of Malcolm's supremacy in northern Britain, and they are clearly his underkings (*subreguli*). Malcolm's residence on Islay and Arran, as described in the contemporary *Prophecy of Berchán*, reveals his ties to the Isles. His authority might have been even greater. Dying in the same year as Malcolm (1034) was a prince named Suibhne mac Cináeda who is styled king of the foreign Gael (*rí gallgóidil*) in the *Annals of Ulster*. Similarity of patronymics suggests that he was a brother of Malcolm who was set up as a subordinate in lands where Viking colonists were settling. Ties between Malcolm and Echmarcach are suggested after the former's death. When Malcolm's great-grandson Malcolm Canmore raided Hexham in 1079, Ailred of Rievaulx claims that he had troops from Galloway and threatened to let them ravage the church if his demands were not met.[17] Just 15 years earlier Echmarcach was called king of the Rhinns of Galloway.

Sighvat and the *Anglo-Saxon Chronicle* agree that this kingly meeting was a peaceful encounter. The poet is openly contemptuous of such poor behavior. Speculation about the meeting connects it with the Scottish conquest of Lothian.[18] The Scots had coveted the area for decades. According to the contemporary *Scottish Chronicle*, raids into it had begun in the ninth century, when Kenneth mac Alpin raided the English six times and attacked Dunbar and Melrose. The initial Scottish annexation of Lothian, probably only as far as the Haddington Tyne, was accomplished half a century earlier, during the reign of the Scots king Idulf (reigned 954–962). Malcolm's later annexation may have worried Cnut, and clearly terrified the local inhabitants. A curious eleventh-century Northumbrian tract called "Concerning the Siege of Durham" (*De Obsessione Dunelmensis*, referring to Malcolm's unsuccessful raid on the town in 1006) claims that Lothian was given to the Scots.[19] The local aristocracy, led by an earl named Eadulf "cudel," placated Malcolm and prevented any more battles by giving him the lands north of the Tweed.

Cnut needed the cooperation of Malcolm, Macbeth, and Echmarcach to guard his northern frontiers while forestalling aid to the Norwegian resistance. Like Sitric Silkenbeard, the Scottish high king and his clients/nobles were in a position to menace England or participate in military adventures outside Britain. Cnut's concerns were real. Malcolm had allowed Domnall mac Eimhin, the mormaer of Mar, to fight for Brian Boru in the Battle of Clontarf. Echmarcach Ragnallsson's ancestors had raided at will around Ireland and Britain. Macbeth, too, had a fleet. *Orkneyinga Saga* states he used it in his battles with Jarl Thorfinn of the Orkneys. Macbeth also used foreign mercenaries, drawing troops from Ireland and, in 1052, employing Norman knights forced to leave the court of Edward the Confessor.[20]

The year after his meeting with Cnut, Echmarcach continued his family's alliance with the family of Brian Boru. In 1032 his sister Cacht married Brian's son Donnchad. While their marriage doubtless was based upon political expediency, it seems to have developed into a union marked by genuine affection. Obituaries for queens are infrequently given in the Irish annals, but the death of Cacht in 1054 is mentioned in the *Annals of Tigernach*. There she is styled "Queen of Ireland," a title that is slightly expansive, yet suggests her husband's affection. Donnchad needed a powerful ally at the time of his marriage. Although he was the king of Munster, he aspired to be the high king of Ireland; his premature claim can be read on the cover of the Stowe Missal.[21] The marriage of Cacht to Donnchad gave him an ally who possessed fleets to attack the Irish coast.

This marriage is a reminder of the longevity of goodwill between families. Friendly relations between the Uí Briain and the Haraldssons began in 984 when Cacht's grandfather Godred Haraldsson joined Brian for a raid on Dublin and continued in 1005 when her father Ragnall died in Munster, possibly at Brian's court. Political alliances could also lead to genuine friendship. When Donnchad went into exile in 1064, he did so in the company of Echmarcach. The alliance between the two families did not stop there, and Echmarcach's daughter Mor married Donnchad's great-nephew.

Echmarcach's alliances suggest why he was successful at Dublin. The flight of Sitric was not a friendly transfer of power. The Irish annals are clear that he was forced to flee. Echmarcach was not Sitric's chosen successor, and there is no record of contact between them prior to 1036. When Sitric went to Rome in 1028 his deputy probably was his son Olaf, who led raids with the Dublin army in 1029, and was lord over the Dublin colony at *Castell Avloed*. Echmarcach's ally and brother-in-law Donnchad could have been crucial for his occupation of Dublin. Donnchad's hostility to his half-brother is visible in 1026, when he attacked Dublin and forced Sitric to give hostages. Another possible ally was another Donnchad, this one the son of the Viking princess Máel Muru and Gilla-Patraic of Osraige, who in 1036 became the provincial king of Leinster. If, as suggested, Máel Muru was the daughter of Godfrey

Haraldsson, then Donnchad was Echmarcach's cousin. There could have been a Scottish connection. Echmarcach's Scottish overlord, Malcolm II, with his Leinster connections had died, but there is no reason to believe that his relations with Malcolm's successor Duncan were anything but cordial. Finally, Echmarcach could have been aided by Sitric's enemies in Dublin.

Echmarcach's first reign in Dublin was brief and unexceptional. Only one event is known: an attack in 1037 on Skreen and Duleek (south of the Boyne). Echmarcach also faced the family of Sigurd the Stout of the Orkneys in the person of his youngest son Thorfinn. After his father's death, Thorfinn resided at the court of his maternal grandfather, the northern Scots king Malcolm of Cenél Loairn (Máel Coluim mac Máel Brigtí, not to be confused with the high king Malcolm II). Malcolm gave Thorfinn the lordship of Caithness. With this support, Thorfinn dominated his elder brothers and become supreme in the Orkneys. After the death of Cnut, Thorfinn led his ships south. According to the poem *Þórfinnsdrápa* ("Thorfinn's *drapa*") by Arnórr Þórðarson, which is preserved in *Orkneyinga Saga*, Thorfinn raided around the Irish Sea where he fought the English and "old Ragnall's family," raiding as far south as the Isle of Man. Apparently Echmarcach fared no better than his father had against the jarl of the Orkneys. The prose narrative of the saga supplies the information that Thorfinn was active in the Hebrides, parts of Scotland and Galloway ("where England and Scotland meet"), and took the fight as far as Ireland; Arnórr claims that the "raven-feaster" (Thorfinn) ruled as far south as Dublin.[22]

In 1038 there was another change of ruler at Dublin, Echmarcach was driven from Dublin by Ivar Haraldsson, a grandson of Olaf Cuaran. The expulsion of Echmarcach from Dublin probably owed something to the raids of Jarl Thorfinn into the Irish Sea, but they were part of wider political turmoil throughout Britain between the years 1034 and 1040. When the Scots prince Malcolm II died in November 1034, a year before Cnut, he was succeeded by his young grandson Duncan, whose path to the throne had been cleared by the old king's assassination of potential rivals. Duncan's hold on the monarchy was propped up by Macbeth, his "underking" or *dux* according to the chronicler Marianus Scotus. This brought additional complications, because Macbeth and Thorfinn were bitter enemies. The Orkney jarl's Scottish grandfather had come to power upon the murder of Macbeth's father (in which he probably had a part). To the south the political uncertainty came to a temporary end when, in 1037, the English nobles tired of waiting for Hardacnut and chose as king his half-brother Harold Harefoot. Neighbors of the English watched the confusion closely; *Orkneyinga Saga* specifically notes that Hardacnut was in Denmark when Thorfinn was raiding around the Irish Sea.

The new king of Dublin, Ivar Haraldsson, was the son of Sitric Silkenbeard's brother Harald who had died in the Battle of Glen Mama in 999. Ivar ruled Dublin from 1038 to 1046. His accession follows Harald Harefoot's elevation to the English kingship. Harald's support for Ivar could explain why his obituary is found in the *Annals of Ulster* when his brief reign of three years ended in 1040. Several years later, Ivar witnessed the end of Cnut's dynasty with the death of Hardacnut in 1042. The last son of Cnut was about 24 years old. In Denmark, Hardacnut's successor was his cousin Svein, known variously as Svein Ulfsson (following his father's name) or Svein Estridsson (after his mother). The English throne was taken by Hardacnut's maternal half-brother and designated heir Edward (later known as "the Confessor"), the son of Æthelraed and Emma, who had been brought back to England by his half-brother in 1041. Both Svein and Edward were threatened with invasion from Magnus of Norway during the early years of their reign.

With the restoration of the Olafssons, Ivar Haraldsson returned to the policies of his uncle, Sitric, with a series of raids into the north of Ireland. In 1044 he raided the minor principality of Uí Fiachrach Arda Sratha and attacked the church of Armagh, where he burned the shrine of Patrick. He also continued the family's feud with the Ulaid that had begun in the year 1000 when Sitric had been refused aid by them. In one of his first acts as king, Ivar led a fleet to Rathlin Island, off the Antrim coast, and plundered it in 1038. In 1045 he raided Rathlin Island again and, at a battle fought at Inispatrick, killed the Ulaidan heir-apparent named Ragnall (ON *Rögnvaldr*) Ua Eochada and 300 nobles. In revenge, Ragnall's brother Niall attacked Fingal.

Ivar also continued the Olafssons' interest in northern Welsh affairs. This brought him into conflict with Gruffudd ap Llywelyn, the greatest of the eleventh-century Welsh princes. Gruffudd was the son of Llywelyn ap Seisyll, the conqueror of the Irishman Rhain. Gruffudd became famous as the unifier of Wales, but the early years of his reign were not easy. A passage in the *Book of Llandaff* remembers his persecution by the "barbarous" English, Irish, and Vikings. The Olafsson fortress at *Castell Avloed* was in the territory of Gruffudd's rival Iago ab Idwal. In 1039 Iago was slain by rivals and succeeded by Gruffudd. Three years later, in 1042, Gruffudd was kidnapped by the Vikings of Dublin. Then a rival named Hywel ap Edwin with a Viking fleet was defeated by Gruffudd in a battle fought at the River Tewy circa 1044. Finally, a fleet from Ireland perished off the south coast of Wales circa 1049.

Elaboration on the first and third items comes from a now lost Welsh chronicle used by the sixteenth-century historian David Powel and the seventeenth-century historian James Ware.[23] They claim that the kidnapping of Gruffudd and the mid-century Irish fleet were led by Cynan ap Iago, the husband of Sitric Silkenbeard's granddaughter Ragnhild. Prior to the first expedition, Gruffudd had seized the Kingdom of Gwynedd and forced Cynan into exile. Cynan fled to Dublin and recruited a fleet. He returned to Wales and captured Gruffudd. As they led their prisoner to the ships, Cynan's mercenaries were attacked by the Welsh. Gruffudd was freed, and Cynan returned empty-handed to Ireland. The alliance between Cynan and Harald (for no war fleet sailed from Dublin without the king's permission) argues that *Castell Avloed* was still controlled from Dublin.

A historiographical point is pertinent here. Sixteenth- and seventeenth-century records contain valuable information from manuscripts that have perished. The important *Annals of Ulster*, for example, survive in sixteenth-century manuscripts, while the *Annals of the Four Masters*, together with the extant copies of the *Chronicon Scotorum* and the *Annals of Clonmacnoise* are all seventeenth-century copies/ reworkings of earlier material. The information given by Ware sensibly expands the information from *Annales Cambriae* and *Brut Y Tywysogyon*. His interest in the matter is confined solely to Dublin. He does not mention either the death of Gruffudd ap Llywelyn or the exploits of Cynan's son Gruffudd. The omission of Cynan from the Welsh chronicles is not unexpected in light of the later fame of Gruffudd as the prince of all Wales. This extended even to his family, and by the twelfth century Cynan's son, also named Gruffudd, was claiming to be the heir of Gruffudd ap Llywelyn. Since Cynan's descendants were important patrons of the literati, a discreet and selective historical memory could be reflected in the extant Welsh records.

The Olafsson supremacy at Dublin lasted until 1046, when Echmarcach returned. According to the *Annals of the Four Masters* he forced Ivar to flee and the Dubliners elected him king, while the *Annals of Tigernach* simply state that he succeeded Ivar. Afterwards all that is known of Ivar is his death in 1054. Like his first reign, there is little about Echmarcach's second rule in the Irish chronicles. During his second reign, Echmarcach might have been responsible for the "Irish pirate ships" that the Welsh prince Gruffudd ap Rydderch hired for an attack up the Usk in 1049. Combining the accounts in the Welsh and English accounts, the fleet attacked at the end of July. Crossing the River Wye, the invaders defeated a force led by Bishop Ealdred of Worcester and devastated the neighborhood. There might be a direct connection with Dublin and the Olafssons. According to Powel at about this time a Cynan ap Iago led a fleet to Wales to regain his inheritance, and Ware claims that it came from Ireland. Once more his plans were thwarted; a great gale blew up and scattered the ships forcing Cynan to return to Ireland. A postscript is in Geoffrey Keating's *History of Ireland* (composed circa 1634), which notes the flight into Ireland circa 1050 of a prince named *Harolt Conan*.[24] The exile Cynan could have been leading Viking pirates from Ireland to Wales, possibly with a diversion to try his luck in Gwynedd.

The main activity of Echmarcach's second reign was economic rather than military. Sometime during the early eleventh century a mint had been set up on the Isle of Man, imitating English issues. Manx coins found in a horde at Kirk Andreas, for example, are copies of Cnut's coinage. Mid-eleventh-century coins produced on Man reflect a significant influence from Dublin. There even has been the suggestion that a colony from Dublin was set up on the Isle of Man in the aftermath of Clontarf. What has not been noted is that the date of the coins roughly coincides with the period of Echmarcach's reign. He might have used his time in Ireland to study the town's financial system and tried to harmonize the coins circulating in his domain with those from Dublin. At the same time an artistic aspect is visible, and borrowings from Dublin can be identified after 1020.[25]

Dublin's influence is also visible in worked wood. Decorated wood is found on items as varied as furniture, housewares, and children's toys. The type of designs produced on the Isle of Man can be identified from the mid-tenth century. Occasionally this identification is made by a comparison with the decoration on the Isle's sculptured stones. In other instances Manx pieces are distinguished by a decorative element with the pelleting of interlace strands within double borders.[26] For a century there was borrowing of artistic styles and imitations of design between Dublin and Man. The distinctly Manx material comes to an end in the mid-eleventh century. This could be no more significant than the adoption of a single style by the Irish and Manx carvers. Yet the change at roughly this time from wood to turf construction in Manx houses suggests an environmental reason: there were not enough trees on the island to continue wood-working as a commercially viable craft.

A reference to trade directly between Dublin and Norway during the reigns of Echmarcach and Magnus the Good is given in the manuscript known as *Morkinskinna*. One of Magnus's retainers named Thorstein Hallsson made a trading voyage between Dublin and Norway without the king's permission. To make matters worse, upon landing in Norway he refused to pay the landing tolls, because of his position at court. Thorstein might have been commanding one of the king's own vessels, for Magnus gave a trading ship, with a full cargo, to the poet Arnórr.[27]

Commercial activity explains why a mint was set up on Man. Like the Dublin mint, the production of coins on the Isle of Man reveals a financial sophistication not usually credited to Vikings. A mint is a sign of increased economic activity under royal control. By the thirteenth-century there is direct evidence of royal control over commercial affairs in the Isle of Man, when permission to enter or leave the Isle of Man required a payment. The kings of the Isles would waive that fee for favored religious houses, in effect giving permission for free admission to or departure from their kingdom as a special privilege. Royal control is also seen in the "king's highway" (*regia via*) on Man like that noted at Dublin. The Manx royal highway formed one of the boundaries for the lands of the monks of Rushen.[28]

Even though the Isle of Man was his main base, Echmarcach's personal home appears to have been in southwest Scotland. He was described as king of the Rhinns by the contemporary chronicler Marianus Scotus after his defeat on the Isle of Man in 1061; under such circumstances retrenchment to the security of one's home region is typical. During the Middle Ages, the area known as the Rhinns was much greater than the modern region. To the Irish, the Rhinns included the Machars, and it extended from the North Channel to Wigtown Bay. Herein is Whithorn, the site of the ancient church of St. Ninian called *Ad Candida Casa* by Bede and *Futerna* by the Irish. The eleventh-century notes attached to the ninth-century Calendar of Oengus remember an Irishman named Findbarr of Moyville who studied at Futerna in the

Rhinns.[29] The strength of Scandinavian settlement in this region is suggested by place names. For example, Tinwald in Dumfriesshire, several miles northeast of Dumfries, comes from Old Norse *Þing-völlr* "field of the Thing" (the local assembly).

Northeast of Whithorn is the coastal fortress of Cruggleton. This was the home of the lords of Galloway in the twelfth century, and it had been inhabited for centuries, beginning with a roundhouse and continuing with a timbered hall. This stronghold might have been Echmarcach's capital. Little now remains of the fortifications because most of the stone castle that replaced the earlier building has fallen into the sea. There is a description of it in the early thirteenth-century story called "The Romance of Fergus." This tale, written circa 1200 for the descendants of the twelfth-century lord of Galloway named Fergus, describes the fort of Cruggleton as situated atop a great rock enclosed by clay and wattle walls. The ramparts gave a clear view for miles around, and within them was an earthen tower. By the beginning of the thirteenth century, this was a very old-fashioned construction, and the author describes it to emphasize how primitive was the region.[30] Serving the fortress was a village, which is mentioned in the twelfth-century *Life* of the Irish reformer St. Malachy written by Bernard of Clairvaux. Malachy probably was visiting the church at Whithorn and as he traveled through the village at Cruggleton he cured a mute girl. He returned to Bangor in Ireland by sailing from Cairngarbh in what is now Wigtownshire, possibly the same port where the twelfth-century *vita* claims a miracle was performed by the staff of Ninian.[31]

The history of Whithorn between the early ninth century and its restoration in the twelfth is obscure; archaeological excavations have revealed interesting material.[32] By the eleventh century there is a similarity in house construction with those at Dublin. Some houses at Whithorn were built in the style found at Dublin rather than those found in the Hebrides or on the Isle of Man. A settlement in the vicinity of the church appears to have been manufacturing leather and iron goods. Among the debris from the Whithorn excavations are Hiberno-Norse style stickpins, beads, and jars.

The inhabitants of the Kingdom of the Isles were not paupers.[33] There has been found on the Isle of Man almost as much silver "ring-money" as has been uncovered in all of Ireland. The wealth of individuals in the Isles is seen in grave goods from the previous century. A lady, aged between 35 and 40 years old, was buried at Cnip Headland on the Isle of Lewis. She was wearing oval broaches, a necklace of colored glass beads, a comb made of antler, a ringed pin, and a belt with a bronze buckle. Placed beside her were knife, whet-stone, and needle case with two needles.[34] At the least, the decorated metals and glass beads were imported. These remains not only testify to the wealth of individuals, but also to their society that could afford to discard such expensive items.

While part of that wealth may reflect raiding, part of it may represent profits from manufacturing. Evidence of earlier commercial activity is found in two graves in the Hebrides. One is at Kiloran Bay, on the Isle of Colonsay, where there was found a balance-beam type scale, together with seven weights; the other grave at Ballinaby on Islay contained a set of blacksmith's tools.[35] Literature gives an impression of how valuable trade and industry were. *Eyrbyggja Saga*, a fourteenth-century work with a genuine antiquarian interest, claims that about this time a lady from the Isles named Thorgunna sailed to Iceland with clothes and fabrics that were the envy of her Icelandic contemporaries. The same saga tells of a trading vessel that was owned jointly by Norwegians and men from the Hebrides.[36] Joint commercial expeditions made by ships from Dublin and from the Isles are remembered in other Norse sagas with historical interests, such as *Orkneyinga Saga*. Trade from Ireland and the Isles specifically is remembered in the Icelandic legal collection known as *Grágás* ("Gray Goose"), in a section concerning Icelandic merchants who die outside the island.

Commercial activity offers one explanation why fights for control of Dublin and the Isles were so fierce or why an Orkney jarl sailed so far from home in order to indulge in, according to the written records, a few brawls with the natives. How different was Echmarcach's domain from that of his neighbors? An insight is provided by comparing the type of goods available in his kingdom with that of his neighbors the Scots. In the Isles were being produced cloth, decorated furniture, and fine jewelry. These goods had an international distribution, to Iceland and beyond. This can be compared with the list of gifts supplied by the Scots monarch Malcolm Canmore for his brother-in-law Edgar Ætheling in 1075, when Edgar was sailing to France. According to the *Anglo-Saxon Chronicle*, the goods included fur robes (made of martin, miniver, and ermine), worked skins, and gold and silver drinking vessels. With the exception of the vessels, probably representing trade, these goods represent manufacturing at a very basic level, little changed from the cargo of Irish goods that arrived in the Loire in the eighth century. The technological and commercial sophistication of Echmarcach's realm made its ruler very wealthy and a target for anyone with a desire for those riches.

Manufacturing or commerce are easily overemphasized and often forgotten is the dominating importance of agriculture. Livestock had a greater status than cereal production, and herdsmen throughout Britain and Ireland benefited from the more benign climate in northern Europe after the millennium. The importance of stock raising among the Viking colonists in Ireland and the Isles is illustrated by physical remains. On the Isle of Man, for example, community cooperation in stock tending is revealed in dykes and in lanes formed by hedgerows. Dykes and hedgerows not only enclosed animals in fields, but also assisted herding by confining the animals within the roads as they were driven. The hedgerows have an in-built chronological guide for estimating their age, which is calculated by counting the number of bramble varieties. Ten varieties indicate a date of construction in the early Viking period of the late ninth/early tenth century, while nine varieties look to a date in the late eleventh century.[37]

The Viking colonists were imitative and borrowed some practices from their neighbors. They seem to have complemented the Old Norse *sel* "shed on a mountain

Map 7. *Isle of Man*

pasture," used for hill-grazing of sheep and goats, with the Irish *áirge*, "dairy." The *áirge* was a summer dairy used in hill pastures remote from the main farmstead where the cattle grazed. These dairies are remembered in the place-name element *eary*, found in place names such as Aresteyne and Eary Glas on the Isle of Man, and *Airigh an Tuim* "Dairy of the Knoll" on the Isle of Lewis.[38] Viking colonists would have been familiar with the idea of transhumance. In medieval Scandinavia there was a time for the herding of livestock to the mountain pastures known as *selmánaðr*, "the month for the removal to the *sel*," around the Irish Sea it was connected with Old May Day (May 11), a festival observed in Ireland, Wales, and the Isle of Man into the modern era. Particularly important were sheep, for their wool was necessary in the manufacture of *röggvarfeldr*, one of the commodities being exported. There was also the collection of winter fuel during the summer grazing. The Vikings' adaptation of turf for fuel was credited to the Orkney lord called "Turf Einar."

The Isle of Man was famous for its fertility. A twelfth-century Irish poem employs the symbolism of apple trees to represent the fruitfulness of the island, while in the thirteenth century the Icelandic historian Snorri Sturluson claims that Man had the finest land in the Isles. Arable farming had played an important role among the Viking settlers.[39] Land being brought under cultivation could be part of the reason for the depletion of the woodlands that is visible by the eleventh century. The Vikings were growing grains such as wheat, oats, and barley that, throughout the Middle Ages, were vital to the Manx economy. The thirteenth-century synodal statutes, composed circa 1229, note that anciently the farmers would gather all sheaves and store them in their barns until the tithe sheaves were collected, possibly as late as All Saints Day; later the tithes were collected while the sheaves were still in the field in order not to inconvenience the farmers.[40]

As king of the Isles and Dublin, Echmarcach presided over a prosperous domain. He had an ally in the powerful king of Munster, and possibly alliances with other Irish princes, too. Allies could be a mixed blessing. If Echmarcach's seizure of the Dublin kingship had been assisted by Donnchad, son of Brian, then that alliance might have been responsible for his expulsion from the town. In 1048 Donnchad went to Dublin where he received a formal submission from Echmarcach. Their combined forces made an expedition into Leinster, in an effort to intimidate Diarmait mac Máel na mbó, the patron of Donnchad's nephew, Tairdelbach. Donnchad and Echmarcach accomplished little more than antagonizing Diarmait. Four years later, in 1052, Diarmait attacked Echmarcach. His raids were originally intended as mere plundering expeditions for Diarmait to gather cattle from the farms around Dublin.[41] He struck north of the Liffey. The *Annals of the Four Masters* claim that he raided from the River Albene to Dublin, while the *Annals of Tigernach* have him raid from the River Delvin to Dublin, which is described as the (latest) extent of Fingal. He achieved completely unexpected success, however, when he was able to storm the Dublin fortress. The *Annals of Tigernach* note the flight across the sea by Echmarcach son of Ragnall, and the son of Máel na mbó took the kingship of the Vikings afterwards. This is the first of its two entries on the capture of Dublin, the second notes that Diarmait took Dublin by force, emphasizing the military triumph. The entire affair could have been ended quickly if the capture of Dublin in 1170 is any guide. Gerald of Wales, in his *Expugnatio Hibernica*, claims that no sooner had the English breeched the town's walls than the king, Arkulf, immediately fled to his ships and sailed to the Isles.

In one stroke Diarmait gained an important source of wealth while destroying the ally of his foe Donnchad. Despite his loss in Ireland, Echmarcach remained king of the Isles and he was still capable of leading raids against Diarmait. In 1061, however, his embattled ally Donnchad decided to submit to Diarmait. This encouraged Diarmait's son Murchad, later that same year, to lead a naval expedition to the Isle of Man, recorded in the *Annals of Tigernach*. The Irish prince forced Echmarcach to pay a tax as an acknowledgement of Leinster lordship. Murchad was well suited for a naval venture, as he had been ruling Dublin for his father. So closely did he become identified with his subjects that Murchad is called "king of the Danes," when defeated in Meath in 1059 by the king Conchobar Ua Máel Sechnaill, and "high king of the Vikings" in a poem lamenting his early death in March of 1070.[42]

A remembrance of Murchad's expedition of 1061 is preserved in the adventure of a Norwegian aristocrat named Guthorm Gunhildarson, found among the miracles of St. Olaf of Norway.[43] Guthorm's mother, Gunhilda, was the sister of two Norwegian kings: St. Olaf and the famous Harald Harada (ON *Hardraði* "Hard-counsel") who invaded England in 1066 and who was the king of Norway at the time of this incident. Guthorm was active around the Irish Sea and maintained a house in Dublin. There he was a friend of the town's king *Margað*, a word that is both the Old Norse word for "market" and for the Irish name Murchad. The adventure of Guthorm and Margad began one July, when they raided around the Irish Sea (later versions of the tale identify Wales as the area of operation) and took much booty. Afterwards they anchored off the Isle of Anglesey in the Menai Straits to divide the loot. Margad demanded all the loot for himself, but Guthorm refused to surrender his share without a fight. A battle was set for the eve of St. Olaf's feast day. Guthorm prayed to his uncle for assistance, promising a tithe of the silver if he had the victory. In the ensuing battle Guthorm and his men, though outnumbered, were victorious. Guthorm kept his word. Snorri mentions that the cross made from the silver in St. Olaf's church at Niðaróss was still on view during his time. The so-called loot could have been the tax paid by Echmarcach to Murchad. No church would knowingly accept property stolen from Christians, but it would accept tax revenues; *Njal's Saga* claims that silver was used to pay the taxes taken from Man and the Isles by Sigurd of the Orkneys, while *Cocad Gáedel re Gallaib* remembers the silver paid for the nose tax.

Hagiography is justifiably suspect as historical evidence, but there are reasons for treating this material with some confidence. Materials about St. Olaf were being collected within a decade of his death at the Battle of Stiklestad on July 29, 1030. One of those collecting information was the poet Sighvat the Black who composed the verse on the meeting of Echmarcach and Cnut in Fife. His *Erfidrápa* ("Memorial Lay") described Olaf's death and several miracles attributed to him. The earliest appearance of Olaf in a church calendar comes from Britain, where his festival is included in a Latin *officium* known as the Leofric Collectar, composed circa 1050. The earliest extant version of Guthorm's adventure is the twelfth-century Latin *vita* of St. Olaf known as *Acta sancti Olavi regis et martyris* ("The Deeds of St. Olaf, king and martyr"), collected by the clergy at Niðaróss.[44]

The saga of Guthorm demonstrates how faint the line between Viking pirate and Christian prince was becoming, especially when it was profitable to cooperate. Around the Irish Sea, Viking and native copied each other. The Irish took over Dublin's connections. Diarmait is styled king of the Welsh in his obituary in the *Annals of Tigernach*, a generous tribute to someone whose territory in Wales was a single fortress. There is even more exaggeration in the late twelfth-century Irish pseudo-prophecy, known by its first line as *Éisdse a Bhoithin go buan* ("Listen, O Báetan, with attention"). Diarmait is described as "Máel" from southern Leinster, and he conquers the Vikings while making Britain, that is, Wales, tributary to him.[45]

After Murchad's successful expedition to the Isle of Man, Echmarcach was forced from the island to Galloway. In 1064 Echmarcach decided to make a pilgrimage to Rome, following in the path of Cnut and Sitric Silkenbeard. He was joined by his brother-in-law Donnchad. Neither man must have expected to return, and both were elderly: Echmarcach was at least 60 years old, while Donnchad was old enough to have commanded troops in the Clontarf campaign of 1014. They both died the next year, 1065, in the abbey attached to the church of St. Stephen the Protomartyr.

Echmarcach's career shows the heights and depths of lordship. His domain fluctuated from a kingdom extending from the Outer Hebrides south as far as Dublin to, at the end of his career, merely the fringe of southern Scotland in the Rhinns of Galloway. The powerful Irish Sea Viking families used their location on the coasts and in the islands to build empires in several lands. Like the Olafssons, Echmarcach depended on allies. The marriage of his sister Cacht to Donnchad mac Briain continued an alliance between their families that began in the last quarter of the tenth century. Even though this alliance had its occasional lapses, such as the Battle of Clontarf, when the Haraldssons fought against the high king Brian, future relations were not harmed. Echmarcach built his alliances on two islands, submitting to Cnut in 1031, and he was the last of Cnut's clients to hold Dublin. The capture of the town by Diarmait in 1052 meant, with the exception of a couple of brief revivals, the end of Viking independence in Ireland. From this time on, Dublin would be independent of direct Irish control only occasionally.

The Olafssons and Haraldssons had built their empires well. Their temporary eclipse in the mid-eleventh century allowed others to use their domains as gateways to the world beyond Ireland. The capture of Dublin by Diarmait mac Máel na mbó in 1052 marked a new era for the Olafssons and the Haraldssons, heralding an obscure period in their history. Until his death in 1072, Diarmait controlled all the eastern Hiberno-Scandinavian towns. His empire extended from Waterford on the southeastern coast to the Liffey Valley; in 1061 was added overlordship of the Kingdom of the Isles. For 20 years the prince of the Irish Sea Vikings was an Irishman, and on his death, the *Annals of Tigernach* remembered him as the king of three peoples: Irish, Welsh, and Vikings. With control of Dublin and the Isles Diarmait became one of the most internationally oriented of the eleventh-century Irish kings. He used the fleets of Dublin and the Isles to interfere in English politics as an ally of the Welsh, Norse, Danes, and exiled English nobles.

The success of Diarmait was, in a way, beneficial for the Olafssons. Goodwill between Diarmait's family and the Olafssons is visible from 1014, when Diarmait's dynasty of Uí Chennselaig fought among the Leinster–Viking forces at the Battle of Clontarf. While Diarmait controlled Dublin, some of the Olafssons continued to reside there. One family was Sitric Silkenbeard's granddaughter Ragnhild, her husband the Welsh prince Cynan ap Iago, and their son Gruffudd ap Cynan, born at Dublin circa 1055. Diarmait was their ally against the Haraldssons.

The expulsion of Echmarcach from Ireland in 1052 had severed the immediate ties between Dublin and the Isles. Diarmait used his new conquest to supply manpower for his pursuit of the Irish high kingship and the destruction of his rival,

Echmarcach's brother-in-law Donnchad. Donnchad was not unaware of the danger from the expulsion of Echmarcach, for he raided Dublin in 1053 and forced Diarmait to surrender hostages. Details of the raid reveal that the territory under Dublin's control was continuing to expand. Donnchad's allies, the men of Teathbha, took prisoners from the church of Lusk, north of Swords. The geography of the region suggests that, in addition to taking control of farmland, the establishment of new harbors was a consideration.[46] Diarmait did not allow Donnchad to hold the initiative for long. In 1054, 1057, and 1058 troops from Dublin were among his forces during raids on Munster. The raid of 1058 is particularly noteworthy, for it was at the invitation of Donnchad's nephew and Diarmait's protégé Tairdelbach Ua Briain, a future claimant of the high kingship.

Together with the increasingly uncertain ethnic distinction between Viking and Irish, there is for the historian the equally difficult question, how great was the connection of commercial wealth with political events? An example of the problem comes from Murchad's raid of 1061 on the Isle of Man, where he took a tax. The invasion brought safety from an attack by Echmarcach and increased prestige. There might also have been more immediate material considerations in Murchad's choice of target. Diarmait could use the wealth from trade and manufacturing of the Viking colonies to pay for his military campaigns in Ireland. The connection of wealth with military expeditions is suggested by the chronology of his career. Only after he had taken control of Dublin did Diarmait lead raids into Munster. Following the successful invasion of the Isle of Man he was able to force his rival Donnchad from Ireland.

Diarmait mac Máel na mbó's capture of the realms of the Haraldssons and Olafssons gave him the opportunity to become involved in affairs beyond Ireland. Often the routes for these contacts were the same as those used for mercantile communication. There is direct and unambiguous Irish involvement in the political affairs of the Anglo-Saxons. For the next half-century, Ireland was a factor to be taken into consideration in the military calculations of those who ruled England, even when the Anglo-Saxon supremacy gave way to the preeminence of the Normans. Three generations of Irish princes—Diarmait, his protégé Tairdelbach Ua Briain, and Tairdelbach's son Muirchertach—were involved in the affairs of their eastern neighbor, all the time using the former domains of the Olafssons and Haraldssons as the avenue for communication.

Even before his capture of Dublin, Diarmait was involved in English affairs. This came about because of an affray on the southeastern coast of England in 1051 involving King Edward's brother-in-law Eustace, the count of Boulogne and husband of his sister Godgifu. Eustace's party had visited Edward's court and they paused to rest at the port town of Dover before boarding ship for the voyage home. A quarrel between the townsmen and the visitors arose, which led to a brawl. When it ended, several of Eustace's party were dead. A furious Edward ordered Earl Godwin of

Wessex, as the lord of the region, to punish the townsmen in the customary fashion by ravaging the town. Whether motivated by feelings of xenophobia, a belief in his security since he was the king's father-in-law (Edward was married to his daughter Edith), or just a desire to show that he was no mere errand boy, Godwin refused to act.[47] His refusal presented Edward with the opportunity to reveal publicly his hatred for his wife's family. Godwin was summoned to the royal court, and when he refused without an assurance of safe-conduct, he and his family were declared outlawed and given five days to leave the country.

Godwin and most of his family fled to Flanders, to the commercial center of Bruges. They found shelter at the court of Count Baldwin V, whose sister Judith was married to Godwin's son Tostig. Two of Godwin's sons, Harold and Leofwine, sailed to Ireland from Bristol in a ship their brother Svein apparently had readied for his personal use. The departure was difficult because of stiff winds they encountered beyond the mouth of the River Avon into the Severn, and they lost many men. The Severn was well known for its dangers to navigation, as William of Malmesbury noted in the twelfth century.[48] What happened when Harold and Leofwine reached Ireland is told in a biography of Edward that was commissioned by their sister Edith in 1065. Upon landing, the brothers were brought to the court of King *Dermodus*, that is, Diarmait mac Máel na mbó. Since Diarmait would not conquer Dublin until the following year, Harold and Leofwine probably had sailed to the port of Wexford, south of Diarmait's home territory of Uí Chennselaig and the Irish port nearest to Bristol. A little over a century later, Wexford was the main port for the early Anglo-Norman expeditionary forces to come into Ireland. Harold and Leofwine were Diarmait's guests from September 1051 to June 1052.[49]

The ship that was waiting for Harold and Leofwine at Bristol leads to two observations. First, Godwin's confrontation with King Edward seems not to have come entirely as a surprise. At least some members of his family had prepared for flight. Second, the choice of refuge for Harold and Leofwine shows that their family was in communication with Diarmait mac Máel na mbó before the flight. Their Irish interests might have been earlier, and Godwin was in attendance upon Cnut at the same time as Sitric. This is the first appearance of Bristol in the written records and also the first notice of ships sailing from a southwestern English commercial port to Ireland, a trade that would become steadily more visible.

Svein Godwinsson's preparation of a ship for his brothers at Bristol argues that Godwin and his family were engaged in trade with ports in Ireland. One item being traded was slaves. Eleventh-century England had a large slave population with a concentration in Godwin's jurisdiction. William of Malmesbury makes two significant statements on this subject. First, in *Life of St. Wulfstan*, he claims that early in the tenure of Wulfstan II as bishop of Worcester (1062–1095), Wulfstan traveled to Bristol where he denounced its trade in slaves with Ireland. The second statement, found in his *Deeds of the English Kings*, is the accusation that Godwin's wife Gytha was involved in the slave trade by selling pregnant girls. William thought those slaves were sold into Denmark, but the Viking colonies around the Irish Sea were sometimes identified as Danish in works such as *Saltair na Rann* and the history of Gruffudd ap Cynan.[50]

There are few details about how the slave trade operated around the Irish Sea, so a glance farther afield is instructive. Archbishop Wulfstan of York, in his "Sermon of the Wolf to the English" written about 1014, describes slave traders traveling with their slaves across the land. The eleventh-century poem on the Irishman Moriuht, who was captured by Vikings, claims that when he was sold at Corbridge, he was identified as being for sale with ivy placed on his head. In what seems to be a deliberate insult, the poet claims that Moriuht was sold for three silver pennies, while he purchased his wife in Rouen for one penny and his daughter for a quarter of a penny and part of a loaf. The difference in price suggests that an adult male was valued at three times an adult female, who was four times more valuable than a female child. An interesting aspect is that Moriuht's wife was preparing to marry her Viking master before she was redeemed by her husband. The Norwegian law code based on the eleventh-century Gulathing Code has detailed regulations for the sale of slaves, including the seller's guarantee that the slave is sound in health.[51]

Now the Irish Sea Vikings entered a new stage in their careers, that of mercenaries. By June of 1052 Godwin and his family were prepared to fight their way back into England. Sometime before June 24, Harold and Leofwine left Ireland with nine ships and sailed across St. George's Channel to the Severn. They raided the northern coasts of Somerset and Devon, took on provisions, and fought a major battle at Porlock. Then they sailed around Land's End and raided along the southern coast. Their father Godwin sailed from Flanders and met his sons off the Isle of Wight. Godwin followed the route used by trading ships. Adam of Bremen was told by sailors that the journey from Cinkfall (Flanders) to Prawle (Devon) took two days and one night. Combining their forces, Godwin and his sons continued their raids. The hostilities persisted for several months until September. Edward abandoned his attempts to fight Godwin when the Anglo-Saxon nobility would not support him. Godwin was reinstated in his lands and given back the offices he had held, becoming stronger than before. The coordination between the fleets reveals communication between Ireland and Flanders as news traveled with cargoes between ports. Orderic Vitalis notes that when the English king William II (William Rufus) landed unexpectedly in Normandy in 1099, he was met by a crowd at dockside eager to learn any news that was brought by crew or passengers.

During the period from 1052 to 1066 the fortunes of Diarmait and his guest Harold Godwinsson prospered. When Godwin died in 1053 Harold became the earl of Wessex and leader of his family, eventually becoming king of England. In Ireland, Diarmait's capture of Dublin gave him power and resources so that he was not only the dominant prince in the east, but his supporters also began to proclaim him high king of Ireland, albeit with reservations. The historical poem "The Lords and Rulers of Ireland after [the conversion to] Christianity" (*Do Flaithesaibh [ocus] amseraib hÉrend iar creitim*) in the *Book of Leinster*, awards Diarmait the title "king of Ireland with opposition" (*rí hÉrend co fressba*).

After Harold Godwinsson's successful return to England, Diarmait's role as powerbroker was enhanced. Nobles in need of troops traveled to Ireland to employ the fleets that Diarmait controlled. One of the first to seek his help was an English noble named Ælfgar, who was the son of Earl Leofric of Mercia. Within his family's lordship was the town of Chester, one of Dublin's main trading partners. When, late in March 1055, Ælfgar was accused of treason and a sentence of outlawry was pronounced against him, he fled to Ireland. The reasons for his misfortunes are now obscure, but seem to have involved some confrontation with Harold Godwinsson's family. Seven months later, in October, he returned to Britain with a fleet of eighteen ships, which could have been supplied only by Diarmait.[52] He allied with his family's traditional foe the lord of Gwynedd, Gruffudd ap Llywelyn. Gruffudd set aside the memory of his clashes with the Olafsson dynasty and apparently had no objections to allying with a protégé of Dublin's new proprietor. He was an excellent choice of ally, for sometime in 1055 Gruffudd had destroyed his southern Welsh rival Gruffudd ap Rhydderch and united the various Welsh kingdoms. Ælfgar and Gruffudd sailed up the Severn and began a campaign that culminated with an attack on Hereford on October 24. Hereford was in the earldom of King Edward's nephew Ralph, who failed to stop the raiders. After that success, Ælfgar and Gruffudd began to raid the English, using Wales as a safe base.

Diarmait became involved on both sides of the conflict, for the pursuit of Ælfgar and Gruffudd was taken up by his former guest Harold Godwinsson. Harold had little success in capturing Ælfgar and Gruffudd when they retreated into the Welsh mountains, and eventually he was forced to negotiate. The result was that Ælfgar was re-established in England, while Gruffudd was brought to an accommodation with the English, probably with the surrender of some territory. The *Domesday Book* account for Cheshire notes that Gruffudd was given lands east of Offa's Dyke by King Edward at some unspecified date, and this would have been a sensible time for such a transfer. When Ælfgar disbanded his mercenary force, they went to Chester for their pay. The Irish part in this alliance helps to explain why excavations in Ireland reveal amounts of pottery indicating an abrupt increase in trade between Dublin and Chester in the mid-eleventh century.

The years from 1055 to 1058 were not happy for the unfortunate Ælfgar. His father died in 1057 and Ælfgar became earl of Mercia. In 1058 he was exiled a second time, again on charges that are obscure. This time he did not flee to Ireland, but went directly to the court of Gruffudd ap Llywelyn. By now the two men may have been connected by more than politics, for Gruffudd was married to Ælfgar's daughter Ealdgytha "Swan-neck" (she later married Harold Godwinsson). While Ælfgar and Gruffudd were assembling their forces, they were unexpectedly joined by the Norse crown prince Magnus, the son of the Norwegian king Harald Hardrada. He had recruited a fleet from the Orkneys, the Isles, and Dublin for his private invasion of England. At this time the Isles were still ruled by Echmarcach Ragnallsson, so Magnus' army contained men from Echmarcach's domain collaborating with those from his foe Diarmait. Magnus joined the Anglo-Welsh army and they invaded England from the Irish Sea. English, Irish, and Welsh records all mention this expedition, with few details. The *Anglo-Saxon Chronicle* notes that some unknown extent of English territory was devastated, the *Annals of Tigernach* state that the fleet did not conquer England, and the Welsh chronicles insist that this force of arms ensured that Ælfgar was re-invested in his lands.[53]

In the mid-eleventh century, the men of Dublin and their overlord Diarmait mac Máel na mbó were aiding not just members of the Anglo-Saxon nobility, but also the Norse royal family in their maneuvers around the Irish Sea. Their involvement in England may have been even greater. In addition to great lords like Harold Godwinsson and Ælfgar Leofricson, there are indications that even lesser Englishmen were finding refuge in Ireland. An interesting document is the twelfth-century biography cum romance of a minor English aristocrat named Hereward, popularly known as Hereward "the Wake."[54] Hereward came from East Anglia and, according to the *Anglo-Saxon Chronicle*, was one of the defenders of the Isle of Ely against King William the Conqueror in 1070. In the biography, Hereward is a thoughtless youth whose bad conduct leads to his banishment from England on the orders of Edward the Confessor. He goes first to Cornwall and thence to Ireland, where he enters the service of the son of the king of Ireland. There Hereward fights in a battle against the "duke" of Munster, whose troops are routed. After a romantic interlude, during which he rescues the messengers of the son of the king of Ireland, he attempts to sail back to England. His flotilla is caught in a storm and blown north to the Orkney Islands. One ship is wrecked there, but Hereward's ship continues around Britain to Flanders, where he is shipwrecked not far from St. Bertin. He is held in close quarters by the local count until recognized by a merchant who remembers seeing him three years previously in Ireland. Hereward is released and proves his usefulness in Flanders, at a date just after the Norman conquest of England. He returns to England to claim his inheritance and defend Ely.

The Irish material in Hereward's history is an accurate reflection of the political situation in Ireland circa 1064, and it strongly supports the argument that this section is historical. Following the chronology of Hereward's adventures, he was in Ireland at least by the year 1064, because he was recognized in Flanders circa 1067 by a merchant who had seen him in Ireland three years earlier. This matches the reign of Murchad at Dublin, at the same time that his father's supporters were claiming that Diarmait was the high king of Ireland, a claim recorded in the *Book of Leinster*. Elsewhere in the narrative Hereward is associated with the prince, not the heir. 1064 was the year Diarmait and Murchad led the decisive invasion of Munster against Donnchad mac Briain. Since Donnchad had submitted to Diarmait previously, his demotion to "duke" of Munster in Hereward's saga highlights his subordinate status, much as Marianus Scotus used the same title to describe Macbeth's status in relation to King Duncan I. Hereward's residency in Flanders reflects good relations between the Flemish and English in the wake of the union of the families of Count Baldwin of Flanders and Godwin of Wessex.

Hereward's journeys from Cornwall to Ireland and from Ireland to Flanders followed the Irish Sea trade routes, and he encountered problems familiar to sailors. His storm-driven voyage to the Orkneys and on to continental Europe is not unique. The *vita* of Findan of Rheinau, a ninth-century Irish recluse on the island of Rheinau, in the Rhine, notes that he was carried by Vikings from Ireland to the Orkneys, whence he found his way to the continent; the *vita* of the Irish saint Énna mentions a storm in the Irish Sea that forced ships to shelter in the mouth of the Boyne.[55] King Æthelraed's raid on the Isle of Man in the year 1000 was due, in part, to a storm that prevented his fleet from sailing to its original destination. Evidence for a reverse of the route taken by Hereward is found in 1070, when the *Anglo-Saxon Chronicle* notes that remnants of the Danish fleet, attempting to sail from the River Humber to Denmark, were blown off course as far as Ireland.

Finally, the merchant in Flanders who had met Hereward in Ireland reflects one aspect of the contacts between the two lands. Commercial activity in Flanders was expanding during the eleventh century, providing a foundation for the greater growth afterwards.[56] The eleventh-century links between Ireland and Flanders are revealed by the rendezvous of the two groups of the family Godwinsson in 1052, the sons from Ireland meeting their father from Flanders off the southern coast of England. The Godwinssons seem to have had affection for Ireland that is revealed in a gift. A cloak at Brussels that was believed to have belonged to St. Brigit is traditionally attributed to a gift made by Godwin's widow Gytha after her flight from Exeter to Flanders in 1067.[57]

The antiquity of these contacts is a matter of debate. Hagiography is an important source of information, always bearing in mind the warning that what the authors did not know for certain, they were not above inventing. Churches made claims of ancient contacts that are difficult to prove, such as the possible connection with Clemskerke of the Anglo-Saxon missionary Willibrord, who as the apostle of the Frisians began his mission in 690 from Ireland, or the activities of the shadowy seventh-century saints named Wiro and Plechelm, supposedly Irish, who were honored at Roermonde in Limburg, Holland.[58] Allusions to contacts between Ireland and Flanders increase during the eleventh century, and some of them suggest that the writers are projecting the trade contacts of their own days into the past.[59] A seventh-century Irish saint named Livinus of Brabant was invented by a writer named Boniface sometime in the early eleventh century. Later in the century, Theofrid of Echternach claims that Willibrord sailed from Ireland to Gravelines on a stone slab, which was exhibited there in the church dedicated to the saint. At the end of the century, the *vita* of the eighth-century Rumbold of Malines (now Mechlin, Belgium), written by Abbot Thierry of St. Trond, makes him a bishop of Dublin.

Not all refugees to Ireland were English. In 1064 their ranks were joined by Gruffudd ap Llywelyn.[60] Shortly after Christmas 1063 Harold Godwinsson led a surprise attack on Gruffudd's fortress at Rhuddlan. Although Harold destroyed the fortress and most of the Welsh prince's fleet, Gruffudd himself managed to escape. He did not survive long; on August 5, 1064 he was slain by a Welsh rival. His death was announced to King Edward by the presentation of his head together with the figure-head from his ship. Gruffudd died in exile, in Ireland. Only the Irish annals know both when Gruffudd died and the name of the man who killed him. Gruffudd is one of only two eleventh-century Welsh princes (the other is his father Llywelyn) whose death is recorded in the medieval Irish annals. The details of Gruffudd's death are absent from the Welsh records. Even though their entries are brief, Gruffudd was so famous that had he been slain in Wales, it is difficult to believe that a Welsh record would not give specific information. The English records are quite clear that he was not in England.

Among the events of 1064 the *Annals of Ulster* note "the son of Llywelyn is slain by the son of Iago" (*mac Leobalem ri Bretan do marbadh la mac Iacoib*). This led to the suggestion that the "son of Iago" was Cynan ap Iago, son of Gruffudd's predecessor as king of Gwynedd, husband of Sitric Silkenbeard's granddaughter Ragnhild, and the father of Gruffudd ap Cynan, the well-known lord of Gwynedd in the late eleventh/early twelfth centuries.[61] Almost a quarter century earlier Cynan had employed the men of Dublin in an attempt to capture Gruffudd ap Llywelyn. The identity of *mac Iacoib* is confirmed by twelfth-century annals from Armagh where, among the events for 1064, is the information "slaying of Gruffudd ap Llywelyn the high king of Wales by Cynan ap Iago" (*marbad Grifrid meic Leobailin airdri Bretaine do Chanan mac Iacco*).[62] Had Gruffudd died in Wales, it is difficult to understand how Irish annals would have the details while the Welsh records are silent.

Additional information about Gruffudd in Ireland comes from Adam of Bremen. Among the triumphs of Harold Godwinsson, Adam states "he beheaded Gruffudd, a king of Ireland" (*decollavit Griphum, Hyberniae regem*).[63] Setting aside the immediate error that Harold beheaded Gruffudd (a misunderstanding of the presentation of the head to King Edward) the description of Gruffudd as an Irish king explains why the Irish annals are so informative about the circumstances of his death, because he died in Ireland.

Memories of Gruffudd's flight to Ireland survived for centuries. An Augustinian named Peter of Langtoft, a canon of Bridlington, writing during the reign of Edward I, composed a chronicle in French verse (of uneven historical value) that notes Gruffudd's flight to Ireland at the time of Harold Godwinsson's raids.[64] Much later Welsh folk tradition also connects Dublin with Gruffudd's death. There is the story found in the Iolo manuscript, a composition of the eighteenth century. This text preserves an earlier tale that Gruffudd was slain by a *Madog Minn*, who was promised a reward of three hundred cows for the deed by Harold Godwinsson. After the event Harold refused to pay and *Madog* sailed back to Dublin.[65]

The death in Ireland of Gruffudd ap Llywelyn at the hands of a man connected by marriage with the Olafssons was not widely broadcast. Despite his later fame as a unifier of Wales, Gruffudd ap Llywelyn's reign was not favorably remembered by everyone. In the late twelfth-century *Journey through Wales*, Gerald of Wales calls him a tyrant who oppressed Wales, while his friend Walter Map (who reverses Gruffudd's names and calls him Llwellyn ap Gruffudd) claims that he treacherously destroyed anyone who might possibly become a rival. Cynan is a shadowy figure at best, although in his son's biography the *History of Gruffudd son of Cynan*, he is called king of Gwynedd. This is generally disregarded because English writers claim that the half-brothers of Gruffudd ap Llywelyn reigned after his death.[66] Cynan ap Iago certainly had the correct ancestry to be king, so he may have been described as lord of Gwynedd by his son's Boswell, who would be eager to establish Gruffudd ap Cynan's right to rule.

Nonetheless, to the Welsh, Gruffudd ap Llywelyn quickly became the symbol of Welsh unity and success. Gruffudd ap Cynan's history is silent about the fate of Gruffudd ap Llywelyn, although it does provide evidence of his elevation to the status of a national hero. During Gruffudd's first expedition to Wales he was given a shirt and tunic made from the cloak of Gruffudd ap Llywelyn as a good-luck talisman.[67] The association is made even clearer when they are presented by a woman named Tangwystyl, the wife of Gruffudd ap Llywelyn's chamberlain. Gruffudd ap Llywelyn's "borrowed robes" signified the passing of legitimate rule over the Welsh, and the episode speaks volumes about the potency of his legend. So by the twelfth century, Gruffudd ap Cynan's biographer would not have wanted to mention any connection between Cynan and Gruffudd ap Llywelyn's death.

The flight of Gruffudd ap Llywelyn to Ireland was only one aspect of the contact between Ireland and Wales that was increasingly visible by the middle of the eleventh century. Part of this increase was due to the Olafssons and Dublin's colony on the Isle of Anglesey. Rule of the colony by Sitric Silkenbeard's son, Olaf, led to the marriage of his daughter with the son of a Welsh princely family. The rise to power of Gruffudd ap Llywelyn had led Olaf's son-in-law, Cynan, to involve Dublin in Welsh dynastic affairs. The early conflict between the Olafssons and Gruffudd was set aside when Gruffudd used the Irish fleet hired by Ælfgar to raid England in 1055, a fleet probably recruited in Dublin, and in 1058 Gruffudd collaborated with the Dublin fleet led by Magnus Haraldsson. Contacts were not limited to princes. Sulien, the future bishop of St. David's (1073–78 and 1080–85), completed his education in Ireland. He might have stayed at the *Tech na mBretan* ("House of the Welsh") within the church precincts at Kells, which is mentioned in the eleventh-century notes to the Calendar of Oengus. Possibly within Dublin's territory, near Brannixtown (county Kildare) was another *Tech na Bretnach*.

In 1066 Diarmait mac Máel na mbó and Harold Godwinsson were at the height of their powers when Harold became king of England on January 6, 1066, the day after his brother-in-law Edward the Confessor died. During his brief reign as King Harold II, Harold Godwinsson initiated a coinage series with a distinctive reverse style.[68] After his death in October 1066, the coin series was soon abandoned and relatively few examples survive. Evidence of how trade followed political goodwill, and the increasing importance of trade between Ireland and England, is provided by the coins of Dublin. The Dublin mint began to imitate the reverse design of Harold's coins almost as soon as they appeared in England; examples of five derivative types survive. Equally revealing is the weight ratio of Irish to English coins. The weight of Irish coins in the eleventh century varied in relation to English coins, but during this period the weight ratio of Irish to English coins was consistently 3:2, and this was maintained for some years after Diarmait's death. This is almost a "fixed" rate of exchange, which was useful mainly between lands with substantial trading interests.

Challenges to Harold's authority came from his brother and abroad. The most serious rival was his brother Tostig, who allied with the Norwegian king Harald Hardrada. Tostig had been forced from his earldom of Northumbria by a popular uprising in 1065. He blamed his brother for his loss and demanded to be restored. When Harold refused, Tostig began to search the courts around northern Europe, looking for a patron who would support him in an invasion. After approaching his sworn brother the Scottish king Malcolm III and the Danish king Svein, he finally won the support of Harald Hardrada by promising him the English throne. Harald had claimed the English kingship, according to Snorri Sturluson, by right of the agreement made between Harald's half-brother, Magnus the Good, and Cnut's son, Hardacnut, Edward the Confessor's half-brother. William of Malmesbury claims that Tostig and Harald made their plans at the court of Malcolm III, although the account in *Morkinskinna* claims that Guthorm Gunhildarson, who had previously defeated Murchad mac Diarmata off Anglesey, was sent by Tostig to the Norwegian court.[69] Tostig and Harald sailed from Norway via the Orkneys to the River Humber in mid-September with a fleet of two hundred ships in addition to numerous lesser vessels. They defeated a Northumbrian force and captured York, but were defeated shortly afterwards at the Battle of Stamford Bridge by Harold Godwinsson, who would be defeated himself several weeks later at the Battle of Hastings by William, the duke of Normandy.

A little known aspect to the invasion of Tostig and Harald Hardrada is their use of troops from Ireland. Adam of Bremen gave a brief account of the Battle of Stamford Bridge, in which he claimed that Harald was assisted by an unidentified "king of the Scots" (*rex Scotorum*).[70] This might be a reference to the Scottish king Malcolm III, but if so then it is mistaken for no other record claims that he was at

Stamford Bridge. Furthermore Adam claimed that an unidentified "king of Ireland" (*rex Hiberniae*) was slain in the battle. The *rex Scotorum* and the *rex Hiberniae* could easily be the same person; one title means king of the *Scotti* (either Irish or Scots) while the other designates a king from Ireland. The Irish annals are silent about the death outside of Ireland of any major Irish king, while the English and Norse records are silent about the presence of any contingent from Ireland at the battle.

Adam of Bremen's account must not be dismissed too quickly as mere confusion, because among his informants was King Svein of the Danes, who had been approached by Tostig to participate in the invasion. Adam was an exact contemporary of the battle and wrote his history less than twenty years afterwards. Ships from all of northern Europe called at Hamburg, and among their crews could have been men who had fought in the battle. Adam also mentions the defeat and death of Harold Godwinsson by William the Conqueror at Hastings in October of 1066, but, not unreasonably, fails to supply the details such as he gives for the Battle of Stamford Bridge. An additional reason for accepting Adam of Bremen's account comes from *Morkinskinna*, which claims that England was defended by troops from many countries, but especially Norse-speakers. The expedition to Britain of Harald Hardrada's son, Magnus, in 1058 is worth remembering in this context, drawing troops from the Orkneys to Ireland. Harald made the Orkneys his base of operations, with his wife and daughter remaining there while he sailed south. The claim that Guthorm Gunhildarson was involved in the negotiations among the Scots, Norwegians, and Tostig is important, especially since he lived at Dublin. This opens a new possibility for either or both the *rex Scotorum* and the *rex Hiberniae*, that he or they were from the Viking colonists among the Gaelic-speakers.

At least one Viking from Dublin fought at Stamford Bridge. In the *Manx Chronicle*, the first item of unique information is the flight to the Isle of Man from Stamford Bridge of a man named Godred Crovan, a member of the Olafsson dynasty, a son of Ivar Haraldsson the former king of Dublin.[71] The flight of Godred Crovan shows that the Olafssons were still involved with the Norwegian royal house. As in 1058, when the *Annals of Tigernach* specifically mention Dublin as supplying troops, there was a tie between Ireland and Norway, which can be dated to the last years of the tenth century and the marriage of the future Norwegian king Olaf Tryggvason to Olaf Cuaran's daughter Gytha. The "Saxon battle" *cath Saxain* is given as one of the important events of 1066 by a contemporary Irish poet named Gilla Cóemgain, who includes it in his chronological poem *Annalad anall uile* for the year 1066: "The Saxon battle of clear course / in which fell the king of Norway," that is the Battle of Stamford Bridge where Harald Hardrada died.[72] Not until the next century did Irish poets interest themselves in the Battle of Hastings. The twelfth-century verse history from Armagh that noted the death of Gruffudd ap Llywelyn at the hands of Cynan ap Iago appends a notice of Hastings to its account of Stamford Bridge: "[A year after the death of Echmarcach] to the death of Edward king of the Saxons and to the battle of Harald from Norway in which died three thousand Norwegians around the king and nine thousand Saxons and to the battle of Harold [Godwinsson] the same [length of time] against the Franks in which died Harold by them."[73]

However important the Battle of Stamford Bridge was to the families living around the Irish Sea, it was the later battle, Hastings, that was far more momentous. After his death, Harold Godwinsson's family dispersed. Several of Harold's children fled to the Danish court where their cousin Svein (whose father was the brother of Harold's mother) was reigning. From there Harold's daughter Gytha (named after her paternal grandmother) left to marry Valdimar II Monomach, the king of Kiev and Novgorod. Another refuge was Ireland. Two of Harold's sons—Godwin and Edwin—along with their cousin, Tostig, retraced the path that Harold had taken a quarter of a century earlier when they fled to the court of Diarmait mac Máel na mbó. Proximity to Dublin could have been among the reasons why Harold's second wife Æthelgytha "Swan's neck," the daughter of Ælfgar of Mercia (previously wife of Gruffudd ap Llywelyn), went to Chester with her children. Her son Harold re-appeared in the Irish Sea in 1098 when he was the pilot for the Norse king Magnus Barefoot during his first invasion. Other members of Harold's family, such as his mother, Gytha, and his sister, Gunnhild, remained in England briefly before fleeing to the continent.[74]

The battles of Hastings and Stamford Bridge were disasters for the Olafssons. The army of the Norwegian king Harald had contained troops from Ireland, including a descendant of Olaf Cuaran. The defeat of Harold Godwinsson at the Battle of Hastings broke the last link between Svein Forkbeard's family, the Olafssons' patrons, and the kingship of England. The same battles were less disastrous for the Haraldssons. William the Conqueror, the victor of Hastings, had familial associations with the kings of the Isles, who had fought for his grandfather Richard II. In the midst of all this was Diarmait mac Máel na mbó. His capture of Dublin in 1052 brought him an international port and a foothold in Wales. Nine years later he added the Isles to his empire when his son Murchad defeated Echmarcach on the Isle of Man. Using the fleets built up by the Olafssons and Haraldssons, Diarmait played kingmaker around the Irish Sea. He supplied troops to the English and their foes. His adventures demonstrate how Irish kings extended their influence outside Ireland. Cooperation between the Irish and Norwegians in 1058 and 1066 illustrate how Diarmait used "Viking" tactics and connections.

A new era opened for all the princes around the Irish Sea. Armies became larger, trade became more important for political plans, and the goodwill of the Church became crucial for a stable reign. The Viking pirates were about to end their period of obscurity in a final struggle for supremacy that was crucial for the Olafssons and Haraldssons.

7

The Contest for Supremacy in the Irish Sea

THE POLITICAL ORGANIZATION around the Irish Sea that had been disrupted so severely by the Viking raiders of the ninth century was very different by the end of the eleventh century. Small kingdoms and political fragmentation had given way to a few powerful families controlling vast empires. Ironically, this had repercussions for the descendants of the Viking settlers, as the Olafsson and Haraldsson dynasties were diminishing in influence under pressure from the great lords. The capture of Dublin by Diarmait mac Máel na mbó might have been seen by contemporaries as a temporary occupation due, in part, to the intrusion into its kingship by an interloper from the Isles. The Irish conquest of the Isle of Man starkly illustrated the real danger to the Viking families; the sea was no longer their refuge. Twenty years later, after Diarmait's death in 1072 and the seizure of Dublin by his protégé Tairdelbach ua Briain of Munster, the permanence of the Irish domination of the Viking settlements was clear. The dynasty of Olaf Cuaran had been unable, or unwilling, to reassert its independence. Less and less were they the masters of their fate. The temporary seizure of the town late in the eleventh century by Olaf Cuaran's descendant Godred Crovan and the efforts by the Irish to recapture it emphasize the importance of the commercial center as a revenue generator for the princes who controlled it.

The Viking towns in Ireland became less frontier settlements between the Celtic and Scandinavian worlds and more avenues for Irish contact with the rest of Europe. This was particularly true for the new masters of England, the Normans. Contacts between Normandy and Ireland began with early Irish missions to the continent. The Irish saint Columbanus had labored briefly around the Seine, where he had blessed a future bishop and saint of Rouen named Ouen. Irish travelers to the continent had entered through ports on the River Seine and, by the ninth century, wayfarers from Ireland could find shelter at *hospitalia Scottorum*, whose maintenance was the subject of correspondence between the bishop of Rouen and Lewis the German. These contacts were remembered in the eleventh and twelfth centuries by the historians William of Jumièges, a student of the school where Columbanus was honored, and Orderic Vitalis.[1]

Antique ties were replaced with modern contact. Bishop Gillebert of Limerick was a friend of Archbishop Anselm of Canterbury; Gillebert had been a monk at Westminster and might have studied under Anselm at Bec.[2] Commercial contacts specifically with Normandy were increasing, and Norman deniers from the mid-eleventh century are found in Dublin as well as in the Isles. A charter issued by Henry of Anjou, the future Henry II of England, confirms the near monopoly on trade from Normandy to Ireland that was enjoyed by the men of Rouen, a situation that the charter claims had existed since the days of Henry I.[3]

The contacts spread more widely than a single port in one region as commercial, ecclesiastical, and political accommodations followed one another. Diarmait mac Máel na mbó's control of Dublin allowed him to extend his influence into Britain as seen in his support of the Godwinssons, revealing the Bristol–Ireland connection, and also in the flight of the Mercian lord Ælfgar to Ireland along the Chester–Dublin trade route. Later in the eleventh century, material excavated at Dublin shows that there was a shift in trade toward southwest Britain and the northern continental ports.[4] Merchants who traveled between Flanders and Ireland are mentioned in the romance of Hereward, while there was a continental orientation in coins minted at Dublin.[5]

The flight of Harold Godwinsson's sons to Ireland after his defeat at Hastings demonstrates the strength of their family's ties with Diarmait mac Máel na mbó, who was seen as a staunch supporter of the Old English Order. His visitors probably presented to him the standard of Edward the Confessor, which Diarmait later presented to his protégé Tairdelbach ua Briain, the king of Munster.[6] Like their father in 1051, Ælfgar Leofricson in 1055 and 1058, and probably Gruffudd ap Llywelyn in 1064, the sons of Harold wanted Diarmait's fleets and troops in order to reestablish themselves in Britain. Harold's mother, Gytha, fled to Exeter, where she hoped to organize resistance to the Normans in the family's southwest stronghold, because of the region's trade connections with Ireland. In 1067 she fled to Flanders rather than surrender to William the Conqueror.

The sons of Harold Godwinsson used the fleets built up by the Olafssons and Haraldssons. In the summer of 1068 Diarmait supplied the first expedition from Ireland under the command of Harold's eldest son Godwin.[7] He led a fleet of fifty-two ships along the trade routes to the Bristol Channel and up the River Avon to Bristol. His attack on the town was unsuccessful. Godwin's fleet then retraced its path and sailed along the coast of north Somerset. The reason for the direction is tied to land ownership. Godwin had held two small estates in Somerset and Devon; his estate at Nettlecomb was not far from the Bristol Channel.[8] In addition to a friendly welcome from his former men, Godwin needed supplies of food and water. As the fleet continued to move westwards around the coast, a battle was fought against Eadnoth, his father's *stallere* ("constable"), who was now in the service of the Normans. The location of their battle is thought to have been Bleadon (east of the River Axe in North Somerset), an estate held by the bishop of Winchester.[9] Once again there were family ties, for Bleadon had been given to the bishop by Godwin's grandmother Gytha. Godwin Haroldsson won a great victory, and Eadnoth fled with his troops. Victory had come at the cost of heavy losses to Godwin's forces. After a plundering expedition around Devon and Cornwall to pay his sailors (a percentage of the loot being the usual wage) Godwin led his fleet back to Ireland.

The Normans were aware of the danger posed by English refugees in Ireland, but there was no easy solution to the problem. William simply could not march his troops into Ireland as a demonstration of his power. An added problem for the Normans was trying to guess who Diarmait would, or would not, support. During the previous decade alone his subjects had fought for the Norwegians, Welsh, and Anglo-Saxons. This probably explains why William set up his loyal follower William fitz Osbern in western Britain. Fitz Osbern guarded the important water gap leading into Britain from St. George's Channel via the Bristol Channel and, sometime in 1067, he was designated *comes palatii* ("Count Palatine") of an area extending from Herefordshire around the Severn and the Bristol Channel to Bristol. As one of William's most faithful companions, fitz Osbern was viceroy when the Conqueror returned to Normandy.[10]

The Conqueror needed to be vigilant on his western coasts. The success of Godwin Haroldsson in 1068 meant that he would return, and it may have encouraged the general English uprising of 1069–1070. That rebellion was especially dangerous as the disaffected Anglo-Saxons allied with the Danes, Scots, and Irish in an attempt to throw the Normans back across the channel. Direct communication between Ireland and Denmark is suggested by the Danish designs that begin to appear on coins minted at Dublin in the mid-eleventh century. More provocative is the discovery in Denmark of a ship constructed in Ireland circa 1042 that was scuttled in 1070 to form part of the Skuldelev barrier. The ship might have transported emissaries from Ireland, possibly some of the sons of Harold Godwinsson, to Denmark in order to coordinate the attacks from the two lands.[11] Such an alliance explains the remark in the *Anglo-Saxon Chronicle* that when the Danish fleet was scattered by a storm off the English coast in 1070, some of the ships ended up in Ireland. Little can be said with certainty, yet the plan appears to have been that raids from Ireland were to start in the summer, leading to uprisings in the southwest that would coincide with rebellion in Northumbria supported by a fleet from Denmark.

The rebellion of 1069 began as a power struggle in northern England that became more international in scope as the year progressed.[12] The earldom of Northumbria had been sold in 1068 by King William to Cospatric son of Maldred, a cousin of the Scottish king Malcolm Canmore. When Cospatric turned his support to Edgar Æthling, the brother-in-law of Malcolm, William gave the earldom to one of his men named Robert de Comines. Robert was ambushed at Durham late in January 1069 by an English army, and then burned to death in the bishop's lodgings. The victorious army next attacked York and captured the town, but not the fortress. After relieving the garrison, King William gave the lordship to his trusted lieutenant William fitz Osbern. Fitz Osbern had completely subdued the region when he joined the king at Winchester for the Easter feast. The Northumbrians were subdued only momentarily and began negotiations with the Danes for assistance.

In the midst of this, in June of 1069, Godwin led another fleet from Ireland across St. George's Channel. He was accompanied by his brother, Edwin, and possibly by their cousin, Tostig. This was a slightly larger flotilla than the previous year, with about sixty-four ships. The raids began where the previous attacks had ended. The fleet sailed south around the Cornish peninsula and fought a battle at the River Tavy before continuing on toward Exeter. *Domesday Book* gives a rare glimpse of the destruction around the Start Bay. Nine manors—Thurlestone, Bagton, Collaton, South Huish, Galmpton, Portlemouth, Ilton, Alston, and Soar—belonging to Iudhael of Totnes were devastated by the "Irishmen" (*homines Irlandes*).[13] Collectively the estates had been rated at 225 shillings in 1066, but their valuation was reduced drastically after the attacks. Seventeen years later they were worth only 150 shillings.

Emboldened by their success, the fleet attempted to capture Exeter. The townsmen were successful in defending themselves, and the invaders sailed off. As had happened in the previous year, the fleet retraced its path. Sailing around Land's End to the north coast of Devon, at the River Taw the Haroldssons were met by Count

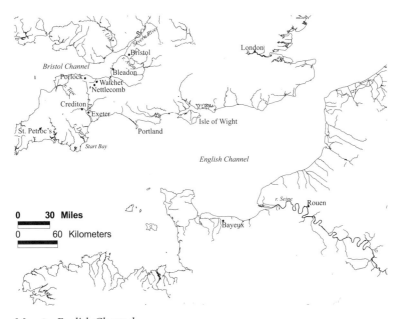

MAP 8. *English Channel*

Brian fitz Eudo. He was the son of the count of Brittany and had recently received lands in the neighborhood. Two battles were fought on June 23. The outcome of the first battle was indecisive, but the second one ended in a rout of the Irish fleet. Brian seems to have distributed lands among followers who made up his private army, and they, rather than a supportive local population, could have provided his victory.[14] The sons of Harold led their forces back to Ireland, never to return. They had raised the standard of rebellion in their native fields and had failed.

The eventual fate of the sons of Harold Godwinsson is unknown. Nine months after their return to Ireland a great plague swept through Dublin. Among the casualties was Diarmait mac Máel na mbó's son, Murchad. Other victims could have included Harold's sons. Their memory might have been preserved in a sword. In 1165 the prince of Ulaid named Eochaid mac Dúinnsléibhe gave to the high king Muirchertach Mac Lochlainn the "sword of the son of the earl." The earl in question might have been Harold Godwinsson and the sword could have been sent to Ulster during the alliance between Diarmait's kingdom of Uí Chennselaig and the Ulaid. If so, this would have been a fitting memento of a failed dream.

The plague at Dublin in 1070 shows that an international port was especially susceptible to disease. A list of these outbreaks illustrates the point. In 1015 there was a disease of the legs and putrefaction in Dublin and Leinster. A plague accompanied by fevers struck the town in 1084, again killing a large number of people. The Tigernach chronicler asserts that it was caused by demons from the northern isles, suggesting that ships from the Northern Hebrides or the Orkneys were being blamed for carrying the disease. Dublin might have been the Irish port of entry for the great plague of 1095–96, and a plague that ravaged southern Ireland in 1117 was especially virulent in Dublin.

The failure of Harold Godwinsson's sons in Britain was part of the general defeat of the Anglo-Saxon insurgents. In the autumn the anticipated Danish fleet arrived in Britain. Testing the defenses from Kent to the Humber, the ships joined a land force raised by Edgar and Cospatric for an attack on York. After capturing the town, the Anglo-Danish force retreated when they learned of the king's approach. The Danes were accused of being too interested in looting with too little appetite for fighting the Normans. As winter approached, the Danes prepared to stay over and resume the fight in the spring. The Normans did not wait for better weather, but reacted immediately, vigorously, and sternly with the famous "harrowing of the North." King William created a path of destruction across Northumbria into Mercia that would not be mended fully until the next century; his path can be traced from *Domesday Book* accounts of flourishing farms in 1066 that were wasteland 20 years later.

With the Normans now having the upper hand, the fiasco of 1069 continued into the next year for the rebels. In 1070 King Svein personally led a flotilla to England in order to relieve and reinforce the Danes who had wintered on the shores of the Humber. As his fleet sailed up the Humber, support from the terrorized and devastated local population never materialized. After coming to terms with William, Svein returned to Denmark. Just as it seemed that matters could not become any worse, in the midst of the retreat a violent storm scattered the Danish fleet. The *Anglo-Saxon Chronicle* notes that some of the ships were forced to sail to Norway, some reached Denmark, and others journeyed to Ireland. While a storm on the eastern English coast could have forced ships simultaneously to Denmark, Norway, and Ireland, it is possible that the ships arriving in Ireland were mercenary vessels simply returning to port or Danes finding a friendly harbor.

The continuing western threat to his newly won kingdom of England was not lost on William the Conqueror. Contemporary and near-contemporary references from English and Norman sources suggest that invasions (and their future possibility) from Ireland were more of a worry to the Normans than they are generally credited with being. A dozen years after the last invasion from Ireland, the Irish were thought to be plotting fresh mischief in league with the Danes. When, in 1082, William's half-brother Odo of Bayeux was tried on a charge of treason, the account of his trial given by Orderic Vitalis claims that William made a speech accusing his brother of taking men from England who were needed to repel attacks by the Danes and the Irish.[15] Orderic is not alone in suggesting that the Irish menace was a worry for the Normans. The *Book of Ely* account of the siege of Ely in 1069 claims that the Conqueror was forced to abandon his blockade because he had to repel invasions from, among others, the Irish.[16]

William the Conqueror placed three major lordships in western England. The lordship given to William fitz Osbern has been mentioned. A second lordship was created around Cheshire. This was entrusted, circa 1071, to a brutal, competent, and loyal warrior named Hugh of Avranches. He is better known as Hugh of Chester, although more accurate is his nickname "the Wolf."[17] By 1086 Hugh had a tight grasp on his territory and also much of northern Wales. His main ally was his kinsman Robert (who had lived in England during the reign of Edward the Confessor) who made his main base at Gruffudd ap Llywelyn's fortress of Rhuddlan. The third lordship was set up on the Welsh border at Shrewsbury, between Hereford and Chester, on the western borders of what had been the Old English earldom of Mercia. King William entrusted it to Roger of Montgomery, who had guarded Normandy in the absence of the duke and, like fitz Osbern and Ranulf of Chester, had supplied ships for the invasion of 1066.[18] William was prepared to chance the creation of possible centers of rebellion in order to guard his western borders.

Rebellion did come. After William fitz Osbern was slain at the Battle of Cassel in 1071, his lordship was given to his son Roger de Breteuil. Roger was less loyal than his father and he participated in the baronial revolt of 1075. When the rebellion failed, he lost his lands and was imprisoned for life. By that time, William seemed to believe that the threat from Ireland was diminished while revolt at home was an increased possibility (despite citing the Irish threat at his half-brother Odo's trial). So William fitz Osbern's lordship was divided, in order to prevent it becoming a base for other rebels.

⚜

In Ireland failure, like success, came in waves for Diarmait mac Máel na mbó. At the beginning of 1069 he had replaced all the Viking dynasties as the most powerful captain in the seas between Ireland and Britain. By the end of the same year his empire began to crumble in a dizzying rush of catastrophes. Perhaps the beginning of the end can be dated to the failure of the Haroldssons' invasion of 1069, with its repercussions reaching beyond England and Denmark. Personal tragedy struck when Diarmait's son, Murchad, died in Dublin of the plague. Almost Murchad's last act was to promise ships and soldiers for a young half-Welsh descendant of Olaf Cuaran named Gruffudd son of Cynan so that he could return to Gwynedd and capture his patrimony. Later that same year Diarmait lost a second son, Glúniairn. His loss extended beyond that of a father because his sons had been trusted deputies in the administration of the family empire. Now Diarmait's hold on his empire steadily slipped as hostilities erupted within his family. Matters became so bad in 1071 that his protégé, Tairdelbach ua Briain, a grandson of Brian Boru and the provincial king of Munster, was forced to enter Leinster and restore order. The end came on February 7, 1072, when Diarmait led his troops north to fight a battle at Odba (county Meath) against Conchobar Ua Máil Shechnaill. His good fortune finally exhausted, Diarmait was captured after being defeated in battle and then beheaded, the customary fashion of execution.

After Diarmait's death at the Battle of Odba, Dublin was seized by Tairdelbach Ua Briain, who promptly busied himself with efforts to be recognized as high king of Ireland. For the next fourteen years, his armies ranged at will throughout the island. Even though the annals politely claim that Tairdelbach was given the lordship of Dublin by its inhabitants, his position was based upon military might. Any loyalty Tairdelbach felt for Diarmait did not extend to other members of his family. Diarmait's brother, Domnall, was in Dublin when Tairdelbach arrived, and he was unceremoniously expelled. The new master of the town gave the title "king of Dublin" to Godfrey son of Olaf son of Ragnall, who made formal submission in the company of three other princes.

All that is certainly known about Godfrey are the names of his father and grandfather. There is the slight possibility that he was the grandson of Olaf Cuaran's son, Ragnall (who was slain at the Battle of Tara in 980), but, in light of the Haraldsson alliance with Tairdelbach's family, it is fairly certain that he was a nephew of Echmarcach, the son of an otherwise unknown child of Ragnall Godfreysson named Olaf. The name Olaf was also that of Echmarcach's cousin, Olaf son of Lagmann, who died at the Battle of Clontarf. There was a direct family link between Echmarcach and Tairdelbach, through the marriage of Tairdelbach's son, Tadc, to Echmarcach's daughter, Mor. Family ties are visible before Godfrey's elevation to the kingship of Dublin. In 1073 his brother, Sitric, was killed during an invasion of the Isle of Man in the company of two young relatives of Tairdelbach.

Other than the date of his submission to Tairdelbach and his death, only one other activity of Godfrey is known—his participation in the selection of a bishop for Dublin. On May 6, 1074, the first incumbent of the metropolitan of Dublin, Archbishop Donatus, died after a reign of probably 46 years (counting from the pilgrimage of Sitric to Rome in 1028). He was buried in the church he had built, Holy Trinity (now Christ Church), and his grave was on the left side of the high altar.[19]

A new bishop for Dublin was consecrated by Archbishop Lanfranc of Canterbury. His name was *Gilla-Patraic*, and he took the name Patrick (*Patricius*) in religion.[20] Patrick had been trained in the monastic life at Worcester. While Patrick's profession to Lanfranc contains the statement that Dublin was a metropolitan, and his predecessor Donatus is described as archbishop in the Irish chronicles, Patrick is described only as bishop. At some point the ecclesiastical status of Dublin was reduced to a bishopric. This might reflect that Godfrey Olafsson's status was much less than that of Sitric Silkenbeard.

According to Lanfranc's letter to Godfrey, Patrick had been sent from Dublin at Godfrey's personal direction. Lanfranc consecrated Patrick according to the custom of his predecessors, a reference to the ordination of Donatus. Such statements were not made idly or willfully, and the earlier ordination could be behind Lanfranc's statement to Pope Alexander II in the spring of 1072 that he had learned from Bede's *Ecclesiastical History* that his predecessors had primacy over Ireland. Bede never said that, although such an interpretation is sensible if Lanfranc knew that the archbishop of Dublin was a suffragan of Canterbury.

Lanfranc's announcement of Patrick's consecration was sent both to Godfrey, called "glorious king of Ireland" and to his overlord Tairdelbach, who is described as "magnificent king of Ireland"; Lanfranc was uncertain of the precise political arrangement, but determined not to offend. The exchange of letters illustrates a desire for good relations on the part of both the Normans and the Irish, and also between the Haraldssons and the Normans. More immediately important to Lanfranc was to establish a definitive right of primacy. Lanfranc seized the opportunity for pastoral work. His letters to Godfrey and Tairdelbach admonish and correct as he urges the kings to patronize reform in their churches. Both kings are directed to correct the marital laxities of their subjects, especially divorce and remarriage. Lanfranc particularly praised Tairdelbach for his good government (mentioned by Patrick) and asked him to stop the irregular ordination of bishops, the uncanonical baptism of infants, and the practice of simony. The archbishop revealed his ignorance of social organization in Ireland by complaining that bishops served in small towns or villages. Other than the Viking towns or a few large churches such as Armagh, there was nothing else.

The government of Lanfranc's king and friend William the Conqueror was constantly in need of funds, and supplying Dublin with a bishop gave the Normans an entrance into a trading partner's community. An illustration of the practical aspects to the interconnection of Church and commerce is seen in 1081. Lanfranc was holding a council at Gloucester when he received a letter from Bishop Domnall Ua hÉnna of Munster (whom Lanfranc addresses as "bishop of Ireland"), concerning the communication of infants. Lanfranc states in his reply that he had asked Domnall's messenger to stay for a few days while he prepared a detailed response, but the courier insisted that he had to leave immediately.[21] Appended to Domnall's letter was a puzzle. This was a friendly overture, but the times had changed. Lanfranc brusquely declined this once common pleasantry and replied that he put away childish things when he became a man (I Corinthians 13:11). The haste of the letter-bearer is that of a sailor whose movements are dictated by the winds and the tides. Even though Gloucester's trade with Ireland becomes visible in twelfth-century documents, this episode is another reminder that there was an antiquity to such connections.

The little that is known about Bishop Patrick comes primarily from his writings, which also give an indication of the intellectual preoccupations in Viking Dublin. Patrick wrote at least five separate works: "The Wonders of Ireland," a poem on the curiosities of Ireland; "The Book of Holy Patrick," a letter to his brethren at Worcester including St. Wulfstan; "Verses," an essay on the fate of the soul; an "Allegory" on the human condition, which is difficult to interpret but seems to look to the fantastic imagery of the voyage literature; and "To a Friend on the Frailty of Life," a second essay on transitory life. The themes, content, and treatment provide insights into Patrick's background. His historical interests, visible in "The Wonders of Ireland," might be responsible for the beginning of an annalistic tradition at Dublin. Annals found in the Black Book of Christ Church and in the records from the Abbey of St. Mary's, Dublin, begin to give information about Dublin while Patrick is bishop.[22]

Patrick was a native of Ireland. Several times in his "Wonders of Ireland" he refers to the island as his "homeland" (*patria*). While Patrick refers to Ireland as "our land," he never refers to the Irish as "our people," but as a separate race. In a passage on werewolves, he notes that they were found among the *Scotti* "Irish." He goes to some lengths to reinforce the idea of distinct identity, as in his comment on the absence of snakes in Ireland: "This island, which the Scots are known to have as their country, holds no snakes." To be a native of Ireland but not to consider oneself "Irish" can mean only that Patrick was a descendant of Viking colonists. He was known to the people of Dublin, who had specifically requested that he be made their bishop. James Ware cites a source claiming that Patrick was an "Easterling" (i.e., descendant of Vikings) and gives a transcript of a, now lost, letter supposedly sent by the citizens of Dublin to Lanfranc.[23] So by the eleventh century, what had formerly been a nest of Viking pirates appears to be producing its own bishop.

Patrick might have been a student of Bishop Donatus of Dublin before being sent for his monastic training in the Benedictine community at Worcester, under the supervision of Bishop Wulfstan II. He certainly displayed that mixture of scholarship and political shrewdness that was so typical of the medieval Benedictine historians. In a survey of the wonders at Tara, Patrick noted that it was the seat of the king of the *Scotti*, but, in an illuminating aside, he states that this was "in former times." His historical revisionism shows Patrick's awareness that his patron Tairdelbach Ua Briain's propagandists were claiming that Cashel had anciently been the superior of Tara, as stated in the *Book of Rights*.

Patrick's place of training, Worcester, had a tradition of interest in the Irish that dated back at least to the tenth century. There were copies of the tract on church discipline known as the *Hibernensis* in the cathedral's library as well as works by the ninth-century Irish intellectual at the Carolingian court named Smaragdus. Interest in Irish affairs continued into the eleventh century; a copy of the letter from Pope Gregory VII to Tairdelbach Ua Briain survives in a Worcester manuscript.[24] By the second half of the eleventh century, the great St. Wulfstan of Worcester had become interested in the Irish. Wulfstan was a valuable intermediary between the Irish and the Normans and one of the most steadfast supporters of both the Conqueror and Rufus. An outspoken opponent of the Irish Sea slave trade, he was also a correspondent with Irish princes, possibly Godfrey or Tairdelbach.[25] During the aforementioned rebellion of 1075, rebellious barons led by Roger of Breteuil were prevented from crossing the River Severn by a force under the command of Bishop Wulfstan. In 1088, when there was a baronial revolt against Rufus, Wulfstan again stood fast for the king against Roger de Lacy and Ralph de Mortimer. He was genuinely respected by the common people, and after his death, Wulfstan became the patron saint of the sailors on the trade routes between Ireland and England.

Patrick's consecration at St. Paul's, London, reveals another aspect to the ecclesiastical ties throughout the Irish Sea. The Olafssons and Haraldssons influenced military affairs between Ireland and Britain for decades. Now the bishopric established by Sitric Silkenbeard gave the Normans their first "foothold" in Ireland. By the end of the eleventh century, Canterbury's interest in Ireland increased, establishing its candidate at Waterford in 1096. At Lanfranc's urging, Patrick might have introduced a community of Benedictine monks into Dublin. A letter from Anselm to a later bishop of Dublin, Samuel Ua hAnglí, written circa 1096, scolds him for expelling the monks from the cathedral.[26]

Lanfranc gave thought to ecclesiastical organization and reform in Britain and Ireland. As with the consecration of Bishop Patrick, Lanfranc promoted his program at the highest levels of society. When, in 1073, Archbishop Thomas I of York requested aid from Lanfranc for the consecration of a bishop of the Orkneys named Ralph, those selected were Wulfstan of Worcester and Peter of Chester.[27] Both men resided in towns that were gateways to the Viking world. Chester's long-standing trading ties with Dublin and the Isles extended to Norway according to Lucian of St. Werburgh's, Chester, who proudly described the ships from Norway that called at the town.[28] Lanfranc may have wanted to bring all the Scandinavian settlements around Britain and in Ireland under the influence of Canterbury. If so his plans came to naught. By the mid-twelfth century Dublin was placed firmly within the Irish orb by the papal legate John Papairo at the Synod of Kells in 1152. At roughly the same time, the English Pope Adrian IV (Nicholas Breakspear) gave jurisdiction over the islands from Man to the Shetlands to the Archbishop of Trondheim.

Bishop Patrick's literary career and reforming interests were formed during his training at Worcester, in the midst of the great reformation of the English church carried out largely by continental clergy, such as Lanfranc.[29] By that time reform movements were sweeping through Europe, and targeted many conservative elements, such as the Irish Church. Pride of place among the abuses, at least in the eyes of the reformers, was secular interference in church affairs. Efforts to eliminate irregular influence had come to a head at the Synod of Sutri in 1046. Simony had been specifically condemned, but this did not go far enough for some. A contemporary tract, *De ordinando pontifice auctor Gallicus*, emphasized that the prohibition against lay interference in church affairs extended even to so prominent a layman as a monarch.[30] This tract seems to have been written in lower Lorraine late in 1047; a place where, and time when, Irish clergy were active. In Ireland secularized officials were powerful. The head of a church, the *comarbai* "heir," and his local representative the *aircinnech* "head" (who oversaw a particular church), were rarely in Holy Orders and usually represented the local aristocracy. Nevertheless, their power in the Irish Church hierarchy was very substantial.

A lively debate on reform had been ongoing among the Irish clergy. The argument is reflected in contemporary eschatological texts.[31] A commentary on the Day of Judgment, known simply as "Judgment" (*Brath*), gives a list of those who were especially in danger of damnation, including the "proud" clergy. What were these arrogant clerics doing? According to another text, the "Vision of Adomnán" (*Fís Adomnáin*), they taught false doctrines, and a group singled out for particular attention were the heads of the monastic schools (*fir léighinn*) who taught heresy. One person's abomination could be another's orthodoxy. Depending on one's views, heresy could have included the theological teachings of Bishop Patrick. Certainly some of his flock in Dublin appear to have been considered candidates for damnation. The "Vision of Adomnán" includes dishonest artisans, cloth makers, and traders among those in greatest danger of judgment. Setting aside the definition of "dishonest," this list encompassed a substantial portion of the inhabitants of the Viking towns who combined manufacture with commerce.

While reformers throughout the eleventh and twelfth centuries, such as Pope Gregory VII or St. Bernard of Clairvaux (in his *Life of Malachy*) emphasized the primitive elements in the Irish Church, they are not objective guides. Bishop Patrick had impeccable reformist tendencies, and the literature shows a debate in the Irish Church about reform. Patrick had been trained in England at Worcester, a house famous for its intellectual interests that extended to Irish texts. His background on the matter of church reform suggests just how different was the intellectual climate at Dublin from what was broadly true in Ireland. Finally, Bishop Patrick does not appear to have been popular in Ireland; among the dozens of copies of his works, not one survives in an Irish manuscript.

The goodwill between Dublin and Canterbury, or, perhaps more accurately, between Tairdelbach and Lanfranc, seems to have been genuine. When Bishop Patrick drowned in the Irish Sea on October 12, 1084, the Dublin–Canterbury connection was renewed. After August of 1085, Lanfranc consecrated an Irish monk named Donngus Ua hAnglí as Bishop Donatus (II) of Dublin at the petition of the king, clergy, and populace of Ireland; the annals of St. Mary's, Dublin, name the king as Tairdelbach. Like Patrick, Donatus had been trained in England, at Winchester.[32]

Whatever his failings as a diplomat, with his support of Patrick, Lanfranc had undisputed authority in one area of Ireland. Ecclesiastical ties may have led to thoughts of political connections. King William could have known of Sitric Silkenbeard's ties to the previous English monarch Cnut. There are some interesting similarities in Cnut and William's relations with their neighbors. Both men directly dealt with the Scots: Cnut with Malcolm II in 1031 and William with Malcolm III in 1072. While leaving no doubt about their supremacy over the Welsh, both were content to leave actual intervention in Wales in the hands of their subordinates. Finally, Dublin was the avenue into Ireland from England. Attacks from the Viking towns were a concern for a Dane and a Norman. For Cnut, his interest in Dublin was parallel with the threat from his Norwegian rival St. Olaf. For William, the danger came from the family of Harold Godwinsson. Precedent was a powerful idea in medieval society, as current church subordination and previous political submission could lie behind the claim that William would have conquered Ireland "without using any weapons" had he lived a little longer.[33]

Godfrey did not long enjoy Patrick's company. According to the *Annals of Inisfallen*, he was expelled from Dublin in 1075 and fled to the Kingdom of the Isles. There he died as his fleet was preparing to sail for the invasion of Dublin. There are several possible reasons why he was expelled. Godfrey might have been involved in the rebellion against William the Conqueror in 1075 led by Roger of Hereford, Ralph of East Anglia, and Waltheof of Northumbria. The Danes were invited to join the coalition, and they supplied a fleet led by their prince Cnut Sveinsson, the son of King Svein Ulfsson. The call for help might have reached across the Irish Sea in memory of Irish raids in England in 1068 and 1069. A eulogy on Cnut (who died in July 1086) written about 1122 by an English cleric named Æthelnoth, claims that Cnut's fame was known as far as Ireland.[34] Another possible reason for Godfrey's banishment is that he was preparing to rebel against Tairdelbach, possibly in alliance with the men of Leinster. During Tairdelbach's absence from Dublin after the flight of Godfrey, Diarmait mac Máel na mbó's kinsmen of Uí Chennselaig inserted their own candidate, his grandson, Domnall, son of Murchad, as lord of Dublin. The return to the old regime was brief. Domnall died in that same year, after an illness that lasted three nights, and Tairdelbach then installed his son, Muirchertach, as king of Dublin.[35]

The Viking lords of Dublin, whether Olafsson or Haraldsson dynasts, had maintained relations beyond Ireland or the Isles as part of their hold on power. Despite an international gateway presented to him through his domination of Dublin,

Tairdelbach did not rush into an alliance outside the island. According to the *Annals of Inisfallen*, in 1079 he received a Jewish delegation, which presented him with gifts and then returned home. This delegation undoubtedly came from William the Conqueror. They might have come from England, where William of Malmesbury claims that the Jewish colony at London had been established by William.[36] Or they might have come directly from Normandy, where there was the largest Jewish population in northern Europe at the time. If the delegation wanted Tairdelbach's permission for settling in Ireland, they were disappointed. Jewish settlement in Ireland waited a century, when men such as Solomon of Cardiff came via Wales and he appears in the twelfth-century list of the merchants of Dublin.[37] Alternatively, they might have consulted with Tairdelbach on the question of trade privileges.

The fortunes of the Olafsson dynasty after the mid-eleventh century clearly demonstrate that any Viking dynasty dependent solely on its own power in Ireland faced extinction. They flourished, however, outside the island in two distinct areas: Wales and the Isles. Wales had been a refuge for royal exiles from Dublin as early as the tenth century, when the family of Olaf Godfreysson fled there after their ouster by Olaf Cuaran. Olaf Cuaran's descendants had followed them there when Sitric Silkenbeard established a base at *Castell Avloed*. The connection between Dublin and Anglesey was continued by Diarmait mac Máel na mbó, whose fleets occasionally operated in conjunction with the Welsh prince Gruffudd ap Llywelyn. That goes far in explaining why Gruffudd fled to Ireland for safety, only to be killed there in 1064 by his rival Cynan ap Iago. Diarmait's son, Murchad, the ruler of Dublin, provided the means for the dynasty of Olaf Cuaran to reestablish itself in Wales, in the person of Sitric Silkenbeard's great-grandson, Gruffudd ap Cynan. Not only did Gruffudd have a long reign as the prince of Gwynedd, but he founded a royal line that became synonymous with Welsh cultural identity.

Unlike so many individuals of this time who are little more than names attached to events, Gruffudd's career can be traced from two documents specifically devoted to him. The first is an elegy probably written in 1137, the year of his death, by Meilyr Brydydd, known by its first line (in translation) "The Lord of heaven, how wondrous is His wonder."[38] Gruffudd, called the son of Cynan, is presented entirely as a Welsh prince; his Irish and Norse ancestry are omitted, although there is the vague statement that he fought a battle somewhere in Ireland. As is common with commemorative poetry, events are presented in general rather than specific terms with Gruffudd as the focus. For example, William Rufus's Welsh expedition is made into an attack directly on Gruffudd.

Later is a prose biography known in English translation as *The History of Gruffudd ap Cynan*. Containing far more specific information, the accuracy of this work is an issue because it was composed long after Gruffudd's death, possibly late in the twelfth century. Unlike Meilyr, this author did not know Gruffudd, but relied on informants. The "facts" seem to be correct, but their chronological order is sometimes confused and impossible.[39] Despite these problems, the history is important for Gruffudd's career and for Irish–Welsh contacts during his life.

Gruffudd's early years among the Viking colonists of Ireland provided contacts that, beginning with his first foray, he exploited by using Irish or Viking mercenaries in his expeditions. The dependence by the Welsh aristocracy on the military resources of the Irish kings increased. Meilyr is silent about Gruffudd's ancestry beyond Wales, but the *History* proudly announces his Irish and Norse forebears, and even attempts to connect him with the Norse prince Harald Fairhair while giving an extensive survey of his Irish connections.

The future lord of Gwynedd was born at Dublin about 1055. His family's estate was located north of the Liffey probably at Baile Griffin, now Balgriffin ("Gruffudd's farm"), south of Swords; in the twelfth century his descendants held lands at Cloghran, just to the north.[40] Like other influential princes, Gruffudd seems to have been destined originally for the Church, and he attended the school at Swords. His career in Wales is not always clear and different interpretations are possible, but it owed its beginnings to the patronage of the family of Diarmait mac Máel na mbó. Gruffudd had been born after Diarmait's seizure of the town, and he lived all his early life under the lordship of the Leinster family. His original appeal for aid against his Welsh enemies, according to his biography, was to a king of Dublin named *Murchath*. This was Diarmait's son, Murchad, who ruled Dublin from 1052 to 1070. His death in March of 1070 has been considered too early for Gruffudd's career, but the *History* claims merely that aid was promised, not given.[41] Without Irish troops, Gruffudd sailed to Wales and landed in the Menai Straits. His first appearance in Wales may have been less noteworthy than implied in his history, possibly little more than a residence of only a few months, during which time he fought some skirmishes before retreating to Ireland, sometime between the deaths of Murchad and Diarmait. He then solicited troops from Diarmait and established a base on Anglesey, his family's ancestral home. Connected with this might be the Viking attack on Bangor circa 1072.

Two princes named Trahaearn ap Caradoc and Cynrig ap Rhiwallon divided Gwynedd between them circa 1075. Gruffudd fought a series of battles against Trahaearn. In his first battle, Gruffudd sent troops from Anglesey to fight Cynrig, who was slain, after which he perambulated all Gwynedd. Gruffudd then led troops to Meirionydd where he defeated Trahaearn in the Battle of Gwaet Erw. This was followed by a revolt in Anglesey, and subsequently Gruffudd was defeated at the Battle of Bron yr Erw by Trahaearn (1075). Gruffudd received the promised Irish aid in 1075 when he returned to Ireland after the Battle of Bron yr Erw, sailing to Wexford, an Uí Chennselaig stronghold. Gruffudd remained in Ireland until 1081 when, probably at the invitation of Rhys ap Tewdwr, he returned to Wales. The assistance given by Diarmait's family to Gruffudd, in addition to their control of the Dublin fortress in Anglesey explains why Diarmait's obituary is in the *Annales Cambriae*.[42]

When he left Ireland in 1081, Gruffudd sailed from Waterford where Diarmait's son Énna ruled. Énna was still ruling the town in 1088, when he was attacked there by the family of his uncle. Gruffudd sailed to Wales with supplies of men and materials where he and Rhys were victorious at the Battle of Mynydd Carn.[43] By this time Tairdelbach Ua Briain was becoming involved in Welsh affairs. His son Diarmait attacked Wales in 1080, but Tairdelbach did not disturb the Uí Chennselaig in their control of any port other than Dublin.[44]

Chronological difficulties in the *History of Gruffydd ap Cynan* together with an Olafsson alliance with the Normans are illustrated by Gruffudd's association with the Norman adventurer Robert of Rhuddlan. His biography claims that prior to the Battle of Bron yr Erw in 1075, Gruffudd is made both to seek Robert's support at the castle of Rhuddlan and then attack him; later the author claims that the Normans entered Wales after the battle. According to Orderic Vitalis, a native of the Anglo-Welsh border who was a friend of Robert's brother and the author of a eulogy on him, Robert was in Wales only 15 years before he was slain by Gruffudd in July of 1093, which places his arrival circa 1077.[45] Gruffudd could not have attacked Rhuddlan castle before or during 1075 because there was no castle there. The earlier castle had been destroyed by Harold Godwinsson in his raid on Gruffudd ap Llywelyn, and the new castle of Robert of Rhuddlan was built only a few years before *Domesday Book*, where it is described as "newly constructed."[46] The association of Gruffudd with Robert follows the goodwill that was being created between Normans and Irish at Dublin.

Gruffudd's campaigns for the conquest of Gwynedd appear to have continued for the next two decades. That he could maintain such a war of long duration is a tribute to the support he received from the Irish. Among his supporters was his foster-father called *Cerit*, from northern county Dublin, and a mercenary named Mac Ruaidhri from Brandon Hill in county Kerry. There was a community of Welsh exiles at Waterford, for when Gruffudd sailed from there to Wales in 1081, his ships' crews included Vikings, Irish, and Welsh.

As one of Olaf Cuaran's descendants was laying the foundations for the dynasty that would become synonymous with Welsh royalty, another was equally occupied in the Kingdom of the Isles. This was the famous Godred Crovan, better known as the legendary King Orry of Manx legend. At almost the last moment before power slipped from his family forever, Godred conquered a new kingdom that his dynasty ruled for the next two centuries. He even revived previous glories when he captured Dublin and ruled as its independent lord. During the reign of Godred's son, Lagmann, the Kingdom of the Isles came under the sovereignty of Norway; until the mid-thirteenth century it was the southernmost territory in the Norwegian colonial empire.

Like his cousin in Wales, the history of Godred and his family is recounted in an important historical text, called the *Chronicle of the Kings of Man and the Isles*, also known briefly as the *Manx Chronicle*. The unique information begins with Godred Crovan fleeing from the Battle of Stamford Bridge. Godred was given sanctuary on Man by its king, Godfrey son of Sitric. Godred was a young man at the time, for the chronicle later comments that he resided on Man during his youth.

Godred was a member of the Olafsson dynasty and his ancestry is described in the *Annals of Tigernach*'s obituary for him in 1095. He was the son of Ivar Haraldsson, the grandson of Olaf Cuaran. Ivar was the king of Dublin from 1038 to 1046 and his father Harald had been killed at the Battle of Glen Mama in 999. The *Manx Chronicle* mixes these names and makes Godred's father an otherwise unknown Harald the Black of *Ysland*.[47] The explanation for the confusion is that Ivar was known to his contemporaries simply as "the son of Harald," as in Tigernach's record of his attack on the shrine of Patrick in 1044, and this became garbled through the years. The *Manx Chronicle*'s *Ysland*, for Harald's home might be the Latin name for Iceland or Islay (although elsewhere in the chronicle it is spelled *Yle*), but is more likely evidence of a francophone influence. *Ysland, Bisland, Hislande,* and *Hysland* are variant spellings of the more common medieval French *Irlande* "Ireland."[48]

The Godfrey son of Sitric, who was Godred Crovan's host, was probably a distant kinsman, illustrating the importance of even distant family connections. Godfrey seems not to have been a native of the Isle of Man because in his first appearance, the manuscript has a line through Sitric and a marginal note "Fingal," but the name Godfrey son of Sitric later is repeated without any comment. Elsewhere there is only one other correction of a proper name, Svein Forkbeard where the original *Suiorth* ("Siward" or "Sigurd") is corrected to *Suan* in the margin. Otherwise, the marginal notes are usually geographical. Godfrey did have a son named Fingal, who succeeded him, but the single appearance of the note suggests that it is the name of a place rather than a person, hypercorrection for Dublin's northern territory. Godfrey son of Sitric appears to have been a native of Dublin.

Godfrey ruled the Kingdom of the Isles under the lordship of an Irish king. In 1066 the Isle of Man was under the control of Diarmait mac Máel na mbó, whose son, Murchad, had defeated the Haraldsson dynast Echmarcach only 5 years earlier. Neither Diarmait nor Murchad resided on the island, so they needed a representative. The solution was to set up someone acceptable to the inhabitants, but not an ally of the deposed Haraldssons. There were good relations between Diarmait and the Olafssons, which suggests where to look for Godfrey's family connections.

The name of his father also leads to the Olafssons in a search for Godfrey's origin. He might have been a son of Sitric Silkenbeard, who had a son Godfrey; giving the same name to several children was not uncommon, and Sitric had two sons named Olaf/Oleif. More likely is that Godfrey was a grandson of Sitric's brother, Glúniairn. In his tract *On the Formorians and Norsemen*, Duald Mac Firbis notes that Glúniairn had a son named Sitric and that he had descendants in Ireland. Nothing else is known of this man, although he might be the unnamed son of Glúniairn, who killed his cousin, Sitric Silkenbeard's son Godfrey, in Wales in 1036. Sitric son of Glúniairn must have been a man of some importance for families to keep his name in their genealogies to the seventeenth century.

After his death circa 1070, Godfrey was succeeded by his son Fingal, who reigned about 9 years, to circa 1079. In 1073 Fingal was attacked by a force from Ireland. Sitric Olafsson, the brother of King Godfrey Olafsson of Dublin, and two Uí Briain dynasts were slain during an attempted invasion of the Isle of Man. A member of the Haraldsson dynasty, Sitric was trying to conquer his patrimony. Diarmait mac Máel na mbó was dead and his family expelled from Dublin, but even without Irish allies the prince of the Isles was a formidable opponent.

Even in their time of obscurity, the Olafssons were powerful and influential, albeit under the sufferance of their Irish masters. The Viking remained a clichéd figure of evil in literature, but by the eleventh century there was no general hostility toward them by the Irish. Powerful princes such as Diarmait were opposed to particular Viking families for specific reasons. While he was hostile to the Haraldssons because of their alliance with the family of Donnchad mac Briain, Diarmait set up his Viking princes to rule over Viking settlements. Irish and Welsh chronicles did not underestimate his power.

Fingal was succeeded by Godred Crovan, who captured the Isle of Man after three invasions. The invasions probably began after Fingal's death; nothing indicates that the two men confronted each other, and the type of hospitality extended by Godfrey to Godred usually meant security for a son. Godred had not been idle during his residence in the Isles and men from the Hebrides followed him on his invasions. The final, and successful, attack saw Godred sailing his fleet into the harbor at Ramsey in the middle of the night, and then hiding a body of men nearby on the slopes of Sky Hill. During the battle the following day, Godred was victorious when his hidden reserves suddenly appeared and overwhelmed the Manx, who were trapped by the incoming of the tide that blocked their path. Godred mixed mercy with victory, and ended the slaughter amid the pleas of the defeated Manx.

Fingal's family might have retired to southwestern Scotland. An entry in the *Annals of the Four Masters* notes the death of a king of the Rhinns named Mac Congail in 1094; these Rhinns have been demonstrated to be the Rhinns of Galloway.[49] The names Fingal and Congal could be confused. This region had been ruled by Echmarcach after his defeat on Man in 1061. Unknown is whether Mac Congail was an independent king or a subordinate of Godred Crovan.

With his victory, Godred behaved like a typical Viking chieftain. He offered his followers two choices: share out the land on the island or plunder it. The majority voted for plunder, and then sailed home with their loot. A few of his followers remained, and Godred gave them the southern part of Man; the northern part was given to the native Manx. This affected only the land-holding aristocracy, and the peasants simply received new masters. The *Manx Chronicle* has two interesting asides. First, Godred allowed the Manx aristocracy to remain, but only on the understanding that no one would claim any hereditary rights to any part of the island. Second, this set a legal precedent that the entire island belonged to the king. In retrospect, Godred's victory was important for establishing a new royal line and for setting a limit to legal memory.

With his victory, Godred Crovan opened a new era in the history of the Kingdom of the Isles. His descendants ruled until the mid-thirteenth century. While some contemporaries remembered Godred's military victories—his Irish sobriquet was *meranach* "the furious"—others remembered a deformity of his hands. In a twelfth-century praise poem addressed to his great-grandson, Ragnall, he is called *méarach* "the fingered." The *Manx Chronicle* calls him *crovan*, probably from Old Norse *kruppin* "cripple," although it is just possibly an adaptation of Irish *crúbach* "claw."[50] Disability was not unknown, and Godfrey's contemporary was the poet Bjorn *inn kruppinhendi* "the cripple-hand," who composed *Magnússdrápa* ("Magnus's *drapa*") in honor of the Norwegian king Magnus Barefoot.

The conquest of the Isle of Man by Godred Crovan signaled a monumental shift in the fortunes of the dynasty of Olaf Cuaran. Regardless of what status they held in Dublin, the Kingdom of the Isles now became their stronghold. Long after their power in Ireland had dwindled, they reigned as kings in the Isle of Man and the Hebrides. Godfrey Sitricsson had been an underking, dependent on his Irish overlord, but Godred Crovan was not. The capture of Man provided Godred with an area of power beyond the powerful Irish princes, although not beyond their orb of influence. Nevertheless, Godred's victory had not been so overwhelming to discourage rivals, and the children from the union between members of the powerful Uí Briain dynasty and the dynasty of Echmarcach Ragnallsson were biding their time.

There is also an ethnic aspect to the Isle of Man. The *Manx Chronicle*, it will be remembered, states that Godred Crovan gave the southern part of the island to his followers while allowing the natives to keep the north. Like his Welsh kinsman Gruffudd ap Cynan, Godred might have relied on the Irish as well as the Vikings of Dublin for support. In 1098 there was a war on Man between the northern and southern parts of the island. The rival commanders were Ottar and MacMaras, both of whom died in the battle. But who was the leader of the natives in the northern half and who was the captain of the newcomers from the southern part?[51] Answering the question based merely on names could be unwise, and MacMaras might have led the newcomers. In the charters in the Book of Kells there is a MacMaras, who was the head of the *reiclés* (a monastic community attached to a church) of Kells.[52] Churches often drew their officers from the local families, and MacMaras probably was a member of the local aristocracy, which, by this time, was using surnames in something approaching the modern sense. The ties of Godred Crovan's family with the churches dedicated to St. Columba, as well as the proximity of Kells to Dublin, make it quite possible that a member of the MacMaras family was one of Godred's mercenaries who settled on Man after his victory.

The location of Godred's stronghold on the island might not have been far from the Tynwald (ON *Þing völlr* "Thing (or assembly) field") that remains the ceremonial center of the island.[53] It is tempting to connect Godred's division of the population into northern and southern groups with the judicial division of the Isle of Man. Late medieval and early modern records reveal that the Isle of Man was divided into two courts—north and south—supplemented by six sheading (ON *séttungr* "sixth part") courts. Before seeing all this in a purely Scandinavian context, by the end of the Middle Ages there was a Gaelic aspect. A guide to procedure called the "Acts of Sir John Stanley," notes that the royal representative in the sheading was a maer.[54] The maer is a Gaelic official, the name comes from Latin *maior* and he was somewhat similar to the *major domus* of the early Middle Ages. In this instance he is the royal representative at the local level, and among his functions was to ensure the security at the meeting of the Thing.

After the triumph of Godred Crovan, the Haraldssons attacked Man again. According to the *Annals of Ulster*, in 1087, a fleet led by "the sons of the son of Ragnall" and the "son of the king of the Ulaid" attacked Man. The raid was unsuccessful and the "sons of the son of Ragnall" were slain. An alliance of the Haraldsson dynasty with the Ulaid reflects temporary instability among the Uí Briain. The great Tairdelbach ua Briain had died on July 14, 1086, at the fine old age of 77; within a month so had his son, Tadc. Tadc was the husband of Echmarcach's daughter, Mor, and their children later made their own invasions of the Isles. Almost immediately after the death of Tadc, war erupted between his brothers Diarmait and Muirchertach. Muirchertach temporarily gained the upper hand and drove Diarmait from Munster. In the turmoil, control of Dublin was retaken by Leinster and the troops used in an invasion of the southern Uí Néill. Even though Muirchertach defeated the Leinster army at Howth the following year, his efforts to bring the eastern coast back under Ua Briain control left Munster open to attacks. In 1088 the king of Connacht joined with the Uí Néill overlord Domnall Mac Lochlann on a raid through Munster that included the burning of Limerick and the destruction of the Ua Briain capital of Kincora.

By the middle of 1072 a new political order had taken shape around the Irish Sea. Harold Godwinsson, Gruffudd ap Llywelyn, Diarmait mac Máel na mbó, his son Murchad, and Echmarcach Ragnallsson were all dead. The men who had dominated Irish Sea affairs for a quarter century had been linked to the region by ancestral ties, and their homes encircled it. They had profited personally from Irish Sea trade, had recruited troops from the shores on the opposite side of the sea, and found refuge across the water; they drew their strength from the Irish Sea and the two who had died in battle—Harold and Diarmait—did so away from it. The men who took their places around the Irish Sea—Tairdelbach ua Briain, William of Normandy, and, later, Magnus "Barefoot"—coveted the region as a part of their empire building, but they personally had no ancestral ties to it. The Irish Sea region with its fleets, towns, and troops would be manipulated and exploited, but no longer was it the end, merely the means to an end.

So far as the Olafssons and Haraldssons were concerned, indeed all the Viking colonists, the failed Norwegian invasion at Stamford Bridge, followed by the destruction of the Anglo-Saxon kingdom after the Battle of Hastings, changed the political and cultural tilt not only of Britain, but also of the Irish Sea. The orientation to the north did not disappear, but it was matched and then superseded by a southwards gaze. The Olafssons and Haraldssons could no longer look to the Irish Sea for security because, as Murchad of Uí Chennselaig had demonstrated in 1061, the Irish princes could follow and defeat them. The Battle of Stamford Bridge, more so than Clontarf, had destroyed the myth of Scandinavian military supremacy. Not merely was a coalition of Viking leaders defeated; the Norwegian king himself was defeated and slain in the midst of the Danelaw. Hastings was a change of a different type, for the infantry style of attack that was used throughout northern Europe had been defeated by mounted troops. The cavalryman became the new model for warfare for the next several centuries.

Success also inspired imitators. After Diarmait mac Máel na mbó had demonstrated how the adaptation of Viking methods could lead to political domination, later Irish kings attempted to control the Irish Sea region directly. They were not alone in their ambitions. They were confronted by the Normans, who had their own agenda for the region and the principalities around it. Added to this were the Viking dynasties, which were not completely in decline. As the Norwegians licked their wounds after Stamford Bridge, the Viking aristocracies in the Isles and Dublin engaged in empire building of their own. The Isles became a base for the reconquest of the Hiberno-Scandinavian towns. From there fleets would do battle in Ireland, the Irish Sea, and Wales. Once again the Haraldssons of the Isles confronted the dynasty of Olaf Cuaran. Now the prize was control of the Isles. The contest was interrupted at the end of the eleventh century when a far more fearsome threat to both the Irish and the Normans would appear in the Irish Sea: the Norse king Magnus Barefoot. He introduced a direct Norse presence in the region that continued until the mid-thirteenth century.

In Ireland, the legacy of Diarmait mac Máel na mbó was a curious mixture of the momentarily brilliant and the enduringly pedestrian, like the dynasties of Olafsson and Haraldsson that he had so ardently attempted to imitate. His capture of the Viking strongholds on the east of Ireland, together with his domination of the Kingdom of the Isles, rescued his dynasty and his kingdom from obscurity. The means of his success would become the guiding policy of his successors for a century, as they fought with the Olafssons, the Haraldssons, and all other comers for control of Dublin. Diarmait's kingdom of Uí Chennselaig became powerful, one of the influential major factors in Irish political and military affairs. Diarmait also demonstrates the inventiveness of the Irish princes, for his alliance with Harold Godwinsson had economic repercussions as well. Diarmait continued the connections of the Olafssons and Haraldssons with the Norwegian royal dynasties, and troops from Dublin and the Isles participated in the invasions of 1058 and 1066. With Diarmait one has a glimpse of the sophistication of the Irish aristocracy. His sheltering of for-eign visitors—be they Anglo-Saxon nobles, Welsh princes, or Norse freebooters—indicates how much the Irish aristocracy was aware of the ebb and flow of events elsewhere in Europe. The range of contacts, the use of fleets, and the willingness to participate in adventures outside Ireland show that activities generally considered "Viking" were adopted, and adapted, by their Irish conquerors.

Less internationally oriented was Diarmait's protégé Tairdelbach. Tairdelbach did correspond with Archbishop Lanfranc, but Canterbury's authority was limited to Dublin during his lifetime. Although a bishop in Dál Cais corresponded with Lanfranc, only two bishops from Ireland were consecrated by him, both for Dublin: Patrick and Donatus II. While Tairdelbach might have helped the Normans by his raid on South Wales in 1080, he was still enough of a mystery for the Conqueror to cite the Irish threat at the trial of his half-brother, Odo, in 1082.

The successes of Gruffudd ap Cynan in Gwynedd and Godred Crovan in the Isles show how easy it is to underestimate the resilience of the Viking dynasties. Their marital alliances are ignored only at one's peril. Despite their best efforts to do so, the Viking colonists in Ireland had not been as successful at assimilating into native society as their counterparts in northern Francia. They were still called "foreigners" by the native Irish writers and rival native factions fought to control their ports. Their military might was still considerable, but ships and troops were not sufficient on their own to guarantee independence.

Gruffudd and Godred both became the symbols of national determination, Gruffudd as the founder of a prominent Welsh princely dynasty, and Godred for the nearly as long-lived lords of the Isles. Their dependence on the resources and the alliances created by earlier generations of Olafssons was not only obvious, but trum-peted by their families' propagandists. The Haraldssons were less successful. We know little about them, possibly because they were not the literary patrons on the scale of the Olafssons, or perhaps because the dynasty in the twelfth and succeeding centuries was so obscure. Yet, as the next chapter will show, they did not disappear without a fight.

8

Lords of the Isles

A͟FTER A PERIOD of obscurity in the middle of the eleventh century, by the last quarter the dynasty of Olaf Cuaran had gained a new prominence in the kingship of the Isles. Medieval writers assigned the triumph to Godred Crovan. When he briefly added Dublin to his domain in the waning years of the century, the Irish Sea Vikings gained a few final years of glory. More important, Godred established his dynasty in one of the few places where they could flourish. His island empire was too poor and remote for the great princes surrounding him. They busied themselves with more profitable and convenient prey. Godred could hurl defiance to one and all from his island redoubts.

Godred's success owed something, however, to favorable circumstances. After he had taken the kingship of the Isles, two great lords—one in Ireland and one in Britain—died. In Ireland, the mighty Tairdelbach ua Briain died in 1086 after a long illness. The *Annals of Inisfallen*, by this time a contemporary Uí Briain record, claim that Tairdelbach wanted his domain to be shared out among his sons Tadc, Muirchertach, and Diarmait. When Tadc died the following month, "in his father's bed" (i.e., peacefully), a fight for the whole inheritance erupted between Muirchertach and Diarmait (who had been named after Tairdelbach's foster-father Diarmait mac Máel na mbó). Muirchertach was initially successful and forced Diarmait into exile, but the discord provided opportunities for their enemies. The second great lord was on the eastern shores of the Irish Sea. The king of England, William the Conqueror, died in Normandy in 1087. He was succeeded by his second son William II "Rufus," but discontented elements among the nobility looked toward Rufus's ineffectual elder brother Robert "Curthose" the duke of Normandy. In the Irish Sea Rufus's policy was a mixture of accommodation and paranoia.

The death of Tairdelbach ua Briain and the subsequent hostilities between his sons led to control of Dublin passing from them for several years. Surprisingly neither the

Olafssons nor the Haraldssons appear to have been involved. In the confusion after the death of Tairdelbach, the princes of Uí Chennselaig seized their opportunity. During the period 1086–1089 the king of Dublin was also the king of Leinster, Donnchad the son of Domnall the Fat. Domnall the Fat was Diarmait mac Máel na mbó's brother, who seized power in Leinster after the deaths of Diarmait and his sons. The speed with which Donnchad seized Dublin once again illustrates its importance to the great Irish lords.

Capturing Dublin was relatively simple, but holding the town was more difficult. Donnchad needed more than just military might, he had to have the active goodwill of the inhabitants. Public displays of generosity were one way to cultivate favor with a populace. The open-handed sovereign was admired and praised throughout medieval Europe. A useful act of largess was a grant of land to the Church. This secured the goodwill of the clergy and was seen as a pious act by ordinary individuals. Donnchad gave an estate called *Clonchan* (probably modern Cloncen near Dalkey) to the cathedral that had been founded by Sitric Silkenbeard.[1] In a delicious piece of irony, a Christian Irish prince tried to win favor from the descendants of pagan Viking pirates by making gifts to their churches. Another member of his family also made a land donation. This was Énna son of Domnall, a grandson of Diarmait mac Máel na mbó's son Murchad; Énna's father had ruled Dublin briefly in 1075. Énna is described as the king of Leinster when he gave an estate called *Realgeallyn*.

The gifts of Donnchad and Énna show their awareness of challenges for control of Dublin, especially from Muirchertach Ua Briain. Early in the eleventh century Dublin's revenues had been useful for the high king Brian Boru, but late in the same century they were essential for his great-grandson Muirchertach's aspirations of domination in Ireland. Dublin was only one town, however, and Muirchertach's schemes required the greater wealth held by all the Viking towns on the eastern Irish coast, an immense task that could not be accomplished easily or quickly.[2] He invaded the lands north of the River Liffey in 1087 and won a battle at a place known as Ráith Etair ("the fortress of Howth"). The location of the fight shows, once again, that care was being taken not to damage the town. Nevertheless, two more years passed before Muirchertach finally regained control of Dublin, in 1089. Donnchad was slain, although the annals are unclear as to whether it was by the hand of Muirchertach, the northern Leinster prince Conchobar Ua Conchobuir Fhailge, or by Donnchad's own kinsmen.

Muirchertach was not the only one with designs on Dublin, and his occupation of Dublin was short-lived. After a reign of a dozen years in the Isles, Godred Crovan felt strong enough to attempt to conquer his ancestral home. In 1091 Godred and his Islesmen sailed up the Liffey and captured Dublin. For a few years, a descendant of Olaf Cuaran was once more lord of the town. The speed of his conquest and the length of his reign show that the Dubliners welcomed the restoration of the native royal family. Nevertheless, Godred's triumph was not due entirely to his abilities. Although a powerful sea lord who could command some of the finest sailors in

Europe, he did not have the resources available to Muirchertach. The timing of the expedition suggests that Godred was aware of other demands on the Irish king's attention. In 1092 Muirchertach was occupied in the west, where the assassination of the king of Connacht provided him with the opportunity to have his lordship recognized in the province. The triumph was marred by another rebellion on the part of his brother Diarmait, who had returned to Munster. Diarmait was again banished, and this time he fled northeast to the Ulaid.

Like his Irish counterpart, Godred needed the wealth of the town. Even though there was manufacturing and trade, the Isles were primarily agrarian. Throughout Europe, revenues from the land were becoming insufficient to provide the wealth needed to maintain royal status.[3] This wealth continued to be generated through trade. Ships capable of long-distance sailing linked the Irish Sea trade with the larger Scandinavian-Atlantic world. The Viking fortress/markets of Britain, Francia, and Ireland remained "border towns" on the southern edge of the Scandinavian world.

The place of Dublin and the Isles in this scheme is illustrated in the medieval Icelandic law of inheritance known as *Arfaþáttr*, now part of the law tracts collectively known as *Grágás* ("Grey Goose"). This legal code was written at the end of the twelfth century, based on laws collected and codified circa 1117.[4] Even though the text survives only in later manuscripts, it clearly describes the period before the mid-thirteenth century. This is demonstrated by a comparison of this text with the ordinances of King Magnus Lagaböter (adopted by the town of Bergen on January 29, 1276), where Ireland and the Hebrides are not mentioned, reflecting the ceding of the Hebrides to the Scots a decade earlier. In the earlier text, a discussion of the circumstances in which the property of someone who dies outside Iceland can be taxed includes the stipulation that a kinsman must be in control of the property prior to its taxation if the deceased died in England, the western islands (i.e., Faroes, Shetlands, Orkneys, Hebrides, and Man) or in Dublin. The passage's insistence that the administering kinsman be one who did not "venture" (*óhætt*) with the deceased shows that this pertains to a merchant. In short, if an Icelandic merchant died in Dublin, his property had to be administered by a kinsman before it could be dispersed.

North America continued to be part of this trading and cultural area. A small piece of evidence is the famous "Maine Coin," a penny minted during the reign of King Olaf the Peaceful, the son of Harald Hardrada. Found in 1957 at Naskeag Point near the Penobscot River in Maine, the coin was discovered among Native American artifacts. The penny was pierced to be worn as a pendant, and probably represents trade between the Vikings and the indigenous population. How long the Viking settlement flourished in North America is not known, but in 1121 Bishop Eirik Gnúpsson sailed from Greenland to minister to the colonists in Vinland, and was never seen again.[5]

Some of the merchant ships sailing from the Irish Sea to Scandinavia had crews and owners from different regions. *Eyrbyggja Saga* mentions one trading ship from Dublin that had a crew of Irish, Hebrideans, and Norwegians, while another ship was owned jointly by Norwegians and Hebrideans. Multiple ownership of vessels by individuals from different lands explains the need for precision in the passage on inheritance in *Grágás*. These were men of consequence and among the Anglo-Saxons a merchant who crossed the sea three times at his personal expense was entitled to the rights of a thane, the lowest rank of aristocrat.[6] There were, however, variations of wealth. *Eyrbyggja Saga* describes what must have been a common sight, the small trader who had only twelve sheepskins and three hundred ells of cloth together with his food for the voyage. International trade brought wealth and prestige for the intrepid.

Godred's capture of Dublin immediately made him the second most powerful prince around the Irish Sea. That prompted a reaction from the most powerful prince: the English monarch William Rufus. England's vulnerability to attack from the Irish Sea that had contributed to William the Conqueror's decision to plant his trusted commanders in western England now had to be addressed by his son. Godred Crovan's conquest of Dublin was followed the next year by a military response from William Rufus. In 1092 William led an army into Cumberland where he advanced as far as Carlisle. He drove out the local ruler, Dolfin, and built a castle.[7] This action has been seen as either a demonstration of power on the part of William or as a fortification project to forestall raids by the Scots.[8] Both ideas probably occurred to him, together with one other: Carlisle's strategic location for defending against raids from the Irish Sea. The Isle of Man was only several hours sailing from the coast of Cumberland. Immediately to the west of Carlisle were the Rhinns of Galloway, still a part of the Kingdom of the Isles. The danger from the Irish Sea had been clearly demonstrated a generation earlier when Thorfinn of the Orkneys had raided the English coast.

William Rufus's behavior in Cumberland is a reminder of how the passage of time changes perception. In hindsight the Norman Conquest was a decisive event, yet contemporaries did not know that. Challengers to the Norman rulers of England were still active, and the attacks were coming from the seas. In 1085 there had been another invasion from Denmark, which failed largely because the Danes were slow in making their preparations. There had been two invasions of England from Ireland. William the Conqueror had cited the threat from Ireland at the trial of his halfbrother Odo in 1082. Tairdelbach's son, Diarmait, had raided Wales from Ireland in 1080. The prince of Gwynedd, Gruffudd ap Cynan, was using troops from Ireland for his campaigns, and with them he had won the important battle of Mynydd Carn in 1081.

There is a legend that Rufus had his own designs on the Irish Sea and Ireland. According to Gerald of Wales, Rufus led his troops across Wales to St. David's, where he saw the outlines of the Irish coast through the mist. He then boasted that he would conquer the island. When the story was told to Muirchertach Ua Briain, he asked if his rival had added "God willing." When told that Rufus had attached no such condition to his threat, Muirchertach replied that he had no reason to worry, for the plan was sure to fail.[9]

William Rufus might have learned about events in the Irish Sea from the clergy, particularly the bishops of the Orkneys. The islands had initially been under the authority of the archbishops of Hamburg/Bremen, but vacancies had sent the bishops-elect of the Orkneys south for consecration. Beginning with Bishop Radulf, who was consecrated circa 1073, the Orcadian bishops of the later eleventh century were consecrated at York.[10] They may have resided in England, for *Orkneyinga Saga* claims that the first bishop of the Orkneys actually to reside in the islands was William the Old, who reigned for more than half a century before his death in 1166. The Orkney bishops would have been useful informants about events beyond the western coasts of Britain because of their authority in the region, which seems to have extended as far as the Kingdom of the Isles.

Little is known of religious life in the Isles immediately prior to or during the reign of Godred Crovan. Only in the middle of the twelfth century, after his son Olaf established the Order of Savigny at the monastery of Rushen, does the episcopal succession become clearer.[11] A brief glimpse of the ecclesiastical structure emerges from a catalogue of the bishops of Sodor (from ON *Suðreys*, "southern isles") appended to the *Manx Chronicle*. The compiler claims that there had been many bishops since the time of St. Patrick, but he provides no names. The list begins in the eleventh century, and for the period before the mid-twelfth century there are three names: Roolwer, William, and Hamond. The only indication of chronology is for Roolwer, who is said to have been bishop before the reign of Godred Crovan.

The names of the bishops in the *Manx Chronicle*, and their order, bear an interesting similarity to the names and succession of contemporary Orkney bishops. Roolwer is a later medieval form of Old Norse *Hrólfr*, from which came the Latin forms *Rolfus* and *Rodulfus* (Anglicized as Ralph and Radulf). The forms *Rooluer* and *Roolfwer* are found in Norwegian documents composed at the same time as the list of Manx bishops was being written in the fourteenth century.[12] Exactly contemporary with Roolwer is Radulf (*Hrólfr*) of the Orkneys; in the eleventh century their names were identical. Bishop Radulf of the Orkneys was consecrated by Archbishop Thomas I (Thomas of Bayeux) of York (1070–1100) circa 1073 and died sometime between 1100 and 1109.

The second name in the *Manx Chronicle* list is William, which is also the name of a contemporary Orcadian bishop. Bishop William the Old of the Orkneys had an episcopate of 66 years (circa 1102–1168) according to *Orkneyinga Saga*, an unusual (but not unknown) length of tenure. The succession is not clear because early in the twelfth century there was another bishop of the Orkneys called Radulf Novell. Sometime between 1108 and 1122, a poet called Simeon of Iona composed a poem about St. Columba, the founder of his church, for the Scots monarch Alexander I and his wife, Sibyl; the dates of the composition are fixed by the commencement of

Alexander's reign and the death of the queen.[13] Simeon mentions that he was working under the direction of William. The poem is clearly an expression of goodwill toward the royal couple and might have been composed in connection with Alexander's elevation to the kingship in 1108.

The third name on the Manx list is Hamond. There has been some discussion as to whether or not Hamond is the same man as Bishop Wimund. A note in a York history reveals that early in the twelfth century, Archbishop Thomas II of York (1109–1114) consecrated a bishop named Wimund who resided on the Isle of Skye.[14] Wimund was probably based at Snizort in Skye. When the canons of Snizort elected their own bishop in the fourteenth century, they may have been encouraged by memories of the earlier prelate.[15] At first glance there does not seem to be any connection between Hamond and Wimund. Hamond comes from Old Norse *Ámundr* while Wimund is a Germanic name that in Old Norse is *Vémundr*. The suspicion that the two men might be the same individual comes from changes in the spelling of place name elements in Normandy, where Wimund becomes Himont/Ymond during the course of the Middle Ages.[16] So a twelfth-century Wimund could have become Himond by the fourteenth century, written as the familiar name Hamond.

That three late-eleventh/early-twelfth century bishops of the Isles had similar (or identical) names and succeeded in the same order as their exact contemporaries in the Orkneys and Skye goes beyond coincidence; they are the same individuals. The influence from the Orkneys into the Kingdom of the Isles did not end with the death of Thorfinn the Mighty. The presence of the Orcadians explains why Godred Crovan's son, Olaf, complained that foreign bishops were exercising authority in his kingdom, and that he wanted one bishop for his entire kingdom. The result was the establishment of an episcopal seat at Rushen, with a bishop selected from the monastery of Furness. The hold of the Olafsson dynasty in the Isles was less secure than the *Manx Chronicle* implies.

With the resources provided by Dublin, Godred became involved in Welsh affairs, allying with his kinsman Gruffudd ap Cynan. In 1094 Gruffudd led a Welsh attack against the Normans in Gwynedd. His target was Hugh of Chester and his followers, who had captured the Isle of Anglesey earlier that year.[17] In seeking aid from his cousin, Gruffudd pleaded his case at Godred's court, "in the islands of Denmark," as the biographer describes them. Godred did not disappoint his kinsman. Sixty war ships were dispatched to Wales. When the ensuing battle was unfinished at nightfall, Godred's fleet returned home. Gruffudd could not resume battle without his allies, so he abandoned the action. To vent his disappointment Gruffudd imitated the piracy of his ancestors, and he attacked a ship sailing from Chester.

Although Godred and Gruffudd had failed to stop Hugh of Chester, they did give the intruders a glimpse of possible retaliation. Gruffudd might have looked as far as the northern isles for aid. The *Life of St. Gwynllyw* claims that Gruffudd used a fleet from the Orkneys for an expedition around the River Usk, in southern Wales. The raiders looted the church of St. Gwynllyw, and the saint's revenge was that all the ships except Gruffudd's were destroyed.[18]

Once again William Rufus was forced to respond to the activities of the Olafssons. A popular uprising in Wales supported by a Viking fleet could push the Normans back into England. The threat of attack from the sea was particularly worrisome in Gwynedd, where the northern coastal strip is narrow and especially vulnerable to an attack from a hostile fleet. The turmoil in Wales alerted the English king to the danger that a new Viking outpost might be placed on Anglesey. So Rufus led an expedition into Wales either late that year or early the next. The campaign gained him nothing except humiliation. The Welsh chroniclers crow that he did not capture so much as a cow.[19] This is not entirely fair to William, since his attention was more firmly fixed on the fight for control of Normandy that he was waging against his elder brother Robert. The Norman campaign of 1094 had profited him little and exhausted his funds, so the Welsh campaign was probably a half-hearted expedition at best.

The dependency of a minor prince's success on the turmoil among his more powerful rivals is illustrated when Godred was expelled from Dublin in 1094. Muirchertach had been reconciled, again, with his brother Diarmait, and he had arranged matters in Connacht to his satisfaction. That freed him to turn his attention back to the eastern Irish coast. Despite the Irish prince's greater resources, removing Godred from Dublin was not easy, and he did not leave without a fight. The contemporary *Annals of Inisfallen*, with their intimate knowledge of Uí Briain affairs, imply that the struggle between Godred and Muirchertach was carried on throughout that year. The final blow came after Muirchertach returned from a campaign in the north of Ireland and captured the town. A confusing account in the *Annals of Clonmacnoise* places the decisive battle southwest of Dublin at Oughterard.

Godred had not been blind to the importance of Dublin in the Irish political scheme, and he knew that the more powerful Irish princes would try to seize it. So an ally was needed to help him hold the town. Godred's solution was to resurrect his dynasty's ancient alliance with the princes of northern Leinster in the person of Conchobar Ua Conchobuir Fhailge the king of Uí Fhailge (located west of the Liffey). Uí Fhailge had enjoyed the patronage of the Uí Briain, and Godred might have hoped to break that union while building up a coalition that would guard his domain in Ireland. Ultimately, however, there was no safety in an alliance. When Muirchertach entered Dublin, Conchobar Ua Conchobuir Fhailge was there, and taken prisoner. Muirchertach returned home, in the words of the Inisfallen annalist, with peace and triumph.

Within a year, Godred was dead. According to the Irish and Manx chronicles, he died from a plague on the Isle of Islay sometime between August and December of 1095. His grave, according to local tradition, is under the standing stone at Carragh Bhan on Islay.[20] Godred may have had a fortress in Finlagan Loch. This is a mile-long loch in the interior of the island where there are the ruins of a castle on Eilean Mór ("the big island"). There the later Macdonald lords of the Isles resided. Just beyond it, and previously connected by a causeway, is a smaller island known as Eilean na Comhairle ("Council Island") where the council of the Isles met during the later Middle Ages.

The plague that killed Godred, and Bishop Donatus II of Dublin among others, began in Bavaria and along the Rhine in 1094; it had spread to Normandy by 1095, accompanied by famine. The pestilence appeared in the Irish Sea region in August 1095, where it lingered for almost a year, until May 1096. This infestation is famous for the hysteria that it spread throughout Ireland, as reflected in the literature on the "panic of 1096" as it was described in the *Annals of Ulster*. The panic reflects the Irish belief in divine retaliation for their role in the death of John the Baptist. Since the tenth century, a legend had evolved that the Irish were particularly responsible for the death of the Baptist, because the decollation had been carried out by an Irish druid named Mog Roth. As divine punishment for their involvement, the Irish were to be visited by devastation that would occur when certain chronological conditions were met: the feast of the decollation of John the Baptist (August 29) would fall on a Friday in a leap year at the end of a chronological cycle. These conditions were ful-filled to some extent in 1096; it was a leap year, and the feast of the decollation of the Baptist was on a Friday. Disaster was believed to have been averted only through the intervention of the clergy, together with public displays of repentance through fasting and prayers.

A literary expression of the panic is the "Second Vision of Adomnán." This is the work of reformers among the Irish clergy, who were particularly critical of lay con-trol of church property that they claimed led the saints to abandon their churches. The author of the "Second Vision of Adomnán" declares that the numerous sins of the Irish brought divine retribution on themselves, because they were behaving as badly as Vikings, except that they did not worship idols. Punishment would be in the form of a pestilence so severe that only a few would survive. The tract closes with suggestions on appeasing the divine wrath.

The casual reference to idolatry in the "Second Vision of Adomnán" is another reminder that the conversion to Christianity proceeded slowly and unevenly within the Scandinavian orb. What type of idolatry might continue to be practiced at a trading port like the Viking towns of Ireland? Some idea can be gleaned from the tenth-century travelogue of the Arabic author Ibn Fadlan, who describes the rites of Swedish Viking (or Rus) merchants preparatory to the beginning of trade. He tells of a very primitive type of worship and offering. The Viking merchant carried offer-ings of bread, onions, meat, and drink to a wooden stake on which a human face was carved; around it were smaller, similarly designed stakes.[21] As the offerings were pre-sented, the supplicant asked for success in his dealings. These idols were known as *trémenn* ("wooden men"). A passage in the Old Norse poem *Hávamál* ("The Speech of Hávi [i.e., Odin]") refers to an offering of clothing made to these figures, "I gave my clothes to two *trémenn* in a field." There was still a pagan sanctuary among the Swedes, at Uppsala; Adam of Bremen claims that they also worshiped stocks of wood set up in the open fields.[22] The Viking ports in Ireland apparently catered to various tastes in religious enthusiasm.

Like Diarmait mac Máel na mbó, one legacy of the Olafsson dynasty that was maintained by Muirchertach after his capture of Dublin was good relations with England. In 1095 the plague killed Bishop Donatus II (Donngus Ua hAingliu) of Dublin on November 23. Muirchertach permitted another cleric who had been trained in England to succeed him, his nephew Samuel. Archbishop Anselm of Canterbury had uneasy relations with Bishop Samuel of Dublin. He reprimanded Samuel for expelling the monks from Christ Church, disposing of books and vestments given by Lanfranc to his uncle, and for traveling through the countryside in the fashion of an archbishop.[23] Anselm's accusation that Samuel was getting above his station is supported by Samuel's brief obit in the Black Book of Christ Church, where his death is announced *Obiit Samuel archiepiscopus Dublin'*.[24] Part of Samuel's transgressions appears to look back to Dublin's initial status as a metropolitan. Samuel's grandiose actions might have been seen by him as a return to the original status of the town. Another part seems to be that he was behaving like the secular clergy that the reformers, such as Anselm, were trying to abolish. The missing books and vestments may have been dispersed because Samuel was treating them as his private property; they were valuable in a society that practiced ritual gift-exchange among the secularized clergy as well as lay society. The expulsion of the monks could reflect the large expense that such a community was to a bishop. Throughout Europe hostility between secular and regular clergy was famous, and Bishop Samuel might have been taking the side of the seculars.

If Samuel was attempting to cast off his subordination to Canterbury, he does not seem to have had the support of Muirchertach, who continued to exchange friendly correspondence with Anselm. More revealing is the relationship between the Irish clergy and Anselm. In 1096 Máel Ísua Ua h-Ainmise (Latin *Malchus*) was consecrated bishop of Waterford by Anselm; among the signatories to the petition was Bishop Domnall of Dál Cais, Muirchertach's home. Also included was Bishop Gillebert (Gilla-espuic) of Limerick, the papal legate (after 1107), author of *De statu ecclesiae* (a tract on liturgical custom), and a personal friend of Anselm. Limerick was the main town in Muirchertach Ua Briain's home territory. Gillebert convened the synod of Rath Breasil (presided over by Muirchertach), which established a diocesan organization in Ireland that brought it into conformity with England.

The English orientation of the see of Dublin that was begun by the Olafssons, with a cathedral founded by Sitric Silkenbeard, was continued by the Irish overlords of the town. The active support of the Uí Briain progressed from the tentative formalities between Tairdelbach and Lanfranc to the personal friendship between

Muirchertach and Anselm. There were some in the Irish churches who were not pleased with this state of affairs, most notably at Armagh. The conflict came into the open upon Bishop Samuel's death in 1121. When Canterbury's candidate named Gregory arrived in Dublin, he found that the head of the church of Armagh, Cellach, was already there and calling himself bishop of Dublin. A transcription of a letter from the people of Dublin to the archbishop of Canterbury claims that the bishop of Armagh was jealous that the citizens preferred Canterbury to the Irish churches.[25]

Another legacy of the Olafssons in Dublin was trade between Ireland and England. Generally the Irish have been seen as more dependent on that trade. Reference is usually made to the story of William of Malmesbury, who claimed that Henry I of England punished Muirchertach by suspending English trade with Ireland.[26] When that trade is viewed within the general context of English and Irish affairs, it appears that it was just as, if not more, important to the Normans. The Normans were constantly in need of revenues, and throughout the eleventh century the Irish had been buying high-value goods such as slaves, horses, and wine. When Bishop Wulfstan preached against the Irish Sea slave trade, the English slaves were going to Ireland, not the other way around. While the *Book of Rights* mentions British horses as high value items in Ireland, there is no contemporary indication in England of Irish horses. All this suggests that in the eleventh century the wealthy side of the Irish Sea was the Irish coast.

The Irish were good customers and their business was valuable. That is why both Bristol and Chester were determined to have their rights to trade at Dublin confirmed by the king. The importance of the early twelfth-century Irish trade for the English can be judged from the charters of King Henry II.[27] Two late twelfth-century documents confirm the trading privileges granted by Henry I that the men of Chester and Bristol had enjoyed with Ireland. These privileges reveal the older trading connections between England and Ireland that preceded the Normans in Ireland. They amounted to monopoly rights, and they were used to reward or punish according to the king's desires. Those charters confirm what other sources note, such as William of Malmesbury's observation on the ships from Norway and Ireland that called at Bristol.[28] The shift toward the ports of the western coast came at the expense of other towns such as York, which was visited by ships of the Danes, Norwegians and *Scotti* (Scots or Irish). Those visits were used by Archbishop Lanfranc of Canterbury as justification for his objections to an archbishop being located at York, where men hostile to the king could naturally and quietly congregate.[29]

Among the cargoes being carried were passengers. The Irish tale of Conall Corc, reworked circa 1000, has Conall take ship at Dublin in order to sail to Scotland. The *vita* of Colman of Ela, composed circa 1100, has an anachronistic episode in which the saint and his companions travel to Rome in a ship sailing from Dublin. Sometimes the passengers are clearly fictitious such as the eighth-century St. Rumbold of Mechlin (Belgium) whom Thierry of St. Trond claims was the bishop of Dublin.[30] Other passengers were real, such as the Welsh prince Owain ap Cadwgan, who, according to *Brut Y Tywysogyon* circa 1108, escaped from Wales by taking passage on a cargo ship from Ireland. In 1130 an Irishman who stole treasures from Clonmacnoise attempted, unsuccessfully, to flee the country from the Viking ports of Waterford and Cork.

While the Irish princes wanted to maintain the commercial viability of the Viking towns, they did not have the expertise of the Olafssons or Haraldssons. Evidence of commercial change comes, once again, from the Dublin coinage. By 1095 the coins produced in Dublin show pronounced signs of decay, and the weight of individual coins was reduced as low as 8 grams. This was far greater than the usual reduced-weight coin of Dublin, and efforts to stay near the previous 3:2 ratio with English coins had been abandoned. Equally revealing was the degraded style of the inscription. For about 30 years prior to 1095 Dublin coins imitated current styles in England, but after 1095 they reverted to copies of the various Æthelraed series. Admittedly the Dublin coins were showing incompetence in design and reduction in weight immediately before, but after 1095 the degeneration in the coinage was dramatic. Reversion to a stylistic model nearly a century old emphasized the precipitous decline. As has been stated succinctly, "where the Hiberno-Norse coinage is concerned, this may be said to be the beginning of the end."[31] The coins after 1095 were little more than tokens distributed locally. This indicates that Muirchertach was uninterested in the nuances of commerce, and more concerned to use the town as a quartermaster store for his forces. Payment of taxes in goods reduced the need to bargain for the best price, a practice at which the Vikings were masters and admired throughout Europe. Dudo of St. Quentin had sneered at anyone who could not strike a favorable deal.

Manufacturing at Dublin was in decline. The twelfth-century version of the poem "Here is a Happy, Graceful History" lists its industrialists as comb makers, cobblers, and a catchall "craftsmen" whose dues were paid in the form of pitchers; manufacturing seems to have become concentrated on domestic wares. A good living was to be made from these goods, however, and the same verse demands a payment in gold from every individual. The reduction of commerce at Dublin reflects another change found throughout Britain during the late eleventh and twelfth centuries—new tastes in style. The goods produced at Dublin were old fashioned, and promotion of new fashions was one way writers described good rule. Scottish kings and queens were praised for the new fashions they were introducing into their domain. The early twelfth-century biography of Queen Margaret (died 1093) praises her encouragement of foreign merchants who brought clothes and jewelry previously unknown to her subjects. When Ailred of Rievaulx noted that his friend, and Margaret's son, King David I had allowed the Scots to exchange their shaggy cloaks for new clothes, he marked the passing of an era. What had been a mainstay of the Irish Sea clothing trade, the *röggvarfeldr* or shaggy cloth that imitated the appearance of fur, was not now fit even for peasants. Ailred's contemporary Gerald of Wales is disparaging about the dark color of Irish wool. Shortly thereafter, the thirteenth-century wool grading scheme used in Flanders ranked Irish wool below the English and Scottish. A decline in manufacturing at Dublin explains why the English had to import so many basic items into Ireland in the first decade of their expeditions. Hand mills, axes, axe handles, nails, planks, shovels, spades, and iron for working into spades were among the cargoes in the supply ships sailing from England to Ireland.[32]

There is also an indication that Dublin was suffering from a population decline. A cryptic remark in the *Book of Rights* claims that the king of Leinster gave to the king of Dublin horses, cows, swords, and thirty women with large families.[33] Was the population of Dublin becoming so small that settlers were being encouraged to move into the town? Why is only Leinster mentioned? The question awaits an answer.

When Godred Crovan was expelled from Dublin in 1094, he returned to the Isles where the Olafssons ruled for another century and a half. Godred had three sons named Lagmann, Harald, and Olaf. Lagmann succeeded his father and, in turn, was succeeded by his youngest brother, Olaf. Names are informative, as they reveal a family's cultural or ancestral heritage. Harald and Olaf might have been named after Godred's grandfather (Harald son of Olaf Cuaran) and great-grandfather (Olaf Cuaran), or after the Norwegian kings St. Olaf and Harald Hardrada. Perhaps both aspects were involved as Godred could revel in ancestral glory while looking towards the Norwegian royal families. The name Lagmann (Old Norse *Lögmaðr*, "lawman") looked towards the Isles. There were the tenth-century "Lawmen" of the Isles who had raided in Ireland, and there was also the earlier king of the Isles named Lagmann son of Godfrey Haraldsson, who was the companion of St. Olaf when they fought for the duke of Normandy early in the eleventh century. Possibly Lagmann's mother was a member of the Haraldsson dynasty, who remembered her kindred when choosing a name for her son.

At the commencement of his reign, Lagmann had to repel an attack from the Isles' former rulers, the Haraldssons. The new champions of the Haraldsson dynasty were the grandchildren of Echmarcach Ragnallsson. Echmarcach had a daughter named Mór, and she was married to Tadc Ua Briain. Tadc was the son of Tairdelbach ua Briain (and the brother of Muirchertach and Domnall) whose death in 1086 "in his father's bed" (i.e. peacefully) had been the spark for a war between his brothers. Tadc and Mór had three sons and a daughter: Olaf, Domnall, Donnchad, and Be Bind.[34] Two of Echmarcach's grandsons—Olaf and Domnall—led invasions of the Isles, in which they attempted to conquer their grandfather's kingdom. The first to try was Olaf. The *Annals of the Four Masters* record that he attacked the Isle of Man in 1096, but was slain in battle. The timing of the attack clearly follows from Godred Crovan's death. As well as the disorder and uncertainty after the death of a powerful prince, this suggests that the hold of the Olafssons in the Isles was believed to be weak, and that Godred's sons could be expelled from the kingdom.

Lagmann's seven-year reign was eventful, even after he had survived a challenge to his kingship. In 1098 his Islesmen sailed three ships to northeast Ireland for a raid on the Ulaid. The *Manx Chronicle* notes that his brother Harald rebelled against him. When Lagmann captured him, he had Harald mutilated. Later, as an act of penance, he took the sign of the cross and went on a pilgrimage to the Holy land, but died before reaching Jerusalem. This has been interpreted as meaning that Lagmann died on the First Crusade (1096–1099). There were not, however, seven years between Godred's death and the Crusade. So it has been suggested that Lagmann ruled contemporaneously with his father, from 1089 to circa 1096.[35] Lagmann, however, was alive and in the Isles in 1098. Verses connected with the first expedition of the Norse king Magnus Barefoot to the Isles in 1098 recall that Lagmann, who is called the lord of Uist, was captured either off the Isle of Skye or off the Isle of Scarba. According to the twelfth-century history preserved in *Morkinskinna*, he resided with the king, who gave him an amnesty, and apparently he was restored to his kingship after Magnus' death in 1103 in Ulster.[36]

Lagmann's identification with Uist suggests that his main residence was there. This, together with his father's death on Islay, indicates that the Olafssons preferred the Hebrides to the Isle of Man, possibly because there was too much support for the Haraldssons on Man. The division of the island by Godred Crovan was resented by the natives, and in the summer of 1098 tensions among the Manx had exploded at the battle of Santwat, when the opposing sides were led by the captains Ottar and MacMaras. There may be some significance in the apparent absence of Lagmann.

The Olafssons' move to the Isles placed them in the path of one of the most colorful individuals of his day, the Norwegian monarch Magnús III Óláfsson. He is better known as Magnus Barefoot, a nickname he acquired during his British expeditions when he began to wear a kilt. In the summer of 1098 Magnus appeared in the seas between Ireland and Britain, where he single-handedly began his personal Viking Age. During the next five years, he decisively established Norwegian lordship over the Isles. Legends about Magnus's adventures circulated in Iceland, Ireland, Britain, and France. To observers, everything about him was larger than life. His banker was a merchant of Lincoln from whom, according to his contemporary Orderic Vitalis, Henry I extorted 20,000 pounds of silver upon learning of Magnus's death.

Magnus's ancestors were a mix of the warlike and the placid. His grandfather was Harald Hardrada, who had died trying to conquer England. In contrast was Magnus's father, Olaf "the Peaceful." Olaf's experiences of warfare in Britain had been decidedly distasteful, and he began his reign by carrying the body of his father, Harald, back to Norway after the Norwegian defeat at Stamford Bridge. More famous were Olaf's commercial interests. He founded the town of Bergen, the main Norwegian port in the later Middle Ages.

For the Irish Sea Viking dynasties, such as the Olafssons, the appearance of the Norwegian king was a mixed blessing. So long as Magnus was in the region, their independence was at an end. Magnus served notice that he intended to take control and eliminate possible rivals when he deposed the jarls of the Orkneys and captured Lagmann of the Isles. In their place he installed his son, Sigurd, who was still a child. Magnus had several sons, but the choice of Sigurd was not a sign of favoritism. Rather it demonstrates once again the importance of an acceptable genealogy. Sigurd's mother, Thora, was English. This British link was maintained by Sigurd when he married Malmfrid, a great-granddaughter of the former English king Harold Godwinsson. Malmfrid's great-uncle Harald Haroldsson (the son of Harold Godwinsson) was the pilot for Magnus on his 1098 expedition. Little wonder that Henry I of England was relieved when he learned of Magnus's death.

Why did Magnus lead an expedition to the Hebrides and Irish Sea? Orderic Vitalis states that Magnus wanted to reassert Norwegian lordship over the Viking settlements in the west. Magnus was able to do so because he was the sole king among the Norwegians. During the battles for the Norwegian kingship later in the twelfth century there were no royal visits to the Isles because the princes were busy protecting their interests at home. Second, there was a long-standing family interest in the region. His uncle, Magnus, recruited troops there in 1058 as did his grandfather, Harald Hardrada, in 1066, both times for an invasion of England. Finally, Magnus needed the revenues that came from colonies in the Irish Sea. Throughout Europe, the cost of royal government increased during the eleventh century. Whenever possible, monarchs took finances out of the hands of the local nobility, eliminating an expensive intermediary who was becoming less effective. At the same time princes searched for ways to augment their revenues, and the Viking colonies between Ireland and Britain were wealthy. A mixture of finances and ineffectiveness are suggested by a scandal recorded by Orderic Vitalis, when Robert de Mowbray robbed four Norwegian merchant ships called canardes (from ON *knörr*) in Northumbria circa 1094.[37] Orderic claims that King William fully compensated the merchants, but the victims (and their king) may have thought differently. So merchants who wanted greater security may have encouraged Magnus in his western expedition.

Contemporaries and near contemporaries speculated about the reasons for Magnus's western expeditions. Medieval accounts such as *Orkneyinga Saga* suggest that Magnus wanted to re-create the glorious Viking days of his ancestors, a fascination in which some of his subjects encouraged him for their own reasons.[38] The saga claims that Hakon Palsson, the future Orkney jarl, urged Magnus to lead an expedition westwards in order that he could be returned to power in the Orkneys. To encourage the king, Hakon noted that Magnus could easily take control of the Orkneys and Hebrides, and then use them as a base for an attack on England in revenge for the death of his grandfather, Harald Hardrada. Magnus liked the idea, but warned that he would treat everybody equally, something that did not please Hakon.

Folklore gives a supernatural explanation for Magnus's expedition. The *Manx Chronicle* claims that Magnus was curious to learn if the body of St. Olaf was uncorrupted and, against the wishes of the clergy, ordered the opening of the tomb. After he had seen and felt the uncorrupted body, an apparition of the saint appeared the following evening, commanding him either to leave the kingdom within a month or to lose his life. Magnus chose the former.[39] Snorri Sturluson tells a somewhat similar story in "Magnus Barefoot's Saga." In his account, Magnus stops at the island of Iona and visits the church of St. Columba. He has it opened, but does not go inside and forbids anyone else to do so.[40] An error in Snorri's story suggests its authenticity. Since the ninth century, Irish works had claimed that Columba's body was at Downpatrick in Ireland, together with the remains of Patrick and Brigit. This was not widely known outside the Gaelic-speaking world, and a late eleventh-century Norse king might have believed that Columba's body rested at Iona. Magnus could have stopped at Iona for provisions. Several accounts claim that there was a market on Iona, and the king forbade his men from plundering it.[41]

The timing of Magnus's expedition suggests that he was informed about affairs in the Isles, which seem to have been becoming chaotic. In addition to the struggle for control of the Isles between the Olafssons and Haraldssons, there were more local conflicts, such as the hostilities among the Manx leading to the Battle of Santwat, when the natives fought the supporters of Godred Crovan's family. Those deep divisions among the Islemen may have been known to Magnus, who, according to the *Manx Chronicle*, landed on Man so soon after the battle that all the slain had not been buried. He would not have wanted another prince to take advantage of the chaos. Orderic Vitalis' erroneous claim that Magnus found the island uninhabited so that he was forced to rebuild houses and bring supplies does suggest hostilities more widespread and lengthy than a single brawl.

Study of Magnus's campaigns around the Irish Sea is made difficult by confusion about the date or order of specific events, even in the works of contemporaries. There is, for example, the question of the year when Magnus first appeared in the Irish Sea. The Irish annals and English chronicles agree that Magnus made his first expedition in 1098, but Orderic Vitalis, who was about 23 years old and living in Normandy in 1098, claims that Magnus made his first royal expedition to Britain in the fifth year of the reign of the English king William Rufus, that is, circa 1092.[42] Magnus was not king in 1092, it was his father Olaf, who died in 1093; to 1094 Magnus shared the kingship with his cousin Hakon Thorir's-Fosterson.

Magnus led his fleet from Norway in the summer of 1098. He sailed first to the Orkneys, where the earls Pál and Erland were removed from office and sent to Norway as captives; his 8-year-old son Sigurd was set up as king with a regency council. Details about Magnus's voyage from the Northern Isles southwards are provided in a versified travelogue by his skalds, or court poets, of whom the most important was named Bjorn Cripplehand. Magnus sailed westward to the Outer Hebrides where he attacked the Isle of Lewis before sailing on to the Isles of Uist and Skye. Traveling south, he landed on Tiree, Sanday, and Mull. He stopped on Iona, Islay, and Kintyre before sailing through the North Channel and entering the Irish Sea, where landfall was made on the Isle of Man. Not unexpectedly the verses present Magnus's voyage in terms of a Viking raid, and there may well have been resistance from local chieftains who did not welcome the benefits to be gained as part of the Norwegian colonial empire.

The last stop was Wales. Magnus's presence was announced in a particularly direct fashion that aided an Olafsson, although neither party knew it. Prior to Magnus's appearance the Normans had continued their advance into Wales. Despite the best efforts of Gruffudd ap Cynan in Gwynedd, with the occasional aid of his kinsman Godred Crovan, in 1098 the Normans launched a new campaign in North Wales. They were led by Hugh of Chester, who was joined by Hugh of Shrewsbury, the son of the Conqueror's friend Robert of Montgomery. Hugh's sons included the savage Robert of Bellême and Arnulf de Montgomery, who sought his fortune in southern Wales. Since the death of Rhys ap Tewdwr in 1093, the Montgomery family had annexed lands across South Wales. Arnulf, the future son-in-law of Muirchertach Ua Briain, was the castellan of Pembroke. Gruffydd ap Cynan had sought allies among other Welsh princes, including the prince of Powys named Cadwgan ap Bleddyn, and his son, Owain.[43]

In July the allies faced the two Hughs, who ravaged North Wales as far as Anglesey. Gruffudd and Cadwgan looked to Ireland for additional troops. According to an aside in the *Brut y Tywysogyon*, Cadwgan's son, Owain, was sent with presents to the court of Muirchertach Ua Briain to induce him to send help; a fleet from Ireland then sailed to Anglesey. Gruffydd was to learn once again that the use of mercenaries was fraught with danger. This time it was disloyalty, when the fleet's commanders met the two Hughs before the battle and agreed to change sides.[44] The refusal of the Irish captains to fight the Normans reflects the ties between the Normans and the Uí Briain, and suggests that Owain could have led the Irish to believe that his opponents were Welsh. Gruffudd and Cadwgan sailed to safety in Ireland, leaving the men of Anglesey to fend for themselves.

Complete disaster for the Welsh was averted by the arrival of Magnus Barefoot, who arrived a few days after the island had been captured. The victors celebrated their victory with a massacre of the local population, after mutilating a priest named Cenred, who seems to have been leading the defense of the island.[45] The arrival of the Norwegians led the Normans to believe that they were being attacked by allies of the Welsh. During the Norwegian archery attack, Magnus and one of his retainers decided to hold an impromptu contest using Hugh of Shrewsbury for their target. Hugh's body was completely protected except for his eyes. They shot their arrows at the same time, one of which found its mark, and Hugh fell dead from his horse. Magnus' competitor graciously (and wisely) awarded the honor to the king. Hugh's death began a rout of the Normans, and the Welsh looked upon the Norwegians as their rescuers.

The Welsh soon learned that their relief was premature. Magnus had no intention of being anyone's protector; he thought the Isle of Anglesey was part of the Kingdom of the Isles. Orderic Vitalis has Magnus utter the diplomatic comment that he had no quarrel with the Normans, but merely wished to reclaim his territory. Viking interest in Anglesey had a greater longevity than usually is thought, and it was not limited to the descendants of Olaf Godfreysson and Olaf Cuaran. Once again, Magnus's action reveals that he was informed about the Irish Sea region. He obviously knew about earlier Viking bases on Anglesey, and the justification given by Orderic is probably an accurate estimation of Norwegian views.

Orderic and Snorri reflect what was generally known of Magnus's land hunger and rationale for his actions, the recapture of what Magnus claimed was anciently Norwegian territory. In Scandinavia, Magnus's tactics were similar to those he had employed around Britain. He repeated his actions on the border between the Norwegians and the Swedes in the summer of 1099. Magnus led his army eastwards as far as the Gaut Elf River and claimed that lands west of the river belonged to the Norwegians, not the Swedes.[46] He then established a garrison on the island of Kvalthinsey in Lake Vänern. Unlike his success in the Irish Sea, there was a different conclusion on the Swedish border. King Inge of the Swedes destroyed the garrison. When Magnus led an army in retaliation, he was defeated by a local force, and the region remained under Swedish lordship.

Magnus's land hunger and military display led to the transfer of some of the Hebrides from Scottish to Norwegian control. These had been part of the ancient kingdom of Dál Riada, roughly the area from Ardnamurchan to the Isle of Arran, the ancestral home of the Scots kings. According to his saga in *Heimskringla*, during this first expedition, Magnus negotiated with Malcolm and Margaret's son, Edgar, for the transfer of the southern Hebrides to Norwegian control.[47] The time was propitious for Magnus's overtures. Since the death of Edgar's father in 1093, his kingship had been contested among three men: Malcolm's brother Domnall *bán* and Malcolm's two sons: Duncan (from his first marriage to Ingibjorg of the Orkneys) and Edgar. Both Duncan and Edgar owed their reigns to the support of William Rufus. Duncan was king briefly in 1093–94, and Edgar succeeded after the deposition of his uncle in 1097. Domnall had been able to overthrow his nephew Duncan in part because of Scottish xenophobia against the French and English troops who supported the family of Malcolm Canmore. Edgar, then, was in the position of trying to keep an imposing opponent at bay with little assurance of popular support.

Snorri's account in *Heimskringla* places the Norwegian-Scottish negotiations after the Battle at Anglesey, late summer or early autumn of 1098. The final agreement was the result of protracted bargaining, but its terms were unambiguous. The Norwegians were to have all the lands to the west of a line that a ship with a fixed rudder could sail. This did not include all the territory coveted by Magnus, who wanted the fertile Kintyre peninsula, so he concocted the type of scheme that added to his legend. When he came to Kintyre he had his ship dragged across the isthmus while he held the tiller, and so claimed the land. Thus the letter, if not the spirit, of the agreement was satisfied.

This information from an Icelandic historian is important because it is generally assumed that there had been no Scottish control in the Hebrides since the mid-ninth century. The historical records tell a different story. The contemporary *Scottish Chronicle* records a Scottish victory over the Vikings at Shiel during the reign of Domnall II (died 900) and a bishop named Fothad was expelled from St. Andrews to the Isles, where he died in 963. Malcolm II lived in exile on Islay and Arran before his accession to the throne in 1005, and John of Fordun claims that after the murder of King Duncan I, Edgar's grandfather, his younger son, Domnall *bán* (Edgar's predecessor) sought refuge in the Hebrides.[48] Orderic Vitalis notes that Edgar's father and mother, Malcolm and Margaret, supplied revenues for repairs to be made at the monastery of Iona. The ceding of Dál Riata gives an indication of how formidable was Magnus, and how weak was Edgar.

Contemporary and later documents confirm that there was substantial emigration into the old Dál Riata lands by both the Viking colonists. Place names show that the Norse name elements in the southern Hebrides are less dense than farther north or on the Isle of Man, and that they are also much later in date, circa the eleventh century.[49] Friendly relations between the Haraldssons of the Isles and the Scots helped, as illustrated by Echmarcach Ragnallsson as part of Malcolm II's retinue in 1031. Godred Crovan died on Islay. Some emigration may have been encouraged by the Scots kings themselves. The *Prophecy of Berchán* claims that during the reign of Edgar's uncle Domnall the Vikings emigrated in large numbers into his realm, so much so that the poet is convinced that he had abandoned Scotland to them. There might have been even more of a personal link for Domnall. His son was named Lagmann, and he died in 1116 while on a raid around the Moray Firth according to the *Annals of Ulster*.

Magnus remained in the Isles for a year, from the summer of 1098 to the summer of 1099, before returning to Norway. He was preoccupied with affairs there for several years and did not return to the Isles until the summer of 1102. Upon his return, Magnus increased the bounds of his domain when he moved into Ireland and took the lordship of Dublin. As part of the transfer of power, Magnus entered into an alliance with Muirchertach Ua Briain. The union was sealed in the customary fashion when Muirchertach's daughter, called Bjadmyn by the Norse (possibly a phonetic rendering of the name Be Bind), was married to Magnus's son, Sigurd. There is some disagreement about the date of the alliance. *Magnúss saga* implies that the marriage was contracted in 1099, but the *Annals of Inisfallen* date it to 1102. The *Annals of the Four Masters* claim that the marriage occurred after Magnus captured Dublin in 1102 and that it was part of a year's truce between Magnus and Muirchertach. The *Annals of Ulster* merely state that Muirchertach and Magnus agreed to a peace treaty of a year's duration. Orderic Vitalis claims that the marriage had been contracted prior to 1098 and was a reason for Magnus's appearance in the Isles. Regardless of the chronology of the negotiations, the union was in name only, since the principals were still children.

The *Manx Chronicle* preserves a somewhat different story in which Muirchertach submits to Magnus. He demonstrates his submission by wearing the Norwegian king's shoes on his shoulders during the Christmas festival, with Magnus's envoys in attendance to ensure that the necessary ceremony is performed. When Muirchertach's nobles complain about the indignity of it, the Irish king replies that he would eat the shoes rather than have the Norwegians destroy any part of Ireland.

This was a busy year for Muirchertach's daughters, as the *Annals of Inisfallen* note that another was married to a "Frenchman," the son of Hugh of Montgomery named Arnulf. There was no more romance involved in this liaison than in the other union, for Arnulf's family was in revolt against Henry I of England. The Montgomery family, led by Arnulf's elder brother Robert of Bellême, had supported Henry's brother Robert "Curthose" in his invasion of England in 1101. Although Henry bought off his brother, Robert, with a pension of 3,000 marks and a promise of amnesty to his supporters, he waited to take revenge on the Montgomery rebels. His opportunity came in 1102 when, after a year during which his spies had compiled a dossier on the Montgomery family, Henry summoned them to his court to answer charges of treason. The brothers, knowing that vengeance, not justice, awaited them, fled. Arnulf and his followers fled to Muirchertach.

There might have been a political connection between these two marriages of Muirchertach's daughters.[50] Sigurd of Norway could have been the spur to Arnulf's matrimonial interests. If the Montgomerys could manage to lure Magnus into at least a tacit alliance, then they would have been a threat by sea and land. Such a connection would have been a powerful bargaining chip in negotiations with Henry. All commentators note that Robert of Bellême was not just a fiend, but also a clever one. There is no evidence of Magnus and the Montgomery family working in concert, but this could be due to Magnus's early death.

Magnus was not content merely to arrange his son's marital affairs; he also reserved some time for his own romantic pleasures. Information about one of his liaisons comes from verses that Magnus supposedly composed. In it he declares his affections for an Irish girl. Although only in his early thirties, Magnus declared that this lady made him feel young again. He had no desire to return to his home without her, for he loved the Irish girl better than his life.[51] There might be a postscript to this dalliance, one that changed the course of Norwegian history. After Magnus's death, the kingship was shared among his three sons. Sometime around the year 1133, a man named Harald Gille arrived at the Norwegian court. He claimed to be Magnus's son, the offspring from a romantic interlude the king had with an Irish lady.[52] In support of his claim he underwent an ordeal, and after successfully completing it he was acknowledged as Magnus's son. His appearance and acceptance at the Norwegian court might have been the impetus for the addition to the law of inheritance credited directly to Magnus's sons Sigurd, Eystein, and Olaf, concerning the right of illegitimate sons of freeborn mothers to inherit.[53] Some time later, Harald organized a rebellion that ultimately installed him as king and, after his assassination, began a contest by his descendants for the Norwegian kingship that led to a civil war paralyzing Norway for generations. Was the mother of Harald Gille the "Irish girl" of Magnus's poem?

Or was the object of Magnus's affections none other than the Scottish princess, and the future wife of Henry I of England, Matilda the daughter of Malcolm Canmore and Margaret? Matilda's real name was Edith, and she did not adopt the better-known name until her marriage to Henry I, because it sounded more "French." Two texts have items that suggest contact between Magnus and Matilda.[54] An item in the manuscript known as *Fagrskinna* claims that King Malcolm of the Scots sent his daughter to the Orkneys to be the wife of Magnus's son Sigurd. This need be no more than a confusion of Malcolm with Muirchertach Ua Briain, whose daughter did marry Sigurd. Or it could be a garbled account of a marriage proposal that was changed by the compiler, who was aware that Magnus already had a wife. The second text is *Morkinskinna* that contains a version of Magnus's saga. There are several love verses attributed to a Magnus. One of the pair is the praise of the Irish girl. The other is attributed to the earlier monarch Magnus the Good, and it tells of the "king's sister who keeps him from sleep" and "warfare in the south."

Matilda was King Edgar's sister, but she was then being educated far to the south with her younger sister Mary in a convent under the care of their Aunt Christine. They were by no means captives, and it is not impossible that the young princesses returned to Scotland occasionally, possibly even meeting a visiting Norwegian king who came personally to handle land negotiations. Family affection was not unknown, even among medieval royalty. Their father Malcolm visited them when he was in England. On one famous occasion he found that their aunt had dressed them in the garb of novices, and in a fury Malcolm ripped the veils from the heads of Matilda and Mary, declaring that he would rather see them dead than nuns. Of course all royal marriages were arranged, and the early stages of negotiation did not require the presence of either the prospective bride or groom. Could a marriage alliance have been contemplated in order to seal the treaty between the Scots and the Norwegians? Even though Magnus was already married, such unions could be ended if the need was pressing. All this must remain speculation.

From 1098 to 1103, it must have seemed to observers that the Viking days they thought had passed into legend were being revived in the Irish Sea. Magnus was as capable a leader as his illustrious forebears, the Viking chieftains of the ninth and tenth centuries. Through a display of military might he had his lordship recognized in the Kingdom of the Isles and in Anglesey. He was able to adapt, and his alliance with the Irish and Scots showed that he was willing to allow diplomacy to substitute for war. By that means he had Dublin formally ceded to him. In short, Magnus was the overlord of all the territory that the Olafssons and Haraldsson had held, as well as Scottish lands outside their control. Romantic he might be, but Magnus was also a shrewd player of the diplomatic game.

Diplomacy, however, did not provide immunity from misadventure. The glorious career of Magnus came to an end on the Irish coast in best "Viking" fashion. The circumstances leading up to his death are not entirely clear. The *Manx Chronicle* and the Irish annals claim that Magnus was invading Ireland when he was slain. His saga by Snorri Sturluson claims that he was actually sailing away from Ireland and had landed to collect provisions that he had been promised by his son's father-in-law, Muirchertach Ua Briain. Muirchertach did not rule the northeast, but he could have implied that he did in order to strike a blow at the Ulaid. In its implication that the Irish prince had been duplicitous, the saga might be correct. Muirchertach had a history of failing to honor his obligations. In 1088 he promised to aid the north Irish prince Domnall Mac Lochlainn in his attack on Connacht, but, as the *Annals of Tigernach* note, he did not fulfill it. Magnus might have incorrectly believed that his ally's authority in Ireland ran as far, and as absolutely, as did his in Norway.

Regardless of the exact circumstances, the Norwegian fleet anchored off the coast of county Down, in the territory of the Ulaid, on St. Bartholomew's Day (August 24) 1103. There they went ashore and collected (or stole) some cattle. On the return to the ships, the king and his party were attacked by the men of the district. Although they fought bravely, the king was slain. Magnus kept his promise to the "Irish girl" and was buried near Downpatrick. In the nineteenth century a grave was discovered on the coast that held the skeleton of a large man with some Viking grave goods. The finder declared it the grave of Magnus Barefoot.[55]

The Norwegian fleet continued its voyage home, pausing in the Orkneys to collect Sigurd, who, if he had ever seen his Irish child-bride, never saw her again. That was not the end of the story. Magnus's sojourn in the west publicly changed the Isles' political orientation. Just what, if any, authority the Norwegian monarch had in the Isles or Dublin prior to Magnus's arrival is difficult to know. Some recognition of lordship explains the number of times the Norwegians had drawn troops from the region. How much was due to long-standing recognition of Norwegian royal rights in the area, or how much to the empire building of the region's Viking dynasties is unknown. After Magnus's death, the limits of Norwegian lordship contracted. Dublin and Anglesey were not part of the later colonial empire. The enlarged Kingdom of the Isles was a Norwegian dependency until the later thirteenth century.

The death of Magnus led to the reinstatement of Lagmann Godredsson. Now the Olafsson dynasty had a new status, as Norwegian clients. Sigurd made known that he intended to maintain domination in the area. He sent Ivar of Fljóðar in one ship with sixty men to collect taxes. The account of his commission is given in *Morkinskinna* and must be regarded as historical, since it is possible that the author of the history met men who had accompanied Ivar. Ivar was an astute negotiator, who offered to collect the taxes only once, and reminded his audience that Sigurd would be fully justified to take revenge for the death of his father. His persuasion was successful, and the taxes were collected.[56] The amount of detail in this episode argues for a personal remembrance, although the location in Ulster, rather than the expected Isles, could reflect confusion about the precise extent of the Norwegian colonial empire. By the mid-twelfth century the dues owed by the lord of the Isles to his overlord were ten gold pieces at the time of his king-making, and this was probably paid in 1152 when the grandson of Godred Crovan, Godred Olafsson, sailed to Norway to do homage to the Norse king Inge.[57]

The death of Magnus and the subsequent return of Sigurd to Norway saw the restoration of Godred Crovan's dynasty in the person of his son, Lagmann. He ruled for about another four years, from late 1103 to the winter of 1108 when he joined his overlord, King Sigurd, on his pilgrimage to Jerusalem.[58] The *Manx Chronicle* states that Lagmann went on this pilgrimage as penance for his part in the mutilation of his brother, Harald. Its phrase *et signo crucis dominicae insignitus*, describing Lagmann's status on his departure, is the customary description of a crusader; crusaders wore red crosses sewn onto their clothing.[59] Lagmann must have joined Sigurd while the latter was visiting the court of King Henry I of England. The Isles king entrusted his youngest brother, Olaf, to Henry. The English king was the only neighboring prince who could guarantee Olaf's safety. The choice of Henry as Olaf's guardian probably was helped by the English king's Scottish connections. His queen Matilda was the sister of the reigning Scots monarch, Alexander I, whose wife Sybil was Henry's illegitimate daughter. Matilda's youngest brother, and future Scots king, David, was living at his sister's court. Years later he would reminisce to his friend Ailred of Rievaulx about life at Henry's court in the company of the other royal youths.

Lagmann was a member of the great Scandinavian crusade that would later be known simply as King Sigurd's crusade. The two men were probably well acquainted from the period when Sigurd had ruled as his father's representative in the Isles. In his lifetime Sigurd was known as Sigurd the Crusader, and his fame endured for centuries. Today he is remembered as the hero of Edvard Grieg's *Sigurd Jorsalfar March* (originally called the "Homage March"), part of the incidental music to the drama *Sigurd Jorsalfar* by Björnstjerne Björnson. In the autumn of 1107 the teen-aged Sigurd sailed from Norway to Britain, where he spent the winter in England as the guest of King Henry I.[60] After recruiting more troops, Sigurd led his fleet south in the spring of 1108.

The little that is known about Sigurd's Crusade comes mainly from two sources: the narrative in *Morkinskinna* and the history composed by Adalbert of Aachen; Snorri Sturluson's account in the saga of the sons of Magnus Barefoot in his *Heimskringla* follows *Morkinskinna*.[61] The fleet sailed south along the Atlantic coast and then through the Straits of Gibraltar into the Mediterranean Sea. The crusaders saw plenty

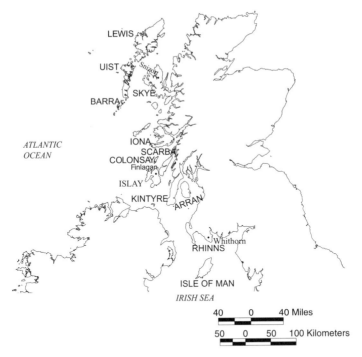

MAP 9. *Kingdom of the Isles*

of fighting, with battles against Muslim princes in the Iberian Peninsula and on the North African coast, before they reached the Holy Land. Sigurd landed at Ascolin and then sailed on to the main crusader port at Joppa. From there he went to Jerusalem. After assisting in the capture of Sidon on December 9, 1110, Sigurd departed. By midsummer of the next year he was back in Scandinavia. Lagmann died before reaching Jerusalem, possibly slain in one of the battles during the journey, and news of his death was announced when the crusaders arrived home in 1111.

The death of Lagmann reopened the contest for control of the Isles. Once again, the Olafssons confronted their rivals, the Haraldssons. Even before the appearance of Magnus Barefoot, they had been making efforts to regain their former territories. Intermarriage between Viking and Irish produced men who were prepared to fight for what they considered to be their inheritance. The seemingly random raids by Irish nobles in the Isles were actually being carried out by descendants of previous Viking rulers.

The defeat of Echmarcach's grandson, Olaf mac Taidc, in 1096 was followed by the arrival of Magnus Barefoot, and almost 15 years passed before Olaf's brother Domnall led his campaign to conquer the Isles. The campaigns of Olaf and Domnall are merged together in the *Manx Chronicle*. According to it, shortly after the death of Godred Crovan and before the arrival of Magnus Barefoot, Domnall was sent by

Muirchertach Ua Briain to rule the Isles at the request of the inhabitants. The *Manx Chronicle* claims that Muirchertach advised Domnall to rule gently, since he was a newcomer to the Isles; instead he ruled badly, and was expelled by the Islesmen.[62]

A more sensible account of Domnall's residence in the Isles comes from the contemporary *Annals of Inisfallen*. There his adventure began in the year 1111, when he went "in an angry mood" to the Isles and took the kingship. This was the same year that Sigurd the Crusader returned home from his crusade, on which Lagmann had died. Domnall's expedition appears to have begun upon hearing the news of his rival's death. Domnall reigned for two years, according to the *Manx Chronicle*, but returned to Ireland after his departure from the Isles. He and his brother Donnchad both died in 1115. The end of Domnall's time in the Isles comes from a cross-reference to the reign of Godred Crovan's last surviving son, Olaf, who had been living at the court of Henry I of England. Olaf died in 1153, after a reign of 40 years, according to the *Manx Chronicle*. This dates the beginning of his reign to 1113, which matches the end of Domnall's reign.

The bounds of Domnall's lordship are given in *An Leabhar Muimhnech*, a late collection of genealogies of important Munster families. He is credited with holding the kingship of the Isles and part of Galloway.[63] This is echoed in the *History of Gruffudd ap Cynan*, where Gruffudd's grandfather, Olaf Sitricsson, is said to have ruled many islands, Man, Galloway, and the Rhinns in addition to Gwynedd and Dublin. With the exception of Gwynedd (where Olaf had his castle), that is actually the territory controlled at various times by the kings of the Isles, most notably by Gruffudd's contemporary and kinsman Godred Crovan. Echmarcach had died as king of the Rhinns, and Magnus Barefoot had taken timber from Galloway for construction on the Isle of Man. The possibility that the compiler of the genealogy in *An Leabhar Muimhnech* had merely inflated the bounds of the kingdom is slight because after the mid-twelfth century Galloway was under the control of the king of the Scots. A later commentator would be expected to reflect the political situation of his day. As late as the early twelfth century southwestern Scotland was still a part of the kingdom of the Isles.

The adventures of Olaf and Domnall mac Taidc, as they tried to take the kingship of the Isles, gave rise to a piece of folklore. In the fourteenth-century *Liber Flavus Fergusiorum* is a story about a man called the son of Tadc son of Tairdelbach Ua Briain.[64] The section of the manuscript with the beginning of the story is damaged, but the legible part has the son of Tadc as a prisoner of the king of Munster. A Viking king named Thorkel and an archbishop named Nenne are with him. The son of Tadc calls upon the devil for assistance to be released from prison. St. Columba intervenes and prevents any diabolical aid because the son of Tadc is his monk. So the devil breathes upon the son of Tadc, who is released from prison and henceforth known as the leper of Lismore.

This is an unusual story. The request for diabolic rather than saintly aid is rare, and the saint seems content to allow his monk to remain in confinement while the devil tries to release him. The son of Tadc emerges with little credit and as a leper, definitely the loser of the tale. As is so often true for the literature of this period, there are some historical parallels. While there is no known prelate of Dublin named Nene, this was the period in which Anselm of Canterbury was scolding Bishop Samuel of Dublin for behaving like an archbishop. According to the *Annals of the Four Masters*, Domnall mac Taidc was "fettered" (i.e. imprisoned) at Dublin by Muirchertach Ua Briain in 1107, but he was released immediately thereafter. Contemporary with Domnall was a Viking named Thorkel, who is mentioned by the *Annals of Loch Cé* as a defender of Fingal during a raid in 1133. Several prominent nobles of Dublin were the sons of Thorkel. One son named Thorfinn was called chief young lord by the *Annals of Ulster* on his death in 1124. He had a brother who died in Wales circa 1144, according to *Brut y Tywysogyon*. In 1146 a Ragnall son of Thorkel who is called the king of Dublin was slain. The family of Thorkel had rivals in the dynasty of a man named Ottar, who came from the Kingdom of the Isles. In 1142 an Ottar son of Ottar intruded into the kingship of Dublin, but he was slain in 1148 by the sons of Thorkel. The folktale alerts us to the possibility that not all was well between Muirchertach and his nephews. Domnall was a concern to his uncle, perhaps because he had designs upon Dublin and had been plotting with one of the powerful residents of the town.

According to the *Manx Chronicle* there was another individual who ruled briefly in the Isles prior to the return of Olaf Godredsson, an obscure person named Ingemund. He was in the Isles less than a year and was slain before being made king, which explains why he is not mentioned in the Irish or English records. Ingemund's appearance could also fall into the period 1111 to 1113, most likely in the year 1113, after the expulsion of Domnall. Ingemund resided on the Isle of Lewis. By the twelfth century Lewis had become an administrative center. The twelfth-century Irish tale "Battle of Ross of the Kings" (*Cath Ruis na Ríg*) has the hero Conall Cernach meeting envoys from Norway on the Isle of Lewis, where he agrees to lead a fleet; the roughly contemporary story "Death of Finn" claims that Finn was the chief of the warrior band of, among other places, the Isle of Lewis while the rest of the Hebrides are called the "thither islands."[65] The chronicle claims that Ingemund was slain because of his vices, but his death may reflect the hostility between those who favored Norwegian lordship, and those who supported the Olafsson dynasty. This is not to ignore the possibility that Ingemund's removal reflects English influence in the region. A bishop for the Isle of Skye was consecrated in England, and to the east of the Isles, the sons of Malcolm Canmore were kings because of support from England. Olaf Godredsson was the ward of King Henry I, who would not be happy with a rival in the Isles. There has been the suggestion that Henry was using economic embargo in order to end Muirchertach's interference in the Isles.[66]

The establishment of Ingemund on the Isle of Lewis shows that the Kingdom of the Isles had almost taken its final shape, extending from Man in the south to Lewis in the north. The boundaries were still fluid at this time. By the later twelfth century the Rhinns of Galloway had been detached from the Isles, and absorbed into the

Scots kingdom. Although the administration details of the Isles are visible only in much later documents, they reveal the unity of the region. At the Thing assembly on Man (probably held then where it is now at Tynwald on St. John's Day) there were sixteen representatives from the Isle of Man and eight from the islands of Lewis, Harris, and Skye; probably the remaining islands south of Skye sent eight so that the Hebrides had as many representatives as Man. If there were sixteen representatives from all of the Isles, then this could reflect the administrative division of the Hebrides into four districts, with their heads at Lewis, Skye, Mull, and Islay, as outlined in a document from the late sixteenth century.[67]

Olaf's fosterage at the English court demonstrates that by the twelfth century the Irish Sea princes imitated and sought the goodwill of the Norman masters of England.[68] The Olafssons had a long history of eagerness to embrace new methods and technologies, and this had served them well. At Henry's court Olaf came into contact with a more varied world than had been the case for his father or brothers. The *Manx Chronicle* claims that he was a friend to all the neighboring kings, underscoring how contact at royal courts influenced behavior. For example, while the guest of the English king, Olaf would have met the future King David I of Scotland, Henry's brother-in-law, whose ancestral lands of Dál Riata were now within the Kingdom of the Isles. Olaf also would have been exposed to the new reforming efforts in the Church. This is reflected in his establishment of the first of the reformed monastic orders in the Isles at Rushen circa 1134. Rushen originally was attached to the Order of Savigny, a monastery of Mortain in Normandy whose founder Vitalis is today known for his mortuary roll (list of condolences) and in his day for the preaching that Orderic Vitalis said had caused his audience to believe that he was peering into their souls. Olaf's enthusiasm for reform was real, and he gave the right of presenting the bishop of the Isles to another Savigniac house, the monastery of Furness in Lancashire, the motherhouse of Rushen.

Olaf's ecclesiastical interests had been shaped during his stay in England. This undoubtedly included a desire to have his bishop in the Isles. Olaf's return to the Isles circa 1113 coincides with the consecration of Hamond/Wimund in the last years of the archiepiscopate of Thomas II of York. Hamond probably died circa 1133, for around that time there are two important changes in the ecclesiastical organization around the northern Irish Sea. The first was the installation of Gilla-Aldan as bishop of Whithorn, the ancient church of St. Ninian. This might be the time when the Rhinns of Galloway became politically separated from the Kingdom of the Isles. The other was the establishment of a bishop resident on the Isle of Man. The first occupant of the see was Wimund. His name is omitted from the Manx list. Some commentators believe that he is identical with the Hamond of the Manx list, while others believe that the Wimund consecrated by Thomas II was actually consecrated by his successor Archbishop Thurstan (1119–1140).[69] One of the witnesses to Olaf's charter to Furness was a *W. monachus*, probably the famous bandit-bishop Wimund whose career was recounted by William of Newburgh.[70]

While Olaf could direct ecclesiastical change (to some extent), less open to manipulation was commerce. As was occurring at Dublin, the economy of the Isles was changing at the end of the eleventh century. A sign of changed circumstances in the Kingdom of the Isles is the absence of domestic coinage and there is no evidence of the mint that had flourished a half century earlier. The manufacturing community— which two generations earlier had allowed blacksmiths to become so prosperous that they could commission monuments with commemorations in runic script— was declining. Craftsmen appear to have accepted that their wares were no longer as highly prized as they once were. In the records of the twelfth century (and later), there is little indication of manufacturing in the Isles other than for local consumption. Evidence of a new economic life in the Kingdom of the Isles, and throughout the Viking settlements, comes from materials that reveal an increasing financial sophistication on the part of the church authorities and from biography. Two of these documents are the Manx synodal statutes in a shorter version that was written circa 1229, and a longer text compiled circa 1292. Both copies of the statutes give elaborate details about the collection of tithes. They are paid mainly in agricultural produce. Craftsmen are not even mentioned in the earlier collection, while the latter regulations have only a brief section where goldsmiths, smiths, builders, those who shoe horses, implement makers, carpenters, and masons are all placed together.[71]

Change was not entirely a bad thing for the Islesmen. The improving climatic conditions of the eleventh century led to increased agricultural production. The Isle of Man was praised for its agriculture from Ireland to Iceland, while the Isle of Arran was famous for its fertility.[72] The Isles were suited for the grazing of sheep, and throughout Europe wool was becoming the important "cash crop" of the era. Winric of Trier wrote a tract titled *Conflictus Ovis et Lini* in praise of wool.[73] The Irish tract *Book of Rights* includes an impressive variety of woolens among its articles suitable for the high status ritual gift exchange. The dominance of livestock rearing in the Kingdom of the Isles is seen in royal grants, such as the license given in the thirteenth century to the Priory of St. Bees that permitted the grazing of sixty head of cattle on the Isle of Man or the substitution of an equivalent number of sheep or swine.[74] Flesh production of a different type was also increasing. An insistence on stricter prohibition of eating meat on certain holy days meant that fishing became another important industry, and Olaf's grandson, Ragnall Godredsson (reigned 1187–1226), distributed royal largesse to religious houses in the form of permission to fish and land the catches. In another grant to St. Bees, Ragnall gave the community land at Ormesham together with fishing rights.[75]

By the twelfth century the Viking pirates that were the scourge of the Church had descendants who were famous for their Christian piety. This study began with the literary hero Havelok the Dane, and it is appropriate to end with him. When, in the mid-twelfth century Geffrei Gaimar began his history of England (*L'Estoire des*

Engleis) with the legend of Havelok, he probably had never heard of Havelok's alter ego Olaf Cuaran. Geffrei's history was only one of the many twelfth-century works in which romance and history are found together, but the creation of a Viking romantic hero with such obvious debts to an authentic tenth-century king of Northumbria could have been due to the residence of Olaf Godredsson at the court of Henry I. Those seeking the patronage of a young princeling might have sought out tales about his family and their deeds, real and imagined. William of Malmesbury mentions that Henry's first queen, Matilda of Scotland, was noted for her patronage of literature, and she might have been the patron of the Anglo-Norman version of the *Voyage of Brendan*.[76] A young Viking prince at the English court might be one explanation why his ancestor Olaf Cuaran suddenly became a man of interest to contemporary writers. William of Malmesbury gives a fulsome account of his career, even confusing him with his cousin Olaf (who died in 941) in the curious account of Olaf dressed as a poet spying on the English positions prior to the Battle of *Brunanburh* in 937. As the last outpost of the wild Viking age, the Kingdom of the Isles became increasingly integrated into the Europe of the High Middle Ages, and the descendants of its pirate founders had transformed into Christian princes.

Conclusion

THE OLAFSSONS and Haraldssons found themselves living in a very different world at the beginning of the twelfth century from that of their tenth-century ancestors. The warriors of the earlier century fought for portable loot and the type of small farms they knew from their homeland. Two centuries later their descendants were fighting for control of trade routes and lordship of kingdoms. During the intervening years the domination of a few powerful dynasties, the exaltation of royal status, and the need for cooperation with the Church became as influential for the fortunes of the Olafssons and Haraldssons as winning battles or accumulating wealth. Change occasionally appears to have been abrupt because the conservatism and interests of the literary class that left written records often obscure gradual development. Even as Dublin became one of the premier trading centers in northern Europe, Gunnlaug Serpent's Tongue praises its king Sitric Silkenbeard in terms fit for a pagan chieftain celebrating his slaughter in battle. Two generations later, in what seems to be an abrupt change, the king of Dublin was being praised by the Christian clergy as the guardian of churches and his subjects' morals, even as his prowess as a sea-warrior was ignored.

Contemporary estimations of the power and ability of Olaf Cuaran and his family were not idle flattery. Olaf's father, Sitric, and uncle, Ragnall, made the first English conquest in Ireland. The Olafssons were also the first of the English invaders to be expelled. Their fortunes followed a circular pattern. They began in Britain and returned to Britain after their expulsion; in the medieval geographical view, the Isle of Man and the Hebrides were not separate from Britain because they had snakes. Less happy were the fortunes of the Haraldssons. Like many other petty princes, they found themselves unable to adapt to changes, such as competing with the powerful dynasties around them. The choice was obvious: submit to outside domination or move to where they could carve out a new dominion. The Olafssons successfully chose the latter, but when the Haraldssons were ousted from control of the Isles and Dublin, they had nowhere else to go. After a generation of attempts to retake their former kingdom, the Haraldssons passed out of view after the deaths of Echmarcach's grandsons, Domnall and Donnchad, in 1115. They had appeared abruptly in the Irish Sea in the tenth century and in the twelfth century they just as suddenly vanished into the mists.

The careers of the Olafssons and Haraldssons reveal an interconnection among the Viking kindreds from Normandy through the Irish Sea to the Orkneys and, beyond, to Scandinavia. The sea was a connector for a shared culture, commercially, artistically, and socially. Merchants from Ireland traded in Rouen, and ships from the Hebrides called at the Orkneys and Iceland. Vikings active in Ireland and Britain settled in northern Francia, while artistic styles found at Everaux are also found in the Hebrides and the Orkneys, where they mingled with symbols also found in Yorkshire. These connections lingered for centuries; in the mid-twelfth century ships from the Irish Sea were still calling at Rouen. The western Viking community took as much pride in seamanship and business acumen as in its martial prowess. Dudo of St. Quentin was probably repeating popular opinion when he mocked the sailor who was an insufficient navigator and sank under the waves, or the would-be merchant incapable of spotting a bargain or haggling successfully.

By the second decade of the twelfth century much had changed in the identities of the Olafssons and Haraldssons. Among the changes from the tenth to twelfth centuries was the increasing difficulty of distinguishing native from Viking. In the early tenth century there was little ambiguity about who was a "Viking" (however it was designated). Often it was as simple as the difference between attackers and attacked. Settlement and intermarriage in the following centuries made the distinction less obvious. Sitric Silkenbeard and his son, Olaf, were described as "foreigners" by the Irish, but they were more Irish than Scandinavian. The reverse was also true. The inheritors of the Haraldssons' claims in the Isles were men whose immediate kin group was the powerful Irish dynasty of Uí Briain.

Another change was religious affiliation. Olaf Cuaran raided many churches, but his dynasty was one of the great benefactors of the Church in the Irish Sea. Not only did his descendants establish a see at Dublin, but they also set up the bishopric of the Isles, later known as the bishopric of Sodor. When Brian Boru destroyed a grove at Dublin dedicated to the Viking god Thor in the year 1000 the town's rulers had been Christian for at least two generations. An Irish writer complained about the idolatry practiced by the Vikings in 1096, but ignored the fact that they had paid for the building of Holy Trinity (now Christ Church) cathedral.

Certainly by the eleventh century the role of the Church in the fortunes of the Viking families was real and important. Conversion of the Vikings to Christianity removed a barrier to trade. The Christian inhabitants of Dublin even employed the churches in business transactions. Gerald of Wales's story about the famous talking crucifix in Dublin's cathedral reveals that merchants used the physical premises of the church to guarantee the validity of contracts. By the twelfth century, sailors on the ships traveling between Britain and Ireland were carrying medallions of St. Wulfstan of Worcester, a bishop who had tried to stop the slave trade of their eleventh-century ancestors. Collections of religious objects reflect the various orientations—cultural, political, and economic—of a community. The relics collected by Archbishop Donatus of Dublin did not include a single Irish, English, Welsh, or Scots saint, even though a Norwegian king, a bishop from Cologne, and a priest from Normandy are represented. By the fourteenth century, relics of the Irish saints Patrick and Laurence had supplemented the collection, together with, from England, Thomas à Beckett and Wulfstan of Worcester.

Some developments throughout Europe during these centuries benefited the Olafssons and Haraldssons. Trade, for example, began to increase during the tenth century, and it continued to do so during the eleventh and twelfth centuries. While the Vikings certainly deserve some of the blame for the disruption of the trade patterns in northern Europe among the successor states of the Roman Empire, they also deserve some of the credit for revitalizing trade. Viking wealth was remembered in literature; the eleventh-century reworking of the Irish tale "The Wooing of Emir" (*Tochmarc Emire*) tells of emissaries from the Vikings bringing gifts of gold and wine.[1] The Olafssons and Haraldssons created a distinct trading zone between Ireland and Britain. The unique position of the Irish Sea region is revealed during the period of Norwegian domination (1098–1266) when Icelandic merchants taking rough woolen cloth (*vaðmál*) to Norway could pay their harbor dues in the Orkneys or Shetlands, but not in the Kingdom of the Isles.[2] Just how economically astute the Viking princes were is illustrated by the sudden decline of commercial life at Dublin that coincided with the expulsion of the last Olafsson prince of the town. A debased currency appeared soon after Godred Crovan was expelled from the town, and Dublin's coinage degenerated into tokens with only a local circulation.

The goods being traded by the Vikings show the wealth of a region generally thought to be primitive and impoverished. William of Malmesbury's famous question about where would the Irish be without English trade would be echoed throughout the Middle Ages. The Olafssons and Haraldssons became wealthy because Irish princes were buying expensive, high-status items such as slaves, horses, and wine. Despite efforts of individuals such as St. Wulfstan of Worcester to end the slave trade between England and Ireland, it continued. The very first text in the Welsh manuscript known as the *Book of Llandaff* is the story of an English slave named Algar, who was sold into Ireland in the twelfth century but escaped to Wales where he lived a life of sanctity.[3] By the late twelfth century the Irish believed that they were being divinely punished for slavery. In the wake of the successful English conquests, an ecclesiastical conference was convened at Armagh in a search of the reason for the invasions. The assembled clergy concluded that the success of the invaders was divine retribution for the generations of English slaves that had been brought into Ireland.[4] Interestingly, there is no mention of the guilt of the Vikings, who had originally bought and transported foreign slaves into Ireland.

Like theology and politics, commerce and politics were intertwined. One reason why the Olafssons and Haraldssons oversaw a successful commercial revival was that they offered security. Control of the seas around them allowed their markets, such as the one at Dublin, to entice merchants. That situation changed rapidly with the collapse of Viking power in Ireland. Piracy in the Irish Sea became a concern by the twelfth century after the Haraldssons' power diminished and the Olafssons were confined to the Kingdom of the Isles. How quickly the situation changed is revealed in an anecdote. About 1113, a delegation from the church of St. Mary's, Laon, made a fund-raising tour through Britain. At Bristol they wanted to buy some new clothes, but were warned not to go out to the Irish ships riding at anchor in the channel because they might be kidnapped and held for ransom.[5]

And who better to be pirates than the descendants of Vikings? In the late twelfth century, Gerald of Wales dismissed the peoples from the Orkneys to the Hebrides as "great pirates."[6] As the Olafssons received less wealth from trade and manufacturing, they had less interest in maintaining order. In 1218 the king of the Isles named Ragnall Godredsson, a descendant of Godred Crovan, had to travel to the English court to make amends for the "excesses" (i.e. pirate raids) of his subjects.[7]

The Olafssons and Haraldssons prospered because they provided a service for those living around them as well as for their own people. Not only did their camps/ports/towns bring in goods, but they were also steady consumers of the raw materials sold by their neighbors. Whether this was livestock and grain to feed the inhabitants of the towns and the crews of the ships calling at the port, or timber for house and boat construction, or minerals for manufacturing, the Vikings were good customers. The neighbors benefited from an increase in power and status, as can be seen in Leinster. At the beginning of the tenth century, Leinster was politically weak and little more than a satellite of the Uí Néill; the leader of the resistance to Olaf Cuaran's father, Sitric, in Leinster was Niall Glúndub from the Northern Uí Néill. Three important Viking strongholds were located in Leinster or its borders: Dublin, Wexford, and Waterford. As commercial activity increased at Dublin from the mid-tenth century, so, too, Leinster's aristocratic families began attempts to throw off outside domination, culminating in the Battle of Clontarf. A generation later Leinster dynasties were becoming national powers. A prince from an obscure family, Diarmait mac Máel na mbó, was able to defeat Brian's son, Donnchad, and claim, with some justification, to be the foremost Irish king after capturing Dublin. As the town declined in the twelfth century, so, too, did the preeminence of all the aristocratic Leinster families. By the High Middle Ages, the economic growth of Dublin and the political fortunes of Leinster went hand in hand.

The success of the Olafssons and Haraldssons was partly due to their own abilities, but also partly to their "victims." While chronicles and sagas alike promote the idea of constant hostility between the native princes and the Vikings, they carefully ignore the fact that opponents could become enthusiastic allies when it suited them. Even a tract such as *Cocad Gáedel re Gallaib*, with its carefully constructed presentation of Brian Boru as the leader of the fight against the Vikings, includes the information that his daughter was married to the king of Viking Dublin, that he employed Viking mercenaries, and that his Irish troops fought using Viking axes. The community of St. Cuthbert lost lands to the Vikings, but its great patron King Edgar might have been responsible for the settlement of the Haraldssons in the Irish Sea region. Olaf Cuaran's father had settled his followers on land belonging to Leinster princes, but the province's overlord, and Olaf's brother-in-law, Máel Mórda, attempted to protect Dublin in 999/1000 against his fellow Irish princes Brian Boru and Máel Sechnaill. This same spirit of collaboration continued into the twelfth century. The English king William II fortified Carlisle probably to forestall raids by Godred Crovan as well as the Scots, but William's brother, Henry I, was the foster-father of Godred Crovan's son, Olaf, who married one of his granddaughters; Olaf's son, Godred, was on friendly terms with his cousin the English king Henry II, and in the thirteenth century Olaf's grandson, Ragnall, was the ally of Henry's grandson, Henry III.

By the twelfth century the Olafssons and Haraldssons were increasingly old-fashioned. This is illustrated by a comment on clothes. Ailred of Rievaulx praised his friend King David I of Scotland for so enriching his subjects that they were able to exchange their shaggy cloaks for precious raiment. An era had ended when only savages now wore the shaggy cloak that had been one of the most widely traded items from the Irish Sea.[8] This helps to explain why the type of commercial achievement that had marked their careers in Ireland did not accompany the move of the Olafssons to the Isles. The Irish Sea region was becoming a supplier of raw materials. When Gerald of Wales noted that the Irish paid for wine from Poitou with skins, pelts, and hides, his list highlights changed economic conditions, for it includes no manufactured goods. He makes this point directly in the statement that there was no manufacturing in Ireland and that the mines were not being worked.[9] His claim is reinforced by a reading of the manifests for the ships supplying the first generation of Anglo-Norman adventurers. In their cargoes are goods as basic as shovels and planks.

That might not be the end of the story. Three powerful men appear suddenly in the twelfth century, seemingly from nowhere: Somerled of Argyll, Fergus of Galloway, and Ottar of the Hebrides. The ancestry of the last two is unknown. Was there any connection between them and the Olafssons or Haraldssons? The powerful lord of Galloway named Fergus controlled an area in southwest Scotland that appears to have been very similar in extent to the domain of the Haraldssons. Ailred of Rievaulx, his exact contemporary, describes him as king. Were the Olafssons or Haraldssons related to the family of a man named Ottar of the Hebrides? This family had occasional control of Dublin in the twelfth century. Finally, there was a connection of the Olafssons with the family of Somerled, who forced the division of the Kingdom of the Isles in the mid-twelfth century. Somerled's family successfully took power in the Isles in the way Mór's son Domnall had been unsuccessful. Somerled married a granddaughter of Godred Crovan, named Ragnhild, the daughter of Olaf and his wife Ingibjorn of the Orkneys. Somerled and Ragnhild had three sons— Dúngal, Ragnall, and Angus—who forced their uncle, Godred Olafsson, to share power in the Kingdom of the Isles with them in the mid-twelfth century.

As the Olafssons and Haraldssons were becoming more submerged into the local society, their Viking ancestors were acquiring a fresh lease on life in literature in Ireland and Britain. Irish sagas of this period were well informed about the political geography of the Viking colonists. The twelfth-century version of the tale "The Battle of Ross of the Kings" (*Cath Ruis na Ríg*) includes a survey of the Kingdom of the Isles and the western Scandinavian world.[10] Sometimes the Vikings were the heroes, even though their real histories might have been less glamorous. The legend of Havelok the Dane as recounted by Geffrei Gaimar took Olaf Cuaran out of the mundane tenth-century world of raids and political maneuver in order to place him in the realms of the romantic hero. The stereotype of the Viking as the enemy remained alongside a more benign view. The eleventh-century *Prophecy of Berchán* includes two ninth-century Vikings—Olaf of Dublin and Ivar—among the Irish high kings, but it also uses the Viking to represent disorder in Ireland, as in one verse that begins with a welcome to thieves and Vikings.[11] Even ancient literary figures, such as the hero Cú Chulainn, contended with the Viking menace. In *Siaburcharpat Con Culaind*, revised in the late tenth or eleventh century, Cú Chulainn forces the inhabitants of Scandinavia to pay taxes.[12]

The Olafssons and Haraldsson transformed life in the seas between Ireland and Britain. A backwater of the Atlantic world where a few boats carried clerics and the occasional cargo of trade goods before the ninth century became an important commercial zone where churches competed to claim the loyalty of the prosperous peoples whose Viking ancestors they had denounced as diabolical brigands. In turn, their success transformed the Olafssons and Haraldssons from pirates living off stolen property to respected, and respectably wealthy, Christian princes.

Notes

Introduction

1. *Achall ar aicce Temair* ("Achall beyond Tara") in Gwynn, *Metrical Dindshenchas*, 1:46–53.

2. Gerald of Wales, *Topographia Hibernica*, 187.

3. Bernard of Clairvaux, *Vita S. Malachiae*, ed. Migne, PL 182, col. 1109.

4. The inscriptions are catalogued alphabetically by site in Olsen, "Runic Inscriptions in Great Britain, Ireland and the Isle of Man," 6:151–232 (esp. pp. 170–216). These should now be compared with, and supplemented by, the readings given in Barnes, "Towards an Edition of the Scandinavian Runic Inscriptions of the British Isles," 32–42; and, for the Isle of Man, Page, "Manx Rune-Stones," 140–42. Their historical importance is argued by Page, "Manx Rune-Stones," 134, and Margeson, "Iconography of the Manx Crosses," 100, and it is the general argument of Sawyer, *Viking-Age Rune-Stones*.

5. Sawyer and Sawyer, *Medieval Scandinavia*, 10–14; and Page, *Runes*, 43–59. The importance of these memorials is stressed by Page, "Scandinavian Society, 800–1100," 145–52.

6. Chadwick, "Literary Tradition," 170–71 (from *Flateyjarbók*). This is similar to the Irish legend of Finn mac Cumaill, who had a tooth of knowledge that he touched in order to gain great wisdom.

7. The pioneers in this study were the Norwegian scholars (father and son) Sophus and Alexander Bugge: Sophus Bugge, "Norsk Sagaskrivning og Sagafortælling i Irland"; and Alexander Bugge, "Bidrag til det sidste Afsnit af Nordboernes Historie i Irland," "Nordisk Sprog og nordisk Nationalitet i Irland," and Duald Mac Firbis, *On the Formorians and the Norsemen*, ed. A. Bugge.

8. *Darraðarljóð* is preserved in *Njal's Saga*; for the Irish context, see Holtsmark, "Vefr Darraðar," 95–96; and Krappe, "Valkyrie Episode in *Njáls Saga*," 471–74. Poole, *Viking Poems on War and Peace*, 128–31, argues for the translation of *darrað* "banner."

9. Liebermann, *Die Gesetze der Angelsachsen*, 1:380–85 (Northumbrian Priest Laws), and 278–371 (laws of Cnut). For the second vision of Adomnán, see Stokes, "Adomnan's Second Vision," 420–43, and Hudson, "Time is Short," 118–21.

10. Hudson, "The Viking and the Irishman," 257–67; *Cogadh Gaedhel re Gallaibh, or the War of the Irish against the Foreigners*, ed. Todd, 180; and Gwynn, *The Writings of Bishop Patrick, 1074–1084*, 1:56–71.

11. *Cogadh Gaedhel re Gallaibh*, ed. Todd, 168 and 180.

12. An important survey is by Chesnutt, "An Unsolved Problem in Old Norse-Icelandic Literary History," 122–34. Specific aspects of a British/Irish connection with Scandinavia are investigated by Turville-Petre, "Um dróttkvæði og írskan kveðskap," 31–55; de Vries, "Les Rapports des poésies Scaldique et Gaélique," 13–26; Mac Eoin, "Some Icelandic Loricae," 153; von Sydow, "Iriskt inflytande på nordisk Guda- och Hjältesaga," 19–29; and Sveinsson, "Vísa í Hávamálum og írsk saga," 168–77, and *Íslenzkar bókmenntir í fornöld,* 251.

13. In *The Chronicle of the Kings of Mann and the Isles,* i, Broderick acknowledges the slight possibility that it was composed at Furness, in Lancashire. A facsimile edition is *Cronica Regum Manniae et Insularum, The Chronicle of Man and the Isles: A Facsimile of the Manuscript Codex Julius A. VII in the British Museum* (Douglas, 1924).

14. For Whithorn, see Hill, *Whithorn and St. Ninian.* Reports on individual sites are also found in publications such as *Proceedings of the Society of Antiquaries in Scotland, Journal of the Royal Society of Antiquities of Ireland,* and *Medieval Archaeology.*

15. Loyn, "Boroughs and Mints," 128, and Dolley and Metcalfe, "Reform of the English Coinage under Edgar," 154.

16. *Cogadh Gaedhel re Gallaibh,* ed. Todd, 114–16; Plummer, ed., *Vitae Sanctorum Hiberniae,* 2:242; and Sweetman, ed., *Calendar of Documents Relating to Ireland,* 1:83.

17. For a survey of the Irish annals with bibliographic references, see Mac Niocaill, *The Medieval Irish Annals.*

18. A good summary of those chronicles is Gransden, *Historical Writing in England, c.550–c.1305,* 29–41.

19. These materials are collected in *Symeonis monachi opera omnia,* ed. Arnold.

20. Two studies are Lloyd, "The Welsh Chronicles," 369–91, and Hughes, "The Welsh Latin Chronicles: *Annales Cambriae* and Related Texts," 233–58.

21. MacNeill, *Phases of Irish History,* 272, and Sommerfelt, "De norsk-irske bystaters undergang 1169–1171," 6, saw the battle as a final effort by the Vikings to prevent domination by the Irish.

22. A brief overview is Holm, "Between Apathy and Antipathy," 162–65. For the former view, see Goedheer, *Irish and Norse Accounts of the Battle of Clontarf,* 19–45 (although he admits there is some unique information, 103–5); for the latter, see Ryan, "Battle of Clontarf," 49–50. Precise points are discussed by: Ó Corráin, *Ireland before the Normans,* 128–32; Leech, "*Cogadh Gaedhel re Gallaibh* and the *Annals of Inisfallen,*" 13–21; Hughes, *Early Christian Ireland,* 288–97; and Ní Mhaonaigh, "The Date of *Cogadh Gaedhel re Gallaibh,*" 354–77, and "*Cogadh Gaedhel re Gallaibh* and the Annals: A Comparison," 101–26.

23. "Ban-Shenchus," ed. Dobbs, *Revue Celtique* 47 (1930), 283–339; 48 (1931), 163–234; and 49 (1932), 437–89. A discussion is by Ní Bhrolcháin, "An Banshenchas," 5–29.

24. *Íslendingabók/Landnámabók,* ed. Benediktsson, 136–40 and 59, respectively.

25. The importance of verse for history is argued by De Vries, *Altnordische Literaturgeschichte,* 1:99, and 2:248–49; Campbell, *Skaldic Verse and Anglo-Saxon History,* 5–15; Jesch, "History in the Political Sagas," 211–13; and Guðmundsson, "On the Writing of *Orkneyinga Saga,*" 204–11.

26. Hudson, "Brjáns Saga," 241–68.

27. Sweetman, ed., *Calendar of Documents Relating to Ireland,* 1:99.

28. The original was on a plea roll of 23 Edward I, memb. 23 (Easter Term) that was in the Public Record Office, Dublin. This was lost in the destruction of the Irish Public Record Office. Before then, a transcript was published by Alexander Bugge, "Bidrag til det sidste afsnit af Nordboernes historie i Ireland," 311–12; for English law and the Ostmen, see p. 276.

29. *Brennu-Njáls Saga*, ed. Sveinsson, 446–48.

30. Gerald of Wales, *Topographia Hibernica*, 167; and Matthew Paris, *Chronica majora*, 3:364–65 (he mentions this blood-pact in connection with the formation of a confederacy in 1236).

31. This follows modern definition, see Jackson et al., *Geology of the Irish Sea*, 1.

32. For Brecan's Cauldron, see Adomnán, *Life of Columba*, ed. Anderson and Anderson, 28; Stokes, ed., *Three Irish Glossaries*, 13–14; and Gerald of Wales, *Topographia Hibernica*, 96. Ranulph Higden, *Polychronicon*, ed. Babington and Lumby, 2:40 (whirlpool in Wales). For Irish sea laws: Wooding, *Communication and Commerce along the Western Sealanes AD 400–800*, 69; and Kelly, *Guide to Early Irish Law*, 276–77. *Sailing Directions (enroute) for Ireland and the West Coast of England*, 48.

33. Crawford, "Distribution of Early Bronze Age Settlements in Britain"; Fox, *Personality of Britain*; and Raftery, "Iron Age and the Irish Sea," 8. For the medieval period, see the works of Bowen: "Britain and the British Seas" (esp. maps on p. 22); *Britain and the Western Seaways*; "The Cult of St. Brigit"; "The Irish Sea in the Age of Saints"; and *Saints, Seaways and Settlement in the Celtic Lands*.

34. Adomnán, *Life of Columba*, ed. Anderson and Anderson, 54; Adomnán, *De Locis Sanctis*, ed. Meehan, 36; Bede, *Historia Ecclesiastica*, ed. Plummer, 1:316 (Arculf), 192 (Egbert), 298 (Wicbert); and Davis et al., eds., *Regesta Regum Anglo-Normannorum*, 3:268–69.

35. Gerald of Wales, *Topographia Hibernica*, 22; Walter Map, *De Nugis Curialium (Courtiers Trifles)*, ed. Tupper and Ogle, 110; *History of Gruffydd ap Cynan*, ed. Jones, 134; O'Neill, *Merchants and Mariners in Medieval Ireland*, 118; and *Íslendingabók/Landnámabók*, ed. Benediktsson, 34.

36. Crumlin-Pedersen, *Skuldelev Ships I*, 327; and McGrail, *Medieval Boat and Ship Timbers from Dublin*, esp. p. 116 for children's toys.

37. Krapp and Dobbie, *The Anglo-Saxon Poetic Records*, 6:16–20; Christensen, *Boats of the North*, 41; and Crawford, *Scandinavian Scotland*, 18.

38. *Lebor na Cert: The Book of Rights*, ed. Dillon, 10 and 40.

39. See, for example, Mackinder, *Britain and the British Seas*.

1. Two Rivers and the Origins of Olaf Cuaran

1. The problem of identifying Ivar is discussed by McTurk, "Ragnarr Loðbrók in the Irish Annals?" 118–19. For a traditional view, see Walshe, *Scandinavian Relations with Ireland during the Viking Period*.

2. Hudson, *Prophecy of Berchán*, 140–42.

3. Olaf the White is mentioned in the twelfth-century "Book of Settlements" (*Landnámabók*) and he is accepted as a historical figure, see *Fragmentary Annals*, ed. Radner, 94–96; and Hudson, *Prophecy of Berchán*, 141. For the verse fragment, see Ó Cuív, "Personal Names as an Indicator of Relations between Native Irish and Settlers in the Viking Period," 87 n. 19.

4. *History of Gruffydd ap Cynan*, ed. Jones, 104–9; see also van Hamel, "Norse History in Hanes Gruffydd ap Cynan," 336–44; and *Achau Brenhinoedd A Thywysogion Cymru* in Bartrum, ed., *Early Welsh Genealogical Tracts*, 99, sections 6a and d (in 6a the name of Olaf's son Glúniairn is substituted for Olaf).

5. Adam of Bremen, *Gesta*, 84.

6. John of Fordun, *Chronica Gentis Scotorum*, ed. Skene, 162; William of Malmesbury, *De Gestis Regum Anglorum*, ed. Stubbs, 1:146; and Geffrei Gaimar, *L'Estoire des Engleis*, ed. Hardy

and Martin, ll. 3509–10. See also Blair, "Olaf the White and the Three Fragments of Irish Annals," 22–23.

7. *Historia de sancto Cuthberto*, in Symeon of Durham, *Symeonis monachi opera omnia*, ed. Arnold, 1:203. For a discussion of this period, see Higham, "Northumbria, Mercia and the Irish Sea Norse, 893–926," 21–30.

8. See the discussions by Stenton, *Anglo-Saxon England*, 331–34 and 353–58; Smyth, *Scandinavian York and Dublin*, 1:63 ff.; and Higham, "Northumbria, Mercia and the Irish Sea Norse, 893–926," 21–30.

9. *Historia de sancto Cuthberto*, in Symeon, *Opera*, ed. Arnold, 1:207–9.

10. Meyer, "The March Roll of the Men of Leinster," 124.

11. Stokes, "Rennes Dindsenchas," 328–29; and *Metrical Dindshenchas*, ed. Gwynn, 3:100–3. See Clarke, "The Topographical Development of Early Medieval Dublin," 29–51, for a geographical overview.

12. Wallace, "The Origins of Dublin," 129–43. For a broad view of Viking settlement, see Young, "Note on the Norse Occupation of Ireland," 11–33.

13. Oengus the Céli Dé, *Félire Óengusso Céli Dé: Martyrology of Oengus the Culdee*, ed. Stokes, 6, 133, 203, and 44.

14. Ibid. 73; and Stokes and Strachan, eds., *Thesaurus Paleohibernicus*, 2:256.

15. Dublin's influence in tenth-century Irish affairs has been noticed since P. A. Munch's consideration of the town as a prime influence in Irish history of the time, see *Det norske folks historie* 1:1.2, 196–202. Steenstrup saw Dublin as the avenue for foreign influences into Irish affairs in the late tenth century, *Normannerne*, 3:128–72. See also Ó Corráin, *Ireland before the Normans*, 104–10, and Sawyer, "The Vikings and the Irish Sea," 86–92.

16. O'Rahilly, *Early Irish History and Mythology*, 3; Griffiths, "Coastal Trading Ports of the Irish Sea," 63; and *Metrical Dindshenchas*, ed. Gwynn, 2:54 and 60.

17. Ó Lochlainn, "Roadways in Ancient Ireland," 471; and Plummer, *Vitae Sanctorum Hiberniae*, 2:135.

18. Wallace, "Archaeology and the Emergence of Dublin," 128–30; and Bradley, *Settlement and Society*, 51–53.

19. Walsh, "Poem on Ireland," 64–74. For *Indiuin*, see *Book of Leinster*, ed. Best et al., 5:1289 (l. 38322); and Hogan, *Onomasticon Goedelicum*, 459–60.

20. Stokes, ed., *Tripartite Life of Patrick*, 1:170 and 186–88: reading Fir Gabrae as referring to Gabar Liphi, now Ballymore Eustace. For chronology, see Jackson, "Date of the Tripartite Life of St. Patrick," 5–45.

21. William of Malmesbury, *De Gestis Regum Anglorum*, ed. Stubbs, 1:136; John of Wallingford, *Chronicle attributed to John of Wallingford*, ed. Vaughan, 47; this used materials from the same lost source as Roger of Wendover and the author of the *Libellus de Regibus Saxonicis*, in addition to unique items, ix–xv; Geffrei Gaimar, *L'Estoire des Engleis*, ed. Hardy and Martin, 2:13.

22. Roger Wendover, *Flores Historiarum*, ed. Coxe, 1:385–86; Roger of Hoveden, *Chronica*, ed. Stubbs, 1:53; and Matthew Paris, *Chronica Majora*, 1:446–47. Wendover was probably the source for Stenton's opinion that Olaf Cuaran was Sitric's son by another wife, see *Anglo-Saxon England*, 340.

23. Æthelweard, *Chronicle*, ed. Campbell, 54.

24. Stokes, *Tripartite Life*, 116; the wording of this passage is somewhat different from the surrounding material.

25. The oldest manuscript of the "Colloquy of the Two Sages" is in Bodleian MS Rawlinson B. 502, from the early twelfth century; an unpublished gloss on the line "stammering women"

is now damaged, but was read by Eugene O'Curry in the nineteenth century as "Saxon women"; Meyer, *Rawlinson B. 502 . . . Facsimile*, f. 62 r. 50, and O'Curry, *Lectures on the Manuscript Materials*, 385.

The problems connected with distinguishing "Viking" from "English" in the Danelaw are discussed by Hadley, *Northern Danelaw*. Richter, "Bede's Angli," 113–14, suggests that after the eighth century all Germanic peoples in Britain were called Saxons by the Irish.

26. Kenney, *Sources for the Early History of Ireland*, 644–47; Bethell, "English Monks and Irish Reform," 132; and Hudson, "Kings and Church in Early Scotland," 162–63.

27. Valante, "Urbanization and Economy in Viking-Age Ireland," 117.

28. *Armes Prydein*, ed. Williams, trans. Bromwich, 2.

29. Hudson, *Kings of Celtic Scotland*, 76–81.

30. William of Malmesbury, *De Gestis Regum Anglorum*, ed. Stubbs, 1:142–43. For a collection of stories about the Battle of *Brunanburh*, see Anderson, *Scottish Annals from English Chronicles*, 69–73, and Campbell, *The Battle of Brunnanburh*.

2. Battle, Marriage, and Empire

1. For text with translation, see Geffrei Gaimar, *L'Estoire des Engleis*, ed. Hardy and Martin, 1:4–34, and 2:3–24. A summary and discussion is *Havelok*, ed. Smithers, xvii–xix.

2. This is similar to Medieval Welsh where Olaf is written *Avloed*, see *History of Gruffydd ap Cynan*, ed. Jones, 102. See also Koster, *Sagnet om Havelok Danske*, 77–79; Storm, "Havelok the Dane and the Norse King Olaf Kuaran," 533; and Dunn, "Havelok and Anlaf Cuaran," 247. Not everyone was convinced of this identification, see Bugge, "Havelok og Olav Trygvesson," 233–72.

3. Asser, *Life of King Alfred*, ed. Stevenson, 67.

4. For Alfred's treaty, see Keynes and Lapidge, *Alfred the Great*, 172. Christian views of non-Christians are found in Dudo, *History of the Normans*, 15–16; and *Cáin Domnaig*, ed. O'Keefe, 196.

5. *Symeonis monachi opera omnia*, ed. Arnold, 1:209, and the later retelling at 1:73.

6. For details about the cult of Odin in the Orkneys, see Crawford, *Scandinavian Scotland*, 196–98.

7. *Anglo-Saxon Chronicle*, 1:110, and Æthelweard, *Chronicle*, ed. Campbell, 54.

8. Marstrander, "Irske Vidnesbyrd om Torsdyrkelse i Irland," 85.

9. *The Circuit of Ireland by Muirchertach Mac Neill*, ed. O'Donovan, 32–36; for comment, see Ó Cuív, "Literary Creation."

10. *Aislinge Meic Con Glinne*, ed. Jackson, ll. 102 and 129–31; and Meyer, "Scél Baili Binnbérlaig," 221.

11. For a selection of opinion on the political situation in Northumbria at this time, see Whitelock, "The Dealings of the Kings of England with Northumbria in the Tenth and Eleventh Centuries," 70–88; Campbell, "Two Notes on the Norse Kingdoms in Northumbria," 85–97; Smyth, *Scandinavian York and Dublin*, 2:111ff.; and Downham, "Chronology of the Last Scandinavian Kings of York," 25–51.

12. Hudson, *Kings of Celtic Scotland*, 83–86.

13. *Historia Regum*, in *Symeonis monachi opera omnia*, ed. Arnold, 2:197.

14. A hint comes from a fourteenth-century copy of the *banshenchas* in National Library of Scotland manuscript 72.1.7 (at folio 5 v 38), where he is made the son of the Scottish princess Máel Muire, daughter of Kenneth Mac Alpin, rather than her great-grandson. This could be

just a manuscript error or a version of Congalach's ancestry that had been circulated in order to justify an expedition beyond Ireland.

15. *Book of Leinster*, ed. Best et al., 1:133.

16. The western Liffey was famous for its waterfowl, and ca. 962 the *Annals of the Four Masters* tell of a lightning bolt that hit the River Liffey not far from Ailenn, killing many swans and ducks. The barnacle goose was famous in the Middle Ages for supposedly being produced by wood and gestating in a shell rather than an egg. Gerald of Wales, who claims to have seen this, mentions that these birds were eaten by some clergy on fasting days because they are not considered to be flesh: Gerald of Wales, *Topographia Hibernica*, 47–49.

17. "Ban-Shenchus," ed. Dobbs, 314 [*Glun Iairn is Mael Sechlaind saidbir a saer-mathair Dunlaith druin Murchertach mac Neill a hathair; i céim ra cathaib ra chuir* ("Steadfast Dúnflaith was the noble mother of Glúniairn and rich Máel Sechnaill; Muirchertach son of Níall was her father, he carried out a march with battalions")] and 188 [*Dunlaith ingen Murcheartaig m. Neill mathair Mail Eachlaind m. Domnaill rig Erind [ocus] Gluin Iaraind m. Amlaib ri Gall* ("Dúnflaith the daughter of Muirchertach son of Níall was the mother of Máel Sechnaill son of Domnall, king of Ireland, and Glúniairn son of Olaf, king of the Vikings")].

18. MacNeill, "Poems by Flann Mainistrech on the Dynasties of Ailech, Mide and Brega," 73 and 80. MacNeill implies that Muirchertach's attack on the Hebrides was in retaliation for Viking attacks on his capitol at Ailech (*Phases of Irish History*, 266).

19. Byrne, *Irish Kings and High-Kings*, 263.

20. O'Donoghue, "Cert Cech Ríg co Réil," 258–77.

21. The number of raids by the Lawmen into Ireland is not clear, see *Cogadh Gaedhel re Gallaibh*, 40, and Mac Firbis, *On the Formorians and the Norsemen*, 3.

22. Editions of the poem include Helgason, *Eddadigte*, 2:72–79, and Dronke, *Poetic Edda*, 2:162–73. For comments on its composition, see Hastrup, *Culture and History in Medieval Iceland*, 107; Young, "Does Rígsðula Betray Irish Influence?" 97–107; Hill, "Rígsðula," 535; and Dronke, *Poetic Edda*, 1:204–8.

23. *Ælfric's Colloquy*, ed. Garmonsway, 33–35 and 39–40. For a summary of Dublin's place in the economic scheme of the north, see Lewis, *The Northern Seas*, 307. More locally, see Gwynn, "Mediaeval Bristol and Dublin," 275–85; Valante, "Urbanization and Economy in Viking-Age Ireland," 133–60; and Wallace, "Archaeology and the Emergence of Dublin as the Principal Town of Ireland," 153–57 (particularly informative is the map at figure 6:12). For Wales, see Charles, *Old Norse Relations with Wales*; Loyn, *Vikings in Wales*; and Redknapp, *Vikings in Wales*.

24. Lucian of Chester, *Liber Luciani de Laude Cestrie*, ed. Taylor, 46.

25. Information about the early Dublin excavations is supplied by Ó Ríordáin, "Excavations at High Street and Winetavern Street, Dublin," 73–85, and "High Street Excavations," 135–40, in addition to his reports in *Medieval Archaeology*: 16 (1972), 168; 17 (1973), 151–52; and 18 (1974), 206. More recent reports are by Wallace, "English Presence in Viking Dublin"; and "Archaeology of Viking Dublin."

26. Hudson, "Changing Economy of the Irish Sea Province," 41–42; Tonning, *Commerce and Trade in the North Atlantic 850 A.D. to 1350 A.D.*; Wooding, *Communication and Commerce along the Western Sealanes*; *Liber Eliensis*, ed. Blake, 107; and Gerald of Wales, *Topographia Hibernica*, 28.

27. Gerald of Wales, *Topographia Hibernica*, 58; and Davis et al., eds., *Regesta Regum Anglo-Normannorum 1066–1154*, 3:268–69.

28. For fruits and nuts, see Geraghty, *Viking Dublin: Botanical Evidence from Fishamble Street*, 33–34 and 50; and Wooding, *Communication and Commerce along the Western Sealanes AD 400–800*, 69–70. For cultivation, see Gerald of Wales, *Topographia Hibernica*, 152; and Warner of Rouen, *Moriuht*, ed. McDonough, 74.

29. *Ælfric's Colloquy*, ed. Garmonsway, 33.

30. Edwards, *The Archaeology of Early Medieval Ireland*, 70; Hewitt, *Medieval Chester*, 137. Gerald of Wales, *Topographia Hibernica*, 28; he notes that Bede claims vines were cultivated, *Historia Ecclesiastica*, ed. Plummer, 1:13.

31. The trade into the region is still being uncovered and its interpretation is often far from certain, see, for example, Welander et al., "A Viking Burial from Kneep, Uig, Isle of Lewis," 165.

32. Wallace, "Economy and Commerce in Viking Age Dublin," 206–7. The chronology is undergoing a revision, see Klæsøe, "Vikingetidens kronologi-en nybearbejdning af det arkæologiske materiale," 128.

33. "Happy, Graceful History," in *Book of Uí Maine*, MS Stowe D. ii. 1, f. 69ra, 20–24; Valante, "Taxation, Tolls, and Tribute"; Wallace, "Economy and Commerce of Viking Age Dublin," 203–18; and Wooding, *Communication and Commerce along the Western Sealanes AD 400–800*, 70.

34. *Cormac's Glossary* in Stokes, ed., *Three Irish Glossaries*, 24; and Blindheim, "Internal Trade in Viking Age Norway," 761–62.

35. Wallace, "Economy and Commerce in Viking Age Dublin," 205; and Brady, "Labor and Agriculture in Early Medieval Ireland," 133–39.

36. Kelly, *Early Irish Law*, 62–63; and Barnes et al., *Runic Inscriptions of Viking Age Dublin*, 39–42.

37. Lang, *Viking Age Decorated Wood*, esp. pp. 4–35; and McGrail, *Medieval Boat and Ship Timbers from Dublin*, 87 and 96.

38. *Lebor na Cert*, ed. Dillon, 88 and 99.

39. Hall, "A Checklist of Viking-Age Coin Finds from Ireland," 71–86; Wallace, "English Presence in Viking Dublin," 209; and Valante, "Urbanization and Economy in Viking-Age Ireland," 106 and 120.

40. *Laxdœla Saga*, ed. Sveinsson, 54.

41. For the "Happy, Graceful History," in *Book of Uí Maine*, f. 69ra, 20–24; and Attenborough, *Laws of the Earliest English Kings*, 114, 134, and 146.

42. Robertson, *Laws of the Kings of England*, 56.

43. Smyser, "Ibn Fadlan's Account of the Rus," 96.

44. Griffiths, "Coastal Trading Ports," 68.

45. Meyer, "Das Ende von Baile in Scáil," 236.

46. Hudson, *Prophecy of Berchán*, 30.

47. Printed by Birch, *Cartularium Saxonicum*, no. 1135, and listed in Sawyer, *Anglo-Saxon Charters*, no. 731. For comment, see John, *Land Tenure in Early England*, 162–66.

48. Dolley and Ingold, "Viking Age Coin-Hoards from Ireland," 245.

49. Byrne, *Irish Kings and High-Kings*, 150; Charles-Edwards, *Early Irish and Welsh Kinship*, 117–25.

50. For Gormflaith, see Dobbs, "Ban-Shenchus," 314: *Cland Murchada mic Fhind Gormlaid gasta gein ríg Lagen leir a mmac mac Briain Donchad deg-main is Sitriuc mac Amlaiph fhéil* ("Of the family of Murchad son of Find was Gormflaith, the clever child of the king of all Leinster; her sons [were] Brian's son wealthy Donnchad and Sitric, the son of generous Olaf"),

and 189: *Gormlaith ingen Murchada m. Find mathair Sitriuca m. Amlaib ri Gall [ocus] Dondchaid m. Briain ri Muman* ("Gormflaith, daughter of Murchad the son of Finn, was the mother of Sitric son of Olaf, king of the foreigners, and Donnchad son of Brian, the king of Munster").

Gormflaith's paternal genealogy is given in *Genelach hUa Fáeláin* in *Book of Leinster*, ed. Best et al., 6:1462; and O'Brien, *Corpus Genealogiarum Hiberniae*, 13 and 423.

51. *Cogadh Gaedhel re Gallaibh*, ed. Todd, 142; and *Brennu-Njáls Saga*, ed. Sveinsson, 441–42. For a study on the name Gormflaith, see Trindade, "Gormlaith," 150–52.

52. McCormick, "Dairying and Beef Production in Early Christian Ireland, the Faunal Evidence," 253–67.

53. Spenser, *A View of the Present State of Ireland*, ed. Renwick, 133, after Lucas, *Cattle in Ancient Ireland*, 59.

54. McCormick, "Dairying and Beef Production," following table on p. 257.

55. Geraghty, *Viking Dublin: Botanical Evidence from Fishamble Street*, 19.

56. Dudo, *History of the Normans*, 28 and 162; and Benton, *Town Origins*, 63.

57. Greene, "Influence of Scandinavian on Irish," 78.

58. The title *rígdamna* as the *Annals of Tigernach* describe Ragnall, means literally, "king-material"; see Mac Niocaill, "The 'Heir-Designate' in Early Medieval Ireland," 326–29.

59. Hudson, "Scottish Chronicle," 154.

60. *Cogadh Gaedhel re Gallaibh*, ed. Todd, 48–50.

61. Crawford, *Earl and Mormaer*, 11–17.

62. "Ban-Shenchus," ed. Dobbs, 313, 188, and 227. This union is identified only by the title Ua Congalach applied to Muirchertach. There was a Leinster dynasty in the kingdom of Uí Failge that was known as Ua Congalach, but that dynasty flourished in the eleventh century.

63. *Þorgils orraskáld, er var með Óláfi kváran í Dyflinni* ("Þorgils grouse-skald, he was with Olaf Cuaran in Dublin"), *Landnámabók*, ed. Benediktsson, 71. On the literary applications of *gercc* "grouse," see *Dictionary of the Irish Language*, G, 74:18–24; and (with the extended meaning of "champion") *Metrical Dindshenchas*, ed. Gwynn, 3:344, l. 84. See also Mackenzie, "On the Relationship of Norse Skaldic Verse to Irish Syllabic Poetry," 356.

3. Pirate Kings of the Islands

1. General Surveys are: Moore, *History of the Isle of Man*, and Kinvig, *History of the Isle of Man*. For classical accounts and myths, see Richmond, "A Forgotten Exploration of the Western Isles," 193–95, and Chadwick, "Literary Tradition," 188.

2. *C. Iulii Solini Collectanea Rerum Memorabilium*, ed. Mommsen, 234–35; for comment, see Dronke, *Poetic Edda*, 2:190–91.

3. Flann Manistrech, *Estid a eolchu cen on*, in *Book of Leinster*, ed. Best et al., 1:43; Stokes, ed., *Three Irish Glossaries*, 31; and Ranulph Higden, *Polychronicon*, ed. Babington and Lumby, 2:42.

4. Stokes and Strachan, *Thesaurus Palaeohibernicus*, 2:260.

5. Bede, *Historia Ecclesiastica*, ed. Plummer, 1:89; and *Chronicle of the Kings of Man and the Isles*, ed. Broderick and Stowell, 71–72.

6. Dicuil, *Liber de Mensura Orbis Terrae*, ed. Tierney, 76; Hudson, "Scottish Chronicle," 149.

7. For a bibliographical survey of the literature, see the series by Michael Chesnutt, "Norse-Celtic Bibliographical Survey," in *Mediaeval Scandinavia* 1 (1968), 135–37; 3 (1970), 109–37; 4 (1974), 119–59; and 5 (1972), 92–95. See also Scott, "The Norse in the Hebrides," 189–215.

8. This legend is little more than a title or an aside, see Flower, *Catalogue of Irish Manuscripts in the British Library*, 1:89–90; Sturluson, *Heimskringla*, ed. Aðalbjarnarson, 1:121; and Orderic Vitalis, *Ecclesiastical History*, ed. Chibnall, 5:222.

9. The payment of tribute is mentioned in the later vernacular Welsh records, for this period the chronology is inexact, see *Brut Y Tywysogyon, Peniarth MS 20 Version*, ed. Jones, 8; Davies, *Wales in the Early Middle Ages*, 116–20; and Davies, *Patterns of Power in Early Wales*, 48–51.

10. *Cogadh Gaedhel re Gallaibh*, ed. Todd, 84.

11. The contemporary Christian Norse king Hakon's subjects wanted him to eat the flesh of a horse and drink its broth before accepting his lordship. Similar is the bizarre rite in western Ireland that Gerald of Wales insists was being practiced in the twelfth century, a king-making ceremony that included the prince bathing in broth from the boiling of horse flesh that he ate. See *Cogadh Gaedhel re Gallaibh*, ed. Todd, 82; Sturluson, *Heimskringla*, ed. Aðalbjarnarson, 1:171–72; Gerald of Wales, *Topographia Hibernica*, 169.

12. For a brief discussion, see Munch, *Det norske folks historie*, 1.1:2, 199–201. Ivar was free a year later, but killed in 977 by the future high king Brian, Mathgamain's brother.

13. *Annals of the Four Masters, s.a.* 960. The number of raids by the Lawmen into Ireland is not clear, see *Cogadh Gaedhel re Gallaibh*, ed. Todd, 40, and Mac Firbis, *On the Formorians and the Norsemen*, 3.

14. Andersen, "Balley/Balla Names in Man," 166; Foote and Wilson, *Viking Achievement*, 91; and Byock, *Medieval Iceland*, 64.

15. There is general agreement that Godfrey attacked Dyfed and St. David's, but not for Llanweithefawr, see *Brut Y Tywysogyon, Peniarth MS 20 version*, ed. Jones, 9 and n. on 145.

16. John of Worcester, *Chronicle*, ed. Darlington et al., 2:432; Thacker, "Anglo-Saxon Chester," 262; and Kapelle, *Norman Conquest of the North*, 37.

17. *Muirfholud mór na macc Arailt co Port Lárgge*, the precise meaning of *muirfholud* is uncertain, see *Dictionary of the Irish Language: M*, col. 193.

18. Hudson, *Prophecy of Berchán*, 137–38.

19. Liestøl, "An Iona Rune Stone," 85; and Wilson, *The Viking Age in the Isle of Man*, 41.

20. Wilson, "Art of the Manx Crosses," 183–85, and Margeson, "Iconography of the Manx Crosses," 96–101.

21. Broderick, "Irish and Welsh Strands in the Genealogy of Godred Crovan," 32 and 37 n. 8; Magnus was not slain in 978 by Brian Boru, it was Harald Ivarsson of Limerick.

22. There is the possibility that the hoard of over 350 coins uncovered at Iona Abbey in 1950 were hidden during this turmoil; Stevenson, "A Hoard of Anglo-Saxon Coins Found at Iona Abbey," 172.

23. Musset, "Pour l'étude des relations entre les colonies scandinaves d'Angleterre et de Normandie," in *Nordica et Normannica*, 145; Etchingham, "North Wales, Ireland and the Isles: The Insular Viking Zone," 145–87; Æthelweard, *Chronicle*, 49; Douglas, "Rollo," 425; Adigard des Gautries, *Les Noms de personnes Scandinaves*, 68–69; Dolley and Yvon, "A Group of Tenth-Century Coins Found at Mont Saint Michel," 11; Grierson, "England and Flanders before the Norman Conquest," 78; and Brett, "Breton Pilgrims in England," 50.

24. *Anglo-Saxon Chronicle*, 1:100. The chronicle's chronology is confused, see Stenton, *Anglo-Saxon England*, 325–26, for dating.

25. Hugh of Fleury, *Hugonis Floriacensis Opera Historica*, MGH SS 9, 384.

26. The material is collected in Adigard des Gautries, *Les Noms de personnes Scandinaves en Normandie*. The wider implications are studied by Musset in three essays: "Pour l'étude

comparative de deux fondations politiques des Vikings: le royaume d'York et le duché de Rouen," in *Nordica et Normannica*, 157–72, "Aperçus sur la colonization Scandinave dans le nord de Cotentin," 34–37, and "Participation de Vikings venus des pays celtes à la colonisation scandinave de la Normandie," in *Nordica et Normannia*, 279–96.

27. Dudo, *History of the Normans*, 69 (William), 140, 156, and 169 (Richard).

28. Storm, ed., *Monumenta Historica Norvegiae*, 90; and Douglas, "Rollo," 425. Sturluson, *Haralds saga Hárfagra*, in *Heimskringla*, ed. Aðalbjarnarson, 1:123–25, claims that Rollo (or Gungu-Hrólfr) was outlawed by King Harald because of his raids on the Norse. Similar material is in *Orkneyinga Saga*, 7; see also Jesch, "Norse Historical Traditions and *Historia Gruffudd vab Kenan*," 145.

29. Richer, *Historiae*, ed. Hoffmann, 65; and Douglas, "Rollo," 420–21.

30. William of Jumièges, *Gesta Normannorum Ducum*, ed. van Houts, 2:xxviii–xxix.

31. *Íslendingabók/Landnámabók*, ed. Benediktsson, 123; while the text notes that Helgi raided round Scotland, Beollan is not described specifically as a "Scottish king."

32. *Annals of Inisfallen*, *s.a.* 940 and *Cogadh Gaedhel re Gallaibh*, ed. Todd, 271–76. See also Chadwick, "The Vikings and the Western World," 13–42; Broderick, "Irish and Welsh Strands in the Genealogy of Godred Crovan," 34 (chart); and Dolley, *Some Irish Dimensions to Manx History*, 15.

33. The *Annals of Ulster* have *Conamhal mac aerri Gall*, but the father is *Gilla Airi* in the *Annals of Tigernach*; the initial M- has disappeared due to lenition.

34. *A New History of Ireland*, ed. Moody, Martin, and Byrne, 9:465–68.

35. Dudo, *History of the Normans*, 114 and 214 n. 358 (followed by William of Jumièges and more recent historians); Flodoard, *Flodoardus canonicus Remensis, Annales*, PL 135, cols. 463–64; and Richer, *Historiae*, ed. Hoffmann, 132 and note (citing the later chronicle of Frutolf claiming Harald as a son of Thurmod, who had raided the northern coasts circa 942, but this seems to be a conjecture).

36. Richer, *Historiae*, ed. Hoffmann, 98 and 134.

37. *Annales Nivernenses*, 89, and Bates, *Normandy before 1066*, 14.

38. Thorsteinsson, "The Two Viking Ages of Britain: A Discussion," 203; and Lauring, *A History of the Kingdom of Denmark*, 49–50.

39. Oakley, *A Short History of Denmark*, 35; and Sawyer and Sawyer, *Medieval Scandinavia*, 56.

40. For a brief summary, see Albrectsen, "Danmark og Normandiet," 22–30.

41. Bates, *Normandy before 1066*, 37; and William of Jumièges, *Gesta Normannorum Ducum*, ed. van Houts, 2:19.

42. Searle, "Fact and Pattern," 135 n. 6.

43. Baylé, "Reminiscences Anglo-Scandinaves dans la sculpture romaine de Normandie," 36.

44. This discussion follows the lists and references given in Blackburn, *Anglo-Saxon Monetary History*, 291–313; Dumas, "Les Monnaies normandes," 84–140; Graham-Campbell and Batey, *Vikings in Scotland*, 233–34; and Dolley, "Continental Coins in the Halton Moor Find and Other Norman Deniers Found in the British Isles," 53–57

45. Bates, *Normandy before 1066*, 36.

46. *Saltair na Rann*, ed. Stokes, 34 (ll. 2349–80). Despite doubts by Greene, "Influence of Scandinavian on Irish," 78, the date of these verses has been firmly set in the late tenth century by Mac Eoin in his essays: "Date and Authorship of *Saltair na Rann*," 57; and "Observations on *Saltair na Rann*," 20. The verses were probably composed by someone who either was a Scot or living in the Scottish domain.

47. *Saltair na Rann*, ed. Stokes, ll. 2377 –80: *Is sin damsír-sin, cét glonn/ robái lon[h]gas na cúllom/ hic saigid for cach gním n[h]garg/ Danair a tírib Danmarg.*

48. Musset, *Les Peuples Scandinaves au Moyen Age*, 82–83; and Nielsen, "Jelling Problems— A Discussion," 156–82, and Lund, "'Denemearc', 'tanmarkar but' and 'tanmaurk ala'," 163.

49. Page, "Manx Rune-Stones," 137; and Spurkland, "Kriteriene for datering av norske rune-steiner fra vikingtid og tidling middelalder," 2 and 7.

50. For two views, see Page, "Manx Rune-Stones," 137 and 139; and Sawyer, *Viking-Age Rune-Stones*, 115 and 146–47.

51. Nicolaisen, *Scottish Place-Names*, 112–13; and Rekdal, "Den nordiske innflytelse," 46.

52. The use of a system of zones was suggested by Crawford, *Scandinavian Scotland*, 93; see also Fellows-Jensen, "Scandinavian Place-Names of the Irish Sea Province," 34 and 39; and Graham-Campbell, "From Scandinavia to the Irish Sea," 148–49.

53. *Historians of the Church of York*, 1:454, after Musset, "Pour l'étude comparative de deux fondations politiques des Vikings: le royaume d'York et le duché de Rouen," in *Nordica et Normannica*, 161. The political turmoil among the Danes also might have had an impact, see Sawyer and Sawyer, *Medieval Scandinavia*, 54.

54. Stubbs, ed., *Memorials of St. Dunstan*, 363–64; *Anglo-Saxon Chronicle*, 1:115; and William of Malmesbury, *De Gestis Regum Anglorum*, ed. Stubbs, 1:164–65. For comments, see Lund, "King Edgar and the Danelaw," 181–95; Bates, *Normandy before 1066*, 33; and Hadley, *Northern Danelaw*, 301–3.

55. IV Edgar 2:1 (issued 962–63) states that the Danes were to choose their own laws, see Robertson, *Laws of the Kings of England*, paragraphs 2a.1 (p. 32), 12 and 13 (p. 36). For comment, see Lund, "King Edgar and the Danelaw," 187; and James, *Britain in the First Millennium*, 251.

56. Powel, *History of Cambria*, 57; and the quotation is Stenton, *Anglo-Saxon England*, 364.

57. John of Worcester, *Chronicle*, ed. Darlington et al., 2:422–24 (*s.a.* 1073); William of Malmesbury, *Gesta Regum Anglorum*, ed. Stubbs, 1:164–65; and Sawyer, *Anglo-Saxon Charters*, nos. 808 and 783.

58. Hudson, *Kings of Celtic Scotland*, 99–100.

59. Richer of Reims uses the phrases *princeps piratarum* or *dux piratarum* to describe the Norman dukes Rollo, William Longsword, and Richard I, see *Historiae*, ed. Hoffmann, 85 (Rollo), 112 (William), and 307 (Richard); while Thietmar of Merseburg uses the phrase *piratarum dux* to describe Cnut the Great's lieutenant Thurgot, see Thietmar, *Chronicon*, ed. Holtzmann and Trillmich, 398.

60. Dolley, "Some Preliminary Observations on Three Manx Coin-Hoards Appearing to End with Pennies of Edgar," 146.

61. Ambrosiani, "Settlement Expansion–Settlement Contraction: A Question of War, Plague, Ecology or Climate?" 245.

62. Cubbon, "Archaeology of the Vikings in the Isle of Man," 19.

63. Lamb, "Climate and History in Northern Europe and Elsewhere," 228–30.

64. Graham-Campbell, "Viking-Age Silver Hoards of the Isle of Man," 55–63 (the chart on p. 55 is helpful).

65. Wilson, "Art of the Manx Crosses," 180.

66. Adam of Bremen, *Gesta*, 92–95. Tschan notes that Adam's "fourteen years exile" looks to the twice seven years that Jacob served Laban in order to marry Rachel (Genesis 29: 16–29), see Adam of Bremen, *History of the Archbishops of Hamburg-Bremen*, 78 n. 113. Campbell thought the whole episode was fable, see "Saxo Grammaticus and Scandinavian Historical Tradition," 11.

67. Sturluson, *Óláfs saga Tryggvasonar*, in *Heimskringla*, ed. Aðalbjarnarson, 1:264–67. The location of Olaf in the Irish Sea must be treated with confidence as his descent on the Isle of Man and his attacks on the Welsh and the Irish are mentioned in skaldic verses composed by Hallfröðr *vendraeðaskáld*.

68. *Orkneyinga Saga*, ed. Guðmundsson, 24; *Eyrbyggja Saga*, ed. Sveinsson and Þórðarson, 76–77; and *Brennu-Njáls Saga*, ed. Sveinsson, 208 and 224, where they confront King Godfrey.

69. Wilson, *Viking Age in the Isle of Man*, 39–40; Dolley, "Palimpsest of Viking Settlement on Man," 175; and Lang, *Viking Age Decorated Wood*, 15.

70. Hudson, *Kings of Celtic Scotland*, 135–36.

71. Ibid. 110–22; and Hudson, *Prophecy of Berchán*, 52.

72. Hudson, *Prophecy of Berchán*, 52, and "Cnut and the Scottish Kings," 355–56.

73. *Cogadh Gaedhel re Gallaibh*, ed. Todd, 136.

74. The claim might reflect now lost materials available to O'Flaherty, see *Ogygia seu rerum Hibernicarum chronologia*, 384.

75. Kapelle, *Norman Conquest of the North*, 37.

76. William of Jumièges, *Gesta Normannorum Ducum*, ed. van Houts, 2:18, and Lawson, *Cnut*, 26.

77. Searle, *Predatory Kinship*, 137–38.

78. Bugge, *Norsk Sagaskrivning og Sagafortælling i Irland*, 9; and Adigard des Gautries, *Les Noms de personnes Scandinaves*, 69. Neveux, *La Normandie des ducs aux rois Xe–XIIIe siècle*, 76, speculates that Lagmann was from the Orkneys.

79. Lund, "King Edgar and the Danelaw," 188–95.

4. Sitric Silkenbeard

1. Dudo, *History of the Normans*, 9.

2. Ibid. 85; and *Ælfric's Colloquy*, ed. Garmonsway, 33.

3. Jones, "Transaction Costs, Institutional Change, and the Emergence of a Market Economy in Later Anglo-Saxon England," 658–78.

4. Hudson, *Prophecy of Berchán*, 178.

5. Round, *Feudal England*, 354, and Gwynn, "Mediaeval Bristol and Dublin," 275–85; for a summary of Dublin's place in the economic scheme of the north, see Lewis, *The Northern Seas*, 307, and Wallace, "Archaeology and the Emergence of Dublin as the Principal Town of Ireland," 153–57 (particularly informative is the map at figure 6:12).

6. For opposing views, see Hodges, *Dark Age Economics*, 180.

7. Fields were being cultivated within the town walls in the tenth century, see Heighway, "Anglo-Saxon Gloucester," 5–12.

8. Webster, Dolley, and Dunning, "A Saxon Treasure Horde Found at Chester," 26–29.

9. Glúniairn was an Irish name, even though there was a Norse name—*Járnkné*—with an identical meaning. Jargna/Iercne is mentioned in the *Annals of Ulster* and the *Fragmentary Annals* as slain after a fight between "Fair" and "Dark" Vikings; his sons were Ottar (died 883) and Eloir (886). Other evidence for this name is scarce, even though there are Norse names beginning *Járn-*; see Lind, *Norsk-isländska dopnamn ock fingerade namn från medeltiden*, cols. 615–16. For discussions, see Bugge, "Nordisk Sprog," 284–85; and Ó Cuív, "Personal Names as an Indicator of Relations between Native Irish and Settlers in the Viking Period," 81.

10. Dudo claims there was opposition to William Longsword because his mother was not Scandinavian; he had his son Richard taken from the town and placed in a manor some miles away; *History of the Normans*, 96.

11. Kelly, *Early Irish Law*, 126; and Charles-Edwards, *Early Irish and Welsh Kinship*, 23 and 468. For bullion, see Graham-Campbell, "Viking Age Silver Hoards of Ireland," 48.

12. Mac Niocaill, *Notitiae as Leabhar Cheanannais 1033–1161*: no. V, ca. 1114–1117 (pp. 20–22); no. III, ca. 1087–94 (pp. 16–18); and no. VI, ca. 1117–1133 (p. 22).

13. Benton, *Town Origins*, 63. Elsewhere in Europe, plots within the towns were valuable. Emperor Otto I and Empress Adelgida gave to the monastery of St. Ambrose five plots of land in Milan that were carefully defined because their value increased by proximity to the market; see Lopez and Raymond, *Medieval Trade in the Mediterranean World*, 54–56.

14. Sitric's sobriquet "silkenbeard" is found in *Orkneyinga Saga*, ed. Guðmundsson, 27, and in *Gunnlaugs Saga Ormstungu*, in *Borgfirðinga Sögur*, ed. Nordal and Jónsson, 74.

15. The poem is edited by Jónsson, *Den Norsk-Islandske Skjaldedigtning*, 1b, 150. For Hallfreð and his poems on Olaf, see Jónsson, *Den Oldnorske og Oldislandske Litteraturs Historie*, 1:549–54; Bugge, "Sandhed og digt om Olav Trygvesson," 1–34; and Frank, *Old Norse Court Poetry*, 62–67.

16. Olaf's saga was composed almost two hundred years after his death by the Icelander Oddr Snorason in the monastery of Þingeyrar from older materials. Information was collected soon after Olaf's death because he was considered one of the Christian missionary kings of Scandinavia. The passage about Gytha in *Orkneyinga* survives in a fifteenth-century Danish version copied from a thirteenth-century original, which may have described Gytha as the sister of the king of Dublin, which a later writer thought referred to Olaf Cuaran rather than his son, Sitric; see *Orkneyinga Saga*, ed. Guðmundsson, 25; and Sturluson, "Olafs Saga Tryggvason" in *Heimskringla*, ed. Aðalbjarnarson, 1:267 (figure iii, table 2). On the importance of these unions, see Jochens, "Politics of Reproduction," 327–49.

17. Dolley, "Introduction to the Coinage of Æthelraed II," 123, dates the beginning of the Dublin mint to 997; later (p. 124) his arguments for the early transfer of the coinage to Scandinavia suggest, rather, a date of 994. See also Blackburn, "Hiberno-Norse Imitations of Watchet *Long Cross* Coins," 195–97.

18. Robertson, *Laws of the Kings of England*, 56–61. For the economic aspects of these treaties, see Stein-Wilkeshuis, "Scandinavians Swearing Oaths in Tenth-Century Russia," 161–63.

19. *Laxdœla Saga*, ed. Sveinsson, 54–56; this reference was pointed out by Dr. Valante.

20. Stolen cattle could be easily recognized by these marks. According to the *Annals of Inisfallen*, to end cattle theft in 1040 the Munster prince Donnchad mac Briain ordered that no cattle were to be confined indoors; possibly because their "brands" could not be easily seen. See also Kelly, *Early Irish Farming*, 119–20 (dogs) and 168 (branding); and Sayers, "Gunnarr, His Irish Wolfhound Sámr, and the Passing of the Old Heroic Order in *Njáls Saga*," 43–44.

21. On Leinster, see Jaski, "The Vikings and the Kingship of Tara," 348–49. For the chronology, see *Cogadh Gaedhel re Gallaibh*, ed. Todd, 112, and 116–18. For Wales, see Maund, *Ireland, Wales and England*, 160, but also see Duffy, "Ostmen, Irish and Welsh in the Eleventh Century," 379–80.

22. *Lebor na Cert*, ed. Dillon, 10: *Biathad mís ó maithib Tomair* ("food for a month from the nobles of Thor"); Tomar is the pagan god Thor, not a ninth-century king as suggested in n. 2, see Marstrander, "Tor i Irland," 82 (for Thor's ring) and 83.

23. Bethurum, *Homilies of Wulfstan*, no. xx, 261–62; Olsen, "Hørg, Hov og Kirke," 85–86; Hogan, *Onomasticon Goedelicum*, 511; and Plummer, *Bethada Náem nÉrenn*, 1:127.

24. Adam of Bremen, *Gesta*, 101.

25. *Cogadh Gaedhel re Gallaibh*, ed. Todd, 112 and 114. For slavery, see Holm, "Slave Trade of Dublin, Ninth to Twelfth Centuries," 317–45; and for feathers (in "Sea Judgments" [*Muirbretha*]), see Binchy, ed., *Corpus Iuris Hibernici*, 6:2155 (l. 20).

26. For imported horses, see Kelly, *Early Irish Farming*, 90 and references; and *Lebor na Cert: Book of Rights*, ed. Dillon, 96 and 98.

27. Foote and Wilson, *The Viking Achievement*, 172 and 174. For the *vita* of Cadog, see Wade-Evans, ed., *Vitae Sanctorum Britanniae et Genealogiae*, 60.

28. *Cogadh Gaedhel re Gallaibh*, ed. Todd, 137. For analysis of food consumption, see Beougher, "Celtic Warfare in Ireland," 39–56.

29. Roesdahl, *The Vikings*, 262–76; Fanning "Hiberno-Norse Pins in Man," 33; *Eiríks Saga Rauða*, ed. Sveinsson and Þórðarson, 235.

30. Abu-Lughod, *Before European Hegemony*, 54–55.

31. Patterson, "Silver Stocks and Losses in Ancient and Medieval Times," 229; Sawyer, "Wealth of England in the Eleventh Century," 160; Hodges, *Dark Age Economics*, 182; and Metcalfe, "Monetary Economy of the Irish Sea Province," 103.

32. Loyn, "Boroughs and Mints 900–1066," 125–26.

33. Dolley, *Sylloge of Coins in the British Museum*, vol. 8, *The Hiberno-Norse Coins in the British Museum*, 38 and 120; the *Crux* issue of Æthelraed II circulated ca. 991–997.

34. *Domesday Book*, ed. Morris, ff. 179a (Hereford) and 172a (Worcester); and Lopez and Raymond, eds., *Medieval Trade in the Mediterranean World*, 59.

35. Campbell, "Observations on the English Government from the Tenth to Twelfth Century," 41.

36. Sweetman, ed., *Calendar of Documents Relating to Ireland*, 1:416–17, dated November 13, 1245.

37. The Welsh item is from Wade-Evans, ed., *Vitae Sanctorum Britanniae et Genealogiae*, 186. The rune stick is mentioned in Sawyer and Sawyer, *Medieval Scandinavia*, 10.

38. Benton, *Town Origins*, 62–63.

39. For Henry III, see Sweetman, ed., *Calendar of Documents Relating to Ireland*, 1:172 (from the Close Rolls of 7 Henry III, dated August 8, 1223); the charters from Christ Church survive in a nineteenth-century transcription, see *Twenty-third Report of the Deputy Keeper of the Public Records in Ireland*, appendix iii, 81 (nos. 498 and 499).

40. Geraghty, *Viking Dublin: Botanical Evidence from Fishamble Street*, 59.

41. Benton, *Town Origins*, 67–79, the figures are extrapolated from Domesday Book.

42. Geraghty, *Viking Dublin: Botanical Evidence from Fishamble Street*, 21, 23, and 68. See also Murry, "Houses and Other Structures from the Dublin Excavations 1962–1976," 57–68; and Wallace, *Viking Age Buildings of Dublin*.

43. Hudson, "Changing Economy of the Irish Sea Province," 49; Valante, "Urbanization and Economy in Viking-Age Ireland," 161–88; and Geraghty, *Viking Dublin: Botanical Evidence from Fishamble Street*, 19.

44. *Cogadh Gaedhel re Gallaibh*, ed. Todd, 78 and 112–14.

45. Dunlop, "British Isles According to Medieval Arabic Authors," 19–20.

46. Kelly, *Early Irish Farming*, 284–85.

47. Larson, *Earliest Norwegian Laws*, 126–27.

48. The others were Mag Mide ("plain of Meath") and Mag Line ("plain of Larne"). See also Ó Ríordáin, "Aspects of Viking Dublin," 43–45; Cope, "Report on the *Coleoptera* from an Eleventh Century House at Christ Church Place, Dublin," 51–56; and Geraghty, *Viking Dublin: Botanical Evidence from Fishamble Street*.

49. *Register of the Hospital of St. John the Baptist*, ed. St. John Brooks, 202; and Gilbert, ed., *Historical and Municipal Documents, Ireland*, 475: *terra Thurkyl*.

50. Gerald of Wales, *Topographia Hibernica*, 135.

51. Kelly, *Early Irish Farming*, p. 390.

52. Wallace, *Viking Age Buildings of Dublin*, 1:47.

53. Valante, "Dublin's Economic Relations with Hinterland and Periphery in the Late Viking Age," 69–83; and Dolley and Ingold, "Viking Age Coin-Hoards from Ireland," 259.

54. *Gunnlaugs saga Ormstungu*, ed. Foote and Quirk, 18; the refrain is *Elr sváru skæ / Sigtryggr við hræ*, while the rest of the suviving poem is: *Kann ek máls of skil/ hvern et mæra vil, / konungmanna kon, / hann er Kvárans son; / muna gramr við mik, / venr hann gjöfli sik, / þess mun grepp vara, / gullhring spara. / Segi siklingr mér / ef hann heyrði sér/ dýrligra brag: / þat er drápu lag*. For a brief discussion of Gunnlaug's compositions, see Jónsson, *Den Oldnorske og Oldislandske Litteraturs Historie*, 1:557–59, and Frank, *Old Norse Court Poetry*, 154.

55. Sveinsson, *Íslenzkar Bókmenntir*, 134–35, reviving Sophus Bugge's theory of an Irish aspect to Icelandic sagas.

56. Lang, *Viking Age Decorated Wood*, 31–34; and Mitchell, *Archaeology and Environment in Early Dublin*, 31.

57. *Cogadh Gaedhel re Gallaibh*, ed. Todd, 192, and *History of Gruffudd ap Cynan*, ed. Jones, 108.

58. According to "War of the Irish against the Vikings," Brian maintained surveillance (*forcomét*) over Fingal, Dublin's territory, and he set up a blockade (*foslongphort*) around the town; he may have attacked Dublin and Leinster about March 17, see *Cogadh Gaedhel re Gallaibh*, 150.

59. Goedheer, *Irish and Norse accounts of the Battle of Clontarf*; Christiansen, *The Vikings and the Viking Wars*, 388–99; and Sayers, "Clontarf, and the Irish Destinies of Sigurðr Digri, Earl of Orkney, and Þorsteinn Síðu-Hallsson," 164–86. Chesnutt, "An Unsolved Problem in Old Norse-Icelandic Literary History," 127, suggests that tales drifted from island to island. Possibly they were like the fragment on the Battle of Clontarf found in Bodleian MS Rawlinson B. 486 f. 36r, beginning *Rocoiraighedh ar dus cath Briain* or the story told by the Frankish historian Ademar of Chabannes, *Chronicon*, ed. Bourgain, Landes, and Pon, 173.

60. *Cogadh Gaedhel re Gallaibh*, 143, and *Brennu-Njáls Saga*, ed. Sveinsson, 440.

61. For comments on this behavior, see Jochens, *Women in Old Norse Society*, 10–11; Jochens, "The Female Inciter in the Kings' Sagas," 100–19; and Jesch, *Women in the Viking Age*, 188–89.

62. Goedheer, *Irish and Norse Traditions about the Battle of Clontarf*, 117–18; Ó Corráin, *Ireland before the Normans*, 130; and Roesdahl, *The Vikings*, 227–28.

63. Thietmar of Merseburg claims that Svein was receiving tribute from the English even before 1013, *Thietmari Merseburgensis Episcopi Chronicon*, ed. Holtzmann and Trillmich, 392.

64. A list is in the *Book of Rights*, ed. Dillon, 42–46.

65. *Orkneyinga Saga*, ed. Guðmundsson, 81.

66. *Annals of Ulster s.a.* 1014; *Cogadh Gaedhel re Gallaibh*, ed. Todd, 164 and 206 (where the earlier *Amlaib Lagmaind mac Gofhraid* becomes *Amlaibh mac Lagmain*). For discussion, see Ó Corráin, "Vikings in Scotland and Ireland," 307.

67. *Cogadh Gaedhel re Gallaibh*, ed. Todd, 150–52; and Crawford, *Scandinavian Scotland*, 68. *Brennu-Njáls Saga*, ed. Sveinsson, 445–46; see also *Orkneyinga Saga*, ed. Guðmundsson, 27. Sveinsson's important analysis can be found in *Um Njálu*, 76, and *Á Njálsbúð, bók um mikið listaverk* (adapted into English as *Njáls Saga, a literary masterpiece* by Schach, see pp. 23 and 30). On the identification of Celtic names, see Craigie, "Gaelic Words and Names in the Icelandic Sagas," 439–54, and Pálsson, "Keltnesk mannanöfn í íslenzkum örnefnum," 195–203.

68. *Song of Dermot and the Earl*, ed. Orpen, 72–74.

69. For discussion with examples, see *Dictionary of the Irish Language*, F 33:65–34:34. Clarke, *Dublin c.840–c.1540*, has several marked on his map, with one at Fair Green, on the west of the town walls, and another at Oxmantown Green, diagonally across the river to the northwest. The others are St. Stephen's Green, Hoggen Green, and the Steine.

70. *Thietmari Merseburgensis Episcopi Chronicon*, ed. Holtzmann and Trillmich, 396.

71. *Cogadh Gaedhel re Gallaibh*, ed. Todd, 158–60 (Vikings) and 160–62 (Irish); and Guibert of Nogent, *Gesta Dei per Francos*, PL 156, 686.

72. *Dictionary of the Irish Language*, T 288:86–287:7; and Dudo, *History of the Normans*, 29 and 135 (chain mail), 135 (helmets), and 141–42 and 149 (weapons).

73. Stokes, "Old Norse Names in the Irish Annals," 249.

74. *Encomium Emmae Reginae*, ed. Campbell, 96–97 (ravens) and 24 (Cnut's banner).

75. Hogan, *Onomasticon Goedelicum*, 356, *vide sub* "drochat dubgaill."

76. *Mariani Scotti Chronicon*, ed. Waitz, 555. Goedheer suggested that the episode is borrowed from Bede's account of the death of Oswald of Northumbria, see *Irish and Norse Traditions about the Battle of Clontarf*, 30–31.

77. *Brennu-Njáls Saga*, ed. Sveinsson, 454–58; Poole, *Viking Poems on War and Peace*, 128–31; and Holtsmark, "Vefr Darraðar," 95–96. The first element in the title might be the name Dörruðr or an archaic word for flag or banner. For an example of Viking banners in Ireland, see MacCarthy, *Codex Palatino-Vaticanus*, 126. For comment on *Njal's Saga* as a source of history, see Hudson, "Brjáns Saga," 241–68.

78. Kluge, "Fragment eines angelsächsischen Briefes," 62–63.

79. Brewer and Bullen, eds., *Calendar of the Carew Manuscripts Preserved in the Archiepiscopal Library at Lambeth*, 5:24–26. The extant Book of Howth, now one of the Carew manuscripts at Lambeth Palace, is from the sixteenth century, but its material was in the archives at Dublin castle during the reign of Edward II (1307–1327). Its preservation might be owed to Walter Islip, the royal treasurer, who in 1317 made a survey of Irish manuscripts; see Bateson, "Irish Exchequer Memoranda of the Reign of Edward I," 497 and 499–500.

80. Dolley, *Sylloge Coins in the British Museum*, vol. 8, *Hiberno-Norse Coins in the British Museum*, 128–29; and Adam of Bremen, *Gesta*, 204.

81. Hudson, *Kings of Celtic Scotland*, 115–16.

5. From Dublin to England and Norway

1. Frank, "King Cnut in the Verse of His Skalds," 107. The standard English language studies of Cnut are Larson, *Canute the Great*, and Lawson, *Cnut*.

2. Henry, "Effects of the Viking Invasions on Irish Art," 68–70, notes the imitation of Ringerike elements in the shrine of the Cathach of Columba (eleventh century), made for the church of Kells by a craftsman with the hybrid Norse-Irish name of Sitric mac Áeda; and Foote and Wilson, *Viking Achievement*, 311. Lang, *Viking-Age Decorated Wood*, 18, argues for the borrowing of Ringerike by Dublin artisans directly from England.

3. Lawson, *Cnut*, 109; she was betrothed in 1035.

4. On this point, see Pelteret, "Slave Raiding and Slave Trading in Early England," 106–11, and *Slavery in Early Medieval England*, 71–72 and 78; Holm, "Slave Trade of Dublin," 317–45.

5. Hudson, *Prophecy of Berchán*, 79; and *Incipit do Flaithesaib [ocus] amseraib hÉrend iar creitim*, in *Book of Leinster*, ed. Best et al., 1:98.

6. A picture is on the map in Clarke, "Topographical Development of Early Medieval Dublin," 34.

7. Chrétien de Troyes, "The Knight of the Cart," 228. Kavanagh, "The Horse in Viking Ireland," 89–121, discusses the riding tack found in excavations at Dublin. The British horse (*ech Bretnach*) was a valued commodity, see Kelly, *Early Irish Farming*, 90–91. In the twelfth-century *Aislinge Meic Con Glinne*, ed. Jackson, l. 1328, a British horse is one of the rewards given to Mac Con Glinne. For other foreign horses, see *Lebor na Cert*, ed. Dillon, 96, 98, and 130.

8. *Instituta regalia et ministeria camerae regum Longobardorum [seu] honoratie civitatis Papie*, ed. Hofmeister, 1452. For comments, see Southern, *The Making of the Middle Ages*, 43–44; and Hudson, "Knútr and Viking Dublin," 334.

9. Very helpful studies with explanatory charts are by Charles-Edwards, *Early Irish and Welsh Kinship*, 478–85, and Kelly, *Early Irish Farming*, 587–95.

10. *Lebor na Cert*, ed. Dillon, 20.

11. Hall, "Check List of Viking-Age Coin Finds from Ireland," 72, gives a useful map of the find locations; for the Fourknocks hoard, see p. 80.

12. Mac Niocaill, ed., *Notitiae as Leabhar Cheanannais, 1033–1161*, 20; *Lebor na Cert*, ed. Dillon, 144. See also Doherty, "Monastic Town in Early Medieval Ireland," 67.

13. The poem on Carmen is *Éstid a Laigniu na llecht* ("Listen, O Leinstermen of the graves") in *Book of Leinster*, ed. Best et al., 4:843–52; the verse on the markets is at p. 852. An edition, with variants from other manuscripts, and translation is by *Metrical Dindshenchas*, ed. Gwynn, 3:2–24. For its location, see Byrne, *Irish Kings and High-Kings*, 141, and the discussion by *Metrical Dindshenchas*, ed. Gwynn, 3:470–71.

14. Wallace, "Archaeology of Viking Dublin," 139; and *Gunnlaugs Saga Ormstungu*, ed. Foote and Quirk, 18.

15. Wallace, "Archaeology of Viking Dublin," 135.

16. The list of the wonders of Ireland was attached to the poem *Lecht Cormaic meic Culennain* ("The grave of Cormac mac Culennáin") by Broccán *Craibdech*, written ca. 1120, in the *Book of Leinster*, ed. Best et al., 1:212. The poem was edited and translated by Dobbs, "On the Graves of Leinstermen," 139–53. For comments, see Clarke, "Topographical Development of Early Medieval Dublin," 29–51; Wallace, "Archaeology of Viking Dublin," 117; and Sims, "Medieval Dublin: A Topographical Analysis," 25–41. A plan of the medieval town is by Clarke, "Topographical Development," 34.

17. Hogan, *Onomasticon Goedelicum*, 419. The *Annals of Tigernach* mention a raid into Fingal in 1053 with an attack on the church at Lusk, while the *Annals of the Four Masters* mentions a raid across Fingal as far as Droichet Dubgaill in 1112. The extent of rural settlement round Dublin by the Viking colonists is examined by Bradley, "Interpretation of Scandinavian Settlement in Ireland," 49–78.

18. The first poem is in *Lebor na Cert*, ed. Dillon, 114–18, with an expanded revision (with more detail about the dues to be rendered to the saint's representative) in the *Book of Uí Maine*, ed. Macalister, f. 68vb.53 – f. 69va.6. The second poem is printed by Smith, "*Mide Maigen Clainne Cuind*," 108–44 (esp. 119–20). The stipends are in *Lebor na Cert*, ed. Dillon, 10.

19. Walsh and Ó Cróinín, *Cummian's Letter De Controversia Paschali and the De Ratione Computandi*, 92. Ryan, "Pre-Norman Dublin," 75, suggests that Olaf ruled Dublin while Sitric was in Rome.

20. The quotation is from Stenton, *Anglo-Saxon England*, 407–8. For Flanders, see *Encomium Emmae Reginae*, ed. Campbell, 36. On the question of Cnut's motives and the legacy of his

pilgrimage, see Gwynn, "Origins of the See of Dublin," 40–55 and 97–112; Flanagan, *Irish Society, Anglo-Norman Settlers and Angevin Kingship*, 11–12; and Lawson, *Cnut*, 136–37.

21. John of Worcester, *Chronicle*, ed. Darlington et al., 2:512–18 (*s.a.* 1031).

22. A transcription of the foundation story is given by Dugdale, *Monasticon Anglicanum*, 3: 1148; and Gwynn, "Some Unpublished Texts from the Black Book of Christ Church, Dublin," 309. An English paraphrase is given by Lawlor, "A Calendar of the Liber Niger and Liber Albus of Christ Church, Dublin," 69. A corrupted abridgement of this material was preserved in an *inspeximus* of Henry VII, itself a copy of an earlier *inspeximus* of Edward VI; it perished when the Public Record Office in Dublin was destroyed. A transcription was made by Bugge, "Bidrag til det sidste afsnit af nordboernes Historie i Irland," 314; it has the foundation by Sitric (called *Cithuricus*) and the donation of *Bealdulig, Rocheir,* and *Portracharn.*

23. Brooks, "Unpublished Charters Relating to Ireland," 338.

24. This discussion follows Poole, *Studies in Chronology*, 185–202.

25. Doherty, "Exchange and Trade in Early Medieval Ireland," 77–78, suggests a connection between trade and pilgrimage in the name Bordgal (county Westmeath) and Bordeaux. Wallace, "Archaeology and the Emergence of Dublin as the Principal Town of Ireland," 155, provides an illuminating map.

26. On the connections of Hornback and Metz with Conrad, see Weinfurter, *The Salian Century*, 7 and 58. Cartroë's *vita* by Reimann (or Ousmann) is printed in *AA. SS. Boll.*, Mart. II, 469–81, his removal to Metz is described on p. 478; a brief discussion is by Kenney, *Early Sources*, 609–10. The charter of Otto III is printed by Sickel in *MGH Diplomatum Regum et Imperatorum Germaniae II*, 2:493; for a discussion, see Kenney, *Early Sources*, 611.

27. Gerald of Wales, *Topographia Hibernica*, 128–29.

28. *Book of Obits and Martyrologies of the Cathedral Church of the Holy Trinity, Dublin*, ed. Crosthwaite, 141. A later insertion adds relics of St. Patrick and St. Laurence O'Toole to that list.

29. Malmros, "Den hedenske fyrstedigtnings samfundssyn," 107–26.

30. Crawford, "Bishops of the Orkneys," 7; and Watt, *Fasti Ecclesiae Scoticanae*, 247.

31. The northern route is described in "The Cattle Raid of Fraech" (*Táin Bó Fraích*), in *Book of Leinster*, ed. Best et al., 5:1134; and the southern route is mentioned in the *vita* of Abban, see Plummer, *Vitae Sanctorum Hiberniae*, 1:11.

32. *Betha Colmáin maic Lúacháin*, ed. Meyer, 80. The *vita* is dated ca. 1122.

33. Ussher, *Whole Works*, 4:488; Richter, *Canterbury Professions* (Donatus, no. 42 (p. 31); and Patrick no. 36 (p. 29)); Gilbert, ed., *Chartularies of St. Mary's, Dublin*, 2:249; Haddan and Stubbs, *Councils and Ecclesiastical Documents*, 2:162; and *Letters of Lanfranc Archbishop of Canterbury*, ed. Clover and Gibson, 66–73. Useful discussions are: Gwynn, "Origins of the See of Dublin," 40–55; Richter, "First Century of Anglo-Irish Relations," 199 n. 16; and Flanagan, *Irish Society, Anglo-Norman Settlers and Angevin Kingship*, 8–18; and Crawford, "Bishops of Orkney in the Eleventh and Twelfth Centuries," 4 n. 12.

34. Hudson, "Knútr and Viking Dublin," 327; and more generally, see Abrams, "Anglo-Saxons and the Christianization of Scandinavia," 213–49.

35. *Callech Finnen* could be read as Ceallach of [St.] Finian's or as St. Finian's nun. For the church legend, see Hogan, *Onomasticon Goedelicum*, 686, and Stokes and Strachan, eds., *Thesaurus Palaeohibernicus*, 2:339. Bróccan's hymn is preserved in the *Liber Hymnorum*; for comment, see Kenney, *Sources for the Early History of Ireland*, 360.

36. Printed in *Corpus Poeticum Boreale*, eds. Vigfusson and Powell, 2:157; Jónsson, ed., *Den Norsk-Islandske Skjaldedigtning*, 1b: 275; and Kock, ed., *Den Norsk-Isländska Skaldediktningen*, 1:141: *Skal svá kveðja / konung Dana, / Íra ok Engla / ok Eybúa, / at hans fari / með himinkröptum, /*

löndum öllum / lof víðara. For a biographical sketch, see Jónsson, *Den Oldnorske og Oldis-landske Litteraturs Historie*, 1:574–77.

37. Svenonis Aggones, *Historia Regum Daniae*, ed. Waite, in *MGH SS* 29:33.

38. This is visible in the contemporary verses about Olaf Tryggvason cited in the previous chapter. The same is true for later prose compositions, as in Olaf's saga, where Conchobar mac Máel Sechnaill, king of Meath and Sitric Silkenbeard's half-brother, is called *Ira konungr*, while Máel Coluim mac Máel Brigtí, the grandfather of jarl Thorfinn of the Orkneys, is *Skota konungr*, see *Saga Óláfs Konungs hins helga*, ed. Johnsen and Helgason, 1:189 and 231.

39. Blackburn and Lyon, "Regional Die Production in Cnut's *Quatrefoil* Issue," 246. The tentative dates for the issue of *Quatrefoil* are 1017 to 1023, see Dolley, *Sylloge of Coins in the British Museum*, vol. 8, *The Hiberno-Norse Coins in the British Museum*, 119.

40. Hudson, "Knútr and Viking Dublin," 324.

41. Wallace, "Economy and Commerce in Viking Age Dublin," 225.

42. *History of Gruffydd ap Cynan*, ed. Jones, 104. The location of *Castell Avloed* is a testimony to the Dubliners' skill at navigation, for the waters around Anglesey are shallow, with a whirl-pool within the Menai Straits; see Hewitt, *Medieval Chester*, 132; and Higden, *Polychronicon*, ed. Babington and Lumby, 2:40.

43. *History of Gruffydd*, 102, 104, and 108. For discussions, see Thornton, "Genealogy of Gruffudd ap Cynan," 79–108; and Jesch, "Norse Historical Traditions and *Historia Gruffudd vab Kenan*," 117–47.

44. This was a clan of Uí Dúnlainge between Kildare and the Wicklow mountains. Máel Corcraig's father, Dúnlang mac Tuaithal, had died fighting for the Leinster–Viking alliance at the Battle of Clontarf. In *Cogadh Gaedhel re Gallaibh*, ed. Todd, 164, he is styled "king of the River Liffey" (*ri Liphi*) and is one of the leaders of the Leinster forces; his fight against the high king's allies from Connacht is described (p. 176).

45. For this obscure individual, see Thornton, "Who was Rhain the Irishman?" 131–48.

46. The original probably was a note from the episcopate of Joseph of Llandaff (ca. 1022–1045). The charter is printed in *Book of Llan Dâv*, ed. Evans and Rhŷs, 253–54, and Haddan and Stubbs, eds., *Councils and Ecclesiastical Documents*, 1:289–90. For discussion, see Davies, *Llandaff Charters*, 126, and *An Early Welsh Microcosm: Studies in the Llandaff Charters*, 96 and 186, no. 253; and Maund, *Ireland, Wales and England*, 188–89.

47. *Encomium Emmae Reginae*, ed. Campbell, 34: the list includes, in addition to England, Denmark and Norway, *Brittania* and *Scothia*; see also Lawson, *Cnut*, 107.

48. This point is made in a different context by Dolley, *Some Irish Dimensions to Manx History*, 21.

49. Printed by Kemble in *Codex diplomaticus aevi Saxonici* as nos. 743 and 744, and Davidson, "Anglo-Saxon Charters at Exeter," no. 11, they are listed in Sawyer, *Anglo-Saxon Charters*, as, respectively, nos. 962, 963, and 971 (pp. 289–91); a charter composed ca. 1027–1031 seems to be the basis for the second and third charters. For discussions, see Chaplais, "The Authenticity of the Royal Anglo-Saxon Diplomas of Exeter," 22–24; Lawson, *Cnut*, 185; and Hudson, "Knútr and Viking Dublin," 330–32.

50. The earlier has Lyfing as bishop a year before he is generally believed to have been elevated, while the second has the wrong number of the indiction and also has a *Hacon dux* as witness. If this was intended for Cnut's nephew Håkon Eiríksson, it is wrong because he died the previous year. Those errors may be nothing more than the usual scribal mistakes; see Lawson, *Cnut*, 66–68, and Keynes, "Cnut's Earls," 65. Two other charters mention a Sitric, but they do not seem to have a connection with the present question. A charter of Cnut from 1019

(S. 956) includes a Sitric the king's thegn, while Abbot Sitric of Tavistock is in a charter of 1045–46 (S. 1474).

51. Hudson, "The Family of Harold Godwinsson and the Irish Sea Province," 93, and "Knútr and Viking Dublin," 331–32.

52. Gwynn, "Some Unpublished Texts from the Black Book of Christ Church, Dublin," 309; and Bugge, "Bidrag til det sidste afsnit af nordboernes historie i Irland," 314. In the Black Book, Sitric is called king, but in the land grants he does not have a title.

53. Keynes, "Cnut's Earls," 65. The writ is printed by Harmer, *Anglo-Saxon Writs*, 345, and she suggests that the reference to Earl Sihtric is ca. 1025 (p. 315). The will is edited by Keynes, "Will of Wulf," 16–21.

54. Dolley and Yvon, "Group of Tenth-Century Coins Found at Mont-Saint-Michel," 11; Richer, *Historiae*, ed. Hoffmann, 123–24; and *Annals of the Kingdom of Ireland by the Four Masters*, ed. O'Donovan, *s.a.* 939.

55. The following discussion is based on Lawson, *Cnut*: 163 and 171 (Osgod), 172 (Odda), 186 (Ælfwine), 164–65 (Thored).

56. For a debate on this issue, see Lawson, "The Collection of Danegeld and Heregeld in the Reigns of Æthelraed II and Cnut," 721–38, and "'Those stories look true': Levels of Taxation in the Reigns of Æthelraed II and Cnut," 385–406; and Gillingham, "'The Most Precious Jewel in the English Crown': Levels of Danegeld and Heregeld in the Early Eleventh Century," 373–84, and "Chronicles and Coins as Evidence for Levels of Taxation in Late Tenth- and Early Eleventh-Century England," 939–50.

57. Musset notes that Cnut preferred to construct a network of alliances both to seize and hold an area, see *Les Peuples Scandinaves*, 158–59. See also Garmonsway, "Canute and His Empire," 18, and Malmros, "Leding og Skjaldekvad," 118–19, who notes Cnut's reliance on ships to guard the kingdom during his absence.

58. Fidjestøl, "Scaldic Studies," 107. "Holy" (*halig, saint*) is used to describe Olaf in the C version of the *Anglo-Saxon Chronicle*, composed ca. 1050 at Abington.

59. Gilbert, ed., *The Chartularies of St. Mary's Dublin*, 1:222 (where it is a boundary marker) and 2:46–47 (list of tenants at the Dissolution); and *Book of Obits and Martyrology of the Cathedral Church of the Holy Trinity, Dublin*, ed. Crosthwaite, lxvi–lxvii and 141. St. Olaf's church/parish was later styled St. Tullocks or St. Doolucks; in 1809 the address where the church had been located was no. 41, Fishamble Street; see Haworth, "Site of St. Olave's Church, Dublin," 177–91.

60. Fell, "Anglo-Saxon Saints in Old Norse Sources," 96; Dickins, "The Cult of St. Olave in the British Isles," 53–80; Vésteinsson, "Christianisation of Iceland," 54; and Lander, *VCH Cheshire*, 3:3.

61. *Saga Óláfs Konungs hins helga*, ed. Johnsen and Helgason, 1:610–12; and Hudson, "Cnut and the Scottish Kings," 359.

62. Sawyer, "The Wealth of England in the Eleventh Century," 160; Graham-Campbell, "Viking Age Silver Hoards: An Introduction," 35.

63. Weinfurter, *The Salian Century*, 79–80. Although Bates, *Normandy before 1066*, 36, points out the significance of the Norman coins found on the Norwegian trade routes along the western Scottish coast, Neveux, *La Normandie des ducs aux rois Xe–XIIe siècle*, 220, sees Normandy's commercial orientation shifting to the south ca. 1025.

64. Dudo, *History of the Normans*, 69, 140, 156, and 169.

65. Le Patourel, *Norman Empire*, 25, following William of Jumièges.

66. The earliest accounts are Norwegian: Theoderic's *Historia de antiquitate regum Norwagiensium*, in Storm, *Monumenta Historica Norvegiae*, 45–46, and *Ágrip af Nóregs Konunga Sögum*, ed. Jónsson, 36.

67. *Orkneyinga Saga*, ed. Guðmundsson, 61. This must refer to the period 1035 to 1040 because Hardacnut was not absent from England after his accession.

68. Bromwich, ed., *Troedd Ynys Prydein: The Welsh Triads*, 256.

6. The Brief Ascendancy of the Haraldssons

1. For the first theory, see *Cogadh Gaedhel re Gallaibh*, 291 n. 22, partially followed in *A New History of Ireland*, ed. Moody, Martin, and Byrne, 9:139. The second theory is suggested by Ryan, "Pre-Norman Dublin," 76, and Duffy, "Irishmen and Islesmen in the Kingdoms of Dublin and Man, 1052–1171," 94–98. Concerning names and ethnicity, see Jochens, "Race and Ethnicity in the Old Norse World," 100–101, and "Politics of Reproduction," 327–49.

2. *Annals of Inisfallen, Facsimile*, ed. Best and MacNeill, f. 23v, column b [for the editors' folio 23e], a superscript emendation in the same hand is *[vel] do Laignib* ("or by the Leinstermen"); the *Annals of Tigernach* blame Diarmait mac Máel na mbó.

3. Hurley et al., eds., *Late Viking Age and Medieval Waterford*, 894; this is possibly a reflection of fairly sparse habitation in the town. See also Ó Corráin, *Ireland before the Normans*, 133, and his "Career of Diarmait mac Máel na mBó," 28.

4. Hudson, "Cnut and the Scottish Kings," 355–56. *Rex inna Renn*, Marianus Scotus, *Chronicon*, ed. G. Waitz (*MGH, SS* 5), 559 (*s.a.* 1087 correctly 1065); and on the location of the Rhinns, see Byrne, "Na Renna," 267. On the topic of age and kingship, see Jaski, "Druim Cett revisited," 343–44.

5. *Ágrip af Nóregs Konunga Sögum*, ed. Jónsson, 26. *Ágrip* was written probably at Trondheim at the end of the twelfth century; it is the oldest vernacular Norwegian history. Comparison with *Historia de antiquitate regum Norwagiensium* by Theodoricus and the anonymous *Historia Norwegiae* suggest that its compiler either used one of these works or a common source in addition to the now-lost Icelandic histories written by Ari the Wise Þorgilsson and Sæmundr Sigfússon.

6. *Ágrip af Nóregs Konunga Sögum*, ed Jónsson, 24 n. on l. 6, and *Encomium Emmae Reginae*, ed. Campbell, 73 n. 1. More recently Driscoll notes that there is no evidence to support this claim, *Ágrip af Nóregs Konunga Sögum*, 97 n. 78. De Vries, however, saw this tract as having an official character, see *Altnordische Literaturgeschichte*, 2:257.

7. Holtsmark, "Historieskrivning: Norge," 595–97; and Frank, "King Cnut in the Verse of His Skalds," 107 n. 8.

8. *Cogadh Gaedhel re Gallaibh*, 150: Brodor iarla ocus Amlaib mac ri Lochland .i. da iarla Cairi ocus tuascirt Saxon uli. The passage is in the medieval (Trinity College, Dublin) manuscript, but it is garbled in O'Clery's seventeenth-century copy.

9. This discussion largely follows the commentary in *Encomium Emmae Reginae*, ed. Campbell, 66–82, but see also Johnsen, "Håkon jarl Eiriksson (998–1030)," 5–24.

10. They are included in several Norwegian king lists, see Storm, *Monumenta Historica Norvegiae*, 182–3.

11. Eyvind's verses are preserved in Sturluson, *Heimskringla*, ed. Aðalbjarnarson, 1:21, 22, 44, 108, 207–8, 280; and see Dronke, *Poetic Edda*, 1:174 and 202.

12. Adémar de Chabannes, *Chronicon*, ed. Bourgain, Landes, and Pon, 172. His geography is not always reliable (he seems to have thought that the ninth-century Northumbrian king

Eadulf lived in Ireland), but he is accurate for his own time. Bachrach proposes an earlier date, August 1006, for this raid "Toward a Reappraisal of William the Great," 13–14. *Iresca* is Adémar's reproduction of ON *Írskr* "Irish," with a superfluous vowel between -r- and -s-; elsewhere he gives *Hirland* (ON *Irland* "Ireland") as an alternative for *Hibernia*.

13. *Anglo-Saxon Chronicle*, 1:157 and 159: *Her for Cnut cyng to Rome.* ₇*þy ilcan geare he for to Scotlande.* ₇ *Scotta cyng him to beah Mælcolm.* ₇ *twegen oðre cyningas, Mælbæþe,* ₇ *Iehmarc* (from the É version). The pilgrimage to Rome refers to the year 1027; Cnut returned to Denmark and was some time absent from England; see Hudson, "Cnut and the Scottish Kings," 350–60.

14. *Saga Óláfs Konungs hins helga*, ed. Johnsen and Helgason, 343 (text normalized): *Hafa allframir jöfrar / út sín höfuð Knúti / færð ór Fífi norðan / friðkaup var þat- miðju. / Seldi Áleifr aldri / (opt vá sigr) enn digri / haus í heimi þvísa / (hann) engum svá manni.* Sighvat was the uncle of Ottar. Although "head" meaning "person" is well attested in Icelandic verse, it also might refer to cattle paid as taxes, see Frank, "Viking Atrocity and Skaldic Verse: The Rite of the Blood Eagle," 339.

15. Later in the Middle Ages this meeting became part of the propaganda war between the English and the Scots. The Scottish chronicler John of Fordun places it in "Cumbria" where it became a confrontation between Scottish resistance and English injustice, see *Johannis de Fordun Chronica Gentis Scotorum*, ed. Skene, 1:183.

16. Hudson, "Cnut and the Scottish Kings," 350–60, and *Kings of Celtic Scotland*, 110–22, and 136–45.

17. *Gallgóidil* should no longer automatically be translated as "Galloway," see Brooke, "Gall-Gaidhil and Galloway," 97–116. For Hexham, see Anderson, *Scottish Annals*, 101.

18. A. Anderson, "Anglo-Scottish Relations," 7–8, and M. Anderson, "Lothian and the Early Scottish Kings," 98–112; and Garmonsway, *Canute and his Empire*, 18. For the annexation, see Duncan, "The Battle of Carham," 106–117; and Meehan, "The Siege of Durham," 1–19.

19. *Symeonis monachi opera omnia*, ed. Arnold, 1:218.

20. Crawford, *Scandinavian Scotland*, 72, and *Orkneyinga Saga*, ed. Guðmundsson, 48–49; *Chronicle of John of Worcester*, ed. Darlington et al., 2:574 (*s.a.* 1052). The Normans were slain in a battle fought against Earl Siward of Northumbria on the Feast of the Seven Sleepers (July 27) in 1054.

21. Duffy, "Irishmen and Islesmen in the Kingdoms of Dublin and Man," 97, who sees a Waterford connection.

22. *Orkneyinga Saga*, ed. Guðmundsson, 61; translation following Pálsson and Edwards, *Orkneyinga Saga*, 75.

23. Either Powel's account or a cognate text was used by Ware: Powel, *History of Cambria*, 87 and 89; Ware, *De Hibernia et antiquitatibus ejus disquisitiones*, 117; and, for a discussion, Hudson, "Destruction of Gruffudd ap Llywelyn," 342–43.

24. Powel, *History of Cambria*, 89; Ware, *De Hibernia et antiquitatibus ejus disquisitiones*, 117; and Keating, *History of Ireland*, 3:29 (he cross-dates to the reign of Donnchad mac Briain). Conan is the Irish form of Cynan, and *Harolt* could have been the name Cynan used among the Vikings of Dublin. Double names, which used the individual's proper name prefaced by an indigenous name, were not uncommon among aristocrats living outside their own land. Cnut's queen Emma, for example, is called Ælfgifu Emma in the *Anglo-Saxon Chronicles*.

25. See three essays by Dolley: "Some Insular(?) Imitations from the 1030s of Contemporary English Pence of Cnut," 86–88, "Hiberno-Manx Coinage of the Eleventh Century," 75–84, and *Some Irish Dimensions to Manx History*, 19–21. Broderick, "Irish and Welsh Strands in the

Genealogy of Godred Crovan," 32, suggests that Magnus and Godred Haraldsson held Man as agents for the kings of Dublin. On styles, see Graham-Campbell, "From Scandinavia to the Irish Sea," 149.

26. Lang, *Viking Age Decorated Wood*, 13.

27. *Morkinskinna*, ed. Andersson and Gade, 163 and 167.

28. A charter granted to St. Werburgh's, Chester, before 1265, gave the community the right freely to enter and exit, buy and sell; *Cartulary or Register of the Abbey of St. Werburgh, Chester*, ed. Tait, lxxix, 211. The text implies that this royal power had an ancient heritage. For the king's highway, see *Chronicle of Kings of Mann and the Isles*, ed. Broderick and Stowell, 87.

29. His feast is at September 28, see Stokes, *Félire Óengusso Céli Dé*, 212.

30. Brooke, *Wild Men and Holy Places*, 118. The excavations of the structures for this period are described by Ewart, *Cruggleton Castle, Report of Excavations 1978–1981*, 14–22.

31. Bernard of Clairvaux, *Vita S. Malachiae*, col. 1096. For the identification of these places, see Lawlor, "Notes on St. Bernard's Life of St. Malachy," 239–43. For Ninian, see Forbes, *Lives of S. Ninian and S. Kentigern*, 152.

32. The following discussion is based on Hill, "Whithorn: The Missing Years," 34–39, and Hill, *Whithorn and St. Ninian*, 48–56.

33. Graham-Campbell, "The Viking-Age Silver Hoards of the Isle of Man," 63; *Eyrbyggja Saga*, ed. Sveinsson and Þórðarson, 137–39; *Orkneyinga Saga*, ed. Guðmundsson, 180–81.

34. Armit, *Archaeology of Skye and the Western Isles*, 197–99.

35. Brown, "Norse in Argyll," 218, 225, and 227.

36. *Eyrbyggja Saga*, ed. Sveinsson and Þórðarson, 33 and 137–39.

37. Allen, "Plant Distribution Patterns as Potential Historical Indicators," 56.

38. For discussions, see Megaw, "Manx 'Eary' and Its Significance," 327–45; Johnston, "Norse Settlement Patterns in Coll and Tiree," 121–22; and Oram, "Scandinavian Settlement in South-West Scotland," 133–35.

39. Ó Cuív, "A Poem in Praise of Raghnall, King of Man," 288–89; Sturluson, *Heimskringla*, ed. Aðalbjarnarson, 3:224; and Foote and Wilson, *Viking Achievement*, 176.

40. That change could be less a concern for the farmers and more a desire to get a full payment. The fines for late or no payment were severe, and failure to tithe dairy produce was two pence for each cow, two pence for every four goats, and eight pence for every eight sheep; see Cheney, "Manx Synodal Statutes," 77.

41. Ó Corráin, "Career of Diarmait mac Máel na mBó," 31.

42. *Annals of the Kingdom of Ireland by the Four Masters*, 2:898: *Cumha áirdríg i nAth Cliath, niba fairbricch co brath mbaoth; . . . Murchadh mac Diarmada déin* ("There is grief for the high-king in Dublin, which will not be exceeded until the terrible Judgment Day; . . . for Murchad son of impetuous Diarmait").

43. Hudson, "The Viking and the Irishman," 257–67.

44. Storm, ed., *Monumenta Historica Norvegiae*, 133–34; *Haralds saga Sigurðarsonar* in Sturluson, *Heimskringla*, ed. Aðalbjarnarson, 3:135–37; and *Saga Óláfs Konungs hins helga*, ed. Johnsen and Helgason, 1:631–33. Reworkings of eleventh-century materials formed the, now lost, twelfth-century vernacular narrative known as "First Saga of St. Olaf" used by Snorri Sturluson for *Haralds saga Sigurðarsonar* and *Saga Óláfs konungs hins helga*.

45. Oxford, Bodleian Laud Miscellany 615, f. 83. An edition and translation was made by Nicolas O'Kearney, *The Prophecies of Saints Colum-Cille, Maeltamlacht, Ultan, Senan, Bearcan and Malachy* (Dublin, 1855, repr. 1925), 32–61.

46. Bradley, "The Interpretation of Scandinavian Settlement in Ireland," 58.

47. On this matter, see a series of articles by Miles Campbell: "The Anti-Norman Reaction in England in 1052: Suggested Origins," 428–41; "Earl Godwin of Wessex and Edward the Confessor's Promise of the Throne to William of Normandy," 141–50; and "A Pre-Conquest Norman Occupation of England?" 21–31.

48. *Anglo-Saxon Chronicle*, 1:175–76; and William of Malmesbury, *De Gestis Pontificum*, ed. Hamilton, 292.

49. *The Life of King Edward Who Rests at Westminster*, ed. Barlow, 25. The E version of the *Anglo-Saxon Chronicle* claims that they enjoyed *griðe* ("protection") in Ireland, see *Anglo-Saxon Chronicle*, 1:176.

50. Postan, *Famulus*, 6; William of Malmesbury, *De Gestis Regum Anglorum*, ed. Stubbs, 1:245 (who is confused about Gytha: she was Godwin's only known wife, not his second; and she was Cnut's sister-in-law, not his sister, see Stenton, *Anglo-Saxon England*, 417); and *Vita Wulfstani*, ed. Darlington, 43, where Wulfstan is credited with ending the Anglo-Irish slave trade.

51. Bethurum, ed., *Homilies of Wulfstan*, 271–72; Warner of Rouen, *Moriuht*, ed. McDonough, 78, 92, and 94; and Larson, *Earliest Norwegian Laws*, 76–77.

52. *Anglo-Saxon Chronicles*, 1:184–85, and Hudson, "The Destruction of Gruffudd ap Llywelyn," 332.

53. For a discussion, see Hudson, "Destruction of Gruffydd ap Llywelyn," 332.

54. *Gesta Herwardi incliti exulis et militis*, in *L'Estoire des Engleis . . . Geffrei Gaimar*, ed. Hardy and Martin, 1:339–404 (esp. 347–54), and Swanton, *Three Lives of the Last Englishmen*, 43–88. An early version claims that its informant was one of Hereward's companions. A still useful summary of scholarship is in Graves, *Bibliography of English History to 1485*, 423–24. Freeman believed the Irish and Flemish episodes particularly likely to be accurate, see *The Norman Conquest*, 4:456. He was followed by Stenton, *Anglo-Saxon England*, 605–6, and Thomas, "*Gesta Herwardi*, the English and Their Conquerors," 216.

55. Christiansen, "People of the North," 148–55; Kenney, *Sources for the Early History of Ireland*, 603; and Plummer, ed., *Vitae Sanctorum Hiberniae*, 2:70.

56. Nicholas, *Medieval Flanders*, 117–19.

57. Ó Fiaich, *Gaelscrínte san Eoraip*, 68–69.

58. Bede, *Historia Ecclesiastica*, ed. Plummer, 299, and Kenney, *Sources for the Early History of Ireland*, 232–3 and 509. For comment on Willibrord, see Grierson, "Relations between England and Flanders before the Norman Conquest," 82 n. 3.

59. *De Sancto Rumoldo Episcopo et Martyre Mechliniae in Belgio* in AA SS, Jul. I, 169–266 (at 255) (Rumbold); *Sancti Livini Episopi et Martyris Vita auctore Bonifacio coaevo* in Migne, *PL* 87, 327–44 (at 329–30) (Livinus); for the points relevant here, see Kenny, *Sources for the Early History of Ireland*, 527 (Rumbold) and 509 (Livinus).

60. Hudson, "The Destruction of Gruffudd ap Llywelyn," 339–40.

61. Walker, "A Note on Gruffydd ap Llewelyn (1039–1063)," 83–94; James, "Fresh Light on the Death of Gruffudd ap Llywelyn," 147; and Charles-Edwards, *Early Irish and Welsh Kinship*, 221 n. 199.

62. Mac Niocaill, "Annála Gearra as Proibhinse Ard Macha," 339; for a discussion of these annals that survive in the fifteenth-century British Library MS Add. 30512, see O'Grady and Flower, *Catalogue of Irish Manuscripts in the British Library (formerly British Museum)*, 2:491.

63. Adam of Bremen, *Gesta*, 155.

64. *Chronicle of Pierre de Langtoft, in French Verse from the Earliest Period to the Death of Edward I*, ed. T. Wright, 2 vols. (Rolls Series 47), 1:394; he claims that Gruffudd returned to Wales and was slain.

65. Lloyd, "Wales and the Coming of the Normans," 138.

66. Gerald of Wales, *Itinerarium Kambriae*, in *Opera*, ed. Brewer, Dimock, and Warner, 6:28–29; *Chronicle of John of Worcester*, ed. Darlington, McGurk, and Bray, 2:596 (*s.a.* 1064); *Anglo-Saxon Chronicles*, 1:191: *se kyng Eadward betaehte [the] land his twam gebroþran*; and Charles-Edwards, *Early Irish and Welsh Kinship*, 220–23 and 294–95.

67. *History of Gruffydd ap Cynan*, ed. Jones, 112–14.

68. Dolley, *Sylloge of Coins in the British Museum*, vol. 8, *The Hiberno-Norse Coins in the British Museum*, 134–35. This is designated the phase V series, in which the Dublin coins exhibit an unusual familiarity with English dies after 1060.

69. William of Malmesbury, *De Gestis Regum Anglorum*, ed. Stubbs, 1:280–82; and *Morkinskinna*, ed. Andersson and Gade, 263.

70. Adam of Bremen, *Gesta*, 196.

71. *Chronicle of Mann and the Isles*, ed. Broderick and Stowell, 61 (*s.a.* 1047 = 1066); Broderick, "Irish and Welsh Strands in the Genealogy of Godred Crovan," 33–34; and Bartrum, *Early Welsh Genealogical Tracts*, 99.

72. *Cath Saxan seol nglaine / i torchair rí Lochlainne*, in *Book of Leinster*, ed. Best et al., 3:503.

73. Mac Niocaill, "Annála Gearra," 340, where the battle is designated *cath Araillt*, "Harold's Battle."

74. For the flight of Harold's family and their fortunes, see Hudson, "Family of Harold Godwinsson," 92–100. Diarmait is named by Orderic Vitalis, *Ecclesiastical History*, ed. Chibnall, 2:224. Gunnhild died at Bruges in 1087 and the plate on her sarcophagus reads *Gunhildis nobilissimus orta parentibus*; Warlop, *The Flemish Nobility before 1300*, 1:57.

7. The Contest for Supremacy in the Irish Sea

1. Kenney, *Sources for the Early History of Ireland*, 489–95 and 600–1; and Orderic Vitalis, *Ecclesiastical History*, ed. Chibnall, 3:60.

2. Ussher, *Whole Works*, 4:513–14 (no. 32). For Gillebert, see Janssens de Varebeke, "Benedictine Bishops in Medieval Ireland," 245.

3. Round, *Calendar of Documents Preserved in France*, 32–34, no. 109, and Davis et al., eds., *Regesta Regum Anglo-Normannorum*, 3:268–69.

4. Gwynn, "Ireland and the Continent in the Eleventh Century," 211; and Wallace, "Archaeology of Viking Dublin," 132.

5. In the Dublin series phase V, Dolley nos. 182–185 show a marked resemblance to coins from Deventer while one penny, Dolley no. 186, suggests an Ottonian model; see Dolley, *Sylloge of Coins in the British Museum*, vol. 8, *The Hiberno-Norse Coins in the British Museum*, 138.

6. *Annals of Inisfallen*, *s.a.* 1068; the standard is identified merely as the banner of the king of the Saxons.

7. The leaders vary according to the source consulted, see Hudson, "Family of Harold Godwinsson," 95.

8. Ann Williams, "Land and Power in the Eleventh Century: The Estates of Harold Godwinsson," 186; Godwin had another estate at Langford (Budville). Neither estate seems to have been attacked, see *Domesday Book: Somerset*, f. 86d.

9. This is named as the site of an important battle in 1068 by a few monastic chronicles following an exemplar written in the southwest, such as the Chronicle of Holyrood, see *Scottish Chronicle Known as the Chronicle of Holyrood*, ed. Anderson, 16, and the *bellum in Bleduna* is at p. 108 (and see n. 5).

10. Douglas, "Companions of the Conqueror," 143; van Houts, "Ship List of William the Conqueror," 159–83; and Hudson, "William the Conqueror and Ireland," 147–49. For the Normans in South Wales, see Walker, *Norman Conquerors*, 34–49.

11. Crumlin-Pedersen, *Skuldelev Ships I*, 329–30.

12. The basic outline is given by Stenton, *Anglo-Saxon England*, 601–2, and by Kapelle, *Norman Conquest of the North*, 112–14.

13. *Domesday Book: Devon*, f. 109b.

14. Le Patourel, *Norman Empire*, 34.

15. Orderic Vitalis, *Ecclesiastical History*, ed. Chibnall, 4:42.

16. *Liber Eliensis*, ed. Blake, 176. While this account is slightly confused, it is a valuable record with many important details; a discussion of its sources and composition, including the reference to the Irish (which the editor identifies with the fleets of the sons of Harold Godwinsson) is at xxxv–xxxvi.

17. Orderic Vitalis, *Ecclesiastical History*, ed. Chibnall, 2:260–62; and Stenton, *Anglo-Saxon England*, 617.

18. Useful discussions are: Douglas, "Companions of the Conqueror," 144; Carlyle, "Political History," *VCH Hereford*, 1:354–57; Harris, "Political History," *VCH Cheshire*, 2:1–8; and Lewis, "The King and Eye," 571–76.

19. Nine *lecciones* were composed about him; see *Book of Obits and Martyrologies*, ed. Crosthwaite, 23. An obit note under November 23 for *Donatus episcopus primus Dublin* refers to Donatus II (1084–1095). For the location of his grave, see Gwynn, "Some Unpublished Texts from the Black Book of Christ Church, Dublin," 333.

20. A general overview is given in Kenney, *Sources for the Early History of Ireland*, 758–59. For the correspondence, see Ussher, *Whole Works*, 4:488–93, and *The Letters of Lanfranc, Archbishop of Canterbury*, ed. Clover and Gibson, 66–73; the acts of Lanfranc are in *Anglo-Saxon Chronicles*, 1:287–92; the profession is edited by Richter, *Canterbury Professions*, 29; and notice of his election is in Gilbert, ed., *Chartularies of St. Mary's, Dublin*, 2:249–50.

21. This point is stressed in the works of writers such as Eadmer whose copying of letters was intended to establish precedent, see Vaughan, "Eadmer's *Historia Novorum*: A Reinterpretation," 264–65. For interpretations, see Gibson, *Lanfranc of Bec*, 121–25; and Holland, "Dublin and the Reform of the Irish Church: Eleventh and Twelfth Centuries," 111–18.

22. *The Writings of Bishop Patrick, 1074–1084*, ed. Gwynn.

23. Ware, *De praesulibus Hiberniae commentarius*, 102, citing a copy of the chronicle of the kings of Man that is either now lost or his error. The letter from Dublin to Canterbury was a manuscript in Cotton's library at Cleopatra E.1, which partly survives (as British Library Cotton MS Cleopatra E.1) and contains professions to Canterbury.

24. Bethell, "English Monks and Irish Reform," 116–17.

25. *Vita Wulfstani*, ed. Darlington, 59. For Wulfstan's ties to the Normans, see Mason, "Change and Continuity in Eleventh Century Mercia," 154–76.

26. The letter petitioning Anselm on Malchus' behalf is preserved by Eadmer, *Eadmeri Historia Novorum in Anglia*, ed. Rule, 76–77. Máel Ísua was consecrated on December 27, 1096 and died in 1135, see: Ussher, *Whole Works*, 4:518–19; Kenney, *Sources for the Early History of Ireland*, 760; and Richter, *Canterbury Professions*, 35. For Samuel, see: Ussher, *Whole Works*, 4:530–31; and Kenney, *Sources for the Early History of Ireland*, 761.

27. Haddan and Stubbs, *Councils and Ecclesiastical Documents*, 2:162–64.

28. Lucian of Chester, *Liber Luciani de Laude Cestrie*, ed. Taylor, 29.

29. Bethel, "English Monks and Irish Reform," 116–18.

30. *De ordinando pontifice auctor Gallicus*, ed. E. Dümmler, in *MGH, Libelli de lite*, 1:8–14, after Whitney, "Reform of the Church."

31. Hudson, "Time is Short," 111–13.

32. For Donatus II, see: *Acta Lanfanci*, in *Anglo-Saxon Chronicle*, 1:290; *Letters of Lanfranc*, ed. Clover and Gibson, 187; Richter, *Canterbury Professions*, 31; and *Chartularies of St. Mary's Abbey, Dublin*, ed. Gilbert, 2:250. Lanfranc's letter is printed in Ussher, *Whole Works*, 4:495–97, and *Letters of Lanfranc*, ed. Clover and Gibson, 154–60 (dated between August 29, 1080 and August 28, 1081). For comments, see: Kenney, *Sources for the Early History of Ireland*, 759–60; and Ó Corráin, "Dál Cais—Church and Dynasty," 52–63.

33. Gibson, *Lanfranc of Bec*, 121.

34. Hudson, "William the Conqueror and Ireland," 152.

35. See two essays by Ryan: "Pre-Norman Dublin," 76, and "O'Briens in Munster after Clontarf," 147–48.

36. William of Malmesbury, *De Gestis Regum Anglorum*, ed. Stubbs, 2:371.

37. Gilbert, ed., *Historical and Municipal Documents, Ireland*, 12.

38. French, "Meilyr's Elegy for Gruffudd ap Cynan," 267.

39. Unfortunately, much of its chronology for Welsh events cannot be checked by the Welsh records in *Brut Y Tywysogyon* and *Annales Cambriae*, which for this period are not as informative as one would hope. A further difficulty is that some versions of those chronicles may have been influenced by the *History of Gruffydd ap Cynan*; see Lloyd, "Wales and the Coming of the Normans," 153–55.

40. *History of Gruffydd*, ed. Jones, 102. Curtis, "The Fitz Rerys, Welsh Lords of Cloghran, Co. Dublin," 13–17, suggests that Gruffudd might have kept ownership of the land even after his establishment in Wales. See also Flanagan, *Irish Society, Anglo-Norman Settlers, and Angevin Kingship*, 62, and for references, see Hogan, *Onomasticon Goedelicum*, 81.

41. The use of *Murchath* for both Murchad and Muirchertach has led to confusion with the Munster prince Muirchertach Ua Briain, see Flanagan, *Irish Society, Anglo-Norman Settlers, and Angevin Kingship*, 62. Muirchertach became king of Dublin late in 1075, and there was not enough time, even discounting the obvious anachronisms, for all the events of that year. Muirchertach's friendly relations with Gruffudd are mentioned later, without any reference to earlier aid.

42. Lloyd, "Wales and the Coming of the Normans," 173.

43. *History of Gruffudd*, ed. Jones, 124; and *Annales Cambriae*, 27–28.

44. Only a few of those events are mentioned outside the *History of Gruffydd ap Cynan*. *Brut Y Tywysogyon* claims that the Battle of Bron yr Erw was fought in 1075 after the slaying of Cynrig. The Battle of Mynydd Carn is placed by both *Brut Y Tywysogyon* and *Annales Cambriae* among the events for 1081. Among the events for 1075 is a notice in the "C" manuscript of the *Annales Cambriae*, also found in *Brut Y Tywysogyon*, that Gruffudd seized Anglesey. Lloyd emends *non obsedit* to *Mon obsedit*, "Wales and the Coming of the Normans," 175 (see explanation at p. 154 n. 2).

45. Robert's brother Arnold was a monk with Orderic at St. Évroul, where Orderic wrote his eulogy for Robert. Orderic is generous toward Robert, claiming a number of conquests unknown elsewhere, so his chronology is unlikely to be condensed; see Orderic Vitalis, *Ecclesiastical History*, ed. Chibnall, 4:134–46, where Chibnall queries Orderic's chronology (4:xxxviii), but accepts it in *Anglo-Norman England*, 46. Davies suggests that Robert could have died anytime between 1088 and 1093; see *Age of Conquest*, 30.

46. *Domesday Book* (Chester), f. 269b.

47. This is also found in the late medieval Welsh genealogy *Achau Brenhinoedd a Thywyso-gion Cymru*, in Bartrum, *Early Welsh Genealogical Tracts*, 99 (6c): *Gwrthrgt mear[a]ch m Har-allt ddu [m] Ifor gamle m Afloyd m Swtrig* (Godred the finger[ed] the son of Harald the black [the son of] Ivarr the old the son of Olaf the son of Sitric).

48. Paton, *Les Prophecies de Merlin*, 1:81–83; and Arnold, *Le Roman de Brut de Wace*, 2:512 (l. 9720) and 700 (l. 13417). Ireland is elsewhere found in the Manx Chronicle as *[H]Ibernia*, and there is the possibility that *Ysland* reflects *Yrland* for *Irland*, the Norse spelling of Ireland with confusion between insular long -*r*- and -*s*-.

49. Byrne, "Na Renna," 267.

50. *Dictionary of the Irish Language: M*, 108:27–28; and Ó Cuív, "A Poem in Praise of Ragh-nall King of Man," 292, stanza 25.

51. Dolley dates the division to the early eleventh century, with a Leinster influence, *Some Irish Dimensions to Manx History*, 17. A *Joh. filius Macmars* witnesses an early charter from the Isles, see *Coucher Book of Furness Abbey*, ed. Brownbill, 6:lxxviii, 709.

52. Mac Niocaill, *Notitiae as Leabhar Cheanannais*, 32 (dated to the second quarter of the twelfth century): *ocus cend ind recléssa .i. mac Maras* "and the head of the recles, that is Mac Maras."

53. Marstrander, "Om Tingsteder pa Man," 384–93; and Crawford, *Scandinavian Scotland*, 205.

54. The text is preserved in BL MS Sloane 4149, and it was edited by Rev. William Macken-zie, *Legislation by Three of the Thirteen Stanleys, Kings of Man*, Manx Society, vol. 3 (Douglas, 1860), 71–102.

8. Lords of the Isles

1. Bugge, "Bidrag til det sidste Afsnit af Nordboernes Historie i Irland," 314.

2. Ó Corráin, *Ireland before the Normans*, 142–43.

3. Harrison, "Offensiva och defensive eliter-om det politiska overskikter under medelti-den," 569.

4. *Grágás*, ed. Finsen, 1:239. For a discussion of political affairs reflected by legal materials, see Johnsen, "Le Commerce et la Navigation en Norvège au Moyen Age," 392–93.

5. Wahlgren, "Maine Penny," 404; and Ingstad, *Discovery of a Norse Settlement in America*, 2:427.

6. *Eyrbyggja Saga*, ed. Sveinsson and Þórðarson, 104; and Benton, *Town Origins*, 55, from the text known as "Customary Practice." These contacts are implied in literary records, see McDougall, "Foreigners and Foreign Language in Medieval Iceland," 180–233.

7. *Anglo-Saxon Chronicle*, 1:227.

8. Scottish raids usually came along the east coast. The last Scots prince known to have raided in Cumberland was Kenneth II ca. 971, although Malcolm Canmore is said to have held parts of Cumberland by force rather than right. Kapelle, *The Norman Conquest of the North*, 150–52, suggests that Rufus and Máel Coluim Canmore had an agreement to divide the spoils at Carlisle among themselves, but see Duncan, *Scotland*, 120–21.

9. *Itinerarium Kambriae*, in Gerald of Wales, *Giraldi Cambrensis Opera*, ed. Brewer et al., 6:109–10.

10. Watt, *Fasti Ecclesiae Scoticanae Medii Aevi*, 248–49.

11. For a discussion of the problem, see Watt, *Fasti Ecclesiae Scoticanae Medii Aevi*, 197–99; and McDonald, *Kingdom of the Isles*, 206–7.

12. Lind, *Norsk-isländska dopnamn ock fingerade namn från medeltiden*, cols. 587–88.

13. Haddan and Stubbs, *Councils and Ecclesiastical Documents*, 2:276.

14. Anderson, *Scottish Annals from English Chroniclers*, 224 n. 1; Watt, *Fasti Ecclesiae Scoticanae Medii Aevi*, 197–98.

15. McDonald, *Kingdom of the Isles*, 209.

16. Adigard des Gautries, *Les Noms des personnes Scandinaves*, 237–38: St. Vigor d'Ymond-ville (earlier *Wimondvilla*), Hymouville (from *Wimonvilla*), and Bois-Himont (from *Bois Wimont*).

17. *History of Gruffudd*, ed. Jones, 136.

18. Wade-Evans, *Vitae Sanctorum Britanniae*, 182–84.

19. Barlow, *William Rufus*, 449.

20. Crawford, *Scandinavian Scotland*, 208–9; and Brown, "Norse in Argyll," 210.

21. Smyser, "Ibn Fadlan's Account of the Rus," 97.

22. For the passage from *Hávamál*, see Helgason, ed., *Eddadigte*, 1:22; and Adam of Bremen, *Gesta*, 9.

23. Kenney, *Sources for the Early History of Ireland*, 761.

24. Gwynn, "Some Unpublished Texts from the Black Book of Christ Church, Dublin," 328.

25. Ussher, *Whole Works*, 4:532–33; details are given by Eadmer, *Eadmeri Historia Novorum in Anglia*, ed. Rule, 297–98, and John of Worcester, *Chronicle*, ed. Darlington et al., 3:148 (*s.a.* 1121).

26. William of Malmesbury, *De Gestis Regum Anglorum*, ed. Stubbs, 2:484–85.

27. Gwynn, "Medieval Bristol and Dublin," 278.

28. William of Malmesbury, *Gestis Pontificum*, ed. Hamilton, 292.

29. Raine, *Historians of the Church of York*, 2:100: "that one of the Danes or Northmen or Scots who coming in ships to York were wont to infest the kingdom should be created king by the archbishop of York and by the natives of his province . . ." after Anderson, *Scottish Annals from English Chroniclers*, 89 n. 6.

30. Vernon Hull, "The Exile of Conall Corc," 940: *Áth Clíath conaccai na llonga oc dul taris. Luid leo taris sair conaccai slébe Alban. Lecait uadib hi tír.* The preceding text is lost because of damage to the manuscript; see *Book of Leinster*, ed. Best et al., 5:1249 (f. 287a). For Rumbold, see *Acta Sanctorum*, Jul. I, 255–57; and Kenney, *Sources for the Early History of Ireland*, 527–28.

31. Dolley, *Sylloge of Coins in the British Museum*, vol. 8, *The Hiberno-Norse Coins in the British Museum*, 135 and 140–42.

32. Anderson, *Early Sources of Scottish History*, 2:68 (Margaret); John of Fordun, *Chronica Gentis Scotorum*, ed. Skene, 1:244 (David); Hudson, "Changing Economy of the Irish Sea Province," 54–55; and O'Neill, *Merchants and Mariners*, 58–60. The specific cargoes brought to Ireland are found in Sweetman, ed., *Calendar of Documents Relating to Ireland*, 1:1–8.

33. *Lebor na Cert*, ed. Dillon, 104.

34. "Ban-Shenchus," ed. Dobbs, 196 and 229: *Mor ingen Eachmarcaig m. Radnaill rig Gall mathair Donchaid [ocus] Domnaill [ocus] Amlaib tri meic Taidc hUi Briain [ocus] Be Bind ingen Taidc* ("Mór, daughter of Echmarcach, the king of the Foreigners, [was the] mother of Donnchad and Domnall and Olaf, three sons of Tadc Ua Briain and [also] Be Bind, the daughter of Tadc").

35. Fryde et al., eds., *Handbook of British Chronology*, 63, the *New History of Ireland*, ed. Moody, Martin, and Byrne, 9:466, and MacQuarrie, "The Crusades and the Scottish *Gaidhealtachd* in Fact and Legend," 132–34, all place Lagmann's death during the First Crusade. Anderson, *Early Sources of Scottish History*, 2:98 n. 2, believed the *Scotti* of the first crusade to have been Irish.

36. *Morkinskinna*, ed. Andersson and Gade, 299; Sturluson, *Magnúss saga berfoetts*, in *Heimskringla*, ed. Aðalbjarnarson, 3:221–22; Anderson, *Early Sources of Scottish History*, 2:109 n. 2; Power, "Magnus Barelegs' Expeditions to the West," 116; Gregory, *History of the Western Highlands and Isles of Scotland*, 6–7; and Scott, "The Norse in the Hebrides," 206.

37. Orderic Vitalis, *Ecclesiastical History*, ed., Chibnall, 4:280.

38. *Orkneyinga Saga*, ed, Guðmundsson, 93–94.

39. *Chronicle of the Kings of Man and the Isles*, ed. Broderick and Stowell, 63.

40. Sturluson, *Magnúss Saga*, in *Heimskringla*, ed. Aðalbjarnarson, 220.

41. *Fagrskinna* ("fair parchment" composed ca. 1200) and *Fríssbók* (*codex Frisianus* composed ca. 1325) in Anderson, *Early Sources of Scottish History*, 2:109; and *Morkinskinna*, ed. Andersson and Gade, 298–99.

42. Orderic Vitalis, *Ecclesiastical History*, ed. Chibnall, 5:223; John of Worcester, *Chronicle*, ed. Darlington et al., *s.a.* 1098; and see Power, "Magnus Barelegs' Expeditions to the West," 116–17.

43. *History of Gruffydd*, ed. Jones, 140; and *Brut Y Tywysogyon*, ed. Jones, 30.

44. *History of Gruffudd*, ed. Jones, 140–42. This diplomatic mission began a long acquaintance that Owain would find useful in 1106 when he fled from Wales to the court of Muirchertach.

45. Orderic Vitalis, *Ecclesiastical History*, ed. Chibnall, 5:219–24; and John of Worcester, *Chronicle*, ed. Darlington et al., 3:86–88 (*s.a.* 1098).

46. Sturluson, *Magnúss Saga,* in *Heimskringla*, ed. Aðalbjarnarson, 3:225–26.

47. The best collection of materials concerning Magnus's Scottish affairs is Anderson, *Early Sources of Scottish History*, 2:102–18 and 127–36. Although *Magnúss Saga* claims that the king was Máel Coluim, it is clear that his son Edgar is intended, because Máel Coluim had been killed five years earlier.

48. *Johannis de Fordun Chronica Gentis Scotorum*, ed. Skene, 1:188.

49. Andersen, "Den Norske Innvandringen til Hebridene i Vikingtiden og den norrøne Bosetningens senere skjebne," 271–82; and Nicolaisen, *Scottish Place Names*, 88–89 (for Galloway, see maps pp. 102 and 106), where the apparent contradiction offered by the distribution of *-dalr* is explained as the difference between influence as distinct from settlement, pp. 94–96.

50. This is claimed by Curtis, "Murchertach O'Brien, High King of Ireland and his Norman son-in-law, Arnulf de Montgomery," 118–19, although he has no direct evidence.

51. *Morkinskinna*, ed. Anderson and Gade, 311; the verse supposedly was uttered by Magnus during the battle in which he received his death-wound.

52. There is uncertainty about the home of Harold, for a discussion, see Anderson, *Early Sources of Scottish History*, 2:171–73; and Gathorne-Hardy, *Royal Imposter*, 23–25.

53. Larson, *Earliest Norwegian Laws*, 327–28.

54. The texts are Fagrskinna, after Anderson, *Early Sources of Scottish History*, 2:117, and *Morkinskinna*, ed. Andersson and Gade, 308–9; for comment, see Poole, "Some Royal Love Verses," 116–17.

55. Briggs, "A Boat Burial from County Antrim," 158–60.

56. *Morkinskinna*, ed. Andersson and Gade, 335.

57. Anderson, "When was Regular Taxation Introduced in the Norse Isles of Britain?" 73–83; and Johnsen, "Betalte Suderøyene og Man skatt eller lensavgift til Norges konge (1153–1263)?" 17.

58. Arguments that Lagmann reigned during the period 1103 to ca. 1110 (possible date of his death) are given by Gregory, *History of the Western Highlands and Isles of Scotland*, 6–7; and Power, "Magnus Bareleg's Expeditions to the West," 116.

59. Gregory, *History of the Western Highlands*, 6–7, who does not specify on which crusade Lagmann participated.

60. Sigurd died on March 26, 1030 when he was 40 years old according to Sturluson, *Magnússon Saga*, in *Heimskringla*, ed Aðalbjarnarson, 3:277.

61. Sturluson, *Magnússons Saga*, in *Heimskringla*, ed. Aðalbjarnarson, 3:239–54. Confirmation is given by William of Malmesbury, *De Gestis regum Anglorum*, ed. Stubbs, 2:485–86. A brief summary is by Musset, *Les Peuples Scandinaves au Moyen Age*, 171–72.

62. Muirchertach also had a son named Domnall, and there has been the suggestion that his child is the man intended by the *Manx Chronicle* as ruling prior to 1096, leading to a later confusion with Domnall mac Taidc, see *New History of Ireland*, ed. Moody, Martin, and Byrne, 9:466 and 468 n. 7. This is possible, but there is no evidence from the records of such an event.

63. *An Leabhar Muimhnech*, ed. Ó Donnchadha, 299.

64. F. 34r. The tale is unpublished, but a summary is given by Gwynn, "The Liber Flavus Fergusiorum," 35–36.

65. *Cath Ruis na Ríg*, ed. Hogan, 10 and 12; and Mac Gearailt, "Cath Ruis na Ríg and Twelfth-Century Literary and Oral Tradition," 132.

66. Ryan, "O'Briens in Munster after Clontarf," 20.

67. Munro, "Lordship of the Isles," 67; and Crawford, *Scandinavian Scotland*, 205.

68. Davies, *Domination and Conquest*, 47–65.

69. Anderson, *Scottish Annals*, 224 n. 1.

70. *Coucher Book of Furness Abbey*, ed. Brownbill, lxxviii, 708 and n. 2. For an account of his career, see McDonald, *Outlaws of Medieval Scotland*, 26–27.

71. Cheney, "Manx Synodal Statutes," 82.

72. Ó Cuív, "A Poem in Praise of Raghnall, King of Man," 288; Sturluson, *Magnúss Saga*, in *Heimskringla*, ed. Aðalbjarnarson, 3:224; Cross and Slover, *Ancient Irish Tales*, 465.

73. *Cambridge Economic History*, 2:626.

74. *Register of the Priory of St. Bees*, ed. Wilson, 75.

75. *Register of St. Bees*, ed. Wilson, 74.

76. Malmesbury, *De Gestis Regum Anglorum*, ed. Stubbs, 2:493–95; and Benedict, *Anglo-Norman Voyage of St. Brendan*, ed. Short and Merrilees, 4–6.

Conclusion

1. See the discussion by Mac Cana, "Influence of the Vikings on Celtic Literature," 81 n. 9.

2. *Hrafns Saga Sveinbjarnarsonar*, ed. Helgadóttir, 22.

3. *Book of Llan Dâv*, ed. Evans and Rhŷs, 1–5.

4. Gerald of Wales, *Expugnatio Hibernica*, ed. Scott and Martin, 68–70.

5. Herman the Monk, *De Miraculis S. Mariae Laudunensis* in Migne, ed., *PL* 156, cols. 985–86; and Tatlock, "English Journey of the Laon Canons," 454–65.

6. Gerald of Wales, *Topographia Hibernica*, 94.

7. Sweetman, ed., *Calendar of Documents relating to Ireland*, 1:123.

8. Ritchie, *Normans in Scotland*, 79–80.

9. Gerald of Wales, *Topographia Hibernica*, 152.

10. Mac Gearailt, "Cath Ruis na Ríg," 132.

11. Hudson, *Prophecy of Berchán*: 25–26 (Olaf), 26 (Ivar), and 31 (foes).

12. *Lebor na Huidre*, ed. Best and Bergin, 281–82; and Mac Cana, "Influence of the Vikings on Celtic Literature," 81.

Selected Bibliography

Manuscript Sources

Dublin, Royal Irish Academy, MS Stowe D. ii. 1: *Book of Uí Maine*.
National Library of Scotland, MS 72.1.7, ff. 4v–5v: *Banshenchas*.
Oxford MS, Bodl. Laud Misc. 615, pp. 82–85: the poem *Éisdse a Bhoitin*.

Primary Sources

Acta Sanctorum quotquot toto urbe coluntur vel a Catholicis scriptoribus celebrantur, ed. J. Bolandus et al., 66 vols. (Antwerp and Brussels, 1643–).
Adam of Bremen, *History of the Archbishops of Hamburg-Bremen*, ed. F. J. Tschan (New York, 1959).
———— *Magistri Adam Bremensis Gesta Hammaburgensis ecclesiae Pontificum*, ed. Bernard Schmeidler (Hanover, 1917).
Ademar of Chabannes, *Chronicon*, ed. P. Bourgain, R. Landes, and G. Pon (*Corpus Christianorum, continuatio Mediaevalis* 129, 1999).
Adomnán, *De Locis Sanctis*, ed. D. Meehan (*Scriptores Latini Hiberniae*, vol. 3, Dublin, 1958).
———— *Life of Columba*, ed. A. O. Anderson and M. O. Anderson (Oxford, 1991).
Ælfric, *Ælfric's Colloquy*, ed. G. N. Garmonsway, 2nd edn. (London, 1947).
Æthelweard, *The Chronicle of Æthelweard*, ed. A. Campbell (London, 1962).
Aggeson, Svein, *Chronicon*, ed. G. Waitz (*MGH, SS* 29), 27–36.
Ágrip af Nóregs Konunga Sögum, ed. Finnur Jónsson (Halle, 1929).
Aislinge Meic Con Glinne, ed. K. H. Jackson (Dublin, 1990).
Anderson, Alan Orr, *Early Sources of Scottish History*, 2 vols. (Edinburgh, 1922).
———— *Scottish Annals from English Chroniclers* (London, 1908).
Anglo-Saxon Chronicle: *Two of the Saxon Chronicles Parallel*, ed. J. Earle and C. Plummer, 2 vols. (Oxford, 1892–99).
An Leabhar Muimhnech, ed. Tadg O Donnchadha (Dublin, n.d.).
Annála Gearra as Proibhinse Ard Macha, ed. G. Mac Niocaill (*Seanchas Ardmhacha* 3, 1959), 337–40.
Annales Cambriae, ed. J. W. ab Ithel (Rolls Series 20, London, 1860).

Annales Nivernenses, ed. G. Waitz (*MGH, SS* 13), 88–91.

Annals of Inisfallen, ed. S. Mac Airt (Dublin, 1951).

Annals of Inisfallen, a Facsimile, ed. R. I. Best and Eoin MacNeill (Dublin, 1933).

Annals of the Kingdom of Ireland by the Four Masters, ed. John O'Donovan, 7 vols. (Dublin, 1851).

Annals of Tigernach: "Fragmentary Annals of Tigernach," ed. W. Stokes, *Revue Celtique* 17 (1896), 6–33, 116–263, 337–420 (for the annals relevant to this study).

Annals of Ulster: *Annala Uladh, Annals of Ulster, otherwise Annala Senait, Annals of Senat; a Chronicle of Irish Affairs from A.D. 431 to A.D. 1540*, ed. W. Hennessy and B. MacCarthy, 4 vols. (Dublin, 1887–1901).

Annals of Ulster, ed. G. Mac Niocaill and S. Mac Airt (Dublin, 1983).

Armes Prydein, ed. Sir Ifor Williams and trans. R. Bromwich (Dublin, 1972).

Arnold, Ivor, ed., *Le Roman de Brut de Wace*, 2 vols (Paris, 1937–40).

Asser, *Life of King Alfred Together with the Annals of St. Neots Erroneously Ascribed to Asser*, ed. W. H. Stevenson, rev. D. Whitelock (Oxford, 1959).

"Ban-Shenchus," ed. M. Dobbs, *Revue Celtique* 47 (1930), 283–339; 48 (1931), 163–234; and 49 (1932), 437–89.

Barnes, Michael, Jan Ragnarr Hagland, and R. I. Page, eds., *Runic Inscriptions of Viking Age Dublin* (Dublin, 1997).

Barrow, G. W. S., *Regesta Regum Scottorum*, vols. 1 and 2 (Edinburgh, 1971–72).

Bartrum, P., *Early Welsh Genealogical Tracts* (Cardiff, 1966).

Bateson, Mary, "Irish Exchequer Memoranda of the Reign of Edward I," *EHR* 18 (1903), 497–513.

Bede, *Historia Ecclesiastica*, in *Venerabilis Baedae Opera Historica*, ed. C. Plummer (Oxford, repr. 1975).

Benedict, *Anglo-Norman Voyage of St. Brendan*, ed. Ian Short and Brian Merrilees (Manchester, 1979).

Benton, John F., *Town Origins: The Evidence from Medieval England* (Boston, 1968).

Bergin, O. J., "Poems Attributed to Gormlaith," in Osborn Bergin and Carl Marstrander, *Miscellany Presented to Kuno Meyer* (Halle, 1912), 343–69.

Bernard of Clairvaux, *Vita S. Malachiae Hiberniae Episcopi*, in Migne, *PL* 182, cols. 1073–1118.

Betha Colmáin maic Lúacháin, ed. K. M. Meyer (Royal Irish Academy Todd Lecture Series, vol. 17, Dublin, 1911).

Bethurum, Dorothy, ed., *The Homilies of Wulfstan* (Oxford, 1957).

Binchy, D. A., ed., *Corpus Iuris Hibernici*, 6 vols. (Dublin, 1979).

Birch, Walter de Gray, *Cartularium Saxonicum: A Collection of Charters Relating to Anglo-Saxon History (A.D. 430–975)*, 3 vols. (London, 1885–93).

Book of Leinster, formerly Lebar na Núachongbála, ed. R. I. Best, Osborn Bergin, M. A. O'Brien, and Anne O'Sullivan, 6 vols. (Dublin, 1955–83).

Book of Llandaff, *Llyvyr Teilo vel Liber Landavensis: The Text of the Book of Llan Dâv Reproduced from the Gwysaney Manuscript*, ed. J. Gwenoguryn Evans and John Rhŷs (Oxford, 1893).

The Book of Obits and Martyrology of the Cathedral Church of the Holy Trinity, Dublin, ed. John Clark Crosthwaite (Dublin, 1846).

Book of Uí Maine, Otherwise the Book of the O'Kellys, ed. R. A. S. Macalister (Dublin, 1942).

Brennu-Njáls Saga, ed. Einar Ól. Sveinsson (Íslenzk Fornrit 12, Reykjavík, 1954) .

Brewer, J. S., and William Bullen, eds., *Calendar of the Carew Manuscripts Preserved in the Archiepiscopal Library at Lambeth*, 6 vols. (London, 1871).

Bromwich, Rachel, ed., *Troedd Ynys Prydein: The Welsh Triads*, 2nd edn. (Cardiff, 1978).

Brooks, E., "Unpublished Charters Relating to Ireland," *Proceedings of the Royal Irish Academy*, 43 (1936), C: 313–66.

Brut y Tywysogyon (Penrith MS 20), ed. T. Jones (Cardiff, 1952).

Cáin Domnaig, ed. J. O'Keefe, *Ériu* 2 (1905), 189–214.

Cartulary or Register of St. Werburgh, Chester, ed. J. Tait, 2 vols. (Chetham Soc. new series 79 and 82, Manchester, 1920–23).

Cath Ruis na Ríg, ed. E. Hogan (Royal Irish Academy Todd Lecture Series 4, Dublin, 1892).

Chrétien de Troyes, "The Knight of the Cart," *Arthurian Romances*, trans. William W. Kibler (London, 1991).

Chronicle of Holyrood, *The Scottish Chronicle Known as the Chronicle of Holyrood*, ed. M. O. Anderson (Scottish History Society, third series 30, Edinburgh, 1938).

Chronicle of the Kings of Mann and the Isles, ed. G. Broderick and Brian Stowell (Edinburgh, 1974).

Cogadh Gaedhel re Gallaibh, or the Wars of the Irish against the Foreigners, ed. J. H. Todd (Rolls Series no. 48, London, 1866).

Corpus Poeticum Boreale, ed. G. Vigfusson and F. Y. Powell, 2 vols. (Oxford, 1883).

Coucher Book of Furness Abbey, ed. J. Brownbill, 2 vols. in 6 parts (Chetham Society, new series 9, 11, 14, 74, 76, and 78, Manchester, 1886–1919).

Cronica Regum Manniae et Insularum, The Chronicle of Man and the Isles: A Facsimile of the Manuscript Codex Julius A. VII in the British Museum (Douglas, 1924).

Cross, Tom Peete, and Clark Harris Slover, *Ancient Irish Tales* (Totowa, N.J., 1981).

Davidson, James B., "Some Anglo-Saxon Charters at Exeter," *British Archaeological Association Journal* 39 (1883), 259–303.

Davies, Wendy, *The Llandaff Charters* (Aberystwyth, 1979).

Davis, H. W. C., H. A. Cronne, R. H. C. Davis, R. J. Whitwell, and Charles Johnson, eds., *Regesta Regum Anglo-Normannorum*, 4 vols. (Oxford, 1913–68).

De Ordinando Pontifice auctor Gallicus, ed. E. Dümmler, *MGH, Libelli de lite*, 1:8–14.

Dictionary of the Irish Language (and Contributions), ed. C. Marstrander, E. G. Quin et al. (Royal Irish Academy, Dublin, 1913–76).

Dicuil, *Dicuili Liber de mensura orbis terrae*, ed. J. J. Tierney (*Scriptores Latini Hiberniae*, vol. 5, Dublin, 1967).

Dobbs, M. E., "On the Graves of Leinster Men," *ZCP* 24 (1954), 139–53.

Domesday Book, gen. ed. J. Morris, 42 vols. (Chichester, 1975–92).

Dronke, Ursula, *Poetic Edda*, 2 vols. (Oxford, 1969–).

Dudo of St. Quentin, [*History of the Normans*] *De Moribus et Actis primorum Normanniae Ducum auctore Dudone Sancti Quintini Decano*, ed. Jules Lair (Caen, 1865).

——— *History of the Normans*, trans. Eric Christiansen (Woodbridge, 1998).

Dugdale, William, *Monasticon Anglicanum*, 3 vols. (London, 1655–73).

Eadmer, *Eadmeri Historia Novorum in Anglia et Opscula Duo De Vita Sancti Anselmi et Quibus Miraculis est*, ed. M. Rule (Rolls Series 81, London, 1884).

Egils Saga Skalla-Grímsson, ed. S. Nordal (Íslenzk Fornrit 2, Rekjavík, 1933)

Eiríks Saga Rauða, ed. Einar Ól. Sveinsson and Matthias Þórðarson, in *Eyrbyggia Saga* (Íslenzk Fornrit 4, Reykjavík, 1935).

Encomium Emmae Reginae, ed. A. Campbell (Camden Society third series 72, London, 1949).

English Historical Documents I, c. 500–1042, ed. Dorothy Whitelock (London, 1955).

Evans, D. Simon, *Historia Gruffudd vab Kenan* (Cardiff, 1977).

Eyrbyggia Saga, ed. Einar Ól. Sveinsson and Matthias Þórðarson (Íslenzk Fornrit 4, Reykjavík, 1935).

Flodoard, *Flodoardus canonicus Remensis, Annales*, in Migne, *PL* 135, cols. 417–90.

Forbes, Alexander Penrose, ed. *The Lives of S. Ninian and S. Kentigern Compiled in the Twelfth Century* (Historians of Scotland 5, Edinburgh, 1874).

Fragmentary Annals of Ireland, ed. Joan Radner (Dublin, 1978).

French, Alexander, "Meilyr's Elegy for Gruffudd ap Cynan," *Etudes Celtiques* 16 (1979), 263–78.

Fryde, E. B., D. E. Greenway, S. Porter, and I. Roy, eds., *Handbook of British Chronology* (London, 1986).

Geffrei Gaimar, *L'Estoire des Engleis*, ed. Sir Thomas D. Hardy and C. T. Martin, 2 vols. (Rolls Series 91, London, 1888–89).

Gerald of Wales, *Expugnatio Hibernica: The Conquest of Ireland by Giraldus Cambrensis*, ed. A. B. Scott and F. X. Martin (Dublin, 1978).

——— *Giraldi Cambrensis Opera*, ed. J. S. Brewer, J. F. Dimock, and G. F. Warner, 8 vols. (Rolls Series 21, London, 1861–91).

Gilbert, J. T., ed., *The Chartularies of St. Mary's, Dublin, with the Register of its House at Dunbrody and Annals of Ireland*, 2 vols. (Rolls Series 80, London, 1884).

——— ed., *Historical and Muncipal Documents of Ireland, 1172–1320* (Rolls Series 53, London, 1870).

Grágás, Íslaendernes Lovbog í fristatens Tid, ed. Vilhjálmur Finsen, 2 vols. (København, 1852–70).

Guibert of Nogent, *Gesta Dei per Francos*, in Migne, *PL* 156, cols. 675–838.

Gunnlaugs saga Ormstungu, in *Borgfirðinga Sögur*, ed. S. Nordal and G. Jónsson (Íslenzk Fornrit 3, Reykjavík, 1938).

Gunnlaugs saga Ormstungu, ed. Peter Foote and Randolph Quirk (London, 1953).

Gwynn, A., "Some Unpublished Texts from the Black Book of Christ Church, Dublin," *Analecta Hiberniae* 16 (1946), 281–337.

Gwynn, Edward, "The Liber Flavus Fergusiorum," *Proceedings of the Royal Irish Academy* 25 (1906), 15–41.

Haddan, A., and W. Stubbs, *Councils and Ecclesiastical Documents Relating to Great Britain and Ireland*, 3 vols. (Oxford, 1869–78).

Harmer, F. E., *Anglo-Saxon Writs* (Manchester, 1952).

Havelok, ed. G. V. Smithers (Oxford, 1987).

Helgason, Jón, *Eddadigte*, 3 vols. (Nordisk Filologi 4, 7 and 8, Oslo, 1962–64).

Herman the Monk, *Hermanni Monachi De Miraculis S. Mariae Laudunensis*, in Migne, *PL* 156, cols. 962–1018.

Higden, Ranulph, *Polychronicon Ranulphi Higden, Monachi Cestrensis*, ed. C. Babington and J. R. Lumby, 9 vols. (Rolls Series 41, London, 1865–86).

History of Gruffydd ap Cynan, ed. A. Jones (Manchester, 1910).

Hogan, Edmund, *Onomasticon Goedelicum* (Dublin, 1910).

Hood, A. B. E., *St. Patrick, His Writings and Muirchu's Life* (Leicester, 1978).

Howlett, R., *Chronicles of the Reigns of Stephen, Henry II and Richard I*, 4 vols. (Rolls Series 82, London, 1884–90).

Hrafns Saga Sveinbjarnarsonar, ed. Guðrún P. Helgadóttir (Oxford, 1987).

Hudson, B., *Prophecy of Berchán: Irish and Scottish Highkings of the Early Middle Ages* (Westport, 1996).

———— "Scottish Chronicle," *SHR* 77 (1998), 129–61.

Hugh of Fleury, *Hugonis Floriacensis Opera Historica*, ed. D. G. Waitz (*MGH, SS* 9), 337–406.

Instituta regalia et ministeria camerae regum Longobardorum et honoratiae civitatis Papiae, ed. A. Hofmeister (*MGH, SS* 30), 1444–60.

Íslendingabók/ Landnámabók, ed. J. Benediktsson (Íslenzk Fornrit 1, Reykjavík, 1968).

John of Fordun, *Johannis de Fordun Chronica gentis Scotorum*, ed. W. F. Skene (Historians of Scotland 1, Edinburgh, 1871).

John of Wallingford, *The Chronicle Attributed to John of Wallingford*, ed. R. Vaughan, in *Camden Miscellany* 21 (Camden Society third series 90, London, 1958).

John of Worcester, *The Chronicle of John of Worcester*, ed. R. R. Darlington, P. McGurk, and Jennifer Bray, 3 vols. (Oxford, 1995–).

Johnsen, O. A., and J. Helgason, eds., *Saga Óláfs Konungs hins Helga, Den store Saga om Olav den Hellige*, 2 vols. (Oslo, 1941).

Jónsson, Finnur, ed., *Den Norsk-Islandske Skjaldedigtning*, 2 vols. (Copenhagen, 1912).

Keating, Geoffrey (Céitinn, Séathrúin), *Foras feasa ar Éirinn: The History of Ireland*, ed. David Comyn and Patrick S. Dineen, 4 vols. (Irish Texts Society 4, 8, 9 and 15, Dublin, 1902–14).

Kemble, J. M., *Codex Diplomaticus Aevi Saxonici*, 6 vols. (London, 1839–48).

Keynes, Simon, "Will of Wulf," *Old English Newsletter* 26 (1993), 16–21.

Keynes, Simon, and Michael Lapidge, trans., *Alfred the Great* (London, 1983).

Kluge, F., "Fragment eines angelsächsischen Briefes," *Englische Studien* 8 (1885), 62–63.

Kock, Ernst A., ed., *Den Norsk-Isländska Skaldediktningen*, 2 vols. (Lund, 1946–49).

Lanfranc of Bec, *The Letters of Lanfranc, Archbishop of Canterbury*, ed. Helen Clover and Margaret Gibson (Oxford, 1978).

Larson, Laurence M., *The Earliest Norwegian Laws being the Gulathinglaw and the Frostathinglaw* (New York, 1935).

Laxdœla Saga, ed. Einar Ól. Sveinsson (Íslenzk Fornrit 5, Reykjavík, 1934).

Lebor na Cert: The Book of Rights, ed. Myles Dillon (Irish Texts Society 46, Dublin, 1962).

Lebor na Huidre: The Book of the Dun Cow, ed. R. I. Best and Osborn Bergin (Dublin, 1929).

Liber Eliensis, ed. E. O. Blake (Camden Society third series 92, London, 1962).

Liebermann, F., *Die Gesetze der Angelsachsen, herausgegeben im Auftrage der Savigny-Stiftung*, 3 vols. (Halle, 1898–1916).

Life of King Edward Who Rests at Westminster; Vitae Ædwardi Regis, ed. F. Barlow (London, 1962).

Lopez, Robert S., and Irving W. Raymond, eds., *Medieval Trade in the Mediterranean World* (New York, 1955).

Lucian of Chester, *Liber Luciani de laude Cestrie*, ed. M. V. Taylor (Lancaster and Cheshire Record Society 64, Manchester, 1912).

MacCarthy, Brian, *The Codex Palatino-Vaticanus no. 830* (Royal Irish Academy Todd Lecture Series 3, Dublin, 1892).

Mac Firbis, Duald, *On the Formorians and the Norsemen*, ed. A. Bugge (Christiania, 1905).

MacNeill, John [Mac Neill, Eoin], "Poems by Flann Mainistrech on the Dynasties of Ailech, Mide and Brega," *Archivum Hibernicum* 2 (1913), 37–99.

Mac Niocaill, G., "Annála Gearra as Proibhinse Ard Macha," *Seanchas Ardmacha* 3 (1959), 337–40.

———— ed., *Notitiae as Leabhar Cheanannais 1033–1161* (Dublin, 1961).

Map, Walter, *Walter Map's Book De Nugis Curialium*, trans. Frederick Tupper and Marbury Bladen Ogle (New York, 1924).

Marianus Scotus, *Mariani Scotti Chronicon*, ed. G. Waitz (*MGH, SS* 5), 481–564.

Metrical Dindshenchas, ed. E. Gwynn (Royal Irish Academy Todd Lecture Series 8–12, 1903–35).

Meyer, K. M., "Das Ende von Baile in Scáil," *ZCP* 12 (1918), 232–38.

———— "March Roll of the Men of Leinster," *Ériu* 6 (1912), 121–24.

———— "National Characteristics," *ZCP* 1 (1897), 112–13.

———— *Rawlinson B. 502: A collection of pieces in prose and verse in the Irish Language compiled during the eleventh and twelfth centuries; now published in facsimile from the original manuscript in the Bodleian Library* (Oxford, 1909).

———— "Scél Baili Binnbérlaig," *Revue Celtique* 13 (1892), 221.

———— ed., *The Triads of Ireland* (Royal Irish Academy Todd Lecture Series 13, Dublin, 1906).

———— *The Voyage of Bran Son of Febal to the Land of the Living* (London, 1895).

Migne, J. P., ed., *Patrologiae cursus completus, Patres . . . ecclesiae latinae*, 217 vols. (Paris, 1844–64).

Morkinskinna, the Earliest Icelandic Chronicle of the Norwegian Kings (1030–1157), trans. Theodore M. Andersson and Kari Ellen Gade (Islandica 51, Ithaca, N.Y., 2000).

O'Brien, M., ed., *Corpus Genealogiarum Hiberniae* (Dublin, 1962).

Ó Cuív, B., "A Poem in Praise of Raghnall, King of Man," *Éigse* 8 (1955–57), 283–301.

O'Curry, Eugene, *Lectures on the Manuscript Materials of Ancient Irish History* (reprinted Dublin, 1873).

O'Donoghue, T., "Cert Cech Ríg co Réil," in Bergin and Marstrander, eds., *Miscellany Presented to Kuno Meyer*, 258–77.

O'Donovan, J., *The Circuit of Ireland by Muirchertach Mac Neill*, in *Tracts Relating to Ireland Printed for the Irish Archaeological Society* (Dublin, 1841), 1–68.

O'Kearney, S., *The Prophecies of Saints Colum-Cille, Maeltamlacht, Ultan, Senan, Bearchan and Malachy* (Dublin, rpr. 1925).

Oengus the Céli Dé, *Félire Óengusso Céli Dé: Martyrology of Oengus the Culdee*, ed. W. Stokes (London, 1905).

Orderic Vitalis, *The Ecclesiastical History of Orderic Vitalis*, ed. M. Chibnall, 6 vols. (Oxford, 1968–80).

Orkneyinga Saga, ed. F. Guðmundsson (Íslenzk Fornrit 34, Reykjavík, 1965).

Paris, Matthew, *Chronica majora (from the Creation to 1259)*, ed. H. Luard, 7 vols. (Rolls Series 57, London, 1872–84).

Paton, Lucy Allen, ed., *Les Prophecies de Merlin*, 2 vols. (New York, 1926).

Patrick, bishop of Dublin, *Writings of Bishop Patrick, 1074–1084*, ed. A. Gwynn (*Scriptores Latini Hiberniae*, vol. 1, Dublin, 1955).

Plummer, Charles, ed., *Bethada Náem nÉrenn*, 2 vols. (Oxford, 1922).

———— ed., *Vitae Sanctorum Hiberniae*, 2 vols. (Oxford, 1910).

Powel, David, *The History of Cambria, now Called Wales, a Part of the Most Famous Yland of Brytaine . . ., trans. H. Lhoyd . . . and corrected, augmented, and continued . . . by David Powel*, ed. W. Wynne (London, 1697).

Raine, James, ed., *Historians of the Church of York*, 3 vols. (Rolls Series 71, London, 1879–94).

Reginald of Durham, *Reginaldi Monachi Dunelmensis Libellus de Admirandis Beati Cuthberti*, ed. James Raine (Surtees Soc 1, London, 1835).

Register of the Hospital of St. John the Baptist without the New Gate, Dublin, ed. Eric St. John Brooks (Dublin, 1936).

Register of the Priory of St. Bees, ed. James Wilson (Surtees Society 126, London, 1915).

Reports of the Deputy Keeper of the Public Records and of the Keeper of the State Papers in Ireland (Dublin, 1869–).

Richer of Reims, *Historiae*, ed. Hartmut Hoffmann (*MGH, SS* 38, 2000).

Richter, Michael, ed., *Canterbury Professions* (Canterbury and York Society 140, Torquay, 1973).

Roger of Hoveden, *Chronica Rogeri de Houedene*, ed. W. Stubbs, 4 vols. (Rolls Series 51, London, 1868–71).

Roger of Wendover, *Flores Historiarum*, ed. H. O. Coxe, 4 vols. (English History Society, London, 1841–44).

Round, J. H., *Calendar of Documents Preserved in France Illustrative of the History of Great Britain and Ireland*, vol. 1 (Public Record Office, London, 1899).

Saltair na Rann, ed. W. Stokes (*Anecdota Oxoniensia*, vol. 1, part iii, Oxford, 1883).

Smith, Peter J., "*Mide maigen Clainne Cuind*: A Medieval Poem on the Kings of Mide," *Peritia* 15 (2001), 108–44.

Solinus, Caius Julius, *C. Iulii Solini Collectanea Rerum Memorabilium*, ed. Theodor Mommsen (Berlin, 1895).

Song of Dermot and the Earl, ed. Goddard Henry Orpen (Oxford, 1892).

Spenser, Edmund, *A View of the Present State of Ireland*, ed. W. L. Renwick (Oxford, 1970).

Stokes, Whitley, "Adomnan's Second Vision," *Revue Celtique* 12 (1891), 420–43.

———— ed., *Félire Óengusso Céli Dé, Martyrology of Oengus the Culdee* (London, 1905).

———— "The Prose Tales in the Rennes Dindsenchas," *Revue Celtique* 15 (1894), 272–484 and 16 (1895), 31–167.

———— ed., *Three Irish Glossaries* (London, 1862).

———— *The Tripartite Life of Patrick with Other Documents Relating to that Saint*, 2 vols. (Rolls Series 89, London, 1888).

———— and John Strachan, eds., *Thesaurus Palaeohibernicus* (Dublin, repr. 1975).

Storm, Gustav, ed., *Monumenta Historica Norvegiae* (Kristiania, 1880)

Stubbs, William, ed., *Memorials of St. Dunstan* (Rolls Series 63, London, 1874).

Sturluson, Snorri, *Heimskringla*, ed. B. Aðalbjarnarson, 3 vols. (Íslenzk Fornrit 26–28, Reykjavík, 1941–51).

Swanton, Michael, *Three Lives of the Last Englishmen* (New York, 1984).

Sweetman, H. S., ed., *Calendar of Documents Relating to Ireland Preserved in Her Majesty's Public Record Office, London [1171–1307]*, 5 vols. (Public Record Office 1875–86, London, repr. 1974).

Symeon of Durham, *Symeonis monachi Opera omnia*, ed. Thomas Arnold (Rolls Series 75, London, 1882–85).

Thietmar, *Thietmari Merseburgensis Episcopi Chronicon*, ed. R. Holtzmann and Werner Trillmich (Berlin, 1957).

Ussher, James, *Veterum Epistolarum Hibericarum Sylloge*, in *The Whole Works of the Most Rev. James Ussher*, ed. C. R. Elrington and J. H. Todd (Dublin, 1847–64).

Vita Wulfstani of William of Malmesbury, ed. R. R. Darlington (Camden Society 40, London, 1928).

Wade-Evans, A. W., ed., *Vitae sanctorum Britanniae et genealogiae* (Cardiff, 1944).

Walsh, Paul, "A Poem on Ireland," *Ériu* 8 (1916), 64–74.

Ware, James, ed., *Ancient Irish Histories: The Works of Spencer, Campion, Hanmer and Marleburrough* (Dublin, 1633, repr. 1809).

——— *De Hibernia et antiquitatibus ejus disquisitiones* (London, 1654).

——— *De Praesulibus Hiberniae Commentarius* (Dublin, 1665).

Warner of Rouen, *Moriuht*, ed. Christopher J. McDonough (Toronto, 1995).

Whitelock, Dorothy, ed., *English Historical Documents, vol. 1, c. 500–1042* (London, 1955).

William of Jumièges, *Gesta Normannorum Ducum of William of Jumième, Orderic Vitalis and Robert of Torigni*, ed. Elisabeth M.C. van Houts, 2 vols. (Oxford, 1992–95).

William of Malmesbury, *Willelmi Malmesbiriensis De Gestis Pontificum Anglorum Libri Quinque*, ed. N. E. S. A. Hamilton (Rolls Series 52, London, 1870).

——— *Willemus monachi Malmesbirensis De Gestis Regum Anglorum in libris quinque*, ed. W. Stubbs (Rolls Series 52, London, 1887–89).

Willibrord, *De Sancto Willibrordo Episcopo Traiectensi et Fresonum Apostolo, Acta Sanctorum* (Nov. 7), 414–500.

Secondary Works

Abrams, Lesley, "The Anglo-Saxons and the Christianization of Scandinavia," *Anglo-Saxon England* 24 (1994), 213–49.

Abu-Lughod, Janet L., *Before European Hegemony: The World System A.D. 1250–1350* (Oxford, 1989).

Adigard des Gautries, Jean, *Les Noms de personnes Scandinaves en Normandie de 911 à 1066* (Lund, 1954).

Albrectsen, Erling, "Danmark og Normandiet," *Skalk* 8 (1986), 22–30.

Allen, D. E., "Plant Distribution Patterns as Potential Historical Indicators," in Peter Davey, ed., *Man and Environment in the Isle of Man* (British Archaeological Reports, British Series 54, Oxford, 1978).

Allen, Ivor, ed., *Le Roman de Brut*, 2 vols. (Paris, 1937–40).

Almquist, B., and D. Greene, eds., *Proceedings of the Seventh Viking Congress-Dublin 1973* (Dublin, 1976).

Ambrosiani, Björn, "Settlement Expansion-Settlement Contraction: A Question of War, Plague, Ecology or Climate?" in Mörner and Karlén, *Climatic Changes on a Yearly to Millenial Basis*, 241–47.

Andersen, Per Sveaas, "Den norske Innvandringen til Hebridene i vikingtiden og den norrøne bosetningens senere skjebne," *Historisk Tidsskrift (Norsk)*, 73 (1994), 265–85.

——— "To What Extent Did the *balley/balla (baile)* Names in the Isle of Man Supplant Place-Names of Norse Origins?" in Fell et al., eds., *Viking Age in the Isle of Man*, 147–68.

——— "When was Regular, Annual Taxation Introduced into the Norse Islands of Britain? A Comparative Study of Assessment Systems in North-western Europe." *Scandinavian Journal of History* 16 (1991), 73–83.

Anderson, A. O., "Anglo-Scottish Relations from Constantine II to William," *SHR* 42 (1963), 1–21.

Anderson, M. O., "Lothian and the Early Scottish Kings," *SHR* 39 (1960), 98–112.

Armit, Ian, *The Archaeology of Skye and the Western Isles* (Edinburgh, 1996).

Attenborough, Frederick L., *The Laws of the Earliest English Kings* (Cambridge, 1922).

Bachrach, Bernard, "Toward a Reappraisal of William the Great, Duke of Aquitaine," *Journal of Medieval History* 5 (1979), 11–21.

Barlow, Frank, *William Rufus* (London, 1982).

Barnes, Michael, "Towards an Edition of the Scandinavian Runic Inscriptions of the British Isles: Some Thoughts," *Northern Studies* 29 (1992), 32–42.

Bates, David, *Normandy before 1066* (London, 1982).

Batey, Colleen, Judith Jesch, and Christopher Morris, eds., *The Viking Age in Caithness, Orkney and the North Atlantic* (Edinburgh, 1991).

Baylé, Maylis, "Reminiscences Anglo-Scandinaves dans la sculpture romaine de Normandie," *Anglo-Norman Studies* 13 (1990), 35–48.

Bekker-Nielsen, Hans, Peter Foote, and Olaf Olsen, eds., *Proceedings of the Eighth Viking Congress-Århus* (Odense 1981).

Bergin, Osborn, and Carl Marstrander, eds., *Miscellaney Presented to Kuno Meyer* (Halle, 1912).

Berglund, B. E., ed., *Cultural Landscape during 6000 years in Southern Sweden* (Lund Ecological Bulletin 41, Lund, 1991).

Bessinger, Jess B., and Robert P. Creed, *Franciplegius: Medieval and Linguistic Studies in Honor of Francis Peabody Magoun, Jr.* (New York, 1965).

Bethell, Denis, "English Monks and Irish Reform in the Eleventh and Twelfth Centuries," *Historical Studies VIII*, ed. T. Moody (Dublin, 1972), 111–35.

Binns, Alan, "The Ships of the Vikings, Were They 'Viking Ships'?" in Bekker-Nielsen et al., *Proceedings of the Eighth Viking Congress*, 287–94.

Blackburn, M. A. S., ed., *Anglo-Saxon Monetary History. Essays in Memory of Michael Dolley* (Leicester, 1986).

——— "Hiberno-Norse Imitations of Watchet *Long Cross* Coins," *Numismatic Chronicle*, seventh series 15 (1975), 195–97.

——— and Lyon, S., "Regional Die Production in Cnut's *Quartrefoil* Issue," in Blackburn, ed., *Anglo-Saxon Monetary History*, 223–72

Blair, Peter Hunter, "Olaf the White and the Three Fragments of Irish Annals," *Viking* 3 (1939), 1–35.

Blindheim, Charlotte, "Internal Trade in Viking Age Norway," in Düwel et al, eds., *Unterschungen zu Handel und Verkehr der vor- und frühgeschichtlichen Zeit im Mittel- und Nord Europa*, vol. 4, 758–72.

Bowen, E. G., "Britain and the British Seas," in Moore, ed., *The Irish Sea Province in Archaeology and History*, 13–27.

——— *Britain and the Western Seaways* (London, 1972).

——— "The Cult of St. Brigit," *Studia Celtica* 8/9 (1973/74), 33–47.

——— "The Irish Sea in the Age of Saints," *Studia Celtica*, 4 (1969), 56–71.

—— *Saints, Seaways and Settlement in the Celtic Lands* (London, 1969).

Bradley, John, "The Interpretation of Scandinavian Settlement in Ireland," in Bradley, ed., *Settlement and Society in Medieval Ireland*, 49–78.

—— ed., *Settlement and Society in Medieval Ireland: Studies Presented to F. X. Martin o.s.a.* (Kilkenny, 1988).

Brady, Niall, "Labor and Agriculture in Early Medieval Ireland: Evidence from the Sources," in Allen J. Frantzen and Douglas Moffat, *The Work of Work: Servitude, Slavery, and Labor in Medieval England* (Glasgow, 1994), 125–45.

Brett, Caroline, "Breton Pilgrims in England," in Gillian Jondorf and D. N. Dumville, eds., *France and the British Isles in Middle Ages and Renaissance* (Woodbridge, 1991), 43–70.

Briggs, C. S., "A Boat Burial from County Antrim," *Medieval Archaeology* 18 (1974), 158–60.

Broderick, George, "Irish and Welsh Strands in the Genealogy of Godred Crovan," *Journal of the Manx Museum* 89 (1980), 32–38.

Brooke, Daphne, "Gall-Gaidhil and Galloway," in Oram, ed., *Galloway: Land and Lordship*, 97–116.

—— *Wild Men and Holy Places* (Edinburgh, 1994).

Brown, Marilyn, "The Norse in Argyll," in Ritchie, ed., *Archaeology of Argyll*, 205–35.

Bugge, Alexander, "Bidrag til det sidste Afsnit af Nordboernes Historie i Irland," *Aarbøger* (1904), 248–315.

—— "Havelok og Olav Trygvesson," *Aarbøger*, second series 23 (1908), 233–74.

—— "Nordisk Sprog og nordisk Nationalitet i Irland," *Aarbørger*, second series 15 (1900), 279–332.

—— "Sandhed og digt om Olav Trygvessøn," *Aarbøger*, second series 25 (1910), 1–34.

Bugge, Sophus, "Norsk Sagaskrivning og Sagafortælling i Irland," *Historisk Tidsskrift* (1901–8), 1–236.

Byock, Jesse, *Medieval Iceland: Society, Sagas and Power* (Berkeley, 1988).

Byrne, F. J., *Irish Kings and High-Kings* (London, 1973).

—— "Na Renna," *Peritia* 1 (1982), 267.

Cambridge Economic History, ed. M. M. Postan et al., 8 vols. (Cambridge, 1966–89).

Campbell, Alistair, *Battle of Brunnanburh* (London, 1938).

—— "Saxo Grammaticus and Scandinavian Historical Tradition," *Saga Book* 13 (1946–53), 1–22.

—— *Skaldic Verse and Anglo-Saxon History* (London, 1971).

—— "Two Notes on the Norse Kingdoms in Northumbria," *EHR* 57 (1942), 85–97.

Campbell, James, "Observations on English Government from the Tenth to Twelfth Century," *TRHS*, fifth series 25 (1976), 39–54.

Campbell, Miles, "The Anti-Norman Reaction in England in 1052: Suggested Origins," *Medieval Studies* 38 (1976), 428–41.

—— "Earl Godwin of Wessex and Edward the Confessor's Promise of the Throne to William of Normandy," *Traditio* 28 (1972), 141–50.

—— "A Pre-Conquest Norman Occupation of England?" *Speculum* 46 (1971), 21–31.

Carlyle, E. I., "The Political History of Herefordshire," *VCH: Hereford*, 1: 347–406.

Chadwick, Nora, "Literary Tradition in the Old Norse and Celtic World," *Saga Book* 14 (1953–57), 164–99.

———— "The Vikings and the Western World," in Ó Cuív, ed., *Impact of the Scandinavian Invasions on the Celtic-Speaking Peoples*, 13–42.

Chaplais, Pierre, "Authenticity of the Royal Anglo-Saxon Diplomas at Exeter," *Bulletin of the Institute for Historical Research* 39 (1966), 1–34.

Charles, B. G., *Old Norse Relations with Wales* (Cardiff, 1934).

Charles-Edwards, T. M. O., *Early Irish and Welsh Kinship* (Oxford, 1993).

Cheney, C. R., "Manx Synodal Statutes, A.D. 1230(?)–1351," *Cambridge Medieval Celtic Studies* 7 (1984), 63–89, and 8 (1984), 51–63.

Chesnutt, Michael, "Norse-Celtic Bibliographical Survey," in *Mediaeval Scandinavia*: 1 (1968), 135–37; 3 (1970), 109–37; 4 (1971), 119–59; 5 (1972), 92–95.

———— "An Unsolved Problem in Old Norse-Icelandic Literary History," *Mediaeval Scandinavia* 1 (1968), 122–37.

Chibnall, Marjorie, *Anglo-Norman England* (London, 1987).

Christensen, Jr., Arne Emil, *Boats of the North* (Oslo, 1968).

Christiansen, Reidar Th., "The People of the North," *Norsk Tidsskrift for Sprogvidenskap*, suppl.: *Lochlann, a Review of Celtic Studies*, 2 (1962), 137–64.

———— *The Vikings and the Viking Wars in Irish and Gaelic Tradition* (Oslo, 1931).

Clarke, H., *Dublin c. 840 – c. 1540, the Medieval Town in the Modern City* (Ordnance Survey, Dublin, 1978).

Clarke, Howard, "The Topographical Development of Early Medieval Dublin," *JRSAI* 107 (1977), 29–51.

———— and Anngret Simms, eds., *The Comparative History of Urban Origins in Non-Roman Europe* (British Archaeological Reports, International Series 255, Oxford, 1985).

Cope, G. R., "Report on the *coleoptera* from an Eleventh Century House at Christ Church Place, Dublin," in Bekker-Nielsen et al., eds., *Proceedings of the Eighth Viking Conference*, 51–56.

Cragie, W. A., "Gaelic Words and Names in the Icelandic Sagas," *ZCP* 1 (1897), 439–54.

Crawford, Barbara, "Bishops of Orkney in the Eleventh and Twelfth Centuries: Bibliography and Biographical List," *Innes Review* 47 (1996), 1–13.

———— *Earl and Mormaer: Norse-Pictish Relationships in Northern Scotland* (Rosemarkie, 1995).

———— *Scandinavian Scotland* (Leicester, 1987).

———— ed., *Scandinavian Settlement in Northern Britain* (Leicester, 1995).

Crawford, O. G. S., "The Distribution of Early Bronze Age Settlements in Britain," *Geographical Journal* 40 (1912).

Crumlin-Pedersen, Ole, *The Skuldelev Ships I: Topography, Archaeology, History, Conservation, and Display* (Roskilde, 2002).

———— "Viking Shipbuilding and Seamanship," in Bekker-Nielsen et al., *Proceedings of the Eighth Viking Congress*, 271–85.

Cubbon, Marshall, "Archaeology of the Vikings in the Isle of Man," in Fell et al., *Proceedings of the Ninth Viking Congress*, 13–26.

Curtis, E., "The Fitz Rerys, Welsh Lords of Cloghran, Co. Dublin," *County Louth Archaeological Journal* 5 (1921), 13–17.

———— "Murchertach O'Brien, High King of Ireland, and his Norman Son-in-Law Arnulf de Montgomery," *JRSAI* 51 (1921), 116–24.

Davey, Peter, ed., *Man and the Environment in the Isle of Man* (British Archaeological Reports, British Series 54, Oxford, 1978).

Davies, R. R., *The Age of Conquest: Wales 1063–1415* (Oxford, 2000).

——— *Domination and Conquest* (Cambridge, 1990).

Davies, Wendy, *An Early Welsh Microcosm: Studies in the Llandaff Charters* (London, 1978).

——— *Patterns of Power in Early Wales* (Oxford, 1990).

——— *Wales in the Early Middle Ages* (Leicester, 1982).

De Varebeke, Hubert Janssens, "Benedictine Bishops in Medieval Ireland," in E. Rynne, ed., *North Munster Studies*, 242–50.

De Vries, Jan, *Altnordische Literaturgeschichte*, 2 vols. (Berlin, 1964–67).

——— "Les Rapports des poésies Scaldique et Gaëlique," *Ogam* 9 (1957), 13–26.

Dickins, Bruce, "The Cult of St. Olave in the British Isles," *Sagabook of the Viking Society* 12 (1937–38), 53–80.

Doherty, Charles, "Exchange and Trade in Early Medieval Ireland," *JRSAI* 110 (1980), 67–89.

——— "The Monastic Town in Early Medieval Ireland," in Clarke and Simms, eds., *Comparative History of Urban Origins in non-Roman Europe*, 45–75.

Dolley, Michael, ed., *Anglo-Saxon Coins: Studies Presented to F .M. Stenton on the Occasion of His 80th Birthday* (London, 1961).

——— "The Continental Coins in the Halton Moor Find and Other Norman Deniers Found in the British Isles," *Hamburger Beiträge zur Numismatik* 4 (1958/9), 53–57.

——— "A Hiberno-Manx Coinage of the Eleventh Century," *Numismatic Chronicle*, seventh series 16 (1976), 75–84.

——— "Introduction to the Coinage of Æthelraed II," in David Hill, ed., *Ethelred the Unready: Papers from the Millenary Conference* (British Archaeological Reports: British Series 59, 1978), 115–33.

——— "The Palimpsest of Viking Settlement on Man," in Bekker-Nielsen et al., *Proceedings of the Eighth Viking Congress*, 173–81.

——— "Some Insular(?) Imitations for the 1030s of Contemporary English Pence of Cnut," *Spink and Son's Numismatic Circular* 88 (1980), 86–88.

——— *Some Irish Dimensions to Manx History* (Belfast, 1975).

——— "Some Preliminary Observations on Three Manx Coin-Hoards Appearing to End with Pennies of Edgar," *Spink and Son's Numismatic Circular* 88 (1975), 146–47 and 190–92.

——— *Sylloge of Coins in the British Museum*, vol. 8, *The Hiberno-Norse Coins in the British Museum* (London, 1966).

Dolley, Michael, and J. Ingold, "Viking Age Coin-Hoards from Ireland and their Relevance to Anglo-Saxon Studies," in Dolley, ed., *Anglo-Saxon Coins*, 241–65.

Dolley, Michael, and D. M. Metcalfe, "Reform of the English Coinage under Edgar," in Dolley, ed., *Anglo-Saxon Coins*, 136–68.

Dolley, Michael, and Jacques Yvon, "A Group of Tenth-Century Coins Found at Mont-Saint-Michel," *British Numismatic Journal* 40 (1971), 1–16.

Douglas, D. C., "The Companions of the Conqueror," *History*, new series 28 (1943), 129–47.

Duffy, Seán, "Irishman and Islesman in the Kingdoms of Dublin and Man, 1052–1171," *Ériu* 43 (1992), 93–133.

——— "Ostmen, Irish and Welsh in the Eleventh Century," *Peritia* 9 (1995), 378–96.

Douglas, David, "Rollo of Normandy," *EHR* 57 (1942), 417–36.

Downham, Clare, "Chronology of the Last Scandinavian Kings of York, AD 937–954," *Northern History* 40 (2003), 25–51.

Dumas, Françoise, "Les Monnaies normandes (Xe–XIIe siècles) avec un répertoire des trouvailles," *Revue Numismatique* (1979), 84–140.

Duncan, A. A. M., "Battle of Carham," *SHR* 55 (1976), 20–28.

——— *Scotland, the Making of the Kingdom* (Edinburgh, 1975).

Dunlop, D. M., "The British Isles According to Medieval Arabic Authors," *Islamic Quarterly* 4 (1957), 11–28.

Dunn, Charles W., "Havelok and Anlaf Cuaran," in Bessinger and Creed, eds., *Franciplegius*, 244–49.

Düwel, Klaus, Herbert Jankuhn, Harald Siems, and Dieter Timpe, ed., *Unterschungen zu Handel und Verkehr der vor- und frühgeschichtlichen Zeit im Mittel- und Nord Europa*, vol. 4 (Göttingen, 1987).

Edwards, Nancy, *The Archaeology of Early Medieval Ireland* (Philadelphia, 1990).

Etchingham, Colmán, "North Wales, Ireland and the Isles: The Insular Viking Zone," *Peritia* 15 (2001), 145–87.

Ewart, Gordon, *Cruggleton Castle, Report of Excavations 1978–1981* (Dumfries, 1985).

Fanning, Thomas, "Hiberno-Norse Pins in Man," in Fell et al., eds., *Viking Age in the Isle of Man*, 27–336.

Farrell, R. T., ed., *The Vikings* (Chichester, 1982).

Faulkes, Anthony, and Richard Perkins, eds., *Viking Revaluations* (London, 1993).

Fell, Christine, "Anglo-Saxon Saints in Old Norse Sources and Vice-versa," in Bekker-Nielsen et al., eds., *Proceedings of the Eighth Viking Conference*, 85–106.

——— Peter Foote, James Graham-Campbell, and Robert Thomson, *The Viking Age in the Isle of Man: Select Papers from the Ninth Viking Congress, Isle of Man, 4–14 July 1981* (London, 1983).

Fellows-Jensen, Gillian, "Scandinavian Place-Names of the Irish Sea Province," in Graham-Campbell, ed., *Viking Treasure from the North West*, 31–42.

Fidjestøl, Bjarne, "The Contribution of Scaldic Studies," in Faulkes and Perkins, eds., *Viking Revaluations*, 100–20.

Flanagan, M. T., *Irish Society, Anglo-Norman Settlers and Angevin Kingship* (Oxford, 1989).

Foote, P. G., and D. M. Wilson, *The Viking Achievement* (London, 1970).

Fox, Sir Cyril, *The Personality of Britain* (Cambridge, 1936).

Frank, Roberta, "King Cnut in the Verse of his Skalds," in A. Rumble, ed., *The Reign of Cnut: King of England, Denmark and Norway* (Leicester, 1994), 106–24.

——— *Old Norse Court Poetry: The Dróttkvætt Stanza* (Islandica 42, Ithaca, N.Y., 1978).

——— "Viking Atrocity and Skaldic Verse: the Rite of the Blood Eagle," *EHR* 99 (1984), 332–43.

Freeman, E. A., *The Norman Conquest*, 6 vols. (London, 1867–79).

Garmonsway, G. N., *Canute and His Empire* (London, 1964).

Gathorne-Hardy, G. M., *A Royal Impostor, King Sverre of Norway* (Oslo, 1956).

Geraghty, Siobhán, *Viking Dublin: Botanical Evidence from Fishamble Street* (Dublin, 1996).

Gibson, Margaret, *Lanfranc of Bec* (Oxford, 1979).

Gillingham, John, "Chronicles and Coins as Evidence for Levels of Taxation in the Late Tenth- and Early Eleventh-Century England," *EHR* 105 (1990), 939–50.

——— "'The most precious jewel in the English crown': Levels of Danegeld and Heregeld in the Early Eleventh Century," *EHR* 104 (1989), 373–84.

Goedheer, A. J., *Irish and Norse Traditions about the Battle of Clontarf* (Haarlem, 1938).

Graham-Campbell, James, "From Scandinavia to the Irish Sea: Viking Art Reviewed," in Ryan, ed., *Ireland and Insular Art, A.D. 500–1200*, 144–52.

——— "Viking Age Silver Hoards: An Introduction," in Farrell, ed., *The Vikings*, 32–41.

——— "Viking Age Silver Hoards of the Isle of Man," in Fell et al., eds., *Viking Age in the Isle of Man*, 53–79.

——— "Viking Age Silver Hoards of Ireland," in Almquist and Greene, eds., *Proceedings of the Seventh Viking Congress*, 39–74.

——— ed., *Viking Treasure from the North West: The Cuerdale Hoard in Its Context* (Liverpool, 1992).

——— and Colleen E. Batey, *Vikings in Scotland* (Edinburgh, 1998).

Gransden, Antonia, *Historical Writing in England, c. 550 – c. 1307* (Ithaca, N.Y., 1974).

Graves, E., *A Bibliography of English History to 1485* (Oxford, 1975).

Greene, David, "The Influence of Scandinavian on Irish," in Almquist and Greene, eds., *Proceedings of the Seventh Viking Congress*, 75–82.

Gregory, Donald, *History of the Western Highlands and Isles of Scotland*, 2nd edn. (Glasgow, 1881).

Grierson, Philip, "The Relations between England and Flanders before the Norman Conquest," *TRHS*, fourth series 23 (1941), 71–113.

Griffiths, D., "The Coastal Trading Ports of the Irish Sea," in Graham-Campbell, ed., *Viking Treasure from the North West*, 63–72.

Guðmundsson, F., "On the Writing of *Orkneyinga Saga*," in Batey et al., eds., *Viking Age in Caithness, Orkney and the North Atlantic*, 204–11.

Gwynn, A., "Ireland and the Continent in the Eleventh Century," *Irish Historical Studies* 8 (1952–1953), 193–216.

——— "Mediaeval Bristol and Dublin," *Irish Historical Studies* 5 (1946/7), 275–86.

——— "Origins of the See of Dublin," *Irish Ecclesiastical Review* 57 (1941), 40–55 and 97–112.

Hadley, D. M., *The Northern Danelaw: Its Social Structure, c. 800–1100* (Leicester, 2000).

Hall, Richard, "A Checklist of Viking-Age Coin Finds from Ireland," *Ulster Journal of Archaeology* 36/37 (1973/74), 71–86.

Harris, B. C.,"Political History," *VCH: Cheshire*, 2: 1–8.

Harrison, Dick, "Offensiva och defensive eliter-om det politiska overskikter under medeltiden," *Historisk Tidskrift* (1997), 555–89.

Hastrup, Kirsten, *Culture and History in Medieval Iceland* (Oxford, 1985).

Haworth, Richard, "The Site of St. Olave's Church, Dublin," in Bradley, ed., *Settlement and Society in Medieval Ireland*, 177–91.

Heighway, Carolyn, "Anglo-Saxon Gloucester," in *VCH: Gloucester*, 4: 5–12.

Henry, Françoise, "The Effects of the Viking Invasions on Irish Art," in Ó Cuív, ed., *Impact of the Scandinavian Invasions on the Celtic-Speaking Peoples*, 61–72.

Hewitt, H. J., *Medieval Chester: An Economic and Social History of Cheshire in the Reign of the Three Edwards* (Chetham Society 88, Manchester, 1929).

Higham, N. J.,"Northumbria, Mercia and the Irish Sea Norse, 893–926," in Graham-Campbell, ed., *Viking Treasure from the North West*, 21–30.

Hill, Peter, "Whithorn: The Missing Years," in Oram and Stell, *Galloway: Land and Lordship*, 27–44.

———— *Whithorn and St. Ninian: The Excavation of a Monastic Town, 1984–1991* (Stroud, 1997).

Hill, Thomas, "Rígsþula," in Pulsiano, *Medieval Scandinavia*, 535–36.

Hodges, Richard, *Dark Age Economics: The Origins of Towns and Trade A.D. 600–1000* (London, 1982).

Holland, Martin, "Dublin and the Reform of the Irish Church: Eleventh and Twelfth Centuries," *Peritia* 14 (2000), 111–60.

Holm, Poul, "Between Apathy and Antipathy: The Vikings in Irish and Scandinavian History," *Peritia* 8 (1994), 151–69.

———— "Slave Trade of Dublin, Ninth to Twelfth Centuries," *Peritia* 5 (1986), 317–45.

Holtsmark, Anne, "Historieskrivning: Norge," *Kulturhistorisk Leksikon for nordisk middelalder*, 22 vols (Copenhagen 1956–78), vi, 595–97.

———— "Vefr Darraðar," *Maal og Minne* (1939), 74–96.

Hudson, B., "Brjáns Saga," *Medium Ævum* 71 (2002), 241–68.

———— "Changing Economy of the Irish Sea Province," in Smith, ed., *Britain and Ireland 900–1300*, 39–66.

———— "Cnut and the Scottish Kings," *EHR* 107 (1992), 350–60.

———— "Destruction of Gruffudd ap Llywelyn," *Welsh History Review* 15 (1991), 331–50.

———— "Family of Harold Godwinsson and the Irish Sea Province," *JRSAI* 109 (1979), 92–100.

———— "Kings and Church in Early Scotland," *SHR* 73 (1994), 145–70.

———— *Kings of Celtic Scotland* (Westport, 1994).

———— "Knútr and Viking Dublin," *Scandinavian Studies* 66 (1994), 319–35.

———— "Time is Short: The Eschatology of the Early Gaelic Church," in Caroline Bynum and Paul Freedman, *Last Things: Death and the Apocalypse in the Middle Ages* (Philadelphia, 2000), 101–23.

———— "The Viking and the Irishman," *Medium Ævum* 60 (1991), 257–67.

———— "William the Conqueror and Ireland," *Irish Historical Studies* 29 (1994), 145–58.

Hughes, Kathleen, *Early Christian Ireland: Introduction to the Sources* (Ithaca, N.Y., 1972).

———— "The Welsh Latin Chronicles: *Annales Cambriae* and Related Texts," *Proceedings of the British Academy* 59 (1973), 233–58.

Hull, Vernon, "The Exile of Conall Corc," *Proceedings of the Modern Language Association* 56 (1941), 937–50.

Hurley, Maurice F., and Orla M. B. Scully, with Sarah W. J. McCutcheon, eds., *Late Viking Age and Medieval Waterford: Excavations 1986–1992* (Waterford, 1998).

Ingstad, Anne Stine, *The Discovery of a Norse Settlement in America*, 2 vols. (Oslo, 1977–85).

Jackson, D. I., A. A. Jackson, D. Evans, R. T. R. Wingfield, R. P. Barnes, and M. J. Arthur, *The Geology of the Irish Sea* (London, 1995).

Jackson, K. H., "Date of the Tripartite Life of St. Patrick," *Zeitschrift für celtische Philologie* 41 (1986), 5–45.

James, Edward, *Britain in the First Millennium* (London, 2001).

James, J. W., "Fresh Light on the Death of Gruffudd ap Llywelyn," *Bulletin of the Board of Celtic Studies* 30 (1982), 147.

Jaski, Bart, "Druim Cett revisited," *Peritia* 12 (1998), 340–50.

—— "Vikings and the Kingship of Tara," *Peritia* 9 (1995), 310–51.

Jesch, Judith, "History in the Political Sagas," *Medium Ævum* 62 (1993), 210–20.

—— "Norse Historical Traditions and the *Historia Gruffud vab Kenan*: Magnús Berfoettr and Haraldr Hárfagri," in Maund, ed., *Gruffudd ap Cynan*, 117–47.

—— *Women in the Viking Age* (Woodbridge, 1991).

Jochens, J., "The Female Inciter in the Kings' Sagas," *Arkiv för nordisk filologi* 102 (1987), 100–19.

—— "The Politics of Reproduction: Medieval Norwegian Kingship," *American Historical Review* 92 (1987), 327–49.

—— "Race and Ethnicity in the Old Norse World," *Viator* 30 (1999), 79–103.

—— *Women in Old Norse Society* (Ithaca, N.Y., 1995).

John, Eric, *Land Tenure in Early England* (Leicester, 1961).

Johnsen, Arne Odd, "Betalte Suderøyene og Man skatt eller lensavgift til Norges konge (1153–1263)?" *Avhandlinger utgitt av det norske Videnskaps-Akademi i Oslo, II. Hist.-Filos. Klasse*, ny serie no. 10 (1966), 1–19.

—— "Håkon jarl Eiriksson (998–1030). Nytt kildemateriale og nye synspunkter," *Det Norske Videnskap - Akademi II. Hist.-filios. klasse. Avhandlinger* n.s. 17 (1981), 1–24.

Johnsen, O. A., "Le Commerce et la navigation en Norvège au Moyen Age," *Revue Historique* 178 (1936).

Johnston, Anne, "Norse Settlement Patterns in Coll and Tiree," in Crawford, ed., *Scandinavian Settlement in Northern Britain*, 108–26.

Jones, S. R. H., "Transaction Costs, Institutional Change, and the Emergence of a Market Economy in Later Anglo-Saxon England," *Economic History Review*, second series 46 (1993), 658–78.

Jónsson, Finnur, "Ágrip," *Aarbøger* (1928), 261–317.

—— *Den Oldnorske og Oldislandske Litteraturs Historie*, 3 vols., 2nd edn. (Copenhagen, 1920–24).

Kapelle, W. E., *The Norman Conquest of the North* (Chapel Hill, N.C., 1979).

Kavanagh, Rhoda, "The Horse in Viking Ireland: Some Observations," in Bradley, *Settlement and Society in Medieval Ireland*, 89–121.

Kelly, Fergus, *Early Irish Farming* (Dublin, 1997).

—— *A Guide to Early Irish Law* (Dublin, 1988).

Kenney, J., *The Sources for the Early History of Ireland: Ecclesiastical*, 2nd edn., ed. L. Bieler (repr. Dublin, 1979).

Keynes, Simon, "Cnut's Earls," in A. Rumble, ed., *The Reign of Cnut: King of England, Denmark and Norway* (Leicester, 1994), 43–88.

Kinvig, R. H., *History of the Isle of Man* (Douglas, 1944).

Klæsøe, Iben Skibsted, "Vikingetidens kronologi-en nybearbejdning af det arkæologiske materiale," *Aarbøger* (1997), 89–142.

Kluge, F., "Fragment eines angelsächsischen Briefes," *Englische Studien* 8 (1885), 62–63.

Koster, K., *Sagnet om Havelok Danske* (Copenhagen, 1868).

Krapp, G. P., and Elliot Van Kirk Dobbie, eds., *The Anglo-Saxon Poetic Records*, 6 vols. (New York, 1931–42).

Krappe, A. H., "The Valkyrie Episode in *Njáls Saga*," *Modern Language Notes* 43 (1928), 471–74.

Lamb, H. H., "Climate and History in N. Europe and Elsewhere," in Mörner and Karlén, *Climatic Changes on a Yearly to Millennial Basis*, 225–40.

Lander, S. J., "The Church before the Reformation," *VCH: Cheshire*, 3: 1–11.

Lang, James, *Viking Age Decorated Wood* (Dublin, 1988).

Larson, L. M., *Canute the Great* (New York, 1912).

Lauring, Palle, *A History of the Kingdom of Denmark* (Copenhagen, 1960).

Lawlor, Hugh Jackson, "A Calendar of the Liber Niger and Liber Albus of Christ Church, Dublin," *Proceedings of the Royal Irish Academy*, vol. 27, section C.1, 1–93.

——— "Notes on St. Bernard's Life of St. Malachy," *Proceedings of the Royal Irish Academy* 35 (1919), 230–64.

Lawson, M. K., *Cnut: The Danes in England in the Early Eleventh Century* (London, 1993).

——— "Collection of Danegeld and Heregeld in the Reigns of Æthelraed II and Cnut," *EHR* 99 (1984), 721–38.

——— "'Those stories look true': Levels of Taxation in the Reigns of AEthelraed II and Cnut," *EHR* 104 (1989), 385–406.

Leech, Roger, "*Cogadh Gaedhel re Gallaibh* and the *Annals of Inisfallen*," *North Munster Archaeological Society* 11 (1968), 13–21.

Le Patourel, John, *The Norman Empire* (Oxford, 1976).

Lewis, Archibald R., *The Northern Seas* (Princeton, 1958).

Lewis, C. P., "The King and Eye: A Study in Anglo-Norman Politics," *EHR* 104 (1989), 569–89.

Liestøl, A., "An Iona Rune Stone and the World of Man and the Isles," in Fell et al., eds., *The Viking Age in the Isle of Man*, 85–94.

Lind, E. H., *Norsk-isländska dopnamn ock fingerade namn från medeltiden* (Uppsala and Leipzig, 1905–15), with *Supplementbind* (Oslo, Uppsala, and Leipzig, 1931).

——— *Norsk-isländska personbinamn från medeltiden* (Uppsala, 1920–21).

Lloyd, J. E., "Wales and the Coming of the Normans," *Transactions of the Honourable Society of Cymmrodorion* (1899–1900), 122–79.

——— "The Welsh Chronicles," *Proceedings of the British Academy* 14 (1928), 369–91.

Loyn, H. R., "Boroughs and Mints 900–1066," in Dolley, ed., *Anglo-Saxon Coins*, 122–35.

——— *The Vikings in Wales* (London, 1976).

Lucas, A. T., *Cattle in Ancient Ireland* (Kilkenny, 1989).

Lund, Niels, "'Denemearc', 'tanmarkar but' and 'tanmaurk ala'," in Wood and Lund, eds., *Peoples and Places in Northern Europe 500–1600*, 161–69.

——— "King Edgar and the Danelaw," *Mediaeval Scandinavia* 9 (1976), 181–95.

Mac Cana, Proinsias, "The Influence of the Vikings on Celtic Literature," in Ó Cuív, ed., *The Impact of the Scandinavian Invasions on the Celtic-Speaking Peoples*, 78–118.

Mac Eoin, G., "The Date and Authorship of *Saltair na Rann*," *Zeitschrift für celtische Philologie* 28 (1960/61), 51–67.

——— "Observations on *Saltair na Rann*," *ZCP* 39 (1982), 1–28.

——— "Some Icelandic Loricae," *Studia Hibernica* 3 (1963), 143–54.

Mac Gearailt, U., "Cath Ruis na Ríg and Twelfth-century Literary and Oral Tradition," *Zeitschrift für celtische Philologie* 44 (1991), 128–53.

Mackenzie, Bridget Gordon, "On the Relationship of Norse Skaldic Verse to Irish Syllabic Poetry," in *Speculum Norroenum*, 337–56.

Mackinder, H. J., *Britain and the British Seas* (New York, 1902).

MacNeill, E., *Phases of Irish History* (Dublin, 1919).

MacNeill, Peter, and Ranald Nicholson, eds., *An Historical Atlas of Scotland, c. 400 – c.1600* (St. Andrews, repr. 1980).

Mac Niocaill, G., "The 'Heir-Designate' in Early Medieval Ireland," *Irish Jurist* 3 (1961), 326–29.

———— *Medieval Irish Annals* (Dublin, 1975).

MacQuarrie, Alan, "The Crusades and the Scottish *Gaidhealtachd* in Fact and Legend," in Loraine Maclean, ed., *The Middle Ages in the Highlands* (Inverness, 1981), 130–41.

Malmros, Rikke, "Den hedenske fyrstedigtnings samfundssyn," *Historisk tidsskrift (København)* 99 (1999), 337–75.

———— "Leding og Skjaldekvad. Det elvte århundredes nordiske Krigsflåder, deres teknologi og organisation og deres placering i samfundet belyst gennem den samtidige fyrstedigtning," *Aarbøger* (1985), 89–139.

Marcus, G. T.,"Early Norse Traffic to Iceland," *Mariner's Mirror* 46 (1960), 174–81.

Margeson, Sue, "On the Iconography of the Manx Crosses," in Fell et al., eds., *The Viking Age in the Isle of Man*, 95–106.

Marstrander, C., "Irske Vidnesbyrd om Torsdyrkelse i Irland," *Nordisk tidsskrift for filologi* 9 (1920), 8–32 and 81–107.

———— "Om tingsteder pa Man," *Norsk Tidsskrift for Sprogvidenskap* 10 (1938), 384–93.

———— "Tor i Irland," *Maal og Minne* (1915), 80–89.

Mason, Emma,"Change and Continuity in Eleventh Century Mercia: The Experience of Wulfstan of Worcester," *Anglo-Norman Studies* 8 (1985), 154–76.

Maund, K. L., ed., *Gruffudd ap Cynan: A Collaborative Biography* (Woodbridge, 1996).

———— *Ireland, Wales and England in the eleventh century* (Woodbridge, 1991).

McCormick, Finbar,"Dairying and Beef Production in Early Christian Ireland, the Faunal Evidence," in T. Reeves-Smyth and F. Hammond, eds., *Landscape Archaeology in Ireland* (British Archaeological Reports, British Series 116, Oxford, 1983), 253–67.

McDonald, R. Andrew, *The Kingdom of the Isles: Scotland's Western Seaboard c.1100–c.1336* (East Linton, 1997).

———— *Outlaws of Medieval Scotland: Challenges to the Canmore Kings, 1058–1266* (East Linton, 2003).

McDougall, Ian, "Foreigners and Foreign Language in Medieval Iceland," *Saga Book* 22 (1987–88), 180–233.

McGrail, Sean, *Medieval Boat and Ship Timbers from Dublin* (Dublin, 1993).

McTurk, Rory, "Ragnarr Loðbrók in the Irish Annals," in Almquist and Greene, *Proceedings of the Seventh Viking Congress*, 93–123.

Meehan, D., "Siege of Durham," *SHR* 55 (1976), 1–19.

Megaw, B., "The Manx 'Eary' and Its Significance," in Peter Davey, ed., *Man and Environment in the Isle of Man* (British Archaeological Reports, British Series, 54, Oxford, 1978), 327–45.

Metcalfe, D. M., "The Monetary Economy of the Irish Sea Province," in Graham-Campbell, ed., *Viking Treasure from the North West*, 89–106.

Mitchell, G. F., *Archaeology and Environment in Early Dublin* (Dublin, 1987).

———— *The Landscape of Ireland* (London, 1976).

Moore, A. W., *History of the Isle of Man* (London, 1908).

Moore, D., ed., *The Irish Sea Province in Archaeology and History* (Cardiff, 1971).

Mörner, N. A., and W. Karlén, eds., *Climatic Changes on a Yearly to Millennial Basis: Geological, Historical and Instrumental Records* (Dordrecht, 1984).

Morral, J., ed., *Medieval Studies Presented to Aubrey Gwynn, S.J.* (Dublin, 1960).

Munch, P. A. *Det norske folks historie*, 6 vols. (Christiania, 1852–63).

Munro, R. W. and J. M., "The Lordship of the Isles," in *An Historical Atlas of Scotland*, ed. MacNeill and Nicholson, 65–67.

Murry, Hilary, "Houses and Other Structures from the Dublin Excavations," in Bekker-Nielsen et al., eds., *Proceedings of the Eighth Viking Conference*, 57–68.

Musset, Lucien, "Aperçus sur la colonization scandinave dans le nord du Cotentin," *Annuaire des cinq départements de la Normandie*, 107 (1953), 34–37.

———— *Nordica et Normannica: Recueil d'études sur la Scandinavie ancienne et médiévale, les expéditions des Vikings et la fondation de la Normandie*, ed. Michel Fleury (Paris, 1997).

———— "Participation de Vikings venus des pays celtes à la colonisation scandinave de la Normandie," *Cahiers du Centre de recherches sur les pays du Nord et du Nord-Ouest* 1 (1978), 107–17

———— *Les Peuples Scandinaves au Moyen Age* (Paris, 1951).

———— "Pour l'étude comparative de deux fondations politiques des Vikings: Le Royaume d'York et le duché de Rouen," *Northern History* 10 (1975), 40–54.

———— "Pour l'étude des relations entre les colonies scandinaves, d'Angleterre et de Normandie," in *Nordica and Normannica*, 145–56.

Neveux, François, *La Normandie des ducs aux rois Xe–XIIe siècle* (Rennes, 1998).

New History of Ireland, ed. T. W. Moody, F. X. Martin, and F. J. Byrne, 10 vols. (Oxford, 1978–).

Ní Bhrolcháin, Muireann, "An Bansenchas," *Léachtai Cholum Cille* 12 (1982), 5–29.

Ní Mhaonaigh, Maire, "The Date of *Cogad Gáedel re Gallaib*," *Peritia* 9 (1995), 354–77.

———— "*Cogad Gáedel re Gallaib* and the Annals: A Comparison," *Ériu* 47 (1996), 101–26.

Nicholas, David, *Medieval Flanders* (London, 1992).

Nicolaisen, W. F. H., *Scottish Place-Names* (London, 1976).

Nielsen, Karl Martin, "Jelling Problems—A Discussion," *Mediaeval Scandinavia* 7 (1974), 156–82.

Ó Corráin, D., "The Career of Diarmait mac Máel na mBó," *Old Wexford Society Journal* 3 (1971), 26–35, and 4 (1972/73), 17–24.

———— "Dál Cais—Church and Dynasty," *Ériu* 24 (1973), 52–63.

———— *Ireland before the Normans* (Dublin, 1971).

———— "The Vikings in Scotland and Ireland in the Ninth Century," *Peritia* 12 (1998), 296–339.

Ó Cuív, Brian, ed., *The Impact of the Scandinavian Invasions on the Celtic-Speaking Peoples* (Dublin, repr. 1975).

———— "Literary Creation and Irish Historical Tradition," *Proceedings of the British Academy* 49 (1963), 233–62.

———— "Personal Names as an Indicator of Relations between Native Irish and Settlers in the Viking Period," in Bradley, ed., *Settlement and Society in Medieval Ireland*, 79–88.

———— "Some Irish Items Relating to the MacDonnells of Antrim," *Celtica* 16 (1984), 139–56.

O'Donoghue, T., "Cert Cech Ríg co Réil," in Bergin and Marstrander, eds., *Miscellany Presented to Kuno Meyer*, 258–77.

Ó Fiaich, Tomás, *Gaelscrínte san Eoraip* (Dublin, 1986).

O'Flaherty, Roderic, *Ogygia seu rerum Hibernicarum chronologia* (London, 1685).

O'Grady, Standish, and Robin Flower, *Catalogue of Irish Manuscripts in the British Library (formerly British Museum)*, 2 vols. (Dublin, 1997).

Ó Lochlainn, Colm, "Roadways in Ancient Ireland," in Ryan, ed., *Féil-sgríbinn Eóin Mic Néill*, 465–74.

O'Neill, Timothy, *Merchants and Mariners in Medieval Ireland* (Dublin, 1987).

O'Rahilly, Thomas F., *Early Irish History and Mythology* (Dublin, 1946).

Ó Ríordáin, B., "Aspects of Viking Dublin," Bekker-Nielsen et al, eds., *Proceedings of the Eighth Viking Conference*, 43–45.

——— "Excavations at High Street and Winetavern Street," *Medieval Archaeology* 15 (1971), 73–85.

——— "The High Street Excavations," in Almquist and Greene, eds., *Proceedings of the Seventh Viking Conference*, 135–40.

——— "Reports," *Medieval Archaeology*: 16 (1972), 168; 17 (1973), 151–52; 18 (1974), 206.

Oakley, Stewart, *A Short History of Denmark* (New York, 1972).

Olsen, Magnus, "Krákumál," *Maal og Minne* (1935), 78–80.

——— "Runic Inscriptions in Great Britain, Ireland and the Isle of Man," in Shetelig, ed., *Viking Antiquities*, 6:152–233.

Olsen, Olaf, "Hørg, Hov og Kirke," *Aarbøger* (1965), 1–307.

Oram, Richard, "Scandinavian Settlement in South-West Scotland with a Special Study of Bysbie," in Crawford, ed., *Scandinavian Settlement in Northern Britain*, 127–40.

——— and Geoffrey Stell, eds., *Galloway: Land and Lordship* (Edinburgh, 1991).

Page, R. I., "The Manx Rune-Stones," in Fell et al., eds., *The Viking Age in the Isle of Man*, 133–46.

——— *Runes* (Berkeley, 1987).

——— "Scandinavian Society 800–1100: The Contribution of Runic Studies," in Faulkes and Perkins, eds., *Viking Revaluations*, 145–59.

Pálsson, Hermann, "Keltnesk mannanöfn í íslenzkum örnefnum," *Skírnir* 126 (1952), 195–203.

Parry, M. L., *Climate Change and Agricultural Settlement* (Folkestone, 1978).

Patterson, C. C., "Silver Stocks and Losses in Ancient and Medieval Times," *Economic History Review*, second series 25 (1972), 205–33.

Pelteret, David, "Slave Raiding and Slave Trading in Early England," *Anglo-Saxon England* 9 (1981), 99–114.

——— *Slavery in Early Medieval England from the Reign of Alfred until the Twelfth Century* (Woodbridge, 1995).

Poole, R. L., *Studies in Chronology and History* (Oxford, 1934, repr. 1969).

Poole, Russell, "Some Royal Love Verses," *Maal og Minne* (1985), 115–31.

——— *Viking Poems on War and Peace: A Study in Skaldic Narrative* (Toronto, 1991).

Postan, M. M., *The Famulus: The Estate Labourer in the XIIth and XIIIth Centuries* (Economic History Review Supplement 2, Cambridge, 1954).

Power, Rosemary, "Magnus Bareleg's Expeditions to the West," *SHR* 65 (1986), 107–32.

Pulsiano, Phillip, ed., *Medieval Scandinavia, an Encyclopedia* (New York, 1993).

Raftery, Joseph, "The Iron Age and the Irish Sea: Problems for Research," in C. Thomas, ed., *The Iron Age in the Irish Sea Province* (London, 1970), 1–10.

Redknapp, Mark, *The Vikings in Wales: An Archaeological Quest* (Cardiff, 2000).

Rekdal, Jan Erik, "Den nordiske innflytelse på irsk og skotskgælisk språk, særlig i ordforråd og stedsnavn," *Maal og Minne* (1987), 39–50.

Richmond, I. A., "A Forgotten Exploration of the Western Isles," *Antiquity* 14 (1940), 193–95.

Richter, Michael, "Bede's Angli: Angles or English?" *Peritia* 3 (1984), 99–114.

———— *Canterbury Professions* (Canterbury and York Society vol. 67, Torquay, 1973).

———— "The First Century of Anglo-Irish Relations," *History* 59 (1974), 195–210.

Ritchie, Graham, ed., *The Archaeology of Argyll* (Edinburgh, 1997).

Ritchie, R. L. G., *The Normans in Scotland* (Edinburgh, 1954).

Robertson, A. J., *Laws of the Kings of England from Edmund to Henry I* (Cambridge, 1925).

Robertson, E. W., *Scotland under Her Early Kings*, 2 vols. (Edinburgh, 1862).

Roesdahl, Else, *The Vikings* (London, 1987).

Round, J. H., *Feudal England: Historical Studies of the Eleventh and Twelfth Centuries* (London, 1895).

Ryan, J., "The Battle of Clontarf," *JRSAI* 68 (1938), 1–50.

———— ed., *Féil-sgríbinn Eóin Mic Néill: Essays and Studies Presented to Professor Eoin Mac-Neill* (Dublin, 1940).

———— "The O'Briens in Munster after Clontarf," *North Munster Antiquarian Journal* 2 (1941), 141–52 and 3 (1942), 1–52.

———— "Pre-Norman Dublin," *JRSAI* 79 (1949), 73–88.

Ryan, Michael, ed., *Ireland and Insular Art, A.D. 500–1200* (Dublin, 1987).

Rynne, Etienne, *North Munster Studies: Essays in Commemoration of Monsignor Michael Moloney* (Limerick, 1967).

Sailing Directions (enroute) for Ireland and the West Coast of England, Defense Mapping Agency, United States of America (Washington, D.C., 1979).

Sawyer, Birgit, *The Viking-Age Rune-Stones* (Oxford, 2003).

———— and Peter Sawyer, *Medieval Scandinavia* (Minneapolis, 1993).

Sawyer, Peter, *Anglo-Saxon Charters - an annotated list and bibliography* (London 1968).

———— "The Vikings and the Irish Sea" in Moore, ed., *Irish Sea in Archaeology and History*, 86–92.

———— "The Wealth of England in the Eleventh Century," *TRHS*, fifth series 15 (1965), 145–64.

Sayers, William, "Clontarf, and the Irish Destinies of Sigurðr Digri, Earl of Orkney, and Þorsteinn Síðu-Hallsson," *Scandinavian Studies* 63 (1991), 164–86.

———— "Gunnarr, His Irish Wolfhound Sámr, and the Passing of the Heroic Order in *Njáls Saga*," *Arkiv för nordisk filologi* 112 (1997), 43–66.

Scott, Sir Lindsay, "The Norse in the Hebrides," *Viking Congress-Lerwick*, ed. Simpson, 189–215.

Searle, Eleanor, "Fact and Pattern in Heroic History: Dudo of St. Quentin," *Viator* 15 (1984), 119–37.

———— *Predatory Kinship and the Creation of Norman Power 840–1066* (Berkeley, 1988).

Seller, W. D. H., "The Origins and Ancestry of Somerled," *SHR* 45 (1966), 123–42.

Shetelig, H., ed., *Viking Antiquities in Great Britain and Ireland*, 6 vols. (Oslo, 1940–54).

Sigurðsson, G., *Gaelic Influence in Iceland* (Studia Islandica no. 46, Reykjavík, 1988).

Simpson, D., ed., *Viking Congress-Lerwick 1950* (Edinburgh, 1954).

Sims, Anngret, "Medieval Dublin, a Topographical Analysis," *Irish Geography* 12 (1979), 25–41.

Smithers, G., ed., *Havelok* (Oxford, 1987).

Smyser, H. M., "Ibn Fadlan's Account of the Rus, with some Commentary and Some Allusions to Beowulf," in Bessinger and Creed, eds., *Franciplegius*, 92–119.

Smyth, A. P., *Scandinavian York and Dublin*, 2 vols. (Dublin, 1975 and New Jersey, 1979).

Sommerfelt, Alf, "De norsk-irske Bystaters undergang 1169–1171," *Avhandlinger utgitt av det norske Videnskaps-Akademi i Oslo, II. Hist.-Filos. Klasse* 4 (1957), 5–30.

Southern, R. W., *The Making of the Middle Ages* (New Haven, 1953).

Spurkland, Terje, "Kriteriene for datering av norske runesteiner fra vikingtid og tidlig middelalder," *Maal og Minne* (1995), 1–14.

Steenstrup, J. C. H. R., *Normannerne*, 4 vols. (Kjobenhavn, 1876–82).

Stein-Wilkeshuis, Martina, "Scandinavians Swearing Oaths in Tenth-Century Russia: Pagans and Christians," *Journal of Medieval History* 28 (2002), 155–68.

Stenton, Sir F. M., *Anglo-Saxon England*, 3nd edn. (Oxford, 1971).

Stevenson, R. B. K., "A Hoard of Anglo-Saxon Coins Found at Iona Abbey," *Proceedings of the Society of Antiquaries of Scotland* 85 (1950), 170–75.

Stokes, Whitley, "Old Norse Names in the Irish Annals," *The Academy* 38 (1890), 248–49.

Storm, Gustav, "Havelok the Dane and the Norse King Olaf Kuaran," *Forhandlinger i Videnskaps-Selskabet i Christiana* 10 (1879).

Sveinsson, Einar Ól., *Íslenzkar bókmenntir í fornöld I* (Reykjavík, 1962).

———— *Njáls Saga: A Literary Masterpiece*, trans. Paul Schlach (Lincoln, 1971).

———— *Um Njála* (Reykjavík, 1933).

———— "Vísa í Hávamálum og írsk saga," *Skírnir* 126 (1952), 168–77.

Tatlock, J. P. S., "The English Journey of the Laon Canons," *Speculum* 8 (1933), 454–65.

Thacker, A. T., "Anglo-Saxon Chester," in *VCH: Chester*, 1: 237–92.

Thomas, Hugh, "*Gesta Herwardi*, the English and Their Conquerors," *Anglo-Norman Studies* 21 (1998), 213–32.

Thornton, David, "The Genealogy of Gruffudd ap Cynan," in Maund, ed., *Gruffudd ap Cynan*, 79–108.

———— "Who was Rhain the Irishman?" *Studia Celtica* 34 (2000), 131–48.

Thorsteinsson, Arne, in P. Sawyer, "The Two Viking Ages of Britain, a Discussion," *Mediaeval Scandinavia* 2 (1969), 163–207.

Tonning, Ole, *Commerce and Trade in the North Atlantic 850 A.D. to 1350 A.D.* (Minneapolis, 1936).

Trindade, W. Ann, "Irish Gormlaith as a Sovereignty Figure," *Études Celtiques* 23 (1986), 143–56.

Turville-Petre, G., "Um dróttkvæði og írskan kveðskap," *Skirnir* 128 (1954), 31–55.

Valante, Mary, "Dublin's Economic Relations with Hinterland and Periphery in the Late Viking Age," in S. Duffy, ed., *Medieval Dublin I* (Dublin, 2000), 69–83.

van Hamel, A. G., "Norse History in Hanes Gruffydd ap Cynan," *Revue Celtique* 42 (1925), 336–44.

van Houts, Elizabeth M. C., "The Ship List of William the Conqueror," *Anglo-Norman Studies* 10 (1987), 159–83.

Vaughan, Sally, "Eadmer's *Historia Novorum*: A Reinterpretation," *Anglo-Norman Studies* 10 (1987), 259–89.

Vésteinsson, Orri, "Patterns of Settlement in Iceland: A Study in Prehistory," *Saga Book* 25 (1998), 1–29.

von Sydow, C. W., "Iriskt inflytande på nordisk Guda- och Hjältesaga," *Vetenskaps-Societeten i Lund. Årsbok* (1920), 19–29.

Wahlgren, Erik, "Maine Penny," in Pulsiano, ed., *Medieval Scandinavia, an Encyclopedia*, 404.

Wainwright, F. W., *The Northern Isles* (Edinburgh, 1962).

Walker, David, *The Norman Conquerors* (Swansea, 1977).

————— "A Note on Gruffydd ap Llewelyn (1039–1063)," *Welsh History Review* 1 (1961), 83–94.

Wallace, P. F., "Archaeology and the Emergence of Dublin as the Principal Town of Ireland," in Bradley, ed., *Settlement and Society in Medieval Ireland*, 123–60.

————— "Archaeology of Viking Dublin," in Clarke et al., eds., *Comparative History of Urban Origins in Non-Roman Europe*, 103–45.

————— "Economy and Commerce of Viking Age Dublin" in Düwel et al., eds., *Untershuchungen zu Handel und Verkehr*, 200–45.

————— "The English Presence in Viking Dublin," in Blackburn, ed., *Anglo-Saxon Monetary History*, 201–11.

————— "Origins of Dublin" in B. G. Scott, ed., *Studies on Early Ireland, Essays in Honour of M. V. Duignan* (Belfast, 1980), 129–43.

Wallace, Patrick, *Viking Age Buildings of Dublin*, 2 vols. (Royal Irish Academy, Dublin, 1992).

Walsh, Maura, and Daibhi Ó Cróinín, *Cummian's Letter De Controversia Paschali and the De Ratione Computandi* (Toronto, 1988)

Walshe, A., *Scandinavian Relations with Ireland During the Viking Period* (Dublin, 1922).

Warlop, E., *The Flemish Nobility before 1300*, 2 vols. (Kortijk, 1975–76).

Watt, D. E. R., *Fasti ecclesiae Scoticanae Medii Aevi ad annum 1638* (St. Andrews, second draft, 1969).

Webster, G., M. Dolley, and J. Dunning, "A Saxon Treasure Hoard Found at Chester," *Antiquities Journal* 33 (1953), 22–33.

Weinfurter, Stefan, *The Salian Century*, trans. Barbara Bowlus (Philadephia, 1999).

Welander, R. D. E., et al., "A Viking Burial from Kneep, Uig, Isle of Lewis," *Proceedings of the Society of Antiquaries of Scotland* 117 (1987), 149–74.

Whitelock, Dorothy, "The Dealings of the Kings of England with Northumbria in the Tenth and Eleventh Centuries," in Peter Clemoes, ed., *The Anglo-Saxons* (London, 1959), 70–88.

Whitney, J. P., "The Reform of the Church," in *Cambridge Medieval History*, vol. 5, ed. J. R. Tanner, C. W. Previté-Orton, and Z. N. Brooke (Cambridge, 1957).

Williams, Ann, "Land and Power in the Eleventh Century: The Estates of Harold Godwinsson," *Proceedings of the Battle Conference on Anglo-Norman Studies* 3 (1980), 171–87.

Wilson, David, "Art of the Manx Crosses," in Fell et al. eds., *Viking Age in the Isle of Man*, 175–87.

————— *The Viking Age in the Isle of Man* (Odense, 1974).

Wood, Ian, and Niels Lund, eds.,*Peoples and Places in Northern Europe 500–1600: Essays in Honour of Peter Hayes Sawyer* (Woodbridge, 1991).

Wooding, Jonathan, *Communication and Commerce along the Western Sealanes AD 400–800* (British Archaeological Reports, International Series 654, Oxford, 1996).

Young, Jean, "Does Rígsþula Betray Irish Influence?" *Arkiv för nordisk Filologi* 49 (1933), 97–107.

————— "Note on the Norse Occupation of Ireland," *History* 35 (1950), 11–33.

Unpublished Works

Beougher, David, "Celtic Warfare in Ireland: A Logistical Perspective" (M.A. 1999, Pennsylvania State University).

Valante, Mary A., "Taxation, Tolls and Tribute: The Language of Economics and Trade in Viking-Age Ireland" (personal communication).

——— "Urbanization and Economy in Viking-Age Ireland" (Ph.D. 1998, Pennsylvania State University).

Vésteinsson, Orri, "Christianisation of Iceland: Priest, Power and Social Change 1000–1300" (Ph.D. 1996, University of London).

Index